ARCTIC OCEAN

ICELAND
Reykjavik

ATLANTIC OCEAN

NORWAY
SWEDEN

FINLAND

GULF OF BOTHNIA

WHITE

Lake Onega

Lake Ladoga

St. Petersburg

Volga
Moscow

Christiania
(Oslo)

Stockholm

BALTIC SEA

R U S S I A

NORTH SEA

DENMARK

Copenhagen

Königsberg

Glasgow GREAT
BRITAIN

Danzig

Vistula Warsaw

Kiev

Dnieper

IRELAND

Dublin

Liverpool

Manchester

Hamburg

Elbe

Berlin

Oder

P O L A N D

CARPATHIANS

Dniester

Birmingham

Amsterdam

Leipzig

Cracow

Pruth

London

ENGLISH CHANNEL

NETH.

BELGIUM

Brussels

Rhine

G
E
R
M
A
N
Y

Prague

AUSTRIA-
HUNGARY

Vienna

Budapest

RUMANIA

Bucharest

BLACK SEA

LUX.

Paris

Seine

Danube

Munich

Loire

FRANCE

Bern
SWITZ.

A
L
P
S

Milan
Po

Danube

Belgrade

Genoa

BOSNIA
Sarajevo

SERBIA

BULGARIA

Sofia

BAY OF BISCAY

Bordeaux

Rhône

I
T
A
L
Y

ADRIATIC SEA

Tiber

MONTENEGRO

OTTOMAN EMPIRE

Constantinople

PYRENEES

Marseilles

CORSICA

Rome

Naples

AEGEAN
SEA

Ebro

PORTUGAL

Lisbon

Madrid

SPAIN

Barcelona

BALEARIC
ISLANDS

SARDINIA

M E D I T E R R A N E A N

Strait of Gibraltar

SICILY

S E A

MALTA
(Br.)

GREECE

Athens

CRETE

EUROPE IN 1890

0 ———————— 500 Miles

NORTH AFRICA

Origins of Contemporary Europe: 1890–1914

J. Kim Munholland

University of Minnesota

Harcourt, Brace & World, Inc.

New York / Chicago / San Francisco / Atlanta

MAPS BY **Jean P. Tremblay**

CHAPTER OPENING PHOTO CREDITS

1 Culver Pictures
2 The Bettmann Archive
3 Radio Times Hulton Picture Library
4 Radio Times Hulton Picture Library
5 Radio Times Hulton Picture Library
6 From a book of illustrations by Edouard Detaille, *Le Panorama: Types et Uniformes de l'Armée Française.* Paris, n.d.
7 Pablo Picasso: Detail from *Three Musicians,* 1921 Philadelphia Museum of Art: A. E. Gallatin Collection
8 Brown Brothers
9 The Bettmann Archive

ISBN: 0-15-567615-6

Library of Congress Catalog Card Number: 76-111323

Printed in the United States of America

PREFACE

When I began teaching twentieth century European history, I was struck by the absence of any book that would provide the students with a general interpretation of the years preceding the outbreak of the First World War. Many students were under the impression that the years between Bismarck's dismissal in 1890 and the assassination of Francis Ferdinand in 1914 constituted little more than a prelude to the First World War, and the origins of that conflict loomed large in their thinking. There is no doubt that the First World War had a decisive impact on the direction of European history in the twentieth century, but Europe was already undergoing significant changes before the war. If one takes a broad look at the prewar years it is clear that many aspects of contemporary Europe had their origins toward the end of the nineteenth century rather than in 1914. Even an understanding of the nature of the war's impact requires a full grasp of the main features of Europe's evolution before 1914. This book was written to help place in perspective the period prior to the war and to balance accounts of diplomatic conflict and national rivalries with a discussion of the social and economic changes that were significantly affecting the lives of the European people.

Because the development of a highly complex, technological, and predominantly urban society has had a deep influence on contemporary Europe, the book opens with a discussion of the industrialization and urbanization in Europe around the turn of the century. The rise of an industrial order contributed to the development of protest movements as well as to the appearance of a "mass society" in which large numbers of people began seeking a wider role in the social, economic, and political life of their states. The first chapter considers some of the social consequences of the rise of an industrial order in Europe, and the second chapter describes some of the movements that emerged to provide channels of protest or participation for those caught up in the industrial system. The protest movements were signs of the social strains emerging in Europe, and the rise of the socialist movement was further evidence of ways in which men sought to provide broader benefits for those laboring under the discipline of the industrial system. By 1905 the political impact of social and economic changes began to be felt throughout Europe. The response in the major states varied according to the existing political structures. Chapters 3 and 4 compare the various European political institutions and practices and discuss the responses made by political leaders to new demands.

In Chapter 5 the diplomatic problems faced by the European states are considered against this background of heightening political debate over social and political demands within each state. As Chapter 6 brings out, Europe's imperial surge at the end of the nineteenth century was a manifestation of Europe's dynamic power, but the eventual containment of that surge indicated the limits of Europe's power on the global scale. Chapter 7 explores the cultural upheaval of European intellectual life at the turn of the century as another manifestation of a new, modernist age, at once dynamic and experimental in its interests. The final two chapters describe domestic and international politics in the decade that preceded the outbreak of war in 1914. By 1914 Europe was well along in its process of modernization.

It is hoped that the approach used in this book will give students an understanding of the rapid and unsettling transition that Europe underwent during the late nineteenth and early twentieth centuries. It is in this sense that the book is a study of the origins of contemporary Europe rather than a more limited investigation of the origins of the First World War.

In the course of writing this book I have accumulated a number of intellectual debts. Without the work of specialists, a synthesis of this period could not have been written. Many of the specialized accounts that have been useful are listed in the Suggested Reading sections at the end of each chapter. I owe a particular debt of gratitude to David S. Landes and Peter N. Stearns for their work in the areas of economic and social history respectively. They are not responsible, of course, for any misinterpretations that I may have made. I am grateful for the constructive advice of Professor Fritz Stern of Columbia who reviewed the plan for the book and Professors John M. Blum of Yale and Robert O. Paxton of Columbia who reviewed the manuscript. Throughout the preparation of this book I have had the valuable assistance of the staff at Harcourt, Brace & World. The conception and writing of the book were encouraged and stimulated by Thomas A. Williamson; Virginia Joyner and Ethel Peirce helped improve the manuscript's style and presentation; the maps and illustrations used in the text were compiled by Susan Haggerty. Finally I would like to thank my students at the University of Minnesota who have served as perceptive and responsive critics over the past six years.

J. K. M.

CONTENTS

CHRONOLOGY

1867	Hapsburg monarchy reorganized into dual state of Austria-Hungary.
1870	Franco-Prussian War; Italian occupation of papal states completes territorial unification.
1871	Foundation of German empire.
1873	Beginning of price decline in Europe, lasting to mid-1890's.
1875	Third Republic established in France.
1879	Germany forms Dual Alliance with Austria-Hungary.
1882	Germany, Austria, and Italy form Triple Alliance; British troops occupy Egypt.
1884	Passage of Gladstone's Reform Act provides nearly universal manhood suffrage in Great Britain.
1884–85	Berlin Colonial Congress sets conditions for European occupation of African territory.
1886–89	Boulanger crisis threatens to topple French Third Republic.
1889	Foundation of Second International in Paris: London dockworkers' and gasworkers' strike.
1890	Bismarck replaced by Caprivi as German chancellor; repeal of anti-socialist laws in Germany; Bismarck's successors fail to renew Reinsurance Treaty with Russia.
1891	Erfurt Congress of German Socialist party adopts Marxism as theoretical basis for party; construction begun on trans-Siberian railway.
1892–94	Resurgence of anarchist outrages.
1894	Franco-Russian alliance; accession of Nicholas II in Russia.
1895	Salisbury forms Conservative ministry in Great Britain.
1896	Defeat of Italian troops in Ethiopia precipitates domestic political crisis.
1898	Climax of Franco-British imperial rivalries in Africa reached at Fashoda; Milan riots lead to government repression; passage of first large naval bill in Germany.
1899	Outbreak of Boer War; formation of Waldeck-Rousseau ministry to resolve Dreyfus affair in France; first Hague Peace Conference; Freud's *Interpretation of Dreams* published.

1900	Boxer uprising put down by international military force in China; formation of Labor Representation Committee in Great Britain; King Umberto of Italy assassinated; Max Planck proposes quantum theory.
1901	Death of Queen Victoria.
1902	Bülow tariff enacted in Germany; House of Lords decides Taff Vale dispute in favor of railway company; Anglo-Japanese treaty signed; Hobson's *Imperialism: a Study* published.
1903	German Socialist party rejects revisionism at Dresden Congress; Witte dismissed as finance minister in Russia; Giolitti emerges as dominant figure in Italian politics.
1904	Anglo-French entente resolves outstanding colonial differences between the two countries; outbreak of war between Russia and Japan; revisionism and French socialists' support for bourgeois government condemned by Amsterdam Congress of Second International; Chekhov's *Cherry Orchard* produced.
1905	Japanese military victory over Russia; revolution erupts in Russia; first Moroccan crisis precipitated by visit of William II to Tangier; separation of Church and state and passage of two-year draft law in France; French Socialist party unified; victory of Magyar nationalists in Hungarian elections; Einstein proposes special theory of relativity; German expressionist painters form "The Bridge" group; "les fauves" are established in Paris.
1906	Liberals win landslide election in Great Britain; Czar agrees to summon Duma; Germany fails to break Anglo-French entente during Algeciras conference on Morocco.
1907	Anglo-Russian entente; Second International passes "peace resolution" at Stuttgart Congress; universal manhood suffrage enacted in Austria; Bülow bloc wins German elections; Braque and Picasso launch cubism in Paris.
1908	Bosnian crisis; *Daily Telegraph* affair; "Young Turks" revolt in Ottoman empire.
1909	Lloyd George proposes his "peoples' budget" in Great Britain.
1911	Parliament Act and National Insurance Act passed in Great Britain; second Moroccan crisis creates war scare; Italy invades Tripoli; revolution in China ends Manchu dynasty; Stolypin assassinated in Russia.
1912	German elections return Socialists as largest party in Reichstag; first Balkan war breaks out; first Irish home rule bill is passed in House of Commons and is vetoed by Lords; most Italian males obtain the vote; France establishes protectorate over Morocco.
1913	Second Balkan war breaks out; large increase in military budget passed by Reichstag; French Chamber establishes three-year draft; London ambassadors' conference establishes state of Albania; Stravinsky's "Rite of Spring" provokes riot in Théâtre des Champs Elysées; first volume of Proust's *Remembrance of Things Past* published.
1914	Formation of industrial alliance among British unions; mutiny of British officers at Curragh in Ireland; Jaurès assassinated; St. Petersburg strikes suppressed by government; assassination of Francis Ferdinand in Serbia; outbreak of the First World War.

Origins of Contemporary Europe: 1890–1914

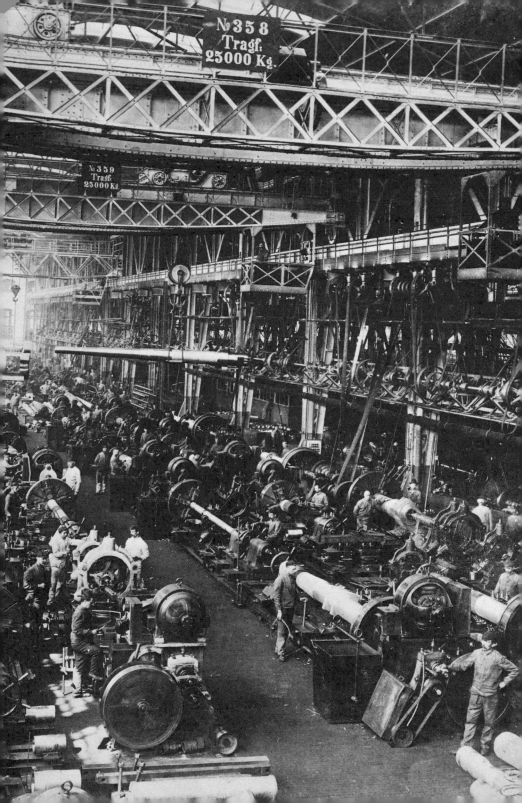

1

EUROPEAN SOCIETY AT THE TURN OF THE CENTURY

The Rise of an Industrial Order

In 1890 the Europeans were in the midst of an era that was bringing revolutionary changes to their ways of life. Because no cataclysmic event marked this transformation, some historians have insisted that the growth of an industrial society in Europe was not a revolution in the sense of causing a sudden and drastic change in society. Yet, in the broad perspective of history, the rise of an industrial, technological society in the nineteenth century equals and possibly surpasses the agrarian revolution of around 10,000 B.C. as a development that gave men the power and skill to exploit their environment to their own advantage.

The magnitude of this revolution may be estimated in terms of the increase in forms and uses of energy through scientific and technological innovation. Before the industrial revolution men relied heavily on animals and manpower for energy. Perhaps no more than 15 or 20 percent of all energy came from other sources such as wind or water. Moreover, the per capita consumption of energy was low, little more than enough to meet demands for food and warmth. Without effective means for extending his labor, man devoted most of his energy to survival. With the advent of industrialization in the nineteenth century, the development of and consumption of energy suddenly increased. It is estimated that the consumption of energy in the world went up 600 percent between 1860 and 1900. Most of this increase was concentrated in the industrial areas of Europe, the United States, and, to a lesser degree, Japan. In these areas the output of energy far outstripped the growth of population, which also increased dramatically. The appearance of an industrial society therefore may be seen as a revolution in the possession and use of energy.

The first evidence of industrialization appeared in England toward the end of the eighteenth century, and it centered around the application of power to the textile, metallurgical, and mining industries. Later the industrial revolution spread to the Continent: to France and Belgium by mid-century and to Germany in the 1860's and 1870's. The industrialization process was not necessarily uniform; certain sectors of the economy of a given state resisted or escaped industrialization altogether, and some countries industrialized more slowly, or later, than others. By the end of the century, however, the industrial order had affected nearly all of central and northwestern Europe and had reached out to the east and southwest.

The introduction of an industrial order brought about certain obvious changes. Productivity increased radically as a result of the use of water and steam power and new machinery in manufacturing. The factory system was established as a means of concentrating the requisites for manufacturing: power, labor, and capital. In the textile industry, for example, the traditional "cottage" industry, by which cloth was produced in homes and collected by merchants, had been just an adjunct to agriculture. The development of water power to drive looms, a more efficient method of making textiles, required that labor be brought to the source of power and placed under one roof. Within the factory, jobs were increasingly specialized and tailored to the standard operations of the machinery. Behind this new form of industry was a capital investment that, even by the standards of the day, might have been considered modest. But some investment was essential to get the factories into operation. Only gradually did the factory system become the dominant system for the production of material goods. Artisans continued to produce on an individual-order basis well into the nineteenth century. Ultimately, however, the artisan class was a major casualty of Europe's industrial revolution.

The industrial revolution also brought about a profound change in transportation, particularly with the development of railways during the first decades of the nineteenth century. During this period nearly every European state and the United States began a railway network, although it was not until the second half of the century that the major European trunk lines were connected and the American transcontinental railways were laid. Because the railways were much more flexible and reliable than the canal and river systems, they successfully challenged these older modes of transportation for bulk goods. The volume of goods moved by all forms of transportation increased to meet the demand of factories for cheap supplies of raw materials and ready access to markets. Once started, industrialization spawned further technological change, and new enterprises emerged; for instance, the making of tools and machinery to run the factories became an industry in itself.

Conditions Inducing Industrial Development

Certain conditions seem to have been important in providing impetus for the development of an industrial order, although not all countries possessed these conditions to the same extent or at the same time. One factor that apparently encouraged industrial expansion was the pressure created by a sudden spurt in population. After 1750 the European population increased at a rate that was without parallel. In the past, sudden increases in population had been followed by famine, plague, or other natural disasters that kept Europe's population at a fairly constant level. A high mortality rate, particularly for infants, tragically served as a further limitation on rapid population growth. In the mid-eighteenth century the introduction of new crops, notably corn and potatoes, established a more abundant supply of nourishment. Better sanitation practices reduced the mortality rate, and earlier marriages led to a sharp increase in the birth rate. The precise effect of the resultant population growth on industrialization is difficult to evaluate, since in some regions it preceded industrialization by perhaps two or more generations. Certainly the excess population in western Europe meant there was a labor supply. The factory system, in spite of harsh working conditions, provided a means of survival for great numbers of people and attracted them into the crowded, burgeoning industrial cities.

In addition to population growth, a favorable climate for investment and innovation was essential for industrial growth. The accumulation of capital, through agriculture and trade, through borrowing from other nations, or through favorable governmental policies, was necessary in order to invest in the machinery and facilities required by the new factories and expanding mines. Britain had been favored in this respect at the outset of its industrial expansion. A profitable overseas trade in the late seventeenth and eighteenth centuries produced a capital surplus that British entrepreneurs were able to draw on. They supplemented these funds with money borrowed in Amsterdam and elsewhere on the Continent.

The political climate of a nation also affected its industrial development. Domestic stability, the establishment of a national market free of internal tariff or other barriers, the creation of laws protecting patents and guaranteeing limited liability to investors, and the abolition of serfdom and of special privileges for certain classes were all acts of government that created favorable conditions in which people were willing to take risks and seek opportunities for profit.

Geographical factors were important influences on the rate of a nation's industrial growth. The proximity of iron and coal to convenient transportation gave Britain and Germany an important advantage in the development of their iron and steel industries; the absence of these resources, on the other hand, hindered the expansion of heavy industry in northern Italy. Finally, an industrializing country required a group of men committed to the notion of modernization, whether for their own gain or for what they considered to be the good of the country. The first entrepreneurs in Britain were predominantly men acting as private individuals; later modernizers, such as Count Sergei Yulievich Witte, the Russian finance minister from 1892 to 1903, placed the welfare of the state at the center of plans for establishing an industrial order.

Why States Varied in Industrial Development

Depending on its circumstances, each state followed a different path to industrialization. These circumstances involved differences in political organization, natural resources, and social structures; but of equal significance was the period in which a state entered the industrial revolution. The industrialization of Britain occurred over the entire nineteenth century; in France industrialization started later and generally lagged behind Britain's rate of growth. In Germany an industrial spurt occurred in the 1850's and 1860's, but the real impulse for industrial development came in the decades after unification. Once started, Germany's growth outstripped that of its European rivals; by the end of the nineteenth century Germany was prepared to challenge

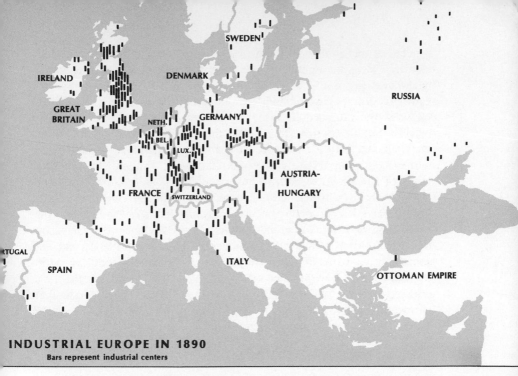

INDUSTRIAL EUROPE IN 1890
Bars represent industrial centers

Adapted from *Les Bourgeois Conquérants,* Charles Morazé. By permission of Max Leclerc et Cie., proprietors of Librairie Armand Colin, (c) Paris, 1957.

Britain as the industrial leader of Europe. Among the late modernizers, Russia began an intensive program of government-sponsored industrial expansion in the 1890's. Italy also commenced a somewhat limited industrial surge in that decade, as did portions of the Austro-Hungarian empire.

Although Great Britain had been the first industrial state in Europe, not all European states repeated the British pattern of development. Since Great Britain had preceded them, continental states could borrow knowledge, techniques, and capital from Britain for their own purposes. But the British industrialization process was not always applicable to these other states. Many of them were not so well favored as Britain in having a geographical location that gave easy access to overseas markets; nor were they so well endowed with convenient transportation at the outset. Many lacked the capital that British merchants had accumulated by the beginning of the industrial revolution. Most important, a later entry into the lists of industrializing nations often meant that a country was initially more "backward"; the process of catching up tended to be more rapid and more strenuous than the rate of industrialization had been in Britain.

This greater effort at mobilizing resources required a more active role for the government and for central banks in stimulating industrial development. In France the government guaranteed bonds for railways. Large banks, such as the Crédit Mobilier, attempted to mobilize the financial resources of the frugal bourgeoisie and make credit available for investment. But the growth of industry in France was held back by the absence of a rapidly expanding market owing to France's comparatively slow population growth, and by the hesitancy of French entrepreneurs, who preferred family-controlled operations with limited production but secure profits. In Germany central banks played a crucial part in financing industrial advance after unification in 1871. Four large banks—the Dresdener, the Deutsche, the Darmstädter, and the Diskontogesellschaft—supplied capital and sometimes provided directors for Germany's flourishing industry. More than any other European country, Germany was noted for the close alliance between banking and industry. Because the banks encouraged more efficient organization, in both industry and finance, Germany's industrial push was characterized from the outset by the growth of large financial institutions and by the consolidation of firms within a particular industry into large cartels.

The Second Industrial Revolution

In 1890 the European states that had been industrialized found themselves on the threshold of a new phase of progress. Historians have identified the development of new industries and the proliferation of products at this time as a second industrial revolution. In some respects this second revolution merely extended the methods and techniques of the earlier one. Older elements of the economy showed a continuing vigor; technological improvements were made in existing industries, such as metallurgy and transportation; and more efficient means were found for the use of power in manufacturing.

But there were distinct differences between the first and second industrial revolutions. The first revolution was achieved in textiles and heavy industry and tended to be the accomplishment of individual entrepreneurs who were able to marshal the capital and labor for the establishment of a plant or development of a mine. The technology of the first revolution was impressive but not very complicated. It was the work of skilled amateurs who, largely through trial and error, hit on successful inventions. Furthermore, with the exception of textiles, the products of the first industrial revolution were not consumed by the majority of the population. Although the lives of many people were transformed by migration to industrial cities, and although cheaper transportation made certain goods less expensive, these effects tended to be indirect. The new phase, on the other hand, saw the emergence of more diversified industries, directed by scientific research, that were capable of producing goods on a mass scale and of supplying power that could serve an enlarged population. Technological advances could be seen in the use of electrical energy, in developments in organic chemistry, and in the wider use of steel in various manufactured products. During this new era the industrial order spread on the European continent and in certain countries overseas, to the extent that Great Britain's industrial supremacy was seriously challenged.

Industrial Organization

The new growth of European industry brought significant changes in the organization and financing of industrial enterprise. The formation of cartels through consolidation of firms and industry-wide agreements, which had been a prominent feature of Germany's industrial expansion, became common in every industrial state. Declining prices and the protracted recession that followed the financial crisis of 1873-74 led manufacturers to seek some escape from the vagaries of an uncontrolled market. By agreeing to limit production or by reaching an understanding on the control of a given market, they found that they could maintain prices at a relatively constant level. By eliminating duplication of efforts, consolidation offered the possibility of greater efficiency and better organization of both production and management. Larger firms were better able to attract the capital needed for expensive new equipment and machinery to improve production techniques. They could also afford a greater investment in research, supplying laboratories in which scientists could search for new products.

The cartels and large firms which developed throughout Europe came to dominate particular sectors of the economy. Smaller firms did not disappear; in fact, their numbers increased, although they represented a proportionally smaller share of the industrial economy. Often these modest enterprises prospered by providing auxiliary services and supplies that could not be produced economically within larger industrial structures. Growth occurred, then, in both the large and the small firms, but the large business or manufacturing organization had become a distinctive feature of industrial society in Europe by the end of the nineteenth century. In the 1890's more than half the labor force in Belgium, Great Britain, Germany, and even France was in concerns that employed more than twenty workers. Some of the concerns developed into giant enterprises. By 1913 the house of Krupp employed about 70,000 workers and the German electrical firm of Siemens-Halske had some 81,000 on its payroll.

Technological Advances

A remarkable series of technological advances, starting in the mid-eighteenth century, lay at the heart of Europe's industrial development. As was noted before, the early triumphs of the industrial revolution depended to a great extent on trial and error. Subsequent improvements or refinements of existing equipment were made by countless tinkerers, foremen, and others who improved machinery on the job. Empirical methods and the inventions of the untrained amateur continued to have an impact on industry throughout the nineteenth century, but science and scientific theory came to play an increasingly significant role. In the 1890's, science was for the first time having a greater influence on technology than technology was on science. Scientific breakthroughs led to the formation of new industries involving chemicals, electricity, and steel. German technicians, scientists, and manufacturers were particularly adept at exploiting the new scientific knowledge. As a result, Germany became the leading industrial state of Europe in these new areas.

The Steel Industry ▪ In a sense the emergence of the steel industry during the latter half of the nineteenth century was an extension of earlier achievements in ironmaking, for steel is simply a form of iron with a different carbon content. Yet this difference gives steel its advantage over other forms of iron: it is less brittle than pig iron, but less malleable and more durable than wrought iron. These advantages were known during early stages of the industrial revolution, but no method had been devised to produce steel cheaply and in quantity. Instruments of steel—knives, scythes, and weapons—thus tended to be small, costly, and highly prized. With the introduction of the Bessemer and Siemens-Martin processes in 1856, mass-produced steel became technologically feasible.

Still, there were disadvantages. Both methods of making steel required high-grade ore with a low phosphorous content, which was expensive and difficult to obtain, particularly on the Continent. The major sources of high-grade ore were in Spain, the United States, and Great Britain. Britain, with convenient access to both its own and Spanish ores, was able to maintain its lead over continental rivals as a producer of iron and steel through the 1870's, until steel production was revolutionized by a simple discovery in 1879.

This discovery, made by two English cousins, Sidney Thomas and Sidney Gilchrist, made it possible to remove phosphorous from molten iron. Their discovery was one of the last triumphs by amateurs (although Gilchrist was a chemist by profession) in the field of metallurgy. It was immediately recognized as a spectacular success. A group of entrepreneurs lost no time in leasing the rights to the Gilchrist-Thomas process. The phosphoric ore deposits of Europe, particularly in the Ruhr basin and Alsace-Lorraine, were open to exploitation. In the following decades European steel production increased one hundred times. In 1870 production of steel in Britain, Germany, France, and Belgium was about 385,000 tons; in 1883 it reached 600,000 tons; and in 1913 more than 32,000,000 tons of steel came from European mills. The age of steel had arrived with a resounding clang.

Of the European states, Germany profited the most from this age. Ruhr industrialists became the leading steelmasters of Europe when steel production in Germany surpassed that of Great Britain in 1893. There are several reasons for this supremacy. German blast furnaces had the largest capacity of any in Europe; German plants were modern; and German transportation could handle larger amounts of ore and finished steel, and move them more rapidly than could British transportation. Unlike German manufacturers, British entrepreneurs were unwilling to make the additional investment that modernization of steel plants and transportation required. Germany's central position on the continent gave it an advantage in supplying central and southeastern Europe, but German steel makers were also able to sell in Britain, much to the chagrin of British manufacturers. The new industrial revolution placed a premium not only on scientific skill but also on the ability to adjust quickly to new opportunities.

Cheap steel revolutionized a number of other industries. Steel replaced iron on much of the rail network in Europe and was widely used in the construction of new rail lines overseas. Shipbuilders increasingly employed steel plating for their hulls. After the turn of the century, steel became the major ingredient in the manufacture of the automobile. Steel was the main component in countless other products and provided new material for the construction industry.

The Chemical and Electrical Industries ■ In addition to steel, chemicals and electricity emerged during the second industrial revolution as new industries with enormous potential for future expansion. In these areas German engineers and manufacturers again displayed a combination of scientific knowledge and aggressive opportunism that vaulted their country into European leadership. German technical and inventive skills were particularly evident in organic chemistry, which was to become a major sector of the chemical industry. The initial innovations in this area came with the development of synthetic dyes as the result of discoveries by German, French, and British technicians. But it was the German manufacturers who were to make the most successful application of these achievements. Early failures in the manufacture of dyes had frightened off British and French entrepreneurs despite the heavy demand of the textile industry. By the turn of the century Germany was manufacturing some 90 percent of the world's dyestuffs.

The discovery of how to make artificial dyes prepared the way for a whole new set of man-made products, including plastics, artificial fibers, and synthetic resins. Businesses required research staffs to develop and test the new goods and materials in an effort to meet, or even to create, new demands. Chemistry also provided the foundation for a wide variety of products that could be employed for useful or destructive purposes—acids for industrial uses, pharmaceuticals, chemical fertilizers, and new types of explosives. In each development, scientific research played a significant role; the practical value of science became increasingly apparent to businessmen, statesmen, soldiers, and ordinary citizens alike.

The electrical industry provides another example of the close relationship that developed between science and technology. In the first half of the nineteenth century the theoretical foundation for the electrical industry was laid by scientists whose names have become incorporated into the vocabulary of electricity: Volta, Ohm, and Ampère, among others, raised electricity from its status in the eighteenth century as a kind of plaything to a science of great theoretical and practical importance. A major advancement came in 1831 when Michael Faraday discovered a way to convert electrical energy into mechanical energy. A whole series of technological discoveries followed this breakthrough; generators, transformers, cables, and batteries were perfected in succeeding years.

By the 1880's means had been found for generating electrical current and sending it over short distances. Small generating plants, either publicly or privately owned, appeared in the 1880's and 1890's to serve local needs, such as municipal lighting. These small plants consumed a great deal of fuel in producing limited amounts of electrical power, and the high cost of their operation excluded many potential consumers. At little cost the harnessing of water on a vast scale could generate enormous power to produce electrical energy, but most sources of hydro-electric power were distant from existing industrial centers in Europe. What was needed was a means of sending power over a wide area from large, centralized, high-capacity generating plants.

In 1891 the problem of power transmission was solved when a Swiss firm sent power to Frankfort from a station more than a hundred miles away by means of high-voltage lines. In the next few years the long-distance capacity of voltage lines increased, and electrical power began to be distributed in integrated power districts. Even a relatively large area such as the Rhineland could be brought under one network. Within such a network large or small industrial plants, cities, and even individual houses could tap the central source for any desired amount of electrical power.

Electricity introduced changes into almost every aspect of European life. For industries, electrical power offered greater flexibility than other sources of power. Because electricity could be brought directly to wherever it was needed, the complicated and inefficient systems of belts and pulleys, used to transmit power in early industrial plants, were eliminated and plants were streamlined. Electrical motors could be designed large or small, depending on the task. These motors efficiently and rapidly transported goods within the factories; such transportation had previously accounted for a considerable portion of production costs. Insofar as electricity was "cleaner" than other forms of power the new industrial era promised to be less grimy and sooty than the preceding one. Electricity also brought the promise of the industrial revolution to areas that lacked coal resources but were well endowed with sites for hydro-electric plants, such as northern Italy and southern France. Since electrical power could be used in small shops as well as in huge concerns, a number of light industries like the manufacture of shoes and articles of clothing became mechanized. Often this meant cheaper, mass-produced consumer items.

Although the electrical industry was in an early stage at the beginning of the twentieth century, the potential of electrical power for domestic uses seemed unlimited even then. As coal had been the energy source for the first industrial revolution, so electricity promised universal power for the mass age. At the turn of the century electricity had already affected the lives of average Europeans living in the cities of industrial states. Every progressive city installed electrical lighting for its streets; streetcars and underground trains powered by electrical motors moved urban workers to and from work with speed and convenience. Some homes and apartments acquired electrical lighting, and a market developed for small appliances such as irons and gramophones. It was technically possible, and even becoming economically feasible, to apply electrical power to almost any task, whether industrial or domestic.

The Impact of Technology

New industrial developments affected the lives of Europeans in many ways. The factory system brought standardization to both industrial and consumer goods. Whatever loss in individuality or quality of the product that may have resulted from this trend was compensated for by lower prices and increased productivity. Manufacture by assembly-line techniques produced cheaper necessities and even brought some luxuries within the financial reach of middle-class Europeans. New items became common; for instance, the bicycle, which came into prominence at the end of the nineteenth century, provided mobility and a sense of freedom to all but the poorest classes. The masses were beginning to participate in the economic life of Europe as consumers, not just as laborers and producers.

Electricity, organic chemistry, and steel symbolized a new era that, if it was not replacing the older age, was at least being superimposed on it in a dramatic way. The concentration of the first industrial revolution on heavy industry, rail construction, and the manufacture of basic textiles met initial demands, but, as was mentioned above, it was confined to a limited sector of the economy. The new age affected all sectors. Electricity brought into every home the promise of vastly increased power. Organic chemistry made possible the production of synthetic goods that few people had imagined before they appeared on the market. Steel became a kind of universal metal (although even newer metals, such as aluminum, were gaining wide acceptance). Steel was used in the construction of ships, automobiles, farm tools, bicycle frames, and apartment buildings—few people living in the industrial states of Europe did not use, ride in, or live in objects made wholly or partially of steel.

Perhaps even more significant for the development of Europe in this new phase of industrial growth was what the economic historian David Landes has called "a gradual institutionalization of technological advance." Scientific research increasingly brought about innovations in a deliberate way: no longer did Europe's industrial society await new discoveries; it made them as a matter of course. The new technology naturally produced strains within European society; gaps widened between regions, between traditional and modern societies, between town and countryside. Moreover, the demands of technology required a readiness for change and an adaptability that fostered social tensions.

Changes in the Economic Structure of Europe

Continuing technological innovation, accompanied by an expansion of plants and products, gave impetus to European industrialization during the last decades of the nineteenth century. Yet, by a curious paradox, at a time when production was going up, trade was increasing, and new levels of prosperity were being reached, the outlook for Europe's economic future was uncertain. The financial panic of 1873 had brought the confident era of the mid-nineteenth century to a close by initiating a decline in prices for industrial goods. Occasional rallies had little effect on the long-range downward trend, which was not reversed until the 1890's. As late as 1896 prices were only about two-thirds of the 1873 level. For this reason, despite expanded production and somewhat higher standards of living for wage earners, the period from 1873 to 1898 has been labeled a depression.

Recently David Landes has argued that the great depression of the late nineteenth century was actually a continuation of a decline in prices in Europe during the whole of that century. He considers the upturn in the 1850's, which reflected an influx of gold from California and Australia, to have been only a temporary reversal of that pattern. By the mid-1860's prices had leveled and in the 1870's began to slide again. Prices started rising in the late 1890's because of a growing demand for goods and a new influx of gold from South African and Alaskan mines, but in the 1880's and early 1890's the steadily dropping prices showed no signs of recovering. The sense of frustration and insecurity within the European business community at that time was in sharp contrast to the relative optimism that prevailed during the temporary boom of the late 1850's and early 1860's.

The Trend Toward Protectionism

The price decline had an important effect on economic development. Increased industrial capacity created a surplus of goods that drove down prices. Increased trade, which brought greater competition from foreign manufacturers, also drove down prices. To protect their domestic markets from this competition manufacturers sought protective tariffs that would eliminate the danger of cheap goods being introduced by foreign manufacturers. Protectionists often found allies among farmers and landowners who suffered from the lower prices of meat and grain caused by the importation of these products from Argentina, Russia, and the United States. Improvements in canning, refrigeration, and transportation had enabled these countries to enter the European market for agricultural products. Between 1874 and 1884, for example, transatlantic rates for grain shipments had dropped by some 60 percent—it became cheaper to harvest grain in Minnesota and ship it to Germany than to grow wheat in East Prussia.

By 1880 higher duties for many items had been imposed by Germany, Austria, and Italy. Other states adopted protectionist measures in the 1880's. The process reached a climax in France with the passing of the Méline Tariff in 1892. Germany's drive toward protectionism, which began with the Bismarck Tariff of 1879, reached an apex with the Bülow Tariff passed in 1902. Only those areas with strong commercial traditions, such as Great Britain, Holland, and Scandinavia, remained faithful to free-trade policies. Even in Britain there were advocates of protectionism; from 1903 on Joseph Chamberlain loudly championed the practice of imperial preference, by which goods traded within the empire would be protected from outside competition.

The trend toward protectionism is obvious, but the influence it had on trade and the European economy is difficult to assess. Protective tariffs did place obstacles in the way of trade in some countries, and they did maintain higher prices for some domestic goods. In spite of these effects, protectionist policies did not seriously curb foreign trade among European states or with non-European nations. The volume of world trade more than doubled in the last quarter of the nineteenth century, and Europe's share remained high, even against competition from the United States and Japan.

The significance of protectionism is that it was symptomatic of the changing character of European economy. A vastly enlarged capacity for production, shared by several nations rather than monopolized by Great Britain, caused a somewhat frantic search for new customers and strenuous efforts to keep existing ones. As a policy designed to control trade and markets, however, protectionism only imperfectly achieved its objective.

Consolidation of Industry

Large firms and cartels, in addition to organizing industry, provided a safeguard against the uncertainties of market conditions during an era of falling prices. Declining prices could be resisted by agreements to divide marketing areas among various firms or by understandings that imposed limitations on production. Sometimes these agreements broke down, causing the system to work imperfectly, but in Germany, for example, cartels and industry-wide agreements were considered legally binding, thereby encouraging consolidation of industry. Agreements on production and prices of merchandise were relatively easy to enforce when firms enjoyed near-monopoly of a given market. Direct mergers enabled reductions in cost of production through tighter organization of management and sales staffs and through consolidation of research and distribution facilities. These savings allowed some firms to maintain profits or at least minimize the squeeze created by declining prices. Although most of these efforts occurred within the framework of national economies, several industries, such as glass manufacturing, adopted common policies that transcended national borders.

The Search for New Markets

The need to find markets for industrial products intensified the scramble for imperial possessions by the European powers. The pressures of market competition by no means accounted entirely for imperialism in the late nineteenth century, but certainly the anxieties of industrialists influenced government policy. The results of colonization, however, were disappointing. Many of the newer territories offered little real profit; in fact they often cost more to administer than could be realized through returns on trade. Asia and Africa proved particularly disappointing as new markets because of extreme poverty in many areas. They became more important as sources for the raw materials on which Europe's industrial economy relied. With the import of raw materials, trade with these areas increased. But the rate of this trade did not grow as rapidly as the development of commerce within Europe and with the United States. Measured by value of exports and imports the industrial nations remained one another's best customers. Germany, for example, was one of Great Britain's most important customers, despite its restrictive tariffs. The increasingly extensive patterns of trade uniting the industrial nations, combined with imperial commerce, created a world-wide economic network of some complexity. A heightened interdependence became a significant characteristic of the new economic patterns in Europe produced by the industrial expansion of the late nineteenth century.

The search for overseas markets by the industrial states of Europe was accompanied by the export of large amounts of capital to distant lands and to other areas within Europe. Britain invested more than one-fourth of its wealth overseas. Of this total, slightly less than half was placed in the empire; the remainder was concentrated in the United States and Latin America. To a lesser degree, France and Germany were also major exporters of capital, most of it invested outside their imperial holdings. France had only 10 percent and Germany less than 7 percent of their foreign investments within their empires. French investments were concentrated in eastern Europe and the Balkans; by 1914 about one-fourth of the French foreign investment was in Russian securities, an economic counterpart to the diplomatic ties that had been formed between the two countries in the 1890's. Germany's foreign investments, which amounted to only 6 percent of its total wealth in 1914, were dispersed, although there was a tendency to invest in Austro-Hungarian, Latin-American, and United States securities.

Often foreign investments, like the French investments in Russia, were politically motivated and were encouraged by the government. Although economic pressures might occasionally be exerted for political ends, foreign investment did not necessarily produce political domination. Nor did capital always follow the flag, as demonstrated by the comparatively light investment in the empires. European capital resources made European states the bankers for much of the world.

Individual investors were attracted to foreign investments by the promise of relatively high profits. Interest rates were low in Europe, and bonds for enterprises such as Mexican or Argentinian railways offered returns of 6 percent or better. To the European *rentier* class, which depended heavily on the income from investments, such rates had a strong appeal. The returns on overseas capital supplemented the European economy.

For Great Britain, the export of capital had become something of a necessity by the end of the nineteenth century. Britain was dependent on imports of foodstuffs and raw materials, and the total amount paid for these imports increased steadily as more goods came into the country. Meanwhile the decline in prices for manufactured goods made it difficult to meet these expenses. Between 1891 and 1906 Britain showed an unfavorable balance of trade. Britain managed to postpone the consequences of this unfavorable balance through overseas investments and commercial services. A series of "hidden exports"—investments, income from insurance services, shipping fees—restored the balance. Profits from these endeavors also enabled Britain to postpone any extensive adjustment to meet the rise of competing industrial powers. The continued prosperity after 1900 convinced the British that, despite the difficulties of a more competitive world market, Britain remained at the center of a world-wide economy and played a crucial role in it. The British banks did in fact provide vital services within the world economy. Although other nations might rival Britain's industrial capacity, few could match the experience of London's commercial banks in handling complex financial affairs on an international level. London bankers arranged the transfer of credit and the payment for goods in remote corners of the world. At the end of the nineteenth century Britain was the world's leading market.

The Spread of Industrialization

Another reason for the growing complexity of Europe's economic structure was the spread of industrialization beyond central and northwestern Europe into Italy and Russia. The Italian push began in the late 1890's and lasted for about a decade. By 1908 Italy was on the way toward an industrial economy, although the modernization was confined largely to northern Italy. The impetus for the drive came from the development of electrical power at Alpine hydro-electric plants. Considerable impetus also came from Italian banks, which provided capital and leadership to Italian enterprises, and from German capital investments. Chemical, engineering, and textile industries and other flourishing manufacturing concerns provided Italy with an important base for economic modernization.

Equally notable were the achievements of Russian industrial development, which began in the late 1880's. Reform-minded finance ministers encouraged the development of domestic industrial production by initiating such governmental policies as protective tariffs for infant concerns, government subsidies, tax benefits, and loans. Although Russia had begun a railway network in the 1860's, the true era of Russian railway construction, including the commencement of the trans-Siberian railroad in 1891, occurred during the 1890's. Government orders for rails created a boom in the steel industry and opened up new iron-producing areas. In the south the Donetz basin became a center for the metallurgical industry. By 1904 the southern provinces accounted for more than 60 percent of Russia's iron production. At this time Russia ranked fourth behind the United States, Germany, and Great Britain in iron production, and its share in the world's steel output increased from 2 to 8 percent. Industry also expanded in the north with the development of metallurgy and textiles in the Moscow and St. Petersburg regions.

The Russian rate of development, beginning from a very modest base, was the highest in Europe. Russia by no means approached the level of western European industrialization, but it had taken significant steps in this direction by the turn of the century. By 1905 about 16 percent of Russia's population lived in an urban environment. Moscow, St. Petersburg, and many of the industrial cities of the south, already of considerable size, were expanding rapidly.

In addition to active government encouragement of industrial growth, Russian manufacturers received assistance from the outside, notably through loans from France and the aid of western European technicians. This assistance tied the Russian economy closely to western Europe. Foreign credits were obtained through the export of grains to western Europe, even in times of famine. In the 1890's Russia was able to stabilize its currency exchange. But these gains were won at the expense of the Russian consumer and the Russian peasant. After the turn of the century, the government came to depend less on foreign loans and more on the development of an internal market for industrial products. Russia's industrial development gradually acquired its own momentum. Russia was still largely an agrarian state, but the direction of its economic development was clearly indicated. Another industrial state was emerging within Europe.

Those nations that were—or were in the process of becoming—industrial states in the 1890's gained a crucial lead over the rest of the world and became a kind of oligarchy of industrial nations. Very few countries since the turn of the century have achieved a similar industrial breakthrough. Those that have made the attempt have faced formidable problems in "catching up." The oligarchy was not exclusive to Europe; Japan and the United States were well advanced in industrial modernization. Also, Russia subsequently surpassed a number of other industrial nations, altering the hierarchy of the industrial elite. But membership in this elite remained fairly constant for nearly half a century following the 1890's.

The People, the Land, and the Cities

Changes in Population

A dramatic increase in the size of the European population paralleled the burgeoning economic and technological development. At the beginning of the nineteenth century the population of Europe, including that of Russia, was about 190 million; by mid-century it had

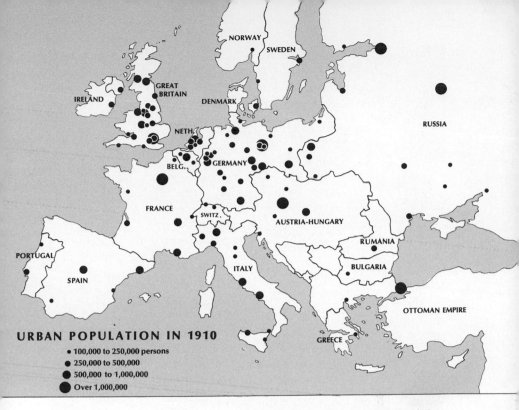

URBAN POPULATION IN 1910

- 100,000 to 250,000 persons
- 250,000 to 500,000
- 500,000 to 1,000,000
- Over 1,000,000

reached 270 million; and at the end of the century some 420 million people inhabited the European continent and the British Isles. This population explosion was part of a general rise in the world's population during the nineteenth century, but it was more dynamic in Europe than elsewhere. In 1800 Europe held about one-fifth of the world's population; in 1900 this proportion had risen to around 27 percent, and these statistics do not include the large numbers of Europeans who emigrated. Europeans, European emigrants, and their descendants accounted for nearly one-third of the people living in 1914.

Improved living conditions furthered the rate of population growth during the last quarter of the nineteenth century. One aspect of the improved conditions after 1870 was an increase in the amount and quality of the food supply. A drastic reduction in the costs of bulk transport by railway and steamship led to an influx of cheap grain from Russia and the American midwest. Improvements in canning and refrigeration enabled Argentine and American beef and Australian mutton to reach Europe in an unspoiled condition and at competitive prices. On the Continent railway tunnels through the Alps gave the north more direct access to a great variety of semi-tropical produce, including citrus fruits. More efficient techniques in dairying and the use of pasteurization permitted relatively inexpensive milk and milk products to reach tables that had not seen such luxuries in the past.

Standards of health in the latter part of the nineteenth century were dramatically improved. Strengthened public health codes reduced the chances of epidemic, as did a growing acceptance of immunization and inoculation. Typhus and cholera, which had broken out on three occasions between 1848 and 1872, had virtually been eliminated from Europe by 1900. Deaths from smallpox, scarlet fever, and other infectious diseases became increasingly rare. Hospital conditions and techniques in surgery became less primitive. In the war of 1870 approximately 10,000 of 13,000 amputations performed by French army surgeons had resulted in death; by the turn of the century more extensive use of antiseptics, chloroform, and aseptic methods, combined with a better knowledge of physiology, improved the chances for survival on the operating table. Hospitals were cleaner and were reorganized in a manner that reduced the possibility of disease being spread within the hospital itself. Perhaps the most impressive contribution to higher standards of health emerged from the discoveries of Pasteur, Koch, and others in the field of bacteriology. Sophisticated laboratory techniques, such as the use of synthetic dyes for microscope slides, facilitated the isolation of different bacteria that could be identified with specific diseases. These processes enabled the development of vaccines for immunization against a wide range of infectious diseases. With the new medicines, including the first antibiotics, that appeared after the turn of the century, pharmacology entered a phase of dynamic growth that has not yet abated.

Curiously, as dietary and medical standards improved, the birth rate for certain western European states began to decline. Apparently this decline was due to a voluntary birth control that reflected changing conditions of family life. Urban families did not have to meet a demand for cheap farm labor, and, in fact, a large family could be a serious burden in the city. With the growing likelihood that each child would survive, birth control in a variety of forms enabled families to avoid the economic burdens of feeding, clothing, and educating a large family. Perhaps this practice reflected a conscious desire to assure a few offspring the advantages of better living standards and better opportunities within an industrial urban society.

While the industrial western states were approaching a balance between lower birth rates and declining mortality, the agrarian regions of eastern Europe retained a high birth rate even as the death rate declined. As a result, the strain of overpopulation in rural areas intensified, because there was little industry in eastern Europe to absorb the surplus. An outlet was found in emigration, and in the late 1880's eastern Europe replaced western Europe as the major source for emigrants. In some areas a wave of migration from east to west occurred; Poles moved in to take the place of the German peasants who moved to the industrial centers of the Ruhr. The influx of Poles alarmed many conservative, aristocratic landowners who exploited cheap Polish labor but displayed a deep-seated hostility toward Slavic peoples.

With increased longevity and lower birth rates in western Europe, the average age of the population was increasing. In Britain, for example, the population under fifteen was 8 percent less in 1900 than it had been in 1850 while the percentage of those between the ages of fifteen and sixty-five went up proportionately. (The aging of the population was even more noticeable in 1950, when only about 22 percent of the British population—as contrasted with 32 percent in 1901— was under fifteen. Similar patterns occurred in other western European states.) With the disappearance of hierarchical rural families, the problem of providing an environment for the elderly was to become acute in the twentieth century.

European society, then, had expanded enormously, and the industrial order in the 1890's held at least a promise of better health, nourishment, and prosperity for the European people. Indeed, scientific and technological discoveries enabled Europe's growing population to enjoy an unprecedented standard of living. Even so, the benefits of industrialization were not equally shared throughout the population.

Class Distinctions

The Upper Class ▪ The upper bourgeoisie profited most from Europe's economic and technological advances in the nineteenth century. In Germany, Great Britain, and France, a very small elite held a preponderance of the nation's wealth; for example, in Britain in 1913 less than 5 percent of the population over the age of twenty-five commanded about 60 percent of the wealth. This disparity of individual income was reflected in living standards. By the turn of the century, styles of life for the newly rich—bankers, industrialists, and financiers —were extremely luxurious. Their homes were equipped with the latest conveniences, from electrical lighting to telephones. Automobiles became fashionable after the turn of the century, despite frequent breakdowns and general unreliability. Country homes or estates provided escape from the city and business affairs, as did trips to vacation resorts and health spas. Servants were essential to maintain establishments in town, in the country, and at the seashore. This lavish consumption was often marked by a certain depressing vulgarity. The upper middle class homes were filled with overstuffed furniture upholstered in expensive and somber fabrics; velvet curtains and sentimental paintIngs in heavy, ornate frames did little to relieve the gloom. Some of the newly rich were patrons of the arts, but they were the exception rather than the rule. In general, taste was imitative and conventional.

Eventually the wealthy bourgeoisie mixed with the aristocratic classes although subtle differences were maintained. In his style of life the wealthy parvenu consciously imitated the ways of his social superiors. Marriages into aristocratic families were highly prized and were worth a considerable dowry. In Great Britain the aristocrats participated relatively freely in trade; they served on boards of directors for large firms, adding the luster of their titles and occasionally some talent to these executive bodies. In France the aristocracy retained a greater disdain for even the superficial appearance of earning a living. The French considered luxury and idleness to be hallmarks of the aristocratic life. But as the luxurious life became increasingly difficult to maintain, more and more aristocrats either married into bourgeois wealth or demeaned themselves with a connection in business. In Germany subtle but important distinctions between men who had made their fortunes and landholding aristocracy remained very much alive, as social novels—particularly those of Theodore Fontane—testify.

For the most part, the European aristocracy continued to pursue the pleasures and idle amusements that had traditionally marked its existence. At the turn of the century, participation in events of the "season" in London or Paris, protracted stays in the country for hunting, and vacations at such spas as Biarritz, Marienbad, and Aix-les-Bains were still characteristic of the aristocracy. But in an age in which the amassing of wealth increasingly depended on commercial or industrial enterprise and less and less on land, it soon became apparent that the aristocrats could not continue their style of life indefinitely. Compromises of necessity, the infusion of new wealth, and the merging of upper bourgeois and aristocratic families forced the aristocracy to adapt its value system to rapidly changing conditions.

A double standard of conventional morality and less conventional behavior existed among the upper class throughout the nineteenth century. At the turn of the century official codes of morality became more flexible than they had been during the height of the Victorian era. Divorce, for example, appeared less scandalous; where it was still prohibited—in Catholic countries—separation, annulment, or simply the taking on of a mistress were all easily arranged. However, the double standard continued to exist in some areas. Women were far from being "emancipated," as several women's rights movements attested. Female deviation from standards of socially acceptable behavior was still considered shocking. After the turn of the century women gradually gained some freedom in society, and certain careers were opened to them, but their freedom was a limited one, and they continually encountered male hostility or skepticism.

Accompanying the loosening of moral codes was a loosening of the paternal authoritarianism in upper-class families. Education enabled children to pursue independent careers; sons of wealthy businessmen often preferred the upper ranks of the civil service or diplomatic corps to employment in the family firm. Military service continued to be regarded as a desirable career, particularly when a commission facilitated access to aristocratic social circles.

The Middle Class ▪ For the middle range of the bourgeoisie the industrial order also brought luxury, although not on quite the same scale. Demand for managers and engineers to run large organizations presented ambitious and talented young men with significant opportunities for social and economic advancement. Social mobility was increased by the education and training available at expanded educational facilities. Some members of the middle class considered dependence on a salary from a large firm as a step down from the tradition of individual dependence and self-reliance. For them the liberal professions, especially medicine and law, satisfied the ideal of independence while providing a comfortable living. A few women even found careers in these occupations, as restrictions on women entering law or medical school were lifted.

Advancement and social achievement came to be measured in economic terms, although certain high-status but low-paying positions, such as the clergy or university teaching, held considerable attraction. The professional middle class could usually save part of their income and frequently accumulated enough wealth to afford an early retirement. For this social group hard work led to a comfortable and satisfying existence.

Somewhat less prosperous than the professional and managerial groups, but more prosperous than the lower working classes, were the white-collar employees, including shopkeepers and clerks and those involved in the expanding governmental and business bureaucracies. This "service" class made up the lower ranks of the middle class. It was the most rapidly growing social group at the turn of the century. (The working class was numerically larger, but it grew at a slower rate.) By 1900 the lower middle class accounted for some 20 percent of the population in Britain and had made an appearance even in nations like Russia where the industrial revolution was in its infancy.

The occupations of this class were in many instances the result of the industrial revolution but were not directly part of it. The salaried clerical employee of a large firm did not consider himself a member of the proletariat. Some members of the lower middle class may have possessed limited savings and perhaps modest investments, but few owned property. The class depended almost exclusively on salaries for survival. Generally these salaries were low, often below wages for some workers. Only foremen and some shopkeepers managed an income high enough to give them a margin of security.

Measured by income level, then, the lower middle class appeared to have more in common with workers than with any other group, but in styles of living and social attitudes they tended to aspire to the values of those immediately above them rather than accept the outlook of the proletariat. Respect for property and a desire for ownership were high with this group. Their "upward mobility" was reflected in their occupational choices. Clerical employment was considered to offer opportunities for advancement into better paying and more respectable occupations. The lower middle class sent many more sons into the ranks of the professions and upper managerial positions than did the working class.

Generally, clerical workers were proud of symbols, such as occupation or dress, that differentiated them from those engaged in blue-collar work. They made sacrifices to obtain better clothing, and whenever possible they sought housing outside working-class districts. The lesser bureaucrats who dealt with workers frequently manifested a petty insistence on rank; indeed, mutual antagonism characterized relations between these two groups.

Despite relatively low pay, the lower middle class resisted most attempts to organize unions among them. Professional organizations like teachers' associations were acceptable, but these groups were not primarily oriented toward bargaining with employers over salaries and working conditions. Individual initiative and a belief in competitive achievement worked against the formation of collective organizations. Where large organizations were formed, as in the German Federation of Salaried Commercial Employees, the members showed a greater anxiety about status than about other considerations, and they held fundamentally conservative, anti-labor, and often anti-Semitic opinions.

Those in the ranks of the lower middle class were not without discontent. First of all, the middle-class comforts they sought could not always be realized on their limted incomes, and the gap between aspiration and achievement was a source of frustration for many. Second, the position of this class within the economy was not at all secure. The threat of unemployment during times of recession carried as much menace for the lower middle class as it did for workers. The small shopkeepers were particularly concerned about competition from large department stores that could undersell them. Profits for the small shopkeeper or artisan were marginal at best, and the danger of competition from "big business" produced a helpless feeling.

With the expansion of this social class, the economic tensions and social discontents carried a possibility for overt political action. In Austria the triumph of the Christian Socialist party in Vienna during the 1890's can be attributed to the political mobilization of the lower middle class; the party program expressed many of the grievances of the little man caught between a revolutionary proletariat and the much more prosperous upper middle class. Demands for protection from big business, the proletariat, and "foreign" or Jewish influence were made. In some states a respect for order and a fear of revolutionary anarchy deflected impulses toward political activism. Nevertheless, a potenitally volatile class had appeared in Europe that was difficult to categorize: it was neither part of the proletariat nor part of the property-owning bourgeoisie. Some members depended on the industrial bureaucracy for employment; others saw themselves threatened by the growing size of Europe's industrial order. Although a certain contradiction marked the attitudes and values of this class, common to all members was a narrow margin of economic security.

The Working Class ▪ From the point of view of political rulers and property owners the working class that was formed by the demands of industrialization seemed to offer the greatest threat to the status quo because of its revolutionary attitude. The steady expansion of industrial enterprises entailed a continued influx of labor into the cities of Europe throughout the nineteenth century. By the 1890's workers made up about one-third of the working population in Belgium, Great Britain, Germany, and France. From that time on, however, the percentage of workers in the industrialized nations remained constant and in some instances even began to decline in relation to the rest of the population. The new class of the second industrial revolution appeared to be the technologists and bureaucrats who proliferated in an environment that increasingly favored large, scientifically oriented firms. Although its growth rate was dropping, the working class became skillful at defending its interests in the industrial order; this was particularly true of the young workers who followed their fathers into the factories. This second generation of workers possessed a greater familiarity with industrial society than did the somewhat disoriented peasants who had initially migrated into the industrial districts.

Living conditions for the working classes were better at the end of the nineteenth century than they had been at any previous time, but existence for one out of three workers was still not much above a subsistence level. Statistics show that real wages increased in France, Germany, and Great Britain until shortly after the turn of the century. Prices had fallen more rapidly than wages after 1873, which meant the average worker had greater purchasing power as long as he remained employed. Recessions and layoffs, of course, canceled some of these gains, but the overall trend was toward improvement in income. With an upswing in prices at the turn of the century, however, workers' real wages increased little, if at all, between 1900 and 1914.

The degree to which workers shared in the general increase of wealth at the end of the nineteenth century is still a matter of debate among economic historians. The debate is aggravated in part by the existence of evidence that does not lend itself to refined analysis. According to one view, the workers' share of the gross national product—admittedly difficult to estimate during this period—actually declined by as much as 50 percent in Germany and by some 25 percent in Great Britain where wage levels tended to be relatively high. Another estimate shows an increase in the share of the gross national product for all salaried employees, but this computation includes white-collar workers and managers and therefore does not accurately describe the income of the working class. From the available evidence it seems clear that the workers benefited less than the middle class from the increase of European wealth at the end of the nineteenth century. The gap between the standards of living was obvious; it could be seen every day in the industrial cities of Europe.

Even so, the last third of the nineteenth century brought a significant improvement in diet, health, sanitation, and literacy for a large segment of the working class. Meat, eggs, sugar, butter, coffee, and wheat (rather than rye) bread appeared more regularly on workers' tables. In Germany, for example, consumption of meat per capita increased some 130 percent between 1860 and 1900; similar gains were registered elsewhere. These gains indicate the low dietary standards that prevailed in Europe prior to the late nineteenth century, but they also suggest that a number of workers could afford more and better food as a result of improved salaries and lower agricultural prices. The less important place that food occupied in the worker's budget enabled him to obtain other necessities. Lower consumer prices, reflecting the economy of mass-produced goods, permitted a wider purchase of clothing of a higher quality. Inexpensive machine-made shoes replaced the wooden sabot for all but the poorest laborers, and warm woolen garments became more common.

Reductions in working hours to an average of ten hours a day by 1914, and an acceptance of Sunday as a day of rest, provided more leisure time for the working class; at the turn of the century Sunday outings to the country or seashore were facilitated by excursion rates offered by railway companies. The more prosperous segment of the working class could set aside a portion of earnings for amusements. Newspapers and novels were popular, as were occasional visits to music halls and, after 1900, to the movies. Although the local bistro still offered an escape from the depressing atmosphere of dingy and overcrowded apartments, the incidence of violence and drunkenness began to decline.

Welfare measures also tempered some of the harsh living conditions for the working class. Health insurance measures and public charity hospitals made improved medical practices more widely available, although such steps were minimal at best. Safety inspections in factories and disability insurance reduced both the physical and economic risks involved in factory employment. Strengthened municipal regulations on sanitation and housing curtailed some of the more flagrant abuses in slum dwellings. The struggle against the spread of slum areas, which many regarded as hopeless in 1850, began to achieve a measure of success. The introduction of streetcars and other forms of urban transportation enabled some workers to seek better housing farther away from the factories. But this greater mobility within the cities, just beginning at the turn of the century, was enjoyed more by the middle class than by the working class. The majority of workers continued to live close to their employment within industrial districts.

The improvement in the workers' living standards was only relative to the preceding years; their gains could not obscure the inequalities that remained. What progress had been achieved seemed little enough reward for the drudgery and monotony of industrial labor. Apartments in industrial towns were overcrowded, dark, and poorly ventilated. Despite stiffer municipal building codes, many apartments were without such conveniences as central heating and running water. Parks in working-class districts were few and were inadequate for serving those who crowded into them. Schools in these areas frequently lacked the equipment and quality of instruction that were available in middle-class districts. By comparison with the middle class, existence for the average worker was drab, uneventful, and "deprived" of many items that the middle class considered necessities.

Below the workers was a category of totally destitute people. The percentage of the population in central and western Europe living in abject poverty may well have declined in the nineteenth century, but significant numbers with incomes that fell below subsistence standards remained in conditions of misery. A survey conducted in the town of York, England, in 1899 revealed that about 10 percent of the population had earnings insufficient "for the maintenance of physical efficiency." The aid provided by charitable organizations for those at the bottom of the economic scale was insufficient. Society preferred to ignore the totally destitute, who lacked any means for expressing their despair. For these, the industrial order held no promises.

Rural Europe

The classes most directly involved in the industrial order lived in the cities, but the rural population—the peasantry, the independent farmers, and the landholding aristocracy—were also influenced by technological changes at the end of the nineteenth century. One of the most consequential changes was the revolution in transportation. As has been mentioned, the drastically reduced steamship rates and the extension of rail lines into fertile grain-producing regions enabled Russian, Canadian, and American grain, and Argentinian beef to reach Europe at competitive prices. The price decline that ensued caused a transatlantic agrarian crisis. The application of mechanized techniques to inexpensive and fertile midwestern American and Canadian land, for example, resulted in an abundance of foodstuffs that suddenly flooded the world market. European farmers could have adopted improved methods and techniques to increase their productivity, but they would merely have added to the surplus already available on the European market. And there was a marked reluctance to invest capital in agricultural machinery when prices were declining.

The Agrarian Crisis ▪ The response of the European countries to the agrarian crisis varied. The most common demand, paralleling the reaction of manufacturers to declining prices, was for protection. Higher duties on a large number of agricultural goods were imposed by Germany in 1879, by France in the 1880's, and by most other continental states soon after. Only Great Britain, Holland, and Scandinavia adhered to free-trade policies in agriculture. Through protective tariffs, prices were maintained at artificially high levels, particularly in wheat-producing areas. The duty on wheat often equaled one-third or one-half the price of American wheat on the European market. Protectionism allowed the wheat farmers to survive, but it by no means assured them great prosperity; it was a measure taken for political reasons to protect a particular social class. For consumers in countries with protective tariffs this policy meant higher prices for agricultural goods than otherwise would have prevailed.

In states where the government maintained free-trade policies, those engaged in agriculture were forced to adjust to conditions of a world-wide agricultural market. The decline of Britain's landed society was one of the more spectacular consequences of the collapse of wheat prices and land values at the end of the nineteenth century. Traditionally this class had supplied Britain's social and political leadership. During the eighteenth and early nineteenth centuries commercial farming had rewarded the British landholders handsomely. In the mid-nineteenth century enlightened landlords enjoyed a final golden age of farming that was characterized by land improvements and expanded production through more intensive cultivation. But the agrarian depression of the 1880's demolished the economic base of the landed class. Agricultural rents, which had reached a peak in 1879, fell rapidly as agricultural prices plummeted. For many landlords income from estates dropped by as much as half within a twenty-year period, and the prospects for recovery were bleak. As indebtedness became more common, increasing numbers of landlords sought to salvage their fortunes in the business world. Gradually the possession of land lost its importance as a prerequisite for social and political advancement. With their landlords financially unable to invest in a declining enterprise, many farmers abandoned their farms for employment in the cities. Both the landed aristocracy and the tenant farmers who survived into the new century represented declining social classes in Great Britain.

Elsewhere in Europe, particularly in Germany, the landed society was more successful in retaining control. The Junkers, the landed aristocrats of Prussia, used their political influence to resist attempts at reform and to organize pressure groups, such as the Agrarian League, which won important concessions for them in the form of high tariffs, subsidies, and favorable labor policies. At the end of the nineteenth century, the Junkers and German business interests formed an alliance of convenience that worked for the preservation of a social and political status quo in the German empire. This alliance brought about the Bülow Tariff of 1902. This tariff raised duties on agricultural goods to unprecedented heights; in exchange for this concession, Junker conservatives endorsed increases for the German naval construction program that the Ruhr industrialists favored. This "rye and steel" alliance was a key factor in German political life because it upheld the landed and upper middle class interests against the demands for reform emanating from liberal and, more important, socialist movements in the country.

Thus, although in both Prussia and Britain there was in the nineteenth century an important landowning class with sizable estates, differences in response to the collapse of grain prices at the end of the century produced different political results in the two countries. By adhering to free-trade doctrines, the landed aristocracy of Britain accepted the decline of their own influence, whereas the Junkers, in seeking protection and allying themselves with industrialists, resisted threats to their social and economic position in Germany. Despite the efforts of the Junkers, the agrarian revolution and the growing industrialization of the country continued to place a strain on their position in German society. Mortgages increased during the last three decades of the nineteenth century, and many landowners found it difficult to make ends meet. Protectionism was only a defensive measure; its acceptance in Germany reflected the political strength of a threatened conservative social class.

Protectionism in France also reflected the political demands of the agrarian sector, but it did not imply the defense of a landowning class controlling large estates. Most French farms were relatively small. Nevertheless, French farmers felt the pressure of slumping prices just as intensely as great landholders, and it is a reflection of the political strength of the countryside that deputies in the French Chamber provided their rural constituents with relief in the form of higher tariffs. Relatively immune to pressures of competition, the small and inefficient French farmer survived into the twentieth century. In other areas with predominantly small landholdings, such as Austria, protection also forestalled threats to the rural economy and delayed modernization of production methods.

The traditional landowning class encountered economic difficulties at the end of the nineteenth century in other regions also. In Russia the amount of land held by the nobility steadily decreased, so that by 1905 this class possessed only 53 percent of the land that it had owned in the 1860's. Land was either sold to pay debts (which were increasingly difficult to meet because of falling agricultural prices), or else leased to peasants. The nobles' complaints were plentiful, particularly in the last fifteen years of the nineteenth century. The establishment of credit facilities through the Nobles' Bank often did little more than postpone bankruptcy. The land passed into the hands of the state, the peasantry, or the growing class of merchants and industrialists. Some nobles survived and even prospered, but they did so only by extensive modernization and conversion to more profitable crops such as sugar beets. Those landowners who could afford improvements and modernization had some chance for economic survival. For the majority, however, the agrarian crisis brought economic failure.

In southern Europe the landowning pattern was feudal. Owners of large estates retained primitive, pre-industrial methods of production. Emphasis was placed on local self-sufficiency, which was often not much above subsistence level, rather than on production for a market; but even in southern Italy and Spain the landed aristocrats felt the pressures of world-wide competition. Although less directly affected by the industrialization, southern Europe did not escape the consequences of the economic transformation brought about by changes in agrarian market conditions throughout the world. Protective tariffs appeared in Italy, Spain, and other southern European countries.

Conversion to New Farming Techniques ▪ In some areas of Europe, notably Scandinavia, Holland, and some parts of Britain and Germany, conversion to more profitable forms of agriculture presented an alternative to protectionism, stagnation, or ruin. Rising living standards increased demands for better food—meat, eggs, and dairy products—and intensive farming became profitable for farmers who had access to the growing urban markets of northern and western Europe. Because perishable dairy goods could not be shipped over great distances, they were not vulnerable to overseas competition. Danish and Dutch farmers were highly successful in responding to new patterns of consumption. Their exports of dairy and meat products to Britain and the industrial cities of northern Europe boomed at the end of the nineteenth century. Even in Britain, where agriculture seemed fatally depressed, those who converted to dairy farming did fairly well.

Conversion to new farming techniques often required capital investments that were beyond the reach of the average peasant or small landholder. Cooperatives, credit unions, and government services aided those who wished to make improvements in production methods. In Denmark, for example, cooperative creameries played a crucial role in developing the Danish dairy industry. By 1909 some 3600 cooperatives had been formed; the prosperity of Denmark reflected the success of this rural program. After the turn of the century, cooperatives proliferated in Russia until there were about 13,000 by the eve of the First World War; by 1910 perhaps one-fourth of Germany's small farmers and peasants belonged to cooperatives, and about 750,000 French peasants, despite traditions of independence, had accepted membership in cooperative societies. These organizations not only offered economies in the purchase of expensive machinery and supplies; they also provided more effective means of reaching a market.

Credit unions and credit societies supplied capital at reasonable rates, thus facilitating the purchase of new equipment. Government subsidies also encouraged certain sectors of the rural economy: the German sugar-beet industry and the French silk and wine industries flourished under such assistance. New techniques were taught at rural schools and training centers. Germany was renowned for the level and extent of its agricultural training. Scandinavia and Holland made significant efforts to educate farmers in the latest techniques. These efforts at agrarian improvement eventually led to an impressive rise in productivity within Europe. Output of wheat, oats, rye, and other grains showed a steady increase, and, of course, the dairy industry prospered. More effective methods of processing brought about higher quality and greater yields of food.

The impulse toward modernization of agriculture was uneven: some areas of Europe adapted rapidly to modern agriculture, particularly where market conditions favored conversion; but many areas continued to use traditional agricultural methods. In many cases the continuing presence of cheap labor on the land made labor-saving mechanization unnecessary. For most of Europe the migration to the cities, although great, did not bring about a rural depopulation. In southern and eastern Europe there was little or no urban-industrial development to absorb the growing rural population; as a result this population remained high and farm wages were depressingly low, a factor that contributed to peasant unrest. Toward the end of the century some rural depopulation did occur in parts of France and Britain, causing farm wages to rise and making the use of labor-saving machinery economically more attractive.

The Condition of European Peasantry ▪ In general, standards of living for the European peasantry were primitive, although the degree of poverty varied from one region to another. In many areas of France, western Germany, parts of the Balkans, and Austria, where small farms were the rule, some peasants with sizable landholdings managed a comfortable existence. Their farms lacked luxuries or conveniences, but harvests usually returned a surplus. Some managed to extend their holdings by purchasing land from those who migrated to the cities. Many farms, however, barely provided subsistence for a single family. Some small landholders, lacking even this minimum, hired themselves out part-time as laborers. Finally, a sizable proportion of the peasantry in western and central Europe were landless laborers, but the numbers in this category began to decline in France, Germany, and Britain at the end of the nineteenth century.

The condition of the Russian peasantry had not been greatly improved by the abolition of serfdom in 1861. Few peasants had been able to purchase land, and the survival of the peasant commune assured deterioration of living conditions and continuation of outmoded agricultural methods. Because peasants could leave the commune only at the cost of renouncing claims to their share in the company's goods and land, many peasants stayed on the land, adding to the natural increase in Russia's rural population in the late nineteenth century. Scattered plots for each family within the commune prevented an efficient use of the land, and the absence of cheap rural credit and of programs of education prevented the introduction of methods that might have improved low yields. Only with agrarian reforms after 1906 was there development of a small landholding class and the beginning of improvement in living conditions for the Russian peasantry.

In areas where large estates predominated, notably Prussia, Hungary, Galacia, and much of southern Europe, living conditions were particularly harsh for the peasants because landowners kept wages or payments in kind as low as possible. Land hunger was acute in these regions because of rural overpopulation. In Prussia migration into the industrial cities offered an escape, but eastern and southern Europe provided no such alternative to farming. Turmoil and discontent began to mark the behavior of the eastern and southern European peasantry toward the end of the nineteenth century.

Urban Expansion

By the end of the nineteenth century different standards and styles of living clearly differentiated the agrarian and the urban-industrial sectors of Europe. Although around 80 percent of the population of eastern and southern Europe continued to depend on agriculture, in western Europe and portions of central Europe the cities and the industrial economy overshadowed the countryside. No longer did the uncertainties of climate determine prosperity or hardship; with assurance of adequate supplies of food from domestic and overseas sources, the western European economy came to be governed by industrial and business cycles.

The shift away from agrarian pursuits was most pronounced in Great Britain, where less than 10 percent of the population were farmers in 1900. In Germany at that time only 35 percent of the gainfully employed worked on the land in forestry or agriculture; and in France, the most agrarian of the industrial states, although half the population was still dependent on agriculture, the numbers were declining. The eclipse of the countryside could be detected also in the diminishing share it had in national income. By 1901 agriculture accounted for no more than 7 percent of the gross national product in Britain and about 30 percent in France. By almost any standard, the role of agriculture within the industrial society of Europe was relatively modest. The changes that had appeared in rural Europe were important, but they paled beside the dynamic growth and expansion of industrial and urban regions.

The vast migration from country to city in western Europe that had begun in the nineteenth century continued after 1900. Fortunately the industrial cities were able to absorb the population growth. The 20-percent increase in the population of Germany and of Great Britain between 1890 and 1914 occurred entirely within the cities.

In southern and eastern Europe migration to the city was not a realistic solution to rural overpopulation. The cities in southern Europe were pre-industrial and offered little in the way of employment or diversion. If anything, living conditions in cities such as Naples were as bad as in the surrounding countryside, where many lived on the verge of starvation. In eastern Europe there were very few cities to which the peasants could migrate. In the last decade of the nineteenth century, emigration offered this rural population the only avenue of escape from impoverishment. The percentage of emigrants to the United States who listed agriculture as their occupation tripled after 1900.

The "new wave" of eastern and southern European emigration to the western hemisphere was predominantly a rural-urban migration across the Atlantic. Some peasants settled in rural areas in the New World and others emigrated only for harvest seasons, but the great majority of Polish, Czech, Italian, Russian, and Slovenian emigrants sought permanent employment in the mines, factories, and cities of North and South America. An international, transatlantic proletariat was thus drawn from the rural and relatively backward areas of Europe. Within Europe, too, there was an international migration of unskilled labor toward those industrial countries with labor shortages. France was second only to the United States as the most popular destination for eastern and southern European emigrants.

The technology of transportation and industrialization at the end of the nineteenth century dramatically changed the size and structure of the cities. Without the industrial revolution, a few European cities at the beginning of the twentieth century might have reached the size that Paris had been in 1800—about 500,000—with the majority of them leveling off at about 200,000. But as a result of the industrialization of northwestern Europe, London was a city of some four and a half million in 1900; Berlin and Paris were approaching two and three million respectively; and St. Petersburg, in relatively undeveloped Russia, had passed the one-million mark. The unprecedented numbers of people living in the cities required that they draw on a world-wide agricultural market. European cities became less dependent on their immediate surroundings for their food needs than at any time in the past. The functions of these cities—the pursuit of commerce and manufacturing or the administration of a state—did not differ so much from those of earlier eras but the scale of operation was far more vast; and the quantitative change brought about a qualitative difference.

The growth of cities in the nineteenth century had been not only rapid but in most cases completely unplanned. Some notable efforts had been made to create a desirable environment: Haussmann's reconstruction of Paris under Napoleon III gave that city its famous boulevards, avenues, and broad vistas; the replacement of Vienna's city walls with the park-like Ringstrasse opened the medieval confines of the inner city. But these were exceptions, and most cities grew haphazardly. In the center of established cities, where commercial, administrative, and other buildings predated the industrial era, new construction was minimal and did not significantly change the appearance. On the perimeter, however, new construction was shaped by the economics of industrialization; the workers' housing had to be close to factories. Clusters of drab, overcrowded tenements around manufacturing plants, which in turn formed a belt around the older city, became a common pattern of cities in the nineteenth century. Parks and open spaces were rare in these working-class districts; often the factories blocked access to rivers, which were used primarily for transportation and the disposal of industrial wastes. Where new cities appeared during the industrial revolution, as in England's Midlands, the German Ruhr, and northeastern France, the cities resembled continuous slums. In many industrial districts the outskirts of one city blended into the suburbs of its neighbor, creating urban conglomeration. Urban sprawl was well under way by 1900.

Toward the end of the nineteenth century, after nearly a hundred years of neglect, some cities made tentative steps toward urban planning. Construction was subjected to closer regulation and inspection, and experiments were launched in housing development through the creation of "garden cities" with open spaces between apartment buildings. A more varied use of materials—steel, reinforced concrete, and glass—presented opportunities for improving on the rather dreary styles that marked the urban environment. The development of public transportation allowed those who could afford it to move to residential suburbs. But these improvements were minor compared to the effort that was needed to control and guide urban growth properly. City planning barely kept pace with the physical expansion of Europe's cities; at best, it simply modified the more depressing features of this growth.

The best and the worst of industrial Europe were to be found in its crowded cities. The pace of life was exciting. The outstanding universities and research institutes, with few exceptions, were located in urban centers. Education became essential for adaptation to a complex society, and the best education and training could be obtained in the cities. For the mass of the urban population, now endowed with at least minimal literacy, the large-circulation dailies brought awareness of a wider world that was not available to the peasant or the average small-town inhabitant. The centers of culture—theaters, museums, galleries, concert halls—that adorned European civilization were in the cities. Yet there could be no doubt that the teeming, populous districts of the cities were depressing and unhealthy. A high incidence of crime made many sections of European cities dangerous. Moreover, the accelerated pace of urban life created anxieties for the city dweller. Traditional ties to family and church weakened, contributing to a sense of isolation and loneliness amid masses of people. The harsh discipline of factory life caused many to long for the unhurried pace of the countryside.

Europe on the eve of the twentieth century was increasingly urban, industrialized, and dynamic. After a long process, lasting most of the nineteenth century but intensified during the final decades of that century, Europe had decisively broken the mold of an agrarian, traditionalist society. In the process the industrial states of Europe acquired an unprecedented amount of power. They were the center of a vast network of transportation that fed their people and supplied raw materials to their factories. A great percentage of the world's capital wealth emanated from the banks of these industrial states. The scientific knowledge and the administrative talent that mobilized Europe's resources were concentrated in the cities of the advanced states. At the base of the industrial expansion of Europe an urban labor force, the most skilled in the world, was prepared to seek a wider share in

European economic and political life. How the advanced European states adjusted to the demands of a mass age, and how they made use of their great industrial and technological power, depended to a great extent on the manner in which politics developed in these states.

SUGGESTED READING

Among the recent works that have assessed the importance of historical changes emerging in Europe at the end of the nineteenth century, Geoffrey Barraclough's *An Introduction to Contemporary History* (New York: Basic Books, 1965) offers a distinctive interpretation. Barraclough sees the year 1890 as marking the beginning of a transition, lasting to 1960, from European-centered history to an era of world history. In *The Economic History of World Population* (Baltimore: Penguin Books, 1962), Carlo M. Cipolla has pointed to the emergence of an industrial society as a development that, like the agrarian revolution of ca. 10,000 B.C., decisively altered the environment of human history. Hajo Holborn's *The Political Collapse of Europe* (New York: Alfred A. Knopf, 1964) is a stimulating general interpretation of European historical development in the nineteenth and twentieth centuries. Kenneth Boulding in *The Meaning of the Twentieth Century: The Great Transition* (New York: Harper, 1964) presents a social scientist's view of contemporary history, emphasizing the impact of technology.

A number of general surveys touch on changing conditions in Europe. Charles Morazé in *Les Bourgeois Conquérants* (Paris: A. Colin, 1957; published in English as *Triumph of the Middle Classes* (World, 1967) emphasizes the uncertainties that by the close of the nineteenth century began to disturb the recently won dominance of the European middle class. Volume X of *The New Cambridge Modern History: Material Progress and World-Wide Problems 1870–1898* (Cambridge: Cambridge University Press, 1962) contains essays on political, social, and economic trends. Another multi-author study—of varying quality—is *L'Europe du xixe et du xxe siècles, 1870–1914* (Milan; Mazorati, 1962) edited by Max Beloff and others. Detailed information on a wide range of topics may be found in Volumes XVIII and XIX of the French series "Peuples et Civilisations": Maurice Baumont, *L'Essor Industriel et l'Impérialisme Colonial, 1878–1904* (Paris: Presses Universitaires de France, 1949) and Pierre Renouvin, *La Crise Européenne et la Première Guarre Mondiale* (Paris, Presses Universitaires de France, 1948). Barbara Tuchman's *The Proud Tower* (New York: Macmillan, 1965) brilliantly evokes some characteristic features of the period, although the author's anti-German and pro-British sympathies are much in evidence. On the eve of the Second World War Carleton J. H. Hayes looked back with deep pessimism on late nineteenth century Europe in his *A Generation of Materialism: 1871–1900* (New York: Harper, 1941). A more recent survey, emphasizing political history, is Maurice Bruce's *The Shaping of the Modern World* (New York: Random House, 1958).

In the realm of economic history and technological development, David S. Landes' article, "Technological Change and Development in Western Europe, 1750–1914," in M. Postan and H. J. Habbakuk (eds.), *The Cambridge Economic History of Europe,* Vol. VI, *The Industrial Revolutions and After,* Part 1 (Cambridge: Cambridge University Press, 1965), is a masterly synthesis of a wide variety of sources and special studies that analyzes the main components of Europe's transition to an industrial order. Problems of European economic development, particularly in Russia and Italy, are examined in Alexander Gerschenkron's *Economic Backwardness in Historical Perspective* (Cambridge, Mass.: Harvard University Press, 1962). The same author provides an interpretation of Russia's agrarian evolution and its impact on economic development in "Agrarian Policies and Industrialization: Russia, 1861–1917" in Part 2 of *The Industrial Revolutions and After,* cited above. Rondo Cameron in *France and the Economic Development of Europe, 1800–1914* (Chicago: Rand McNally, 2nd rev. ed., 1967) has reassessed the French contribution to European industrialization. Charles P. Kindelberger in *Economic Growth in France and Britain* (Cambridge, Mass.: Harvard University Press, 1964) questions the value of using the historical experiences of these two states as effective models for determining the factors that promote or inhibit economic growth. Several older studies remain useful to students of the period, including Herbert Feis's *Europe the World's Banker, 1870–1914* (New Haven: Yale University Press, 1930), and John H. Clapham's *The Economic Development of France and Germany, 1815–1914* (Cambridge: Cambridge University Press, 4th ed., 1935). William Ashworth in *An Economic History of England, 1870–1939* (New York: Barnes & Noble, 1960) and William H. B. Court in *British Economic History, 1870–1914* (Cambridge: Cambridge University Press, 1966) offer useful guides to understanding Britain's response to the new economic challenges.

European social history has been treated in random fashion by scholars. Peter N. Stearns, however, has provided a valuable synthesis of disparate trends in his survey of European social development, *European Society in Upheaval* (New York: Macmillan, 1967). A less scholarly but entertaining insight into European society emerges from James Laver's *Manners and Morals in the Age of Optimism, 1848–1914* (New York: Harper, 1967). Upper-class behavior and values provide themes for Ernest K. Bramsted, who makes effective use of social novels as sources in his *Aristocracy and Middle-Classes in Germany: Social Types in German Literature, 1830–1900* (Chicago: University of Chicago Press, 1964, rev. ed.), and for F. M. L. Thompson, in his *English Landed*

Society in the Nineteenth Century (Toronto: University of Toronto Press, 1963), an analysis of the impact of the agrarian crisis on Britain's traditional ruling elite. A neglected topic is the question of population migration within Europe, although Frank Thistlewaite's article, "Migration from Europe Overseas in the Nineteenth and Twentieth Centuries," in Herbert Moller (ed.), *Population Movements in Modern European History* (New York: Macmillan, 1964), puts the trans-Atlantic emigration in perspective.

2

THE SEARCH FOR A
NEW SOCIETY

The rise of an industrial order in the nineteenth century brought a high degree of regulation into the lives of the European working classes. In the past, the life cycles and daily tasks of the European peasantry had been controlled in the sense that their means of existence had been governed predominantly by forces of nature, but these natural forces did not operate in the mechanistic and predictable way that the factory system did. Work in factories was paced by the functioning of man-made machines that ran in accordance with schedules established by supervisors and factory owners. This unremitting discipline provoked sporadic protests and rebellions in the course of the nineteenth century. Increasingly objections arose to a system that appeared to be a harsh exploitation of man by his fellow man.

Because the factory system was a human invention, it occurred to many of its critics that its inequities might be remedied by human action. By 1890 a number of competing social theories, recommendations for change, and methods of organization had appeared. The most important of these were anarchism, syndicalism, trade unionism, and socialism. Supporters of each doctrine agreed that the existing political and economic arrangements of society perpetuated the injustices of the factory system, and that radical change was needed. But they disagreed both in their visions of what the new society would be like and in the methods that were to be used in attaining it. The different approaches to a new society will be taken up in detail in this chapter, but first some consideration should be given to earlier trends in European social thought that prepared the way for later movements.

Early Social Theorists

A number of social theorists who appeared at the time of the first stirrings of an industrial revolution left distinctive legacies through their writings or deeds. Among the most important of the early theorists were the British classical economists of the late eighteenth and early nineteenth centuries. This group had no intention of overturning the industrial order; instead they proposed laws to explain and justify the functioning of a capitalist industrial system. They argued that natural laws operated in economic development much in the way that they operated in the realm of science. Adam Smith, the founder of the classical school, insisted that if each individual pursued his economic interests in a free market, all of society would benefit. Governments were to stand aside from this competition and limit themselves to maintaining a few public services such as schools, courts, and armies to protect the society from invasion and internal disorder.

Smith tended to be optimistic about the benefits that would accrue from this laissez-faire system, but two of his successors, Thomas Malthus and David Ricardo, drew depressing conclusions from their studies of the political economy. Malthus anticipated perpetual misery for the bulk of mankind because the population, unchecked by wars, plagues, or other disasters, tended to increase faster than the food supply. Unless men practiced birth control, which he called "moral restraint," the vast majority would be condemned to bare subsistence or even starvation. Ricardo carried this analysis further by pointing out that wages would be at a subsistence level as long as a rapidly growing population assured a labor surplus. Employers would naturally purchase labor as cheaply as possible, particularly since, as Ricardo insisted, the price of goods was determined by the amount of labor expended in production. Labor surplus and competition for jobs combined to drive wages to a minimum.

Ricardo's "iron law of wages" and his "labor theory of value" were used by widely different schools of theorists to justify their views. Ricardo was cited, along with Malthus and Adam Smith, by those who believed that government interference was an unnatural and harmful disruption of economic life. Suffering and hardship, according to this view, were unavoidable consequences of a freely operating capitalism. An opposing view questioned the value of capitalism. The laws of classical economic theory were used by Karl Marx to demonstrate the inherent contradictions in capitalism, the very system for which the laws were formulated. With support from Hegelian philosophy, Marx forged a new theory that predicted capitalism's collapse as a result of its own contradictions. From this process, Marx insisted, socialism would emerge triumphant.

The classical economists' justifications of the existing system were rejected by those who favored an industrial society based on cooperation rather than competition. In Great Britain the leading advocate of this school was Robert Owen, a manufacturer who had risen from the working class but had retained a sympathetic understanding of the plight of its members. At his cotton mill in New Lanark, Scotland, Owen formed a model industrial community that included respectable housing, schools, churches, and medical services. Much to the horror of his fellow manufacturers, Owen raised wages and curtailed child labor.

The urge toward a cooperative, communal society was a strong one. In France, for example, Charles Fourier advocated a cooperative organization of society into large estates, or phalansteries, in which each member would fulfill a useful function according to his talents and in which a careful balance between agriculture and manufacturing was to be maintained. The only attempts to put cooperative ideas into practice, however, came in the wilderness areas of the United States, removed from the industrial revolution but considered virgin territory for social experiments. Robert Owen sponsored a cooperative community at New Harmony, Indiana. Unfortunately, this community did not live up to its name and collapsed as a result of disagreements among its members. Other utopian communities also failed despite the good intentions of their founders. These wilderness societies appeared to be an escape from an industrial order rather than a transformation of it. Only the paternalism of Owen's New Lanark offered a realistic course of action within the context of an industrial society, and its success depended on the benevolence of management. In other circumstances the company town became a parody of Owen's intention and served only as one more instrument for exploitation.

A different form of paternalism was suggested by the French

writer Henri de Saint-Simon. Saint-Simon rejected his aristocratic heritage during the French Revolution to adopt the cause of the oppressed. He left a series of inchoate writings and a group of ardent admirers who formed a Saint-Simonian school to develop and expand the ideas of the master. They called not for an egalitarian social order, but for a structured society composed of useful and productive individuals identified by Saint-Simon as "industrialists" and including scientists, engineers, laborers, financiers, and even farmers. The goal of society was productivity to the extent that all members would be supplied with what they needed, but those who were most productive were to be most amply rewarded. Scientific methods were to be applied rigorously in the production of goods, and the various producers were to be bound together into a corporate whole. Saint-Simonian doctrines had a wide influence later in the nineteenth century. Many of the state socialists surrounding Napoleon III considered themselves Saint-Simonians as did a number of entrepreneurs in the Second Empire. At the turn of the century theorists of syndicalism took up, in modified guise, Saint-Simon's concept of industrial enterprise as the basis of social organization.

Another critic of laissez-faire capitalism was the Frenchman Louis Blanc, who shared a Saint-Simonian belief in the necessity of work for all but disagreed with Saint-Simon's system of rewarding the most productive members of society. "From each according to his abilities, to each according to his needs" was a phrase coined by Louis Blanc that expressed his conception of social and economic equality. Blanc believed that government had a responsibility to provide its citizens with a livelihood. As a member of the provisional government during the revolutionary days of 1848, Blanc advocated the establishment of national workshops designed to give employment to all in need of work. Blanc's support for such policies anticipated the development of democratic state socialism in the twentieth century. In 1848, however, his schemes only excited the hostility of those who feared state competition with private enterprise, and the national workshops were abandoned after a few weeks.

Most workers were so preoccupied with survival in the industrial order that elaborate schemes for social reform seemed remote from their pressing needs. In the early nineteenth century a few workers' organizations were formed to gain immediate improvements in working conditions and pay. In the 1830's, for example, a vast union of British workers appeared under Owen's guidance. Although it collapsed not long after its formation, it was a precursor of later industrial trade unions organized on a national basis and incorporating a large segment of the working population. The initial efforts at organization in Great

Britain at least drew attention to existing labor conditions; as the result of parliamentary inquiries into the problem, the workers gained some minimal standards for working hours and conditions. For most of the nineteenth century, however, the formation of labor unions and the development of a political consciousness on the part of workers were slow and sporadic.

An important influence on social theorists of the late nineteenth century was the tradition of intransigent revolutionism. The long, often futile, process of organization and of the formulation of legislation to improve conditions was rejected by the revolutionists, who resorted to terrorism as a form of protest against social inequities. August Blanqui, a devoted revolutionist active around the middle of the century, held that the existing order had to be swept away by revolutionary violence before a new society could be built. A conspiratorial elite was to wage a relentless war against the possessors of wealth. Blanqui formed a number of secret societies for the purposes of revolutionary terrorism; the members were often unknown to one another but were prepared to lead the revolution on signal from their leader, Blanqui himself. Although his attempts at revolution failed, his total commitment to the idea of revolution anticipated a similar devotion on the part of men such as Lenin, and his reliance on a closely knit elite to lead the revolution foreshadowed Lenin's insistence on a disciplined group that would provide the phalanx for a cataclysmic upheaval.

Pierre Proudhon, a contemporary of quite a different temperament from Blanqui, was equally important for his impact on late nineteenth century social movements. Proudhon's writings, which called for a rejection of all forms of authority and coercion, became a major source of inspiration for anarchism. The son of a poor artisan, Proudhon grew up in the French provincial town of Besançon. In his adolescence Proudhon worked in the countryside at rural tasks, and he never forgot the bucolic delights that he experienced. "What a pleasure," he later wrote, "to roll in the long grass . . . to run barefoot under the hedges." Not surprisingly he found that urban employment, which he experienced in Lyons and Paris, confined his spirit. He protested against all institutions and customs that imposed on individual free-dom—the Church, the state, factory discipline, urban life itself. Above all, he felt that private property represented the most damaging form of oppression, for it gave one individual great economic power over another. When Proudhon announced that "Property is theft," he launched one of the nineteenth century's most potent revolutionary slogans. The very basis for capitalist middle-class society was thereby condemned.

Proudhon had little sympathy for the utopians and their schemes for reordering society: he felt that men such as Saint-Simon simply offered the substitution of one form of oppression for another. Instead, society as it was organized then was to be abolished. At the most, men would voluntarily participate in small groups of artisans and farmers who would provide enough food and goods to meet their own modest needs. The ideal was held to be Besançon and its surrounding district, untouched by either the industrial world or the demands of a complex state. Within each small, voluntary community—linked together only through a very loose federalism—goods were to be exchanged on a barter basis, thereby eliminating bankers, financiers, credit associations, and the pernicious "rule of gold" that plagued modern society.

Proudhon assessed the difficulties of any voluntary relationship that relied on man's good will. In a sense he possessed a French peasant's cynical and somewhat suspicious evaluation of human motivation. Therefore Proudhon preached moral reform of the individual as a necessary prelude to true freedom. But this path to liberty aside from being difficult, was obstructed by a paradox. As a moralist Proudhon called for an end to human violence and acquisitiveness, yet as a man of action he called for destruction of institutions that encouraged these traits. Many of his followers turned to violence in an effort to destroy society. Proudhon struggled with his own violent tendencies, although in his writings he urged that man's propensity toward violence be sublimated into peaceful, rational behavior.

Proudhon assumed an important place among nineteenth century libertarian thinkers. In wanting absolute freedom he carried the desire for individual freedom and liberty to its logical extreme. He expressed a provincial distrust of the city and a desire to break the bondage of social constraints that were part of the intellectual heritage left by Jean-Jacques Rousseau. Finally, Proudhon anticipated the populist hatred for capitalism and "bigness" that was to emerge in a variety of forms during the twentieth century. But it is as an early spokesman for anarchist principles that Proudhon is best known.

Anarchism

Proudhon's writings inspired a number of anarchist groups that emerged in many parts of Europe during the 1860's. Another important figure in that particular surge of anarchism was Michael Bakunin, an impoverished Russian aristocrat who traveled about western and southern Europe promoting his dream of an anarchist brotherhood that would liberate men from the shackles of coercive social and political institutions. His efforts met with some success. In France alone the anarchists claimed several thousand sympathizers by the end of the decade, and anarchists were active in Spain, Italy, Russia, and Switzerland.

Many of those who embraced anarchism, such as artisans, found the individualist aspects of anarchist doctrine appealing. They were inspired by humane, noble ideals that looked to the liberation of the individual, but they were also prepared to endorse violence as a means to that liberation. Behind what later became known as "propaganda by the deed" was a belief that political assassination and other extreme gestures would expose the injustices of society. The anarchists would strike at authority by destroying the occupants of high office. By creating a climate of fear and distrust the anarchists hoped to precipitate the disintegration of the social order.

Through the 1860's anarchist activities seemed to be confined to propaganda and exhortation and to Bakunin's efforts to form clandestine anarchist groups in southern Europe. The European governments seemed content to keep their eye on anarchist activities through police spies and harrassment. But the increasing strength of the anarchist movement toward the end of the decade became the source of greater concern, and when the anarchists passed from the realm of theoretical exhortation to that of violent action, the European governments stepped up their repression. In the aftermath of the 1871 Paris Commune, for example, the French government executed, imprisoned, and exiled a number of anarchists who had participated in the revolutionary uprising. Other governments, equally frightened by the threat that the anarchists' hostility to the state posed, followed suit, and by the mid-1870's the movement began to languish in western and southern Europe. On the eve of his death in 1876, Bakunin lamented to a fellow anarchist, "The revolution for the moment has returned to its bed."

Only in Russia did anarchism remain active with a series of violent attacks on public figures. This campaign culminated in the assassination of Czar Alexander II in 1881. With Alexander's assassination, however, the Russian government severely repressed all suspected anarchist groups and effectively curbed anarchist violence. Throughout Europe the harrassed anarchists became disheartened in the 1880's, and the movement seemed to have subsided.

Yet anarchism had not died out. Bakunin and other anarchists of the 1860's and 1870's had inaugurated, in the phrase of the Italian historian Franco Venturi, a "revolutionary mentality," and this mentality was to reawaken with explosive force in the 1890's. The revival of anarchist activity in that decade was marked by an even greater tendency toward terrorism and violence than had been apparent in the earlier phase. This activity took place in nearly every country in Europe, as well as in the United States and Latin America.

Although their wide occurrence led many people to attribute the anarchist acts to an international conspiracy, they were usually the work of isolated individuals. The impression of a vast anarchist conspiracy seemed to be confirmed by the anarchists themselves, many of whom went to their deaths shouting "Long live anarchy!" At their trials anarchists coolly predicted vengeance on their executioners and judges. But this behavior reflected faith in the movement rather than knowledge of a plot. Anarchists assumed that others would step forward to sacrifice themselves, as they had done, in the name of the movement. By definition anarchism did not permit organization to plot a systematic campaign of terror—it was simply the means that certain individuals, wrenched by an overwhelming sense of injustice, considered necessary to achieve the ideal of an absolutely free society.

Anarchism in France

France experienced some of the more sensational anarchist deeds during the 1890's with a series of attacks against institutions, assassinations of government figures, and bombings of innocent patrons in outdoor restaurants. One of the first events in the anarchist revival in France came in 1886 when an anarchist threw a bottle of vitriol into a crowd of stockbrokers at the Paris Bourse. The anarchist who had hurled the bottle boasted at his trial that his action was an "act of propaganda by the deed for anarchist doctrine."

The Chamber of Deputies was another object of anarchist hatred. In 1893 August Vaillant dropped a homemade bomb from a visitors' balcony in the Chamber and injured several deputies on the floor. Although no one had been killed, Vaillant was condemned to death. The severity of his sentence indicated the growing public panic at a whole series of anarchist acts of terror that had occurred in France in the early 1890's. Anarchism seemed an irrational and frightening force to the average middle-class Frenchman. Nerves became frayed as papers bannered more and more headlines of anarchist deeds.

About the same time that Vaillant carried out his attack on the Chamber of Deputies, another anarchist, Emile Henry, initiated a series of calculated attacks on the bourgeois order. Henry was a brilliant student who had dropped out of the prestigious Ecole Polytechnique to devote himself to the anarchist cause. In 1892 he left a bomb in the Paris offices of the Carmaux Mines, a company that had just brutally smashed a strike. Four policemen lost their lives when the bomb exploded as they were removing it. A year later another of Henry's bombs went off in the Café Terminus near the Gare St.-Lazare in Paris, killing one and wounding nineteen others. On this occasion Henry was caught after a short chase. While awaiting trial, he wrote an analysis of his actions. He had chosen the Café Terminus precisely because its clientele were predominantly "good little bourgeois who make 300–500 francs a month." They shared responsibility for social injustice with the men of great wealth, and they were perhaps even more responsible, Henry concluded, for the bourgeois tended to be the most hostile to the classes immediately below them. In any event, Henry noted that "there are no innocents" in bourgeois society. Like his predecessors, Henry went to his death predicting the ultimate triumph of the cause.

Equally chilling to the middle classes was the career of François Ravachol. A man of sallow complexion and sinister appearance, Ravachol began his anarchist activities in March, 1892, after an earlier career of crime. Within three weeks he was caught and brought to trial. The trial itself created a sensation. Fearing anarchist retaliation, the government took elaborate security measures in the courtroom. During the trial it was revealed that Ravachol had murdered shopkeepers for small sums and robbed graves for jewelry. The brutality of Ravachol's acts led the middle class to condemn all anarchists as criminals. Many anarchists initially disassociated themselves from Ravachol, claiming that he was not representative of the movement. But with his execution at the hands of the state he earned his martyrdom. In the 1890's he became a legendary figure for anarchists and was immortalized in song and poetry. His contempt for authority and his defiant cry of "Long live anarchy!" came to typify the anarchist movement in France.

The climax of anarchist terror in France came in 1894 when the president of the republic, Sadi Carnot, was fatally stabbed by an Italian anarchist during a state visit to Lyons. Again, this was an independent act, although the assassin claimed that his deed was a measure of revenge for Carnot's refusal to grant Auguste Vaillant a pardon. Under pressure of the public hysteria provoked by Carnot's assassination, the French police intensified their pursuit of anarchists and harrassed those who were suspected of anarchist tendencies. Homes were searched on the least pretext, and many anarchist newspapers were suspended during the anti-anarchist campaign of 1894–95. In the summer of 1894 thirty journalists, some of whom mixed anarchist views with Bohemian living, were brought to public trial and accused of having encouraged acts of violence. The government's case, however, was not on solid ground. When the presiding judge, in a desperate moment, accused art critic Félix Fénelon of holding a conversation with an anarchist behind a lamppost, Fénelon drily retorted, "Can you tell me, Your Honor, where is 'behind a lamppost'?" Because the political views of the accused were insufficient grounds for indictment for terrorism, the jury acquitted the journalists of charges of inciting violence.

Among some French intellectuals anarchism became a fashionable attitude. Many artists and writers shared the anarchist's contempt for respectable bourgeois values, and insofar as they held political opinions they declared their sympathy for anarchism. For example, when informed that an anarchist had bombed the Chamber of Deputies, the poet Laurent Taillade responded, "Of what importance are the victims, as long as the gesture is beautiful?"

In the final analysis, however, such aesthetic posing simply confirmed rather than destroyed middle-class prejudices, and the forces of order in France stood in firm opposition to anarchists of all shades. In fact, "anarchism" became a term of abuse that the middle classes used indiscriminately in condemning many movements of social reform. In the last half of the 1890's the anarchist movement began to lose its momentum. Instead of producing a revolutionary effect, the acts of terror only elicited measures of repression and a decided lack of sympathy from bourgeois society. Even the anarchists themselves came to regard their acts as futile.

Jean Maitron, the historian of French anarchism, has estimated that at its height anarchism could count on no more than a thousand activists and some 4500 subscribers to anarchist newspapers. Yet if anarchist methods were deplored, the anarchist distrust of authority and reservations about the direction of modern society appealed to many Frenchmen who considered themselves to be individualists. Maitron has estimated that perhaps as many as 100,000 Frenchmen sympathized with anarchist objectives if not with their methods. As a state of mind, anarchism found a significant place in a nation uncertain about its commitment to an industrial society, and the movement left a legacy that outlasted the period of "propaganda by the deed."

Anarchism in Other Countries

Political assassinations and other acts of violence had occurred in Spain, Italy, the United States, and Russia by the turn of the century. In Germany the anarchist movement was feeble, although anarchists made an abortive attempt on the Kaiser's life in the 1880's. Elsewhere the number of high officials and heads of state who fell victim to assassinations was on the increase. In 1897 the Spanish premier Canovas was shot by an Italian anarchist. The assassin in his justification for the deed cited Canovas' suppression of strikes and his position as head of an oppressive government. The following year another Italian anarchist stabbed the Empress Elizabeth of Austria, wife of Francis Joseph, as she boarded a steamer on Lake Geneva. Ironically the empress, a gentle and rather tragic figure, had little political influence and was living apart from the emperor.

In 1900 King Umberto of Italy, who had survived two previous attempts on his life, was assassinated by an anarchist who had been commissioned by a group of Italian anarchists living in Patterson, New Jersey. Umberto's assassination was a calculated revenge for the Italian government's attack on the workers during the 1898 Milan uprising. Thus, it was one instance of a widespread plot rather than an isolated act by an individual. Although the plot did not extend beyond the assassination itself, it had unanticipated repercussions. After having read of this deed, a recent emigrant to the United States from the Austro-Hungarian empire plotted and carried out the assassination of President McKinley in 1901. This particular act turned public opinion in the United States against anarchism and, as elsewhere, brought increased police suppression of anarchist meetings and harrassment of anarchist leaders.

Attacks against state officials were also renewed in Russia in the 1890's. One of the most spectacular assassinations (later used by Joseph Conrad in his novel *Under Western Eyes*) ended the life of the hated minister of the interior, V. K. Plehve, in the summer of 1904. Anarchists had carried out some sensational terrorist acts in Russia by 1905; yet, at no time did they threaten the established structure of society. When revolution did break out in Russia that year, it was not directly as a result of anarchist activity, which had only a limited impact.

As an attitude toward society, anarchism had a longer life and a greater influence in Russia. Many anarchists cherished the mythology associated with direct, violent terrorism long after the turn of the century. Other anarchists condemned blind acts of violence but continued to call attention to the basic inequalities of organized society. Among the intellectual spokesmen for the pure form of anarchism was Prince Peter Kropotkin, a gentle Russian nobleman and scholar of geography who devoted his life to the anarchist cause. His participation in the populist agitation of the 1870's led to his arrest and imprisonment in 1874. Two years later he escaped from prison and eventually found a haven in England, where he spent most of his later years. Kropotkin refused any form of compromise with the organized state, and he insisted that reform and revolution, rather than individual acts of terror, would lead to a new society. For anarchists who recoiled from terrorism yet remained hostile to an industrial society, Kropotkin's ideal of free cooperation among men of good will seemed a hopeful alternative. But its realization remained elusive.

The Impact of Anarchism

In many ways anarchism represented a sharp outcry against the impersonality of industrial organization, and it continues to appeal to those alienated by the apparent callousness of an industrial system and a bureaucratic state. Yet anarchism had its greatest appeal and most lasting influence not in the industrial states of Europe but in the less developed rural areas of Spain, southern Italy, and parts of Russia. The ideal of a voluntary society without private property quite naturally appealed to peasant groups that had long possessed strong communal traditions. When these backward rural districts experienced the depression produced by declining agricultural prices, the response was one of despairing rebellion against a landholding system that had always been oppressive. There was little prospect of relief from the government, which had always seemed remote and had supported the large landowners against the peasants whenever its influence did appear. Moreover, when population pressures led to migration from rural areas to the industrial centers, the newly arrived peasants found life in Barcelona, Milan, St. Petersburg, or Rostov bewildering and hostile, and they turned to social movements with strong anarchist strains that offered hope for a less coercive way of life.

Anarchism appealed to another group that found itself alienated from the industrial order and saw its economic status threatened—the artisans. In northern Europe significant numbers of artisans adopted anarchism as a protest against the competition of mass manufacturing. Large institutions, whether industrial or political, conflicted with the artisan's strong sense of independence and self-reliance.

The mass of the population directly involved in the industrial society did not rally to the anarchist idea. In most advanced industrial states the growing trade unions and socialist political parties offered more realistic prospects for achieving social justice. Rather than pursue wholesale opposition to an industrial order, workers were urged to seize control of factories and take over the political machinery of the state in order to convert the industrial system into a benevolent rather than an oppressive system. Many of those who may have been tempted by anarchism turned to a greatly modified version of this movement in adopting revolutionary syndicalism after the turn of the century. Syndicalism offered a greater organization and sense of solidarity than was to be found among the pure anarchists.

Syndicalism

The syndicalists shared the anarchists' basic distrust of political parties and representative institutions, regarding them as nothing more than instruments for perpetuating social injustice. Meaningful changes in society could occur only through direct, concerted action on the part of the workers themselves. This attitude was expressed by the French syndicalist Emile Pouget, who declared, "The aim of the syndicate is to make war on the bosses and forget about politics."

But syndicalism deviated from anarchism in several important respects. Emphasis was placed on solidarity and discipline among the workers rather than on individualism. Also syndicalism rejected the despairing rebellion against industrial capitalism implicit in anarchist views, in favor of a program that would replace the old order with workers' control of industry. The syndicalists intended to establish a mass base for common revolutionary action through their own organizations and unions rather than rely on isolated protests to undermine society. The industrial order was to be kept in a state of tension by means of sudden strikes and even acts of sabotage; continued industrial strife ultimately would weaken capitalism until a vast general strike would initiate the revolution. Since syndicalism advocated organization of workers, its policies were easily adopted by the previously existing workers' unions. A wary coexistence with socialist parties might be accepted for tactical reasons, but the autonomy of purely workers' organizations was to be preserved.

Syndicalism exhibited considerable strength in France where the workers' distrust of politicians was particularly strong. From the time when workers' unions were first formed in the 1880's a clear distinction had been maintained between these organizations and political parties that claimed to speak for the worker. The major French union, the General Confederation of Workers (C.G.T.), tended toward syndicalist ideals. This tendency became dominant in 1906 when the union congress, meeting at Amiens, passed resolutions calling for an escalation of strike activity that would culminate in a revolutionary general strike. From the turn of the century French trade unionism opted for industrial militancy rather than action through accepted political channels.

Syndicalism made inroads in Italy and Spain, where it emerged as a strong rival in the working classes to both the purely anarchist and the socialist movements. In Italy, the syndicalists formed the National Secretariat of Resistance in 1904. That group quarreled on a number of issues with the socialists who dominated the trade unions, and within a few years the syndicalists broke away from the moderate General Confederation of Labor (C.G.L.). They attracted to their ranks the migrants from the Italian countryside who were employed as unskilled workers in the cities.

The trade unionism that revived in Spain at the turn of the century took on a distinctively syndicalist orientation, gaining as adherents those Spanish anarchists who leaned toward collective action. The fact that the syndicalists promoted general strikes as a means of breaking down the capitalist order attracted anarchists to their side. In 1902 violence erupted in Barcelona when a strike conducted by metalworkers expanded into a general strike. Although the strike ultimately failed, its initial and prolonged success caused syndicalist doctrines to spread rapidly among workers in Barcelona, until eventually a syndicalist organization, Solidad Obrera, was formed in Catalonia. By 1905 Spanish anarchism, still strong in rural areas and particularly influential in Barcelona itself, had to share with syndicalism its influence among workers.

In Russia anarcho-syndicalism also gained strength at the expense of purely anarchist groups. After the revolution of 1905 the Russian working class considered strike activity more effective than political assassination and terrorism as a means of undermining confidence in czarist rule. By 1905 in many other areas of Europe anarchist terror tactics were being replaced by the equally militant but more coherently organized syndicalist movement. Because syndicalism was directed toward a seizure of the industrial order and not a rejection of it, it represented a greater maturity on the part of workers in their response to the industrial order.

Trade Unionism

Not all workers' unions in Europe at the end of the nineteenth century accepted syndicalism either in doctrine or in practice. Generally European unions wanted to modify rather than radically change the existing system. They favored action that produced tangible results rather than attempts to promote revolutionary fervor among their membership. And the average unionist wanted immediate gains, not feverish hopes. Insofar as they were satisfied, these material ambitions diminished revolutionary zeal among the working classes. Moderate union organizations avoided political connections as much as possible, but this policy was less the result of a preference for strike action over parliamentary debate than of a belief that the unions' struggles for better pay, hours, working conditions, and the like did not require political support. These concessions could be won directly from employers without the intervention of the state. Although strikes could be used to reinforce demands, they were not necessarily seen as revolutionary measures or even preparations for revolution.

Even the attempt to win concessions within the existing system required organized, concerted action. During the early stages of industrialization trade unions had evolved slowly, their histories marked by legal battles as well as physical violence. Gradually many countries recognized the workers' rights to association, thereby permitting them a means of redress of grievances within the existing social order. Final restrictions on trade union organizations in France were not removed until 1884, and those states, such as Russia, that refused to acknowledge a legal status for trade unions forced their workers' movements onto the path of illegal and revolutionary activity. Where unions were considered legitimate organizations, they frequently entered the political arena and acted as moderating influences within socialist movements. But these unions moved toward political action very cautiously and maintained clear distinctions between their special concerns and those of the socialist movements in which they participated. This was particularly true in Germany and Britain, the two European states that by the 1890's possessed the most powerful union movements.

Unionism in Britain

Although the British workers had longer experience than workers in other countries in dealing with problems of industrialization, the British workers only gradually organized themselves into national groups. An early attempt at creating a vast national organization, Robert Owen's "Grand National" of the 1830's, had failed, and for most of the nineteenth century the great majority of British workers lacked unions to speak for their interests. Certain of the more highly skilled or traditional trades had craft organizations, but they were frequently timid in their demands and expectations. In the last half of the nineteenth century the organization of national industrial unions proceeded laboriously from industry to industry and region to region. Union organizers faced the hostility of the employers, the general public, and the government. It was thought that unions fell under the common law prohibition against organizations that acted in restraint of trade. Toward the end of the 1860's the climate for establishing national unions temporarily improved. After investigating a violent workers' strike in the cutlery trades of Sheffield in 1866, a royal commission produced a report recommending that some recognition be given to trade unions' legal rights. At the same time a meeting of British unions in a Trades Union Congress recommended that a parliamentary committee be established to press for favorable factory legislation. This flurry of union activity lasted into the 1870's and served as a stimulus to the reforms granted by Disraeli and the Conservative party in 1875 that established minimum health and sanitation standards for urban dwellings and gave the unions the right to strike. But by the end of the decade unionism stagnated; the British Trades Union Congress seemed content with gains that had been won, and further campaigns for labor legislation were abandoned. The unions, partly as a result of their conservative approach to labor problems, lost support after having boasted about a million and a half workers organized and represented in the Trades Union Congress in 1874.

The New Unionism ▪ A revival of union activity, or "new unionism," swept over the British labor movement at the end of the 1880's. This revival took place for a number of reasons: the trade depression during the decade created unemployment for many workers; a growing solidarity among the working class occurred as the result of increased literacy; and a new generation of union organizers emerged who were dissatisfied with the restraint of the traditional leadership. Tom Mann, a young and aggressive member of the Amalgamated Engineers, denounced the failure of union officials to lead strikes against employers, a complaint that was echoed by fellow unionists. At about the same time a leader of the Scottish miners, James Keir Hardie, also bitterly criticized union officials who appeared more concerned with maintaining good relations with Liberal politicians than with achieving benefits for the working class. Tom Mann and Keir Hardie represented a renewed vigor and dynamism within British trade unionism, although their aggressive tactics alarmed many older members.

The new unionism reached many areas, but its influence was most clearly evident in the growing belligerence of the London gasworkers and dockworkers. In the summer of 1889 the workers of the

South Metropolitan Gas Company formed a union that demanded and won the eight-hour workday, a radical concession for the time. Their accomplishment inspired a similar effort among the London dockers who organized a strike that also drew in stevedores, coalporters, and other workers associated with the dockers. After almost five weeks of struggle during which the strikers nearly surrendered because of a lack of strike funds, the Lord Mayor of London arranged a conciliation meeting. The dock managers made extensive concessions, notably in raising hourly rates, but balked at yielding an eight-hour day. Nevertheless, the London strikes of 1889 marked a significant achievement for labor and served to encourage unionism throughout Britain. Soon gasworkers everywhere demanded an eight-hour day, and dockworkers' unions won sizable support among dockers in Scotland. A General Railway Workers Union was organized to represent those unskilled railway workers who had been excluded from an older railway union.

In some areas the new unionism brought conflict between the newer and older unions and, as has been mentioned, between younger and older leadership. The main issue of contention was the demand for an eight-hour day, which veteran labor leaders considered impractical and radical. Although the differences between groups were intense, a split within British labor was avoided. In fact, union membership increased so that by 1895 approximately one-fifth of the British labor force belonged to some form of union.

The Formation of a Labor Party ■ As the labor movement continued to grow and conflicts between labor and management intensified, some unionists urged that a political party be formed representing the working class independent of both the Conservatives and the Liberals. The older union leadership held back, preferring to work for specific gains from employers and leaving their political interests to those Liberals who sympathized with labor's problems. They resisted involvement in theoretical arguments associated with socialist politics. The younger generation shared this skepticism of theoretical quibbling, but displayed less reserve than their elders in calling for political action. Keir Hardie, who had been elected a member of Parliament in 1892, was among the strongest advocates of political involvement. He and his colleagues pressed the trade unions to accept the need for a separate labor party. After some years of persuasion a delegation from the Trades Union Congress got together with representatives from Keir Hardie's Independent Labor party, the Fabian Socialists, and the Marxist Social Democratic Federation to form the Labor Representation Committee (L.R.C.), later to become the Labor party in the elections of 1902–03. The L.R.C. marked a first step toward political action on the part of British unions.

Lingering doubts of conservative unionists about this course of action were removed when a court decision that placed labor in a highly vulnerable position revealed the need for a labor party. In August, 1900, workers for the Taff Vale Railway Company in South Wales went on strike when the company dismissed a signalman. The strike was unplanned, but it quickly gained the moral and financial support of the national railway union. The railway company in turn sued the union for damages. Eventually the case reached the House of Lords where it was decided that union officials were financially liable for damages suffered by the company during the strike. The decision stunned all British unions, for it deprived them of the strike weapon that they thought had been assured by Disraeli's reform legislation in 1875. When the House of Lords imposed restrictions on picketing activity in another decision a few weeks later, the unions felt further threatened. Obviously the tactics of dealing directly with employers would be ineffective under these new conditions, which placed the unions at a distinct disadvantage.

Unionists resolved to undo the harm of Taff Vale and its aftermath by supporting candidates who pledged to reverse these decisions. In the elections of 1906, which swept the Liberal party into power, the Labor party sent twenty-nine members to the House of Commons where they joined some twenty-five Liberals pledged to advancing the cause of labor through legislation. The newly elected House of Commons responded to labor's political pressure, and the Taff Vale decision was reversed by legislation. For many unionists this success demonstrated the advantages of political action in support of the working classes.

Unionism in Germany

The German unions had won the right to organize on the eve of Prussia's victory over France in 1870. Under the new empire union organization continued, but anti-socialist legislation of 1878 seriously hampered their development. Even when this legislation lapsed in 1890, most German workers remained outside formal organizations. In the following fifteen years, however, union membership increased from a quarter of a million workers to nearly a million and a half, and this steady growth continued up to the outbreak of war in 1914.

Many types of union organizations developed, including a number of Christian unions and groups that derived from earlier mutual-aid societies. By far the largest and most important unions were the socialist unions organized nationally under the German Trade Union Commission. The leader of this "Free Union," Karl Legien, favored the pursuit of moderate gains through collective bargaining with employers. Legien was prepared to establish good relations with employers who met the demands of labor. Evolutionary improvement rather than revolutionary challenge characterized his approach to industrial conflict. Legien's outlook had a lasting influence on the German trade union movement; syndicalism, for example, gained few supporters among the German unions.

Initially, Legien and the union leaders were content to leave politics in the hands of the German socialist party. But, with the impressive gains in membership during the 1890's, the German unions found themselves drawn toward a more direct participation in socialist politics. Indeed the unions appeared to be providing a sizable proportion of the party's electoral strength. Like the party itself, German unions had acquired something of a stake in the existing social system. Many unionists were reluctant to jeopardize the considerable gains that had been won. Alarmed by the revolutionary rhetoric of the German socialist theoreticians, some union leaders assumed an active role in party affairs in an attempt to moderate the course of the socialist movement. By 1905 the German unions were having an increasing influence on the direction of German socialism. Within the unions themselves, extensive services were developed for the members, and bureaucracies were established to administer these services. For many German workers and their families the union became a way of life; they looked to the union rather than to revolutionary theoreticians for guidance.

Unionism in Other Parts of Europe

Unions also acquired influence and power elsewhere in northern Europe. Generally the unions that were able to make gains did so in a gradual fashion by working within existing social and political institutions and following whatever doctrine the socialist parties expounded. In Scandinavia, unions flirted briefly with syndicalist ideas, but after the failure of a general strike in Sweden they turned more and more toward political action. In Denmark and Sweden the alliance between unions and farmers' cooperatives created an atmosphere more favorable to negotiation and compromise than to revolution. In the Low Countries and in Switzerland, despite strains of syndicalism and anarchism, the unions also tended to be evolutionary in their approach to achieving changes in the industrial system and in society itself.

Elsewhere in Europe trade unions were weaker and less well disciplined than in the northern regions. Conflicts between militant and moderate workers' groups hindered the development of a dominant union organization in France, for example. The formation of the General Confederation of Workers quelled some of this factionalism, but relatively few workers actually joined the organization; in 1904 it could claim only some 150,000 members. The hostility of syndicalists within the unions to politics interfered with the formation of close ties between French labor and the socialist party. Union membership in Italy also remained low and was strongly influenced by syndicalism. As in France bitter factional quarrels between militant syndicalists and moderate socialists divided the unions. The apparent triumphs of the moderate General Confederation of Labor over syndicalists were really only temporary tactical gains that were by no means decisive. Wildcat strikes and rural uprisings, encouraged by the syndicalists, took place without the sanction of the General Confederation. Eventually the syndicalists broke away completely from the confederation. The trade union movement in Spain was strongly influenced by the presence of both anarchism and syndicalism within its ranks. The Spanish National Confederation of Labor was clearly anarcho-syndicalist in its political sympathies and had a wider following than its rival, the socialist General Union of Workers. Quarrels between anarcho-syndicalists and socialists weakened the nascent Spanish labor movement. Here, too, the actual members organized in unions were relatively small compared with those in Britain and Germany.

Unionism also reached eastern Europe, although under even more difficult circumstances than elsewhere. In the Austro-Hungarian empire unions appeared in the industrial districts of Bohemia, Vienna, and Budapest, despite legal restrictions on union activity. The greatest difficulty faced by these unions was the problem of rivalry between nationalities that threatened to divide labor against itself. The Czechs wanted a separate trade organization that would recruit Czech workers not only in Bohemia but throughout the empire. This proposal alarmed the German-speaking socialists for it posed the threat of a rival group competing for the loyalty of the workers. The continuing conflict over Czech separatism within the Austrian union movement paralleled wider national conflicts within the socialist movement itself. However, the struggle for universal suffrage provided a common issue to offset divisive tendencies; in the period from 1893 to 1907 all the trade unions supplied demonstrators for this cause. These demonstrations suggested the growing power of the union movement, although the unresolved internal divisions remained a potential source of weakness. In the Hungarian half of the empire the development of unionism was complicated by the question of support for rural labor. The trade unions tried to extend their movement to include rural laborers by statements of sympathy for their problems and attempts at organization in the countryside, but the movement remained oriented toward the urban goals of the Budapest socialists. Still, their hostility toward the ruling elite provided the rural and the industrial proletariats with a common basis for action, and in the 1890's trade unionism was spreading in Hungary, although not so rapidly as elsewhere.

The formation of unions in Russia in the latter part of the nineteenth century was by clandestine activity because technically unions were illegal. The intensification of industrial unrest in the 1890's, however, provided a favorable climate for establishing some solidarity among Russian workers. The unions that emerged in the industrial cities tended to be locally based because poor communications and the repressive government policies hampered all efforts to form a network of unions. One of the most successful local unions appeared in St. Petersburg in the mid-1890's and played an important part in the industrial strikes of 1896–98. This union was one of the first to issue political demands, which became more prominent among Russian clandestine unions at the turn of the century. The political orientation of the Russian labor movement was again seen in the strikes that occurred in southern Russia in 1902–03; if the Russian unions remained fragmented, there was nevertheless a growing political consciousness and discipline among the expanding working class.

The growth of trade unions in all countries touched by the industrial revolution revealed a widespread urge for practical action to alleviate poor working conditions. Although directly representing only a minority of the workers, unions spoke for the entire working class in their dealings with industrial owners. In most areas, except those in which syndicalism was strong, unions tended toward moderation within the ranks of socialism. Trade unions generally attempted reform rather than revolution in the process of seeking some adjustment or transformation of the industrial system. The reformist tactics pursued by most unions had produced significant gains and concessions by the turn of the century, although working conditions, housing, and wages still could not compare with standards of living for the middle classes. The increasing enlistment of workers in labor and socialist movements suggested that they were aware of such differences and were determined to eliminate them. Small gains encouraged greater expectations.

One of the most important lessons that workers learned from the industrial order was the advantage to be gained from organization and discipline. Workers gradually realized that they need not strike out desperately against the rigors of the industrial order. They could modify conditions and gain a fairer share of the industrial produce by joining unions empowered to bargain with employers and by participating in socialist parties committed to defending their interests and promoting the cause of social justice.

Socialist Parties

While the unions were providing the workers with strength in bargaining for better wages and conditions, the need for political action was less readily seen. The short-range goals of better pay and working conditions seemed to be more urgent matters at first. By the turn of the century however, growing numbers of the European working class were becoming "politicized" through the influence of socialist parties, which reached the worker through pamphlets and other propaganda literature. Although some leaders of the socialist parties came from the working class itself, most of them were middle-class intellectuals who had been deeply impressed by the works of Karl Marx and his analysis of the ills and injustices of capitalism. Through the influence of these men, Marxism provided the foundation for the political programs of the socialist parties. In 1870 Marxism was merely one among many competing theories of society and social evolution; by the 1890's it had outdistanced rival beliefs.

The Influence of Marxism

Perhaps the most influential aspects of Marx's teaching were his analysis of capitalist society and his prediction of its ultimate transformation into a new classless and propertyless society. His analysis seemed to correspond to the actual conditions and trends within capitalism in the mid-nineteenth century. For those at the lower economic levels of the industrial order, his prediction, backed by his interpretation of historical trends, carried great hope for altering that order.

Marx and his close collaborator, Friedrich Engels, observed the miserable conditions of the British laborer and concluded that deprivation was inevitable under a capitalist economy. Borrowing arguments from the British classical economists, Marx decided that the value of goods derived from the amount of labor expended in production. But workers were not paid wages that fairly compensated their efforts. In order to obtain capital for further investment, industrialists squeezed profits—or "surplus value"—from workers by keeping wages as low as possible. Since workers did not receive adequate compensation and could not, therefore, purchase the goods they helped produce, capitalism faced recurring problems of overproduction. Cyclical waves of boom and bust were thus an inescapable part of the capitalist economy and would become successively sharper and more protracted as time went on. Competition for markets would become desperate, driving capitalists to seek outlets overseas. Only the most efficient and ruthless would survive; the smaller producers would be driven into bankruptcy by the competition. Marx anticipated that the number of producers would shrink while the ranks of the proletariat swelled until the workers burst forth in a revolutionary upheaval causing the capitalist system to topple. Simply stated, the widening gulf between exploiters and exploited would make the system unstable to the point of revolution.

Capitalism held little immediate hope for the worker. Marxists in the latter half of the nineteenth century were sustained by a confident belief that history would reward the oppressed. This assurance was based on a doctrine of dialectical materialism that Marx had derived from the writings of the German philosopher, Friedrich Hegel. Hegel had proposed that history progressed as the result of continuing tensions between antagonistic elements in society. Out of clashes between opposites, new forms arose that Hegel called a synthesis. Furthermore, history unfolded according to laws in a determined process that could neither be ascribed to chance nor altered in any way. Thus, all historical development was inevitable. Marx accepted this, but he disagreed with Hegel on two critical assumptions. Hegel insisted that history revealed the workings of a great idea, which he equated with God. Marx claimed that ideas did not guide history; rather, ideas or ideals were themselves manifestations of material forces, of which economic relationships were the most important. Religious organizations, political institutions, and social relationships were shaped by the underlying economic structure of society. Materialism, not idealism, was at the heart of historical evolution. Marx did not rule out the influence of ideas or religions once they had come into existence. Marx's famous statement, "religion is the opium of the people," suggests that he recognized the power of religion, however delusive he may have considered it. But basically he thought economic forces were the most powerful factor in society.

Marx also disagreed with Hegel's assumption that historical development had reached its highest synthesis in the German state. For Marx the dialectic was still going on and was leading toward another clash of opposing social forces. Just as the commercial middle class had opposed the feudal aristocracy and replaced it as the ruling element in society during the English upheaval of the seventeenth century and the French Revolution of 1789, so the proletariat, formed from artisans and peasants by the industrial revolution, now opposed the bourgeoisie and would eventually replace it. At some unspecified date a collision was bound to occur; according to Marx the task of socialists was to prepare for this day by instilling a sense of discipline and class-consciousness in workers. A continuing and unrelenting class warfare was the prospect that Marx set before the workers of Europe.

The long-range purpose of the socialist parties was clear, then, from the Marxist point of view. But while awaiting the revolution, what tactics were they to adopt? Was it possible to work for measures that would alleviate conditions for the working class? From 1890 until the eve of the First World War this problem plagued all socialist parties in Europe confronted with the requirements of both revolutionary doctrine and practical action.

Revolution Versus Reform

During the 1890's socialist parties could be found in nearly every European state, and in many areas the socialists won sizable followings. One party that commanded the respect of socialists throughout Europe was the German Social Democratic Party; this party's history dramatized the difficulties involved in reconciling a belief in revolution with the demands of practical politics.

A unified German socialist party had been formed in 1875 when a Marxist group and a number of socialists, somewhat less doctrinaire, came together. The statement of principle that they produced—the Gotha program—was so moderate in its demands that it provoked a scathing attack from Marx himself. But Bismarck, the German chancellor, had been sufficiently alarmed at the appearance of this small party to introduce in 1878 a ban on socialist party activity, although socialist candidates would be permitted to stand for elections to the Reichstag without benefit of organized support. The party organization then moved to Switzerland where it published newspapers and pamphlets that were smuggled into Germany. This period of clandestine activity, during which socialists were made to feel that they were enemies of the German state, left its mark on the party. They acquired a strong sense of discipline and unity with several results. Socialist hostility toward the state grew until cooperation with other groups was impossible when the party returned to Germany after 1890. Frequently the invocation of party unity only set aside fundamental differences within the party without actually resolving them. Moreover, the demands of socialist solidarity, which gave the party its strength, inhibited adaptation to new political conditions.

With the lapse of the anti-socialist laws in 1890, the party sought to establish a theoretical basis for its political actions within the German empire. At the Erfurt Congress of 1891, Marxism became the fundamental doctrine of the party, indicating a more radical theoretical stance than had been adopted at Gotha. The Erfurt program was largely the work of Engels and Karl Kautsky, who emerged as the leading spokesman and theoretician for orthodox Marxism within the German Social Democratic Party. The language of the Erfurt statement suggested a commitment to revolutionary principles. Although direct references to class warfare were avoided, it was made clear that no compromise with bourgeois society would be tolerated and that the growing gulf between rich and poor made revolution inevitable. The Erfurt program confidently expected that increasing crises within the capitalist order would soon bring its collapse, after which a "socialization of the means of production" would take place and society would be governed by a "dictatorship of the proletariat."

In addition to the revolutionary rumblings of its Marxist tenets, the Erfurt program also included a set of practical demands that the party hoped to obtain through political action while awaiting the revolutionary crisis. The party called for an eight-hour day for all workers, a progressive income tax, universal male suffrage in the state of Prussia as a prelude to democratization of imperial politics, payment of Reichstag delegates, abolition of labor by children under fourteen years of age, election of important public officials in the bureaucracy, and a number of other measures that were essentially moderate. Even these modest proposals seemed radical in the context of German politics, for their adoption would have initiated a thorough transformation of German political life.

The gap between the theoretical and practical portions of the Erfurt program anticipated what was to become a vexing problem for German socialists after 1891—a sharp division between the reformist and revolutionary, or radical, wings of the party. The Erfurt program did, however, provide a temporary unity for the party, since it justified both tendencies. In the immediate aftermath of Erfurt the radicals believed their position had been firmly adopted by the party, and they pointed to the revolutionary predictions in support of their belief. Toward the end of the 1890's, however, the moderate elements of German socialism began to criticize pure Marxism, and by the turn of the century the "revisionist" controversy threatened to divide the party into warring factions.

The "Revisionist" Controversy

Revisionism affected every European socialist party to some degree. The man most responsible for launching this controversy was Eduard Bernstein, a German Social Democrat whose *Evolutionary Socialism* became the best known of several pamphlets, books, and articles on revisionism. Bernstein observed that at the end of the nineteenth century certain of Marx's predictions were not being fulfilled. Class conflicts did not appear to be deepening, and, more significantly, capitalism still showed abundant signs of life. Bernstein's statistics showed that wage-earners' incomes had actually gone up in many areas and that the middle classes were increasing numerically, not withering away as Marx had predicted. Moreover, the small investor was sharing a limited part of capitalism's profits; even the peasant and the small landholder were able to exist in modest comfort. The "law of increasing misery," which Marxists posited as fundamental to capitalism, simply failed to operate, according to Bernstein and the revisionists.

The revisionists' main contention was that if capitalism was not headed for an immediate, destructive crisis, then the socialists had to reconsider their theoretical assumptions as well as their political tactics. Revolutionary conflict might eventually be unnecessary if socialism, working from within the existing system, could bring about the proper evolutionary changes in society. Rather than maintain an inflexible hostility to other bourgeois political parties, socialists might contemplate tactical political alliances with democratic groups to achieve specific programs. A misguided insistence on doctrinaire politics, the revisionists warned, condemned the German socialist party to sterile isolation.

The orthodox Marxists within German socialism, led by Kautsky, attacked revisionism in the party newspapers and at party congresses. Kautsky denied the premises of revisionism by interpreting the facts differently. He saw the party's participation in Reichstag elections and in the Reichstag itself as a way to build a revolutionary consciousness, and he regarded the victories of the party at the polls as evidence of the forthcoming revolutionary surge. He insisted that class conflicts were intensifying and that socialism should not ally itself with moribund political parties drawn from the bourgeoisie or peasantry. Although Kautsky sympathized with democratic procedures, he nevertheless refused to deviate from "pure" Marxism: the party's role should continue to be the preparation of the working class for a revolutionary future through discipline and opposition to compromise with existing institutions.

To substantiate his thesis that a crisis of capitalism was brewing, Kautsky pointed to the growing competition among industrial powers as reflected in the scramble for empires. This argument was advanced by the radical wing of the Social Democratic Party, represented by Rosa Luxemburg, a brilliant writer and polemicist who showed no sympathy for the moderate tendencies of some of her socialist colleagues. Anticipating arguments made later by Lenin and others, Rosa Luxemburg identified imperialist rivalries as last-ditch efforts to find markets for surplus industrial production, thereby confirming Marx's prediction. Although workers might derive profit from the jobs created by imperialist enterprise, these gains were won at the expense of exploitation overseas and, at best, were simply temporary benefits that obscured the real crisis. Bernstein's reformist objectives were measures that deflected the workers from revolutionary purposes. At the same time, however, Rosa Luxemburg also criticized Kautsky's position as a do-nothing approach that lulled the workers into thinking that they merely had to wait for an inevitable revolution. She called on the party leadership to stimulate revolutionary zeal within the working classes.

Revisionism was formally rejected in 1903 at the Dresden Congress, after a heated and protracted debate. But what appeared to be a triumph for orthodox Marxism proved to be only a hollow victory as the party continued to drift toward reformism. There were several reasons for the continuing revisionist orientation. First, many moderate socialists, though no longer calling themselves "revisionists," persisted in advocating reforms within the existing system. In the years after Dresden these elements carried more and more weight in party councils. The Bavarian section of the party, for example, urged practical programs and alliances with bourgeois parties, if necessary, to achieve these programs. This tactic was a sensible one in Bavaria, where liberal electoral laws made the state government far more progressive than in Prussia and hopes of gaining concessions from the government were more realistic. Second, the trade unions, under the strong influence of Karl Legien, served as a moderating influence on those members who eventually entered party activities. Finally, the growth of the party itself contributed to reformist tendencies. Between the elections of 1890 and 1903 socialist support doubled from one and a half million to three million voters, while the number of active party members increased proportionately. The party's expansion required a considerable bureaucracy to handle services for its members, like educational libraries and vacation tours. Meeting the requirements of everyday party affairs bred a certain caution into the administration; as a result, the party bureaucrats tended to be less revolutionary in outlook than the party theoreticians. The leadership became somewhat reluctant to support proposals that might bring reprisals against the party itself. The discrepancy between theory and practice within German socialism widened in the years after Dresden until the party ultimately split along those lines.

In Britain, Italy, and France socialists also faced, within differing political contexts, the need to reconcile programs for immediate gains with a dogmatic opposition to working within the capitalist system. In Britain the potential divisiveness of the dispute did not reach the proportions that it assumed in Germany largely because the strictly Marxist component of the Labor party, the Social Democratic Federation, had a minor role in party affairs. The major elements that had participated in the formation of the Labor party—the Trades Union Congress, the Fabian Society, and the Independent Labor party— were reformist in outlook. The Trades Union Congress had traditionally pursued immediate gains and had only entered politics when it felt that its interests could be protected through political action. The Fabian Society, composed for the most part of middle-class intellectuals, believed that socialism could be achieved through measures enacted by Parliament. Because they judged the existing Liberal party to be unwilling to press for such goals as nationalization of industries, the Fabians participated in the formation of a Labor party and emerged as the major theoreticians for the party on most issues. Finally, Keir Hardie's Independent Labor party also preferred to seek gains through political rather than revolutionary action. As we have seen, the Labor party did achieve a modest success in the elections of 1906 and was able to have an influence on the direction of British politics that was greater than the numerical strength of the party would suggest.

In Italy the socialist party leadership favored gradualist tactics and formed a kind of tacit alliance with the government following the turn of the century. After Giovanni Giolitti came to power as prime minister in 1903, he tried to woo the socialists by offering one of their leaders, Filippo Turati, a post in the government cabinet. Although Turati declined the offer, he found that he was quite close to Giolitti on matters of social reform and labor legislation. Turati and Leonida Bissolati, editor of the party newspaper, *Avanti*, represented the reformist strain within Italian socialism. But they faced opposition within the party from more radical members. To placate the radicals the Italian socialists adopted the formula devised by the Germans at Erfurt. At their Rome Congress of 1900, they accepted a program that encompassed both minimum and maximum demands. This compromise, however, failed to halt conflicts within the party, which continued until the eve of the First World War when the radicals gained a victory and proceeded to expel the moderate faction.

Socialists in France were more prone to collaborate with bourgeois parties than were the Italians. The reform socialist Jean Jaurès argued that France's deficiencies in social legislation could be remedied if socialists entered into political alliances with other reform-minded parties. Moreover, he called for cooperation with other groups if it became necessary to defend the republic from its enemies. Jaurès was highly optimistic about the prospects of gaining power through what he called "the revolutionary instrument of the ballot." Confident that the future of French politics was to the left, he felt that socialism could not long be denied dominance. His assumptions were challenged by Jules Guesde, a rival for leadership of French socialism. Guesde's strict Marxist views made him wary of Jaurès' propensity for cooperation with bourgeois elements. Guesde suspected that Jaurès had become the dupe of his political allies.

Ultimately the controversy between Jaurès and Guesde about collaboration reached the 1904 Amsterdam Congress of the Second International, an international socialist organization. The assembled delegates reviewed the dispute and were asked to reach a decision that would be binding on the French socialist party. At issue was more than a quarrel within one national group. The Amsterdam Congress was faced with the general question of cooperation with non-socialist parties for tactical purposes. Under the influence of the German delegation, which had just the previous year condemned revisionism at Dresden, the Amsterdam Congress decided in favor of Guesde. During the debates the French socialists were admonished to end the factionalism that had plagued their movement. Although he had vigorously defended his position at Amsterdam, Jaurès accepted the International's judgment, and settled into an uneasy alliance with Guesde. In 1905 a unified French Section of the Workers' International was formed to represent all socialist groups in French politics.

The French socialists shared with their Italian colleagues certain difficulties arising from the attitude of the labor unions toward politics. The ties between the trade unions and the socialist party were weaker and stormier than in either Germany or Britain, where the unions exerted a moderating influence on the party. The French and Italian unions were smaller but more deeply imbued with syndicalist opposition to political action. In the French unions there was doubt as to the wisdom of following either Guesde's orthodox Marxism or Jaurès' reformist policies.

The progress and impact of socialism depended to a large extent on the degree to which socialist parties anticipated having some influence on political life; the prospects varied from one state to another. At the Amsterdam Congress Jean Jaurès pointed out that the German socialists could indulge in doctrinaire orthodoxy because they had little chance to wield power, given the political structure of their country. The Reichstag lacked the power and practical authority of the Chamber of Deputies in France. Therefore, Jaurès claimed that the defense of non-cooperation represented no sacrifice for the German socialists. "Behind the inflexibility of theoretical formulas which your excellent Comrade Kautsky will supply you with until the end of his days," Jaurès observed, "you concealed from your own proletariat, from the international proletariat, your inability to act." As events in France proved, reformism was a more promising course of action in those states in which parliament provided a channel to political authority. In areas such as eastern Europe, where channels were either narrow or blocked, socialist politics assumed a more revolutionary cast.

Despite impressive gains in the 1890's, in no country did socialist strength approach a parliamentary majority by 1905. But the excitement and dynamism of the movement created the impression that socialism was the wave of the future. For workers in the European states this trend was the source of considerable hope; for the conservatives, socialism evoked the specter of revolution and was cause for alarm. Preoccupied with the threat of class warfare, conservatives failed to appreciate the democratic tendencies at work among the reformist wings of most socialist parties. Some states passed rather comprehensive measures of social-welfare legislation, hoping to undermine the workers' grievances and weaken the appeal of socialism. But these attempts, notably in Germany, failed to have the desired effect, and socialist parties continued to grow and to be hostile to the ruling classes.

International Socialism

One reason for the fear socialism evoked among the middle classes was its claim that class differences transcended national boundaries and that all workers therefore shared the same ambition of overturning the existing social order. The rulers of Europe considered socialism to be an international movement and condemned it as treasonous as well as revolutionary. But the notion of international solidarity became an article of faith for the socialists themselves. Through unity the socialists of all nations hoped to gain strength and bring in a new era of universal peace and social justice.

The First International

The earliest attempt at international cooperation was the First International, founded by Karl Marx in 1864. This organization did not attract a wide membership and had a brief and stormy existence. The meetings became battlegrounds in a struggle between Marxists, who saw themselves as hard-headed, realistic revolutionaries, and the more romantic anarchists who followed the lead of the colorful Michael Bakunin. After a particularly heated meeting of the First International at the Hague in 1872, Marx decided that future cooperation with the anarchists was hopeless and arranged the collapse of the First International by transferring its headquarters to the United States, where it was neglected. Bakunin and others tried to keep the International functioning in Europe, but by 1877 it had expired.

The Second International

The economic difficulties of the 1880's, combined with the growing activity of trade unions and the emergence of socialist parties, revived interest in an international organization that would provide a forum for discussions of theoretical and practical problems arising out of the workers' movement. The impulse for calling an international congress came from a number of sources. Both the British Trades Union Congress and the German socialists agreed independently that an international meeting should be held. Labor groups in France and the United States wished to convene an international meeting for the purpose of coordinating agitation in favor of the eight-hour day, a concession that had recently been won in Australia. In 1888 a meeting of representatives from the British Trades Union Congress, members of the moderate French Possibilist group (a reformist group committed to working for realistic changes), and other delegates from the Continent was held in London. The French were asked to host an international meeting the following year, the centenary celebration of the French Revolution. It was hoped that this occasion would rally the many socialist factions and create an atmosphere of common purpose.

Expectations of international unity were not to be realized, in part because of basic conflicts within the French socialist movement itself.

The French Marxists were highly suspicious of any meeting sponsored by the rival Possibilist group. They received encouragement from the German Social Democratic Party, which wanted an international meeting that would be clearly under the control of Marxists. Two separate meetings, both claiming to represent the international workers' movement, convened in Paris on Bastille Day, July 14, 1889. Some gestures were made in the direction of reconciliation, as delegates drifted from one meeting to another, but the differences were not resolved. Of the two meetings, the Marxist assembly attracted a larger and more impressive following from several countries, and its deliberations marked the birth of the Second International. The French provided the largest delegation, but the discipline and sober determination of the German delegation gave them an important influence from the outset.

This first meeting of the Second International was chaotic; a great deal of time was consumed in reports from national delegations. Only at the last minute did the socialists pass resolutions on substantive issues. One resolution called for an end to standing armies and the abolition of war as a means of national policy. The method for achieving these goals was left vague, but from this time the socialists considered themselves a potential force for preventing the outbreak of war. Another resolution urged socialists to press for universal suffrage where this goal had not been achieved. Finally, the delegates accepted May 1 as a labor holiday. This date had originally been chosen by the American Federation of Labor as a day on which a mass demonstration would be held in favor of a universal eight-hour working day. With the reservation that each national delegation would decide on the nature of the demonstration, May 1, 1890, was accepted as the date for an international workers demonstration. The practical achievements of this demonstration were negligible. In Germany the trade unions did nothing because they were fearful of provoking a return of the anti-socialist laws that had only recently been lifted. In Great Britain, the law-abiding unions confined themselves to speeches and demonstrations on the first Sunday after May 1, thereby avoiding loss of a day's labor. In Austria, however, the demonstrations occurred in an orderly and impressive fashion. There were no outbursts of violence, although the government had taken the precaution of reinforcing the police. May Day took on a symbolic significance for the labor movement and reminded the propertied classes of labor's potential strength on an international scale.

Initially the organization was to welcome diverse groups within its ranks, but the old quarrel between Marxists and anarchists made this impossible. The Marxist majority passed several resolutions that condemned fruitless acts of terror and violence, an obvious rebuke to anarchists. For a while the anarchists continued their participation in the International; however, by the mid-1890's it had become obvious that they were no longer welcome. The anarchists' departure marked a triumph for Marxism within the Second International but did not entirely eliminate anarchist influence. Many trade unions, particularly in France, Spain, and Italy, were also suspicious of a large organization devoted to political problems. Because the Second International was reluctant to alienate these supporters, the formulas that condemned the anarchists were stated in very general terms.

During the 1890's the International debated the value of working within existing political systems. Many of the arguments over revisionism that had torn the national parties recurred within the International. For the most part, the policies that had prevailed in the party congresses of the German socialists became the standard for international socialism: revisionism was condemned, and opportunistic deals with other political groups were censured. Political action was encouraged only if socialist parties retained their independence and avoided becoming satellites of bourgeois groups. In spite of this standard, differences between the intransigents and the reformists threatened to bring about an open conflict. To avoid a schism it was agreed at the Paris Congress in 1900 that for tactical gains socialists might participate with other parties on a temporary basis and to meet an emergency situation. Generally, the International solved its doctrinal disputes by simply preventing an opportunity for direct confrontation with the issues. Resolutions passed at the congresses, for instance, tended to be couched in general terms.

The Paris Congress of 1900 also established an International Socialist Bureau with headquarters in Brussels. The purpose of this organization was to provide a permanent office that could coordinate the activities of national parties between congresses. In the next decade and a half the secretariat efficiently guided the Second International, providing a formal structure for European socialism. But the secretariat, like the congresses themselves, lacked coercive power to compel loyalty from the national parties, which accepted only those decisions reached by the International that they wanted to accept. For the most part, the International secretariat avoided divisive issues and acted to resolve quarrels within the International.

One of the more important issues that came before the Second International was the question of national rivalries and the threat of war that they brought. A basic premise of the Second International was that class loyalty took precedence over patriotism among the working classes. On this basis, the socialists were convinced that they could check the warlike propensities of national governments and that they thus held the balance of peace in their hands. Resolutions passed during the 1890's generally condemned expenditure for military or colonial purposes as being both dangerous and wasteful. Socialist parties consistently voted against these credits in national budgets. Socialists were also called on to organize demonstrations whenever an international crisis developed, although these resolutions did not specify what the nature of the demonstration would be. At Paris in 1900 the possibility of a general strike in the event of war was suggested, but the proposal received only brief consideration and nothing was done to implement it.

As the debates on the prevention of war and imperialism developed it was seen that the socialists differed over tactics and even over the question of the impact that war or imperialism might have on the evolution of society. For example, at the Paris Congress Rosa Luxemburg had proposed that capitalism would collapse from tensions engendered by imperialist rivalries for markets among the great powers. In this event, the objective of socialist parties was a preparation of the working class for its revolutionary task on an international scale. In making this speech, Rosa Luxemburg echoed Engels who had predicted in 1887 that war among capitalist powers would be a terrible event, but it would produce "a general exhaustion and the establishment of conditions for the final victory of the working class." War and revolution were thus linked. Most socialists, however, recoiled from the implications of an analysis that allowed them to expect to benefit from a capitalist war. The great majority, despite revolutionary doctrine, were committed to the peaceful conquest of power. Consequently, as the intensity of national rivalries mounted after 1904-05, the Second International found itself debating more and more on steps that might be taken to prevent war. One of the strongest believers in using socialism to ensure peace was Jean Jaurès, who devoted much of his time to this problem. His interest reflected a broader concern that international crises were assuming dangerous proportions and might sweep Europe into war either deliberately or by miscalculation.

With the outbreak of the Russo-Japanese War in 1904 and the tensions evoked by the Moroccan crisis of 1905 the fragile nature of European peace was dramatically illustrated. The Second International offered the possibility of an alternative to national rivalries—namely international cooperation—if it could unite the working classes in the cause of peace. This possibility was still untested, whatever hope it may have held for Jaurès and others who shared his views. But it was an important aspect of the search for a new society.

SUGGESTED READING

The most extensive survey of European socialism is G. D. H. Cole's *A History of Socialist Thought*, 5 vols. (New York: The Macmillan Co., 1963); Parts 1 and 2 of Volume 3, *The Second International*, concern the prewar decades. A perceptive analysis of the interplay between Marxist doctrine and socialist practice within the context of nineteenth century economic and political conditions may be found in George Lichtheim's *Marxism: a Historical and Critical Study* (New York: Praeger, 1961). The same author's more recent *Origins of Socialism* (New York: Praeger, 1969) is an excellent introduction to the subject. *European Socialism: a History of Ideas and Movements*, 2 vols. (Berkeley: University of California Press, 1959), by Carl Landauer and others, offers a detailed comparative approach. A convenient, brief treatment of international socialism from 1889 to 1914 is James Joll's *The Second International, 1889–1914* (London: Weidenfeld and Nicolson, 1955).

Among the books that deal with the evolution of socialism within individual countries, Carl E. Schorske's *German Social Democracy, 1905–1917: the Development of the Great Schism* (Cambridge, Mass.: Harvard University Press, 1955) stands out as a model of analysis, clearly delineating the internal dilemmas and divisions of German socialism. Peter Gay in *The Dilemma of Democratic Socialism: Eduard Bernstein's Challenge to Marx* (New York: Collier, 1962) focuses on Bernstein and the revisionist controversy. The process of molding a socialist party in Great Britain is described in detail by Henry Pelling in *The Origins of the Labour Party, 1880–1900* (Oxford: Oxford University Press, 2nd ed., 1965). Pelling and Frank Beasley have carried the story down to the election of 1906 in *Labour and Politics, 1900–1906* (London: Macmillan, 1958), showing the way in which Labour gained a foothold in Parliament. One of the best accounts of the Fabians' influence is A. M. McBriar's *Fabian Socialism and English Politics: 1884–1918* (Cambridge: Cambridge University Press, 1962). A good approach to the study of socialism in France is found in Harvey Goldberg's laudatory biography, *The Life of Jean Jaurès* (Madison: University of Wisconsin Press, 1962). Aaron Noland in *The Founding of the French Socialist Party, 1893–1905* (Cambridge, Mass.: Harvard University Press, 1956) discusses the factions that ultimately came together to form a unified party. A solid, reliable account of French socialism may also be found in the appropriate chapters of Val R. Lorwin's *The French Labor Movement* (Cambridge, Mass.: Harvard University Press, 1954).

As yet there is no satisfactory study of syndicalism, although scholars are at work on the topic. The most detailed and comprehensive history of anarchism is George Woodcock's *Anarchism, a History of Libertarian Ideas and Movements* (Cleveland: The World Publishing Co., 1962). A briefer treatment, covering a broader time-span, may be found in James Joll's *The Anarchists* (Boston: Little, Brown and Company, 1965).

3

POLITICS AT THE TURN OF THE CENTURY IN WESTERN EUROPE

The Political Temper of the Time

The social and economic changes at the end of the nineteenth century confronted each state with the need to adapt its political institutions to the new conditions. The trend was toward an age of "mass politics." The political arena had broadened perceptibly as greater literacy and more accessible forms of communications brought an awareness of common problems to emerging social classes. Urbanization concentrated the population in compact districts, facilitating the organization and mobilization of large numbers of people. Social groups that formerly had been excluded from political life were now demanding some influence and even a share of political power. Those in power struggled to find a formula that would accommodate or channel these new political forces while permitting them to retain their own social and political strength.

A broadening of the channels for popular political expression could be seen in the extension of the franchise. By 1890 both Germany and France had enjoyed universal male suffrage for a generation. The reform acts of 1867 and 1884 brought Britain near this goal, although some British adult males were still without the franchise by the turn of the century. The Austrian half of the Hapsburg monarchy obtained universal male suffrage in 1907; in Russia the newly formed legislative assembly (the Duma) was elected in 1906 by a fairly wide electorate. Italy's high illiteracy rate limited progress toward universal suffrage, but as educational standards improved the electorate expanded accordingly. Giolitti's electoral reforms in 1912 eliminated most restrictions on the right to cast a ballot in Italian elections. Some enclaves in Europe resisted any widening of the franchise—for example, property qualifications assured the landowning classes a continuing predominance in the electorate of Hungary and within the Prussian portions of the German empire. But the trend at the turn of the century was toward universal suffrage; in 1907 the Norwegians even took the unorthodox step of granting the vote to women.

The enfranchisement of new classes greatly affected the techniques employed by political parties. An expanded electorate required a more extensive organization and discipline than were provided by the informal electoral alliances of the mid-nineteenth century. The process of political organization was most advanced in Great Britain where both Liberals and Conservatives established national and local committees to handle party business. On the Continent the disciplined socialist parties, especially the German Social Democrats, provided a wide range of services for their membership. The effectiveness of the socialists' discipline induced other political groups to adopt similar practices. Even where formal party organizations were weak, as in France, most parties had their own newspapers and published pamphlets in an effort to win popular support. At this time two new elements in political life emerged in Europe—pressure groups, designed to gain particular legislation for their constituents, and professional political organizers. At the turn of the century politics was becoming a vocation rather than an avocation of amateurs.

Liberalism, Radicalism, and Conservatism

The socialists appeared to be the principal beneficiaries of the broader franchise, but, either by choice or by exclusion, nowhere did they hold significant governmental positions. When the socialist Alexandre Millerand accepted a post in the French cabinet in 1899, his participation provoked a major crisis. The real power remained in the hands of liberals and conservatives. Generally the middle classes tended toward liberalism, whereas the upper classes were inclined to embrace conservative views. Of the two doctrines, liberalism had a wider impact, particularly in western Europe, during the last third of the nineteenth century. Measures such as franchise reform had a liberal rather than a conservative cast, and liberals readily identified themselves with notions of progress in both the economic and political spheres. Liberal ideology emphasized the freedom of the individual. The classical liberal theorists believed that man could direct his affairs toward productive ends and control his own destiny through the use of reason. The government's role was to provide uniform standards of justice while interfering in each citizen's affairs as little as possible. Liberals favored vigorous parliamentary institutions that would protect the rights of citizens and prevent any abuse of political power by arbitrary executive authority. Finally, most liberals assumed that those chosen to govern would be the best qualified—that is, those endowed with a superior education and independent economic means.

European liberals were moderate men who placed faith in gradual progress toward greater political freedom. But the conditions that had increased the ranks of liberal parties now posed serious challenges to liberal theories. A complete doctrine of laissez-faire was untenable as government intervention in the lives of citizens became increasingly necessary. The vast increase in population and the dislocations caused by industrialization promised to produce a waste of human resources unless governments made some effort at planning and providing direction to society. The trend toward industrial consolidation and monopoly created large business and manufacturing concerns that threatened to destroy small private enterprises unless governments introduced protective measures. With the appearance of mass politics, liberals had to adjust to participation of social groups that they considered to be unqualified by their education and class to rule. Furthermore, parties organized along class or sectarian lines offended a liberal tenet that each man could be expected to reach intelligent, informed, and rational political decisions through the exercise of his judgment alone. Liberalism increasingly was compelled to adapt its doctrine and tactics to the changing political climate at the end of the nineteenth century.

While liberalism was providing a mildly progressive position in most states (except Russia, where liberalism clashed with czarist autocracy), a related doctrine, radicalism, was successfully competing for allegiance. Radicals and liberals shared certain assumptions—strong belief in representative government, limits to arbitrary authority, and uniform justice—but they differed on certain political issues. Perhaps the most important distinction centered on the role of religion in society. Radicals, whether nonconformists in Britain or anticlericals in France and Italy, wished to remove religion from any connection with the state, whereas the liberals held no tenet on this issue.

Radicalism also displayed a more egalitarian ethos than liberalism, which assumed that a natural hierarchy of talent and wealth would emerge in a free society. Radicals aggressively championed the interests of the "little people" against the pretensions of the high and mighty, the arbitrary power of the state, and the threats of collectivism. A broadly based political democracy for all (male) citizens was a militant faith for radicals, yet they did not embrace any sweeping doctrine of social and economic reform. Radicals had no interest in causing a wholesale revision of the capitalist system; in fact, when they gained power—as in France after 1900—they showed themselves to be staunch defenders of order. By the turn of the century radicals were beginning to look apprehensively over their shoulders as they sensed the growing appeal of socialism among the European working classes.

The main contention of the conservatives was that any changes in society and politics should be made consonant with past traditions. To liberals and radicals, conservative respect for the past appeared to be no more than a defense of old privileges, but conservatives thought that the weight of traditional authority and procedures helped contain the disorderly tendencies to be found in society. During the later nineteenth century, when they feared that their power and influence were declining, many conservatives seized on nationalist slogans in an effort to find broader popular support. Arguing that conflicts of class and ideological interest threatened the unity of the state, conservatives appealed to patriotic feelings that would cut across class lines. In some areas in Austria-Hungary and the Russian and German empires, local nationalism was directed toward liberation from dynastic control and was, therefore, an element of instability rather than the basis for cohesion. But the nationalist doctrine predominant among the ruling groups in these empires reflected a belief in their own national and even racial superiority and was used to justify domination over "lesser" people and to promote expansionist dreams, thereby creating a mission for society.

In the late nineteenth century a combination of aggressive nationalism and racism found a full expression in the pan-German and pan-Slav movements in central and eastern Europe, which were intent on a reunion of their respective nationalities under a single authority. Assumptions of national superiority also supplied the western European imperialists with a rationale for overseas rule. The French justified colonial conquest as a "civilizing mission," and British rulers assumed that they brought the benefits of stable administration and wholesome institutions to the people of their empire. Such arguments attracted a significant following in Europe, among liberals as well as conservatives. But the conservatives in particular seemed inclined toward essentially violent and emotional doctrines. In the atmosphere of super-heated nationalism and imperialism that emerged in the 1890's, conservatives found a new voice and successfully escaped the eclipse that had appeared possible in the 1870's and 1880's.

In most European states conservatives retained important positions in the military establishments, diplomatic services, and higher bureaucratic posts throughout the nineteenth century. They were thus in a position to use their influence to perpetuate their power and to make the emerging technological forces serve their own ends. As the English historian George Kitson Clark has observed in his *Making of Victorian England:* "The process of social and economic development may increase the power of those elements in society which demand change, but it may also increase the power of forces to whom changes, at least those changes which are most insistently demanded, are increasingly repugnant."* The technological revolutions of the nineteenth century brought new classes into prominence and even into existence, but they did not guarantee the political triumph of those classes. Instead they created a widespread prospect for political conflict throughout Europe.

The Components of Political Power

Although each state experienced its own distinctive political development, certain common features of political power could be found across Europe. By 1890 most states, with the major exception of Russia, possessed some form of representative assembly at the national level. The function of the assembly was to act as a legislative arm for the state. Normally, budgets and laws were submitted to this chamber by the government for approval or modification; in some states the parliamentary assembly had the right to initiate legislation. The authority that European parliaments possessed in practice varied from one country to another. In France the influence of the Chamber of Deputies was extensive, and in Britain the power of the monarchy had been greatly reduced to the advantage of the prime minister, his cabinet, and the House of Commons. In Germany and Austria-Hungary, where the royal houses continued to play important roles,

*London: Metheun & Co., 1962, p. 289.

many significant political decisions took place outside the halls of parliament. In Russia, of course, prior to the calling of a Duma in 1906, the power of the Czar was limited only by the inefficiencies of his bureaucracy. But in a majority of European states parliaments had some degree of political power, and even where this power might be limited, the executive authority's consultation with parliament was considered important for successful government.

Other institutions in addition to representative assemblies had a share in the political power of the European nations. The monarchy, for instance, continued to have both a formal and an informal authority. A constitutional monarchy was the most common form of government in Europe; only France, a republic, Switzerland, a democratic federation, and Russia, an absolutist monarchy before 1906, deviated from this standard. In several constitutional monarchies ministers were selected technically at the monarch's discretion, although they usually assured themselves a working majority in parliament. Royal influence was frequently exercised in appointments to higher administrative posts and to supreme military commands.

Governmental bureaucracies represented another instrument of state power often outside direct parliamentary control or supervision; the state bureaucracies provided the means for transmitting and enforcing political decisions. The bureaucracy of a state, guided by legal codes meant to prevent an arbitrary exercise of power, was reasonably efficient and free from corruption. Bureaucracies and courts were expected to enforce the laws of each state in an objective manner. Special privileges and obligations for different social classes had been abolished in most of Europe by the end of the nineteenth century, although this ideal was abused or distorted in some regions. Each citizen presumably had the same rights and duties as his fellow countryman.

An additional and crucial element in political power was the military, which had an influence in both international and domestic politics. Increased military strength, the result of technological improvements, supplied the sinews for each state's foreign policy and also served as a deterrent to domestic violence or revolution. The loyalty and support of the army became critical to the government in times of domestic political crisis.

All these elements—representative institutions, remnants of monarchical authority, an effective bureaucracy, and a modern military organization—provided the basic ingredients of political power in Europe at the end of the nineteenth century. Because the contest for domestic political power turned on the relative strength of these elements in each nation, every European government reflected its own pattern of development. In three major states of western Europe—Great Britain, France, and Italy—the transition from the nineteenth to the twentieth centuries was accompanied by a political crisis that led to a renewed strength for representative institutions within the balance of domestic politics. The passage was not always smooth and did not guarantee political tranquillity, but fairly vigorous representative institutions in these states offered a means for mediating the conflict between the forces producing social change and the elements of traditional authority.

Great Britain Between Imperialism and Reform

The first step in Great Britain's transition from an era in which aristocrats and members of the wealthier middle classes ruled more or less by habit to an era of popular politics came in the period 1890–1906. In these years the Conservative party, reflecting traditional upper-class leadership, dominated British politics, and imperialism appeared to be the most important issue before the country. Yet subtle changes were occurring. In retrospect the period may be seen as one in which political lines were being redrawn.

The Liberal and Conservative Parties

Throughout the mid-Victorian era Britain's two political parties, the Conservatives and Liberals, were in power alternately. They established the tone and style of political discourse, mirroring the upper-class characteristics of their leadership. The parties did not show deep class divergence, although the Liberals drew heavily on support from manufacturing and commercial interests of the cities, nonconformist religious groups, and some wealthy landowners of Whig persuasion, whereas the Conservatives counted on the loyalty of country squires and the Anglican clergy. Of the two parties, the liberals showed a stronger interest in political reforms, especially measures that would protect the rights of the individual and the rights of Parliament against royal power. Liberals also criticized the influence of the Anglican church, a position that gained votes among radical, nonconformist elements with an antipathy for the Anglican establishment. Because by their standards arbitrary royal government had presented serious threats to liberties in the past, the Liberals favored imposing clearly defined limits on governmental power. For instance, they opposed governmental interference in economic affairs, thereby expressing the preference of the manufacturing class for a laissez-faire economy.

The Conservatives were less wed to laissez-faire doctrines. In the nineteenth century under the leadership of Benjamin Disraeli they displayed a strong sense of social responsibility; they proved to be willing to pass measures that would alleviate the economic hardships associated with the industrial revolution. Disraeli bequeathed a dual legacy of social conscience and enthusiasm for the British empire to the Conservatives, and these two issues were to supply the party with ammunition in competing with the Liberals. From the late 1860's to the mid-1880's the two parties appeared equally balanced, although the Liberals' strong faith in progress convinced them that the future would confirm the rightness of their politics. Under the leadership of William Gladstone the Liberal party in Britain acquired a moral tone that at times seemed rather too self-assured.

Neither party was indifferent to the demands of the disenfranchised who wished for a voice in the political process. Competition between the parties for new electoral support resulted in an extension of the franchise during the last half of the nineteenth century. The Reform Act of 1867 doubled the electorate by enabling the urban lower middle classes and skilled workers to vote. But about two-thirds of the male population was still unrepresented in electoral politics. In 1884 Gladstone pressed for an additional reform that established virtually universal male suffrage (only excluding some 15 percent). The following year parliamentary seats were redistributed according to a formula that more nearly reflected equal representation for each voter. Of course, there were still political inequities: many seats were considered "safe" for one party or another, and women were not permitted to vote. But the extension of the franchise was regarded by its proponents—and opponents—as a step toward democratization.

The expansion of the electorate induced significant changes in political techniques. Both parties strengthened their internal organizations by establishing committees to maintain contact with their followers during off-years. Party leaders began stumping the country in an effort to woo new voters. The first to do so was William Gladstone, the Liberal leader who charmed large crowds with his eloquence during the campaigns of 1879. Although Queen Victoria found his performance unseemly and Disraeli, his Conservative opponent, denigrated its effectiveness, the elections of 1880 swept the Liberals into office. Henceforth both parties made every effort to carry their programs to the people. The parties in Great Britain during these years began to resemble modern political parties.

The Eclipse of the Liberal Party, 1885

Even though the Liberals were skeptical of the capacity of the masses to guide their own political destinies, they nevertheless assumed that their party would benefit from an era of popular politics. This expectation seemed confirmed in the election of 1885, held under provisions of the second reform act. As a result of that election the Liberals held a majority of eighty-six over their rivals. But this majority exactly equaled the size of the Irish delegation, a separate faction in Commons, led by Charles Stewart Parnell. Parnell could not provide the Conservatives with a majority, but he could deny a majority to the Liberals. Parnell would turn over his votes to Gladstone only in exchange for political concessions to Irish demands for home rule, an issue that had simmered since the union of Britain and Ireland in 1801. When Parnell found that Gladstone had in fact already accepted the idea of home rule for Ireland, a bargain was made. If Gladstone could maintain control of his own party, the Liberal-Irish combination could control the Commons decisively. Unfortunately, Gladstone neglected to consult his colleagues on the issue of home rule, and this failure proved costly for the Liberals. When Gladstone presented his Home Rule Bill in 1886, ninety-three Liberals, headed by the dynamic Joseph Chamberlain, voted against it. The measure lost by thirty votes, forcing Gladstone to resign. The split within the Liberal party over Ireland was one factor that prepared the way for a Conservative dominance in Parliament.

Imperialism was another issue that split the Liberal party and helped foster its eclipse. Although Gladstone had never retreated from the concept of an empire, he was known to be a "little Englander," a man who would gladly curb Britain's overseas commitments. He felt that Britain should not assume the burden of directing the affairs of other people. The Liberal party came under sharp attack for its neglect of Britain's overseas responsibility. For example, the Gladstone ministry felt the brunt of the outrage over the death of General Gordon outside the gates of Khartoum in January, 1885. This disaster was attributed to an unaccountable delay in sending reinforcements to Gordon. The public outcry should have alerted the Liberals to the growing popular attention that was being directed toward Britain's overseas "sporting wars," but the party remained divided. Gladstone and his followers continued to believe that imperialism was not entirely moral. A minority of Liberal imperialists disagreed; they wished that Britain would meet and even increase the burdens of its imperial charge. This internal disagreement weakened the party, confronted with an electorate that favored a vigorous overseas policy.

The elections of 1885 revealed important shifts in voting patterns. The Liberal party lost votes in many urban areas where formerly they had enjoyed support from business interests and nonconformist workers. In part this loss was caused by Parnell's request that Irish Catholics in the cities vote for Conservatives, but it also indicated that the desire for imperialism and the resentment at General Gordon's death were livelier in the cities than in the countryside. Many rural districts that formerly had been bastions of conservativism went over to the Liberals. In some instances this rural support reflected a vote of appreciation by rural workers who had gained their franchise with Gladstone's 1884 reform. But the electoral importance of the cities was steadily increasing, and the Liberals could no longer take them for granted.

The election of 1886, which the Conservatives called immediately after Gladstone's defeat on the home rule issue, gave them a comfortable working majority in Parliament. The electorate clearly indicated that they had little sympathy for Ireland, and an era of Conservative dominance in British politics began.

The Ascendancy of the Conservative Party, 1886–1902

Imperialism, opposition to home rule, and vague talk of social reform supplied the Conservative party with the basis for political supremacy during the two decades following 1886, except for a brief Liberal interlude in the early 1890's. The prime minister for most of this time was Lord Salisbury of the Cecil family, whose members had served British monarchs since the time of Queen Elizabeth. Salisbury represented the traditional, landed, ruling class of Britain down to his own personal idiosyncracies—one of his favorite forms of exercise was riding an oversized tricycle about the gardens of his estate. But his abilities were formidable. His opponents lived in dread of his sarcasm, which could neatly demolish any foolishness. Moreover, Salisbury seemed little concerned whom he offended, for he stood at the pinnacle of social and political achievement. His main interest was in foreign affairs; domestic problems were generally treated with casual neglect during his ministries. He had no intention of giving home rule to the Irish, whose capacity for government he scorned.

Quite different in temperament and background was Joseph Chamberlain, a former Liberal who found himself uneasily allied with Salisbury and the Conservatives after 1886 because of his opposition to home rule. Chamberlain came from a family that had made its fortune in manufacturing. This was the class to whom Gladstone's moral fervor appealed, and Chamberlain began his political career within the radical tradition of the Liberal party. At one time a reform mayor of Birmingham, Chamberlain displayed a conscience that marked him as a champion of the oppressed and a firm opponent of special privileges. In fact, during his Liberal years, Chamberlain had at one point attacked Salisbury himself as the spokesman for those "who toil not, neither do they spin." Such views made Chamberlain's defection to the Conservatives something of a puzzle. His departure left the Liberals without their strongest advocate of social reform. But his insistence on maintaining the union with Ireland was decisive; after the split over home rule, Chamberlain's faction, the Liberal Unionists, voted with the Conservatives. Even on the issue of social-welfare legislation Chamberlain found a Conservative tradition that he could adopt. Under his influence the Disraeli mixture of imperialism and social reform was revived, although imperialism continued to be the more important of the two.

The Conservatives' position was buoyed by the celebration of Queen Victoria's jubilee in 1887. At that time Britain was at the zenith of its power; it commanded the world's largest empire and possessed enormous industrial capacity. Few people then could discern the limits of this achievement or foresee the prospects of a lesser role in the future. There was another side, however, to this image of Victorian glory. Toward the end of 1887 a series of meetings called by the Marxist Social Democratic Federation, and attracting a wide assortment of radicals, had been held in Trafalgar Square. The commissioner of police tried to limit the impact of these assemblies by selectively prohibiting them. When on one Sunday a meeting was held in defiance of a ban, the police marched in to disperse the crowd. The result was a violent clash in which two men lost their lives. "Bloody Sunday" left a bitter memory for British radicals, and it portended a growing intensity of ideological conflict in Great Britain. A second rumbling, more significant in the long run, came two years later with the London gasworkers' and dockers' strikes of 1889.

Salisbury characteristically paid little attention to these domestic discontents. The course of foreign and imperial affairs seemed to confirm for him the official boasts of unparalleled accomplishment. Furthermore, the problem of Irish home rule was posing little difficulty.

The Irish cause suffered a setback when Parnell was named core-spondent in a divorce case. Adultery meant political disaster in Victorian England; Parnell's reputation was dealt a fatal blow just when his career appeared to have reached a peak.

The Liberal Interlude, 1892–95 ▪ Even though Salisbury faced no major crisis, his majority began to slip in a series of by-elections. The results of a general election in 1892 revealed a slight shift in sentiment but hardly any evidence of more than a temporary dissatisfaction with the Conservative stewardship. Although neither party won a majority, the Liberals in alliance with home-rulers did have an edge over their opponents. The Liberals thus returned to power, but once more they displayed internal disagreements and malaise. Gladstone, now in office for the fourth and last time, again introduced a home-rule measure and again was defeated. When he retired in 1894 after sixty-one years of active parliamentary life, he acknowledged a new era was at hand that he did not fully comprehend. His departure exposed further rifts within the Liberal party that had temporarily been bridged out of respect for him. Lord Roseberry, Gladstone's successor, alienated many Gladstonian Liberals by his enthusiastic endorsement of imperialism. After little over a year in office he resigned on a minor issue.

Although the accomplishments of the Liberal interlude were largely negative, the rotation of office did keep alive a two-party tradition and in two respects the Liberals anticipated future developments. First, they succeeded in passing a graduated tax on inheritances. By modern standards this tax was not great, but the principle of gradation in payment had been accepted and the way was opened to a possible redistribution of wealth through taxation policy. Second, Liberals in the House of Commons proposed many measures that were vetoed by the House of Lords between 1892 and 1895. This experience foreshadowed a later constitutional conflict between Commons and Lords that was to reach a crisis stage after the Liberals returned to power in 1906.

In the general elections of 1895 the Liberals were decisively defeated by the Conservatives and their unionist allies, who obtained a majority of some 150 seats. This electoral swing indicated that the British voters did not trust Liberals either on imperial questions or on the issue of home rule in Ireland (which many regarded as a kind of imperial possession), and it demonstrated a further loss of Liberal strength in urban constituencies. Increasingly the urban middle classes, particularly the more prosperous businessmen and manufacturers, were transferring their allegiance to the Conservative party, and those urban workers who did not vote Conservative demonstrated their dissatisfaction with a rather sterile liberalism by abstaining. Liberal attempts to revive their radical traditions offered nothing but vague statements on the subject of industrial relations and social policy. Home rule, disestablishment of the Anglican church in Wales and Scotland, and advocacy of local liquor control were hardly issues that had much appeal among the working classes. The founding of Keir Hardie's Independent Labor party in 1893 represented early stirrings of working class defection from liberalism, although significant numbers did not turn toward socialism until after the turn of the century.

In 1895, then, the Liberals found themselves in a dilemma: their reforms were inadequate to satisfy urban workers, yet they had alienated many middle-class supporters. Moreover, the party was pressed for campaign funds; in 124 of 670 constituencies there was no Liberal candidate to contest the election. Although the popular vote for the Liberals had not been far behind that for the Conservatives, the decline of the Liberal party seemed to be at hand. Gladstone the great statesman was gone, and the Liberals were driven to patching together support, much of it from the assorted grievances to be found in the "Celtic fringe" of Ireland and Wales.

Conservatives and the Empire ▪ The Conservatives came back into office in 1895 with great confidence. Lord Salisbury presided over a cabinet containing what the young Liberal H. H. Asquith described as "an almost embarrassing wealth of talent and capacity." Members were drawn predominantly from the landed aristocracy that had ruled England for centuries; but the motor force, sometimes an erratic one, within the cabinet was supplied by the commoner and former Liberal, Joseph Chamberlain, who took the colonial office. He brought his impressive energies and talents to a post that many politicians had considered to be second rank; under Chamberlain it acquired central importance. His interest in social reform continued, but imperialism commanded most of his efforts.

The imperial problem that overshadowed all others during the Conservative decade of 1895-1905 was the tension of the relations between Britain's South African possessions at the Cape and the neighboring Boer republics, the Transvaal and the Orange Free State. The discovery of gold in the Witwatersrand in the late 1880's had brought British subjects flooding into the Transvaal, an independent state governed by Dutch farmers whose ancestors had settled there in the seventeenth century. The Boers, who resented the newcomers or Uitlanders, placed strict limitations on their political rights and heavily taxed their earnings. Encouraged by the famous colonial entrepreneur,

Cecil Rhodes, the Uitlanders began conspiring against the Boer government and its uncompromising president, Paul Kruger. The growing tension between the Boers and the Cape Colony first exploded in 1895 when a raiding party, led by Dr. Jameson and encouraged by Rhodes, was captured by the Boers en route to Johannesburg, where they had hoped to stir an uprising against Kruger and his government. The Jameson raid had extensive repercussions: Rhodes was discredited— at least temporarily—for his conspiracy; foreign opinion condemned the high-handed action of British officials in South Africa; and the Dutch inhabitants of both Transvaal and the Cape Colony itself united in their hostility to Great Britain.

As incidents between Uitlanders and Boers mounted, the prospect of war also increased. Efforts at negotiation fell through when the British high commissioner at the Cape, Sir Alfred Milner, lost patience with the stubborn Boers. Both sides issued ultimatums and began moving troops. On October 9, 1899, the Transvaal Boers, supported by the Orange Free State, launched an attack on the Cape Colony. The opening stages of the war revealed a surprising lack of organization and preparation among the British forces. The Boers were well-stocked with Krupp guns, which they used skillfully, and they exploited their knowledge of the local terrain to advantage. During a "black week" in December, 1899, British forces suffered a series of unexpected defeats. Undeterred by news of these disasters, the British government sent Lord Roberts to retrieve the situation; after a series of brilliant campaigns he entered Johannesburg on May 31, 1900. By the summer's end the Boer armies had been defeated in the field. Lord Roberts returned to England, leaving his chief of staff, Lord Kitchener, to mop up.

But the war was not over, despite the celebrations in the streets of London, for the Boers' guerrilla tactics kept Kitchener occupied for the next two years. He finally obtained victory only through drastic expedients that used much manpower and money, and brought great suffering to the people of South Africa. He organized vast drives to trap his opposition by herding them into barbed wire entanglements and confronting them with surrender or annihilation. His forces burned farms and placed in concentration camps those who were suspected of supporting guerrillas. The loss of life caused by disease in these camps was appalling. This guerrilla phase of the war was not very heroic. It became distasteful to the British public, and won the sympathy of Europe for the Boers' struggle.

The Boer War of course had widespread political repercussions in Great Britain. As the party most clearly identified with imperialism, the Conservatives initially profited from the patriotic sentiment engendered by the war. The only opposition to the war came from a faction of the Liberal party and served to divide that party further. In order to exploit this division and to profit from news of Lord Robert's triumph, the Conservative party called a general election for October, 1900. The "khaki" election was held amid great emotional tension. Abuse was heaped on those who spoke in opposition to the war and they were labeled traitors or worse. Demagoguery, much deplored at the time by high-minded politicians on both sides, crept into the decorum of Victorian politics in Great Britain. Under these supercharged conditions the Conservatives returned in 1900 with a sizable majority but less triumphantly than they had hoped—their majority in the House of Commons was slightly reduced. Nevertheless, they had a six-year mandate, and their Liberal opposition appeared hopelessly divided. Few could foresee a total reversal of these positions at the next general election.

The Decline of the Conservative Party, 1902–05

In 1902 Lord Salisbury retired as prime minister and was succeeded by his nephew, Arthur Balfour. Many had expected Joseph Chamberlain to become prime minister on Salisbury's retirement. Although a man of unquestioned talent, Chamberlain was not trusted by moderate Conservatives, who believed that he was a somewhat erratic and unsettling influence in British politics. His defection from the·Liberals had been welcomed but had also raised a few eyebrows in Conservative circles. Events of the next few months were to confirm Chamberlain's tendency to go his own way, whatever the consequences for his party.

The Education Bill of 1902 ■ Balfour's initial test came on a significant domestic issue, the Education Bill of 1902, which provided extensive and long overdue reforms of British schooling. Essentially the act gave the state primary responsibility for educational standards by reducing differences in curriculum and quality of instruction among various church, private ("public" according to British usage), and public institutions. The administration of education was to be streamlined by eliminating a number of local boards of education in favor of county or borough councils. Technical training was to be expanded and made more rigorous. A portion of taxes was to be used—even in denominational schools—to increase salaries and raise standards generally. Although the bill permitted state support for religious schools, it in effect pushed the British educational system, which had traditionally been closely tied to religious institutions, toward a greater degree of secularization. Any church school accepting tax money had to meet minimum requirements and religious instruction could be given only on a voluntary basis.

The education bill represented a crucial step in strengthening Britain's educational system, but it was violently attacked by non-conformists who disliked seeing Anglican schools supported by public taxation. Taxpayers even threatened a tax strike. The Conservatives began losing by-elections after 1902 as voters turned against the party that had championed the measure. The passage of the bill was an important reason for the Liberal party's success at the next general election.

The Issue of Tariff Reform ■ Another decisive issue that caused divisions among the Conservatives was Chamberlain's imperial tariff scheme to establish a protective tariff to end Britain's traditional free-trade commercial policy. This measure was taken by many Conservatives to be evidence of Chamberlain's tendency to pursue his own objectives within the ranks of the Conservative party. Chamberlain's proposal carried a great deal of political dynamite; free trade had become a sacred tenet of British policy in the course of the nineteenth century. Agrarian interests might have wanted protection from foreign competition, but the inhabitants of the industrial cities preferred cheap, imported foodstuffs to expensive domestic produce. And political strength was increasingly to be found in the cities. Chamberlain realized this and he also understood that a protective tariff would provoke retaliation from other manufacturing and trading nations, but he felt that the loss would be more than offset by the economic security of a unified, world-wide empire.

Chamberlain's plan reflected his growing concern with Britain's position as a world power. To pay for foodstuffs, as well as other raw materials, Chamberlain pointed out, Britain had to export manufactured goods. At the turn of the century British manufacturers encountered increased competition on the world market and within the empire itself. It was embarrassing to find German, American, French, and Japanese manufacturers gaining a share of the trade in India, Britain's most valuable overseas possession. Chamberlain readily perceived a shifting balance of international politics behind the rise of these vigorous industrial states. The United States had demonstrated international ambitions by defeating Spain in 1898 and by taking an interest in China, as revealed in the Open Door Notes of 1899 and 1900. Meanwhile Germany was bidding for a world policy, which Emperor William II identified as a "place in the sun." Chamberlain also regarded Russia as a great land-empire of enormous potential that threatened British power in China, India, and the Near East.

Chamberlain's tariff scheme would utilize an empire of some 400 million to offset the growing power of new rivals and to maintain Britain's status as a world power. Furthermore, income from the tariff would finance domestic social reforms to accompany the increase in jobs secured by eliminating overseas competition. The scheme seemed to offer something for everyone: protection for manufacturers, foodstuffs and raw materials from the empire for the urban dwellers, security for workers, and a grandiose vision of continuing imperial greatness for the whole nation.

Chamberlain's vision and energies outreached his colleagues in the Conservative party. His ideas on tariff reform, first formulated in 1902, were not discussed until parliamentary debates over the budget in the following year. The vehement dispute between protectionists and free-traders eventually engulfed the cabinet itself. In an effort to reduce the division within the cabinet Chamberlain resigned, as did some outspoken free-traders. Balfour reorganized the government and managed to retain power, but the division within the Conservative ranks was out in the open. The Liberals rallied quickly. As Chamberlain toured the country to drum up support for protectionism, he was followed by H. H. Asquith, a rising star in the Liberal party, who skillfully countered his position. The steady losses suffered by the Conservatives at by-elections indicated that the country had become disenchanted with Conservative leadership. Near the end of 1905 Balfour resigned.

The Return of the Liberal Party, 1906

Balfour's successor, called by the king, was Henry Campbell-Bannermann, a Liberal whose considerable political skill had helped guide the party through nearly seven years of crisis and internal bickering. Accurately sensing the mood of the country, Campbell-Bannermann immediately called for a general election. The election of 1906 was a landslide for the Liberals by any standard. They gained an absolute majority of 132 seats over all other parties, and since the Irish delegation and the labor contingent would support them on most issues, they could normally count on a majority of 356. As unequivocal supporters of free trade, the Liberals picked up support from urban voters who feared rising prices under protectionism and so turned against Chamberlain. "No more Joe," the Liberals chanted, as Chamberlain went down to defeat in his Birmingham constituency, sharing the fate of many Conservative stalwarts, including Balfour himself.

The Liberal party had profited from Conservative divisions and mistakes without offering much in the way of an alternative program. Even so, the Liberal victory of 1906 was a decisive event in British political life, for it ushered in a reform era of unprecedented scope. Of those who came into the Commons with the Liberal landslide, nearly half had never served in Parliament before; they tended to be more open to new ideas than the members they replaced. Equally important, a shift in the social composition of Parliament occurred. With the defeat of the Conservative party the landed aristocracy faded into the background. An "establishment" continued to govern England, but a great number of middle-class professional men, businessmen, and even labor officials became part of it. Symbols of change could be found in the abandonment of older conventions. Dress in the House of Commons became informal, for example. Some 150 of the Liberals in Parliament were nonconformists (suggesting the extent of dissatisfaction with the 1902 Education Act), and they were at once reform-minded and impatient with traditional formality.

Insofar as the Liberals had a mandate, it was for change and for a consideration of problems that had been neglected over nearly two decades. During the campaign the Conservatives had tried to evoke memories of the Boer War, but imperialism—and particularly Chamberlain's brand of imperialism—did not have much appeal in 1906. The voters wanted reforms in domestic politics that would improve general standards of living, provide old-age, unemployment, and health insurance, and reduce economic, social, and political privilege. The Liberals did not entirely abandon imperialism, but they turned the focus of their attention to problems of modern society, or rather yielded to pressures to do so. After the Liberal victory a slightly larger percentage of the nation's gross national product was spent on social services than on armaments, whereas before 1906 more had been spent on armaments. This was one sign of the times. In meeting the demands of the twentieth century the Liberal party rejected the laissez-faire principles of its Gladstonian years and laid nineteenth century liberalism to rest.

The Republic in France

In France, no less than in Great Britain, the fifteen years between 1890 and 1905 marked a political watershed. By the end of this period the republican form of government had secured a wide acceptance among the French people, largely as a result of successfully overcoming a series of challenges to its legitimacy. In Britain, political debate occurred within the context of a generally accepted political structure; in France conflict often centered on the very nature of the country's political system. The French had experienced ten different modes of government in the century following the Revolution of 1789, and no regime was considered necessarily permanent.

For anti-republicans, the Third Republic, established in the 1870's after the fall of Napoleon III, had no greater claim to legitimacy— and in the eyes of royalists and Bonapartists it had far less—than some of its predecessors. Even Adolphe Thiers, who had helped shape the Third Republic, concluded rather negatively that this was the government that divided Frenchmen least. Reluctant acceptance of the republic by no means ended the divisions; any form of compromise among the disputing political factions was handicapped by the doctrinaire rigidity that characterized their arguments. Bismarck, Germany's chancellor, celebrated the Third Republic's domestic disputes as a source of French weakness. He maintained that France lived in a "state of morbid fermentation," which eroded the nation's political strength.

It appeared that French politics at the end of the nineteenth century was marked by disruptive political quarrels and fundamental political instability. Actually, the situation was somewhat different. To be sure, conflicts between monarchists and republicans, Catholics and freemasons, Parisians and rural dwellers all produced an impression of continuing discord. However, the Third Republic established a curious equilibrium that was based on the desire of the French middle classes for social stability, order, and a maintenance of the status quo. For the peasants who were small property owners, one great fear was "reaction"—a return of the old regime and a possible reversal of the property arrangements that had been confirmed by the French Revolution. Another fear was of revolutionary upheaval that would threaten existing property arrangements. Provincial landowners wanted a government that would protect them from both dangers. For the wealthy bourgeoisie the greatest source of alarm was the specter of social revolution. The Third Republic occupied the middle ground between the feared extremes; as long as it could preserve the status quo it was a system acceptable to the majority of French citizens. This was, as the political scientist Stanley Hoffman has phrased it, a "stalemate" society, committed to only gradual change at best. Because of its precarious balance the Third Republic rallied support from many different groups when it appeared threatened by extremist disruptive forces; its dominant trait was a defense of the existing social order.

French politics showed a greater continuity than the frequent changes of government would suggest. One element of this continuity was the bureaucracy that ran the affairs of state on a day-to-day basis; another was the consistent return of the same men as office-holders from one government to the next. Governments were drawn from an elite of deputies considered to be of ministerial potential regardless of party affiliation. Thus at the end of the nineteenth century France presented a paradox of stability amid a rapid succession of governments. Political conflict took place within a specified arena—parliament and negotiations for governmental positions—while the rest of the country possessed a social structure that resisted change to perhaps an unhealthy degree.

Emergence of the Third Republic

The Third Republic's political system emerged from the unusual political circumstances that prevailed in France after the defeat suffered in the Franco-Prussian War. In 1871, thoroughly exhausted by a war that had been both disastrous and hopeless, the French people elected a national assembly that was committed to seek peace terms with Prussia. The great majority of the deputies were royalists, for the Bonapartists had been discredited by the defeat and capture of Napoleon III, and the republicans appeared to want war to the bitter end. Once peace had been signed, the royalist-dominated assembly set about the task of establishing a basis for governing France. Given the character of the assembly, some form of constitutional monarchy was anticipated, but the royalists were divided between Bourbon and Orleanist factions. They finally agreed on the Comte de Chambord as king of France, but he insisted that he would rule France only under the Bourbon flag and not the French tricolor. Over this seeming trifle, monarchist hopes foundered and the royalists were forced to devise some other form of government until a more reasonable candidate for the throne appeared.

Between 1871 and 1875 a series of by-elections happened to return a succession of republican deputies, thus reducing the monarchists' majority and indicating that public opinion had swung to the idea of a republic. In 1875 a republican form of government was agreed on by a one-vote margin. Political power was to be shared by a chamber of deputies elected on the basis of universal male suffrage, a senate selected by a limited number of electors, and a president chosen by the chamber and senate. The first president of this republic was Marshal MacMahon, a royalist who considered himself a temporary occupant of the office until agreement on a king for France could be made. In this manner the Third Republic was founded, but it was at first literally a republic of "Dukes"—fundamentally conservative and designed as an expedient pending a restoration of the monarchy.

Yet the republic soon came to reflect more than the maneuvers of the Dukes. In the elections held in 1876 for the Third Republic's first Chamber of Deputies the republicans won a majority of the seats. During the electoral campaign, republican politicians emphasized that the republic would be a moderate one and that it would be the best guarantee of stability. On this basis, a number of republican parties won support from the middle classes and the peasantry. Electoral success did not produce a clear republican triumph, however, for conservatives still dominated the Senate and a monarchist held the presidency.

A test of strength between republicans and monarchists rapidly developed when Marshal MacMahon dismissed a moderate republican premier in the spring of 1877 and replaced him with the Duc de Broglie, a monarchist whose views were more palatable to him. When the Chamber refused to grant Broglie its confidence, MacMahon exercised his constitutional right and dismissed it. Despite every effort to persuade and coerce the voters, MacMahon and his followers were unable to displace the republicans in the next election. Rejecting the alternative of a coup d'état against the republic, MacMahon yielded to popular sentiment and appointed a premier who commanded a majority in the Chamber. This episode had far-reaching implications for the political development of the Third Republic. Henceforth the Chamber of Deputies became the dominant element in the French state, and the power of the presidency was greatly reduced in practice. MacMahon's successors under the Third Republic contented themselves with being relatively powerless figureheads and never attempted to dissolve the Chamber.

The republicans further consolidated their hold on French political life in 1879 when MacMahon, finding that his political position had become awkward, resigned from office. His departure permitted the election of a moderate republican, Jules Grévy, to replace him. Elections for the Senate the same year brought a republican majority to the upper house, so that by the end of the 1870's the republicans controlled the major levers of political power. Loyal republicans also gained key positions in the bureaucracy. Only the army and the diplomatic service offered careers to monarchists who wished to serve the French nation in some way, despite their distaste for the republic.

Factions Within the Republic

Republican success did not immediately usher in an era of political stability in the 1880's. The monarchists and Bonapartists both remained very much opposed to the republic in republican hands; in the 1880's a scattering of socialists appeared. Equally important, no consensus among the republicans themselves existed. Instead, several republican parties within the Chamber reflected various shades of political views and had their own identities. There were a variety of designations (for example, Democratic Left, Republican Union), but three major tendencies might be noted. Moderate republicans were represented by President Grévy, who believed that the task of a republic was to pursue a gradualist policy; from their point of view the best government was the one that governed least. Somewhat to the left of them were the "opportunists," followers of Léon Gambetta, a republican who had shed some of his earlier radicalism in the process of seeking acceptance for the republic. The opportunists were mildly reform-minded, interested in building solid republican institutions. To their left was a group of radicals, led by Georges Clemenceau, who argued for a secular republic purged of any trace of political inequality. Staunchly egalitarian in outlook, the radicals identified themselves with the Jacobin tradition of the French Revolution; they boasted of having "no enemies to the left."

Had the republicans possessed the discipline of a single party, they would easily have controlled French politics. But they often quarreled with one another, closing ranks only when the republic seemed in danger. Relations between republican parties were clouded by personal rivalries and animosities. Every cabinet that was formed from these groups had of necessity to be a coalition, and measures presented to the Chamber had to be acceptable to each element supporting the cabinet, or else the government fell. Frequent changes of government (although, as has been mentioned, not always of governing personnel) became common.

The absence of national party organizations enabled deputies to pursue personal ambition or to follow the whims of shifting opinion in parliament. To be sure, candidates were elected from individual districts and had party endorsement, but electoral campaigns tended to be fought on local issues and personalities rather than party platforms. The committees formed by the parties shortly before each election to obtain support in as many districts as possible were only temporary arrangements. Once elected, the deputies felt little party loyalty. It was not until 1901 that the radicals formed a permanent organization, and even then it remained relatively weak throughout the Third Republic.

Because of the multiplicity of candidates, in many districts elections frequently failed to produce a majority for one man or party on the first ballot and a second ballot had to be held. At this point agreements were sometimes made among parties of similar views to withdraw weaker candidates and throw support to the party with the best chance of winning the runoff. This practice, if pursued rigorously, might have encouraged the formation of "blocs," but generally it amounted to little more than temporary bargaining between parties. Cabinets continued to be formed on the basis of agreements among individual deputies or groups within the Chamber of Deputies.

Although they had many disagreements, one issue was capable of rallying the republicans. For many republicans the influence of the Catholic church appeared to pose some threat to the republic itself because of the strong monarchist sentiment within the Church. In the 1880's republican politicians introduced reforms in education designed to create a state-sponsored educational system that would be secular in its orientation and be free to all school children in the primary grades. The Catholics in turn condemned the republic for encouraging atheism. The reforms were passed, however, and the Church was displaced as the major educational institution in France. Although the republicans hesitated to force a separation of Church and state, they did display definite anticlerical attitudes. They agreed that the schools had a responsibility for promoting republican secular ideals among French youth. A rather strongly nationalistic republicanism, combined with a secularist positivism, became the underlying ideology of the state educational system. These reforms had a great impact as they virtually eliminated illiteracy in a whole generation, but they also left a legacy of hostility between the Church and the republic.

In other areas, notably imperial expansion and social reform, the republican parties showed less solidarity. Debates over French advances into Tunisia, Tonkin, and West Africa produced some dramatic moments in the French Chamber. The most sensational of these brought the downfall of Jules Ferry in 1885. Ferry was a talented republican politician who had sponsored the educational reforms of the early 1880's. He gradually became converted to the cause of French overseas expansion; but his political enemies, fearing that he might become too powerful, used this issue against him. Accused of wasting money and men in Asia, Ferry was driven from office and narrowly escaped an ugly crowd demanding the life of "Ferry the Tonkinese." Despite these pyrotechnics, the Third Republic retained its hold on Tonkin and continued to advance into tropical Africa, thereby lending credence to the argument that much of the anti-imperialism of the 1880's was the result of political rivalries and personal opposition to Ferry himself, rather than to his policy of expansionism. Once committed to the empire, politicians of the Third Republic showed little inclination to retreat from their position.

Disagreement among republicans appeared more clear-cut over

social reforms. Clemenceau and the radicals claimed that moderate and opportunist republicans had lost their reforming zeal; Clemenceau blamed them for supporting imperial adventures while domestic social reforms languished. There was some truth in this assertion, for the moderate republicans showed little willingness to reawaken social fears among rural constituents. The French countryside recalled with considerable alarm the revolutionary overtones of the Commune that had been established briefly in Paris in the spring of 1871. Moderate republicans used every opportunity to assure the provinces that the republic would not bring social revolution. Full amnesty for exiled communards was not granted until 1880, for example, and unions did not receive official recognition until 1884. This reluctance to confront the question of social reform weakened the appeal of many republican parties among the working classes of Paris and the industrial regions.

A growing militancy on the part of the peasants and workers became apparent in the 1880's. The economic slump of that decade, particularly acute after the crash of 1882, affected towns and countryside alike. The French farmer began agitating for protection while the worker turned to direct strike action to enforce his demands for higher wages. The government was forced to respond. The rural interests received a generally favorable hearing as protectionist agricultural tariffs were voted. But the response of the moderate republicans to the workers' demonstrations was to suppress them. Conflict between the working class and the government became severe during the Decazeville coal miners' strike of 1886 when the government had to call in troops. Against this background of economic distress and political tension a threat to the institutions of the Third Republic appeared in the figure of General Boulanger.

The Republic Challenged: the Boulanger Crisis

General Boulanger had originally been a darling of the radicals. In the mid-1880's he acquired a reputation as a general of the people when, largely through radical pressure, he was appointed war minister in 1885 and proceeded to improve conditions in the barracks for the average soldier. Whenever Boulanger appeared on horseback for parades in Paris, he was warmly cheered by the crowd. The radicals hoped that Boulanger would use his office to curb the conservative political tendencies of the officer corps. He did discipline a few officers who indiscreetly proclaimed their contempt for the republic. Largely as a result of his bellicose speeches, Boulanger also became identified with the idea of revenge against Germany for the Franco-Prussian War. His aggressive statements alarmed moderate republicans, who forced him out of the war ministry and eventually assigned him to a provincial command. Meanwhile, however, Boulanger became the favorite of conservatives intent on exploiting his popularity for their own purposes of altering the structure of the Third Republic in favor of a restoration of the monarchy. A series of electoral campaigns, financed by the monarchist Duchesse d'Uzes, was organized on Boulanger's behalf. He easily won the by-elections for which his name was put forward. Because he was not permitted to serve as deputy while on active duty, he resigned the office after each election. But the campaign continued, and Boulanger was wildly cheered wherever he appeared.

The movement reached a climax in the spring of 1889. Boulanger's popularity increased during the preceding year and the government unwisely placed him on the retirement list, enabling him to campaign openly. In January 1889 he won a parliamentary election in a former republican stronghold in Paris. The way appeared open to a seizure of power if Boulanger decided to act. But the republicans, at first hesitant and confused, began to rally. After Boulanger's electoral victory the minister of the interior indicated that he had evidence implicating Boulanger in treasonous activity and that he planned to call the general before the Senate for a hearing. Boulanger was frightened into an inglorious flight to Belgium, for he had little stomach for a serious confrontation. Embarrassed by the hasty departure of their leader, Boulangists saw their movement collapse. In the elections of 1889 the conservatives lost heavily, while the opportunists gained.

Despite its comic-opera conclusion, the Boulanger episode had significant repercussions in French politics, particularly in the French right. The ill-advised connection with Boulanger finally discredited the monarchist cause. Henceforth right-wing opponents of the republic turned elsewhere to express their dissatisfactions with the regime. Many, for example, adopted a militant nationalism, which in the aftermath of the Franco-Prussian War had actually been an attitude more commonly found among radical republicans. Others championed authoritarian political movements that had anti-Semitic characteristics, as a way of expressing contempt for a "decadent" republican rule.

Some conservatives abandoned the struggle against the republic altogether and decided to work within it. An emergent liberal Catholic movement offered prospects in the 1890's for a moderate-conservative coalition in French politics. Following the lead of Pope Leo XIII, who had suggested that good Catholics could live within the secular republic, the *ralliement,* or "rally" to the republic, attracted several distinguished Catholic politicians. The movement never became strong however because the upper level of the Catholic hierarchy in France discouraged efforts to find agreement with moderate republicans. Their influence was unfortunate, for the apparent willingness of many opportunists to drop the anticlericism of the 1880's had offered a hope for reconciliation of the republic and the Church.

In the early 1880's Léon Gambetta had dreamed of a reconciliation among Frenchmen that would end the country's internal divisions. France, he had argued, should no longer be a "broken mirror" but should recover some internal unity. He believed that a moderate republic offered the best prospect for a reconciliation of divided elements. In the 1890's his successors among the opportunists hoped for a tranquil period during which they would be able to heal the country's social and political wounds, but the passions aroused by the Dreyfus affair shattered this hope and brought a bitter struggle between pro- and anti-republicans.

The Republic Triumphant: the Dreyfus Years

The significance of the affair that shook France at the end of the 1890's still has not been fully assessed by historians, and even the events that transpired are the subject of controversy. As an introduction to the impact of the Dreyfus affair on the Third Republic, some of the main events preceding and surrounding the affair should be noted.

In 1892 a political scandal erupted in France that anticipated some of the more somber moments of the Dreyfus controversy in bringing anti-Semitic and anti-parliament sentiments to the empire. The scandal was known as the Panama affair, taking its name from a bankrupt company that had hoped to build a canal across the Isthmus of Panama. In an effort to avoid bankruptcy, at the last minute some officials of the company had obtained authorization from parliament to hold a national lottery to raise funds. When the lottery failed to produce enough capital to save the company, the enterprise foundered. In the aftermath it was revealed the company officials had bribed some members of parliament into agreeing to the lottery-loan scheme. A parliamentary investigating committee glossed over this embarrassing episode, but the anti-parliamentary conservatives exploited the Panama affair in an effort to discredit the Third Republic. Their criticism was accompanied by a wave of anti-Semitism. Two financiers connected with the Panama Company were of Jewish origin, a circumstance that provided Eduard Drumont, the publisher of an anti-Semitic newspaper, with an occasion to attack the nefarious influence of this "foreign race" that was polluting French soil. The feelings aroused by the Panama affair, although of limited impact on French politics at the time, added depth to what was to come five years later in the Third Republic's most serious test.

In 1894 French military counterintelligence received a memorandum that had been discovered in a wastebasket in the German Embassy in Paris. This memo revealed a leak of classified military information from a well-placed source, presumably a French staff officer. A hasty investigation produced a suspect—Captain Dreyfus, a Jewish officer serving a two-year tour with the general staff. The evidence against him was inconclusive; two handwriting experts disagreed over whether Dreyfus had been the author of the memorandum. Perhaps the army would have dropped the case had not Eduard Drumont learned of it and hinted that Jewish money was going to free a traitor. Reacting to this pressure, the army decided to court-martial Dreyfus, and in December he was sentenced to life imprisonment. The minister of war, General Mercier, who at first had hesitated even to prosecute Dreyfus, now let it be known that he had definite proof of Dreyfus' guilt. At this point few Frenchmen were prepared to challenge this opinion.

During the next two years the matter simmered but was not forgotten. Dreyfus' family conducted a search for evidence to support their conviction that he was innocent. Meanwhile a new chief of the army's counterintelligence office, Colonel Picquart, decided to reopen the Dreyfus file. Military information had continued to reach the German Embassy, and Picquart suspected that an officer of dubious character, Major Esterhazy, was the source of the leaks. At least Picquart found that Esterhazy's handwriting closely resembled that of the memorandum attributed to Dreyfus. When he examined the file, Picquart was astonished at the lack of real evidence against Dreyfus. Picquart had little sympathy for Jews, but he nevertheless became convinced that an injustice had been committed by the army. These views placed him in a difficult position, however. His military superiors had no intention of reopening the case; they informed Picquart that they had further evidence of Dreyfus' guilt. When Picquart persisted in his doubts, he was reassigned to southern Tunisia.

Before his departure, Picquart expressed his views of the case to his lawyer who, in turn, discussed them with Senator Scheurer-Kestner, a highly respected politician. When Scheurer-Kestner asked the government to look into the matter, Premier Jules Méline denied that there was any need for concern over the Dreyfus case, and the war minister continued to maintain that the evidence against Dreyfus was conclusive. In part, this assurance rested on new evidence that had been manufactured by Major Henry, a counterintelligence officer with a talent—or at least a propensity—for forgery. Perhaps to please his superiors, or for other, unknown reasons, Henry had been stuffing the file with false documents incriminating Dreyfus. Despite this "evidence" and Méline's efforts to silence doubters, a Dreyfusard party came into existence in 1898 demanding a revision of the conviction. Lines of conflict were being drawn. The army denied any miscarriage of justice and hinted darkly that anyone doubting its word sullied its honor and integrity; from the army's point of view the Dreyfus case was purely a military affair and not subject to partisan political meddling. For the Dreyfusards these attitudes seemed a mockery of justice and represented an attempt by the officer corps, whose loyalty to the republic was suspect, to forge a privileged place for itself beyond the reach of republican standards.

The affair caused a crisis in 1898. At the beginning of the year Esterhazy was tried for treason and acquitted by a military tribunal, an event that caused wide celebration among anti-Dreyfusards. Two days later the novelist Emile Zola published his famous "I Accuse!" letter in Clemenceau's newspaper, *L'Aurore;* in this letter Zola claimed that the acquittal had been reached on orders from the army's high command. The publication of Zola's letter divided Paris over the issue of Dreyfus' guilt, and the division ran along lines of political sympathy. Conservatives, nationalists, anti-Semites, and many Catholic groups led the opposition to any reconsideration of Dreyfus' conviction. Reconsideration, they argued, would destroy confidence in the army and encourage disrespect for all institutions that guaranteed the country's security and social order. The Dreyfusards insisted that justice under the republic had to be absolute and without exception; if Dreyfus had been condemned arbitrarily, then no citizen was secure in his civil rights. They argued that their opponents really aimed at subverting the republic by mocking its institutions and its justice. A number of intellectuals and republican politicians allied with the Dreyfusards. The whole case came to be redefined in political terms as a struggle between those who favored the republic and those who opposed it.

Throughout 1898 sentiment ran high. At this time a majority of the population believed that Dreyfus was guilty; excited crowds surged through the streets of Paris demanding the death of Zola and all Jews. Then toward the end of the year a series of events undermined the anti-Dreyfusard position. In an effort to silence its critics, the war ministry brought some of the evidence before the Chamber. The Dreyfusards, supported by Colonel Picquart, claimed that the evidence had been tampered with and that at least one of the documents was an outright forgery. The latter assertion was confirmed by another counterintelligence officer. Finally, Major Henry confessed his part in supplying the false evidence and then committed suicide in prison. Esterhazy further damaged the anti-Dreyfusard cause by prudently leaving the country.

A retrial of Dreyfus could no longer be denied. In September 1899 a new court-martial returned another verdict—guilty once more, but with "attenuating circumstances." The Dreyfusards were outraged at this decision, although they had some consolation when the president of the republic pardoned Dreyfus immediately afterward. The conclusion to the affair came in 1906 when the Chamber voted for the rehabilitation of Dreyfus and gave him and Colonel Picquart, who had been forced out of the army during the crisis, promotion in rank. Justice eventually was achieved for the man who at times seemed lost amid the political and moral combats that were taking place in his name.

The Aftermath: 1899–1905 ■ The consequences of the Dreyfus affair are as significant as its drama. Continued clashes in the Chamber and in the streets between Dreyfusards and anti-Dreyfusards kept the country in a state of turmoil. At the height of the crisis a Dreyfusard bloc of republican parties was impelled to join in defending the republic against its opponents. In February 1899 the anti-Dreyfusard Paul Déroulède, an ultra-nationalistic pamphleteer and political adventurer, attempted a coup d'état against the regime. The army refused to follow him on this occasion, but the abortive coup confirmed the suspicions of those who thought that the anti-Dreyfusards wished to bring the republic to its knees. A major political turning point came when a moderate republican, René Waldeck-Rousseau, formed a broadly based ministry that included radicals, moderates, and one socialist, Alexandre Millerand, and that enjoyed the support of Jean Jaurès and his socialist allies in the Chamber.

The first order of business for the Waldeck-Rousseau government was to settle the affair as gracefully as possible on Dreyfusard terms. The pardon of Captain Dreyfus in the fall of 1899 accomplished much of this. Although the scars of the affair remained in evidence for years to come, the intense phase of agitation had abated by 1900. During the next few years the Dreyfusard coalition was able to maintain its grip on French politics because of its unified opposition to the antirepublican tendencies of the army and the Church. The Dreyfusards used their triumph in fact to curb the influence and power of these institutions.

The army's anti-republicanism was not surprising. For years it had offered refuge for upper-class opponents of the republic. Those officers who had pronounced republican sympathies found themselves socially ostracized by their colleagues, and it was rumored that republican views hindered careers and promotions. This situation was reversed by General André—war minister under Waldeck-Rousseau. André assumed direct supervision of army promotions, thus taking on himself a task that had previously been carried out by the upper echelon of the army's officer corps. As part of his policy, he began keeping records of the officers' political and religious views; members of the masonic Grand Orient Lodge assisted in the collection of this information. Promotion boards responsible for selecting officers for advancement were frequently guided by these files rather than the old "informal" system by which orthodox conservative views influenced the boards. When these practices became known to the public in 1904, André was forced to resign, but a deep distrust between the army and the republic had already been sown.

The following year the government reduced the term of compulsory military service from three to two years. More men were to be drafted for shorter service, after which they would go into the reserves. The intent of the law was to equalize service obligations and to create a draft reserve that—it was believed—would serve as a liberal counterweight to the conservatively oriented officer corps. The French army officers considered the law an act of vengeance directed against the army. This measure, combined with the André policies, brought the relationship between the army and the French state to a low point. The military profession lost prestige: applications for officer candidate schools declined sharply, and within the army several officers resigned from active service.

Many Catholic organizations, especially the ultra-conservative Assumptionists, had been rabidly anti-Dreyfus. Waldeck-Rousseau's cabinet had been sensitive to the dangers of the Church's hostility to the republic, but it remained for his successor, Emile Combes, to wage war against the Church. The election of 1902 produced a stunning victory for the republican parties and above all for the radicals. Waldeck-Rousseau resigned following the elections when he realized that the anticlerical sentiment of the new Chamber outdistanced his more moderate attitude. Combes felt no such restraints. Once a seminary student, Combes had later turned against the Church with a single-minded passion. Beginning with an expulsion of the Catholic orders in France, Combes's campaign culminated in a break with the Vatican that ended the Concordat signed by Napoleon a century before. Although angry opposition to the government's action was expressed in some regions, particularly when the government began an inventory of Church property, the move was acceptable to most of the French people. The elections of 1906 showed no reaction against the government since the radicals, who had been most outspoken in their anticlericism, remained the dominant force in the Chamber.

In some ways the break with the Vatican, however abrupt and bitter, cleared the way to an eventual *modus vivendi* between the Church and state in France. As the clerics ceased to be paid by the state, and as churches became private associations, the Church was deprived of a direct role in politics. Anticlericism abated as a political issue, after over a century in which it had excited strong passions. The way was opened to a pragmatic settlement of differences. At the same time, one of the issues capable of arousing republican solidarity—anticlericism—was on the wane.

The Primacy of Radicalism ▪ The radicals emerged as the main beneficiaries of the Dreyfusard revolution, which shifted the balance of political power in the French Chamber to the left. The campaigns against the army and the Church represented a double triumph for the radical party; since the 1880's it had insisted that the influence of these traditionally conservative institutions be isolated from the political life of the country. The radicals dominated the coalition formed in 1899 to settle the affair and were swept into the Chamber as the largest party by the elections of 1902. From that time, they played a crucial role in the formation of every government until 1940. The victory of the radicals also assured the achievements of the Third Republic's first generation—universal education impregnated with a republican ethos, confirmation of the republic against monarchist reaction, and an assurance of a secular republic. These were measures that the radicals approved.

As it turned out, however, radicalism's success did not lead to a program of social reforms that would meet the needs of a new era. The radicals abandoned much of their interest in social-welfare legislation just at a time when France had finally reached industrial maturity after decades of sporadic economic growth, and industrialization introduced new fissures into French society, notably a conflict between the *patron,* or factory owner, and his employees. The radicals' attitude toward the social question was to ignore it as much as possible. The danger in this attitude, of course, was that it produced cynicism and a sense of alienation from the state on the part of the working classes. But the radicals seemed willing to accept this risk, for they found political support elsewhere.

This support came from the "little people," the artisans, tradesmen, and peasants who were skeptical of, if not hostile to, many of the changes, as well as the very pace of change, that were part of the industrial order. After political gains had been made and the republic had been secured, the radical party assumed a basically defensive role in French society. The leading exponent of radicalism, Alain, maintained that a deputy's primary responsibility was to defend the ordinary Frenchman from the machinations of the high and mighty or from any group that threatened the social order. This attitude reflected the egalitarian outlook that was fundamental to radicalism, but it also confirmed the "little people" in their suspicion of political authority and attracted them to the radical doctrine. While the radicals were winning votes in the small towns and rural areas, the socialists were gaining in the industrial regions, former radical strongholds.

The emergence of the socialists to the left of the radicals caused an important shift in the political basis of French radicalism. Traditionally the radicals had proclaimed that they had no enemies to the left, but after the turn of the century they seemed unwilling to consent to the demands of French socialism. This reluctance contributed to the breakup of the Dreyfusard coalition that had been forged at the turn of the century. The socialist leader Jean Jaurès had hoped that this alliance between men of good will would ultimately work out a program of social reform. But the radicals' unwillingness to move in this direction gave ammunition to Jules Guesde, Jaurès' rival within French socialism; Guesde successfully argued that socialists could expect nothing from a bourgeois republic. In 1905 the socialists, having formed a unified party, stood aloof from parliamentary combinations. In the next decade radicalism began to move to the right; unable and perhaps unwilling to ally with the socialists, the radical party began forming alliances with moderate and even conservative parties.

While the socialists were combining on the left, enemies were also uniting to the right of the radicals. Monarchism and clericalism had declined as meaningful threats to the republic, but during the height of the Dreyfus crisis a new organization made its appearance—the *Action Française*. Ostensibly royalist in its politics, it attracted many authoritarian, anti-republican elements. Those who disliked modern society and felt that traditional French institutions and customs were being submerged in the materialistic republican state found an outlet for their grievances in the doctrines of this movement.

The radicals managed to hold the middle ground in French politics. Their triumph signaled the acceptance of republican institutions by the majority of the French people. To the average Frenchman the parliamentary republic seemed the best method for guaranteeing stability. A strong commitment to the republic developed in the population at large. It was not until the depression of the 1930's that the

French people lost faith in the political institutions of the Third Republic.

The Italian Political System

Like Britain and France, Italy made an uneasy passage into the twentieth century by a process that confirmed the importance of parliamentary institutions in its political life. But Italy's political development at the turn of the century was handicapped by circumstances with which neither Britain nor France had to contend. The country lagged behind northern Europe in its economic development because of the absence of coal and iron resources. Sharp geographical divisions, corresponding to serious social and economic cleavages in the state, further weakened the nation. Italy appeared relatively backward and torn by internal divisions that threatened the very basis of the country's constitutional system. In addition a colonial defeat brought about a severe political crisis at the end of the nineteenth century. Italy successfully coped with its domestic problems, however, and entered an era of gradual social and political progress that continued up to the First World War.

The Unification of Italy, 1848–70

Italy's unification in the mid-nineteenth century had seemingly fulfilled the dreams of Italian patriots. With unification, or *risorgimento*, would come prosperity and greatness, according to Italian nationalists of the first half of the century. The concept of the *risorgimento* elicited considerable romantic enthusiasm, but this ebullience was dampened somewhat by the failure to achieve unification during the revolution of 1848. Instead Italy became unified under the auspices of the skillful Piedmontese prime minister, Count Camillo di Cavour. Rather than depend on the spirit of unity generated by the *risorgimento,* Cavour placed his trust in the hard-headed—although occasionally risky— methods of diplomatic power politics. There were some flamboyant episodes connected with Italian unification, such as Garibaldi's descent on Sicily with a band of red-shirted volunteers, but Cavour carefully and somewhat nervously kept these acts in check.

By 1861 most of Italy was under the House of Savoy, the ruling family of Piedmont-Sardinia. The king of Piedmont-Sardinia became the new king of Italy. Piedmontese administrative practices and political institutions were extended to all of Italy and the Piedmontese constitution of 1848 became the basis for the Italian government. By this constitution Italy acquired an upper house, or senate, whose members were appointed by the king for life, and a lower house, or Chamber of Deputies, elected on the basis of a limited suffrage (no more than 2 percent of the population were eligible to vote). Cavour believed that a centralized, constitutional monarchy would provide the strongest sinews for holding Italy together.

The Italian territory was further extended with the acquisition of Venice and its hinterland in 1866 and the seizure of Rome in 1870, a stroke that embittered the Pope who lost all his territorial holdings except for the land occupied by the Vatican and St. Peter's Church. Henceforth the Pope considered himself a "prisoner" of the Italian state, and, needless to say, relations between Church and state were strained. Some Italian-speaking peoples remained outside Italy's borders, notably in the Austrian South Tyrol. Ardent nationalists agitated for the transfer of this district to Italy, but few politicians did more than pay lip-service to irredentism; most Italians in Europe had been brought under one government.

The course of Italian history after unification appeared rather prosaic and disappointing to those ardent patriots who had read deeply in *risorgimento* literature and looked forward to an era of prosperity. The lack of resources prevented a sudden industrial expansion, and in many areas unification actually produced economic dislocations. In addition the unified state began with a heavy public debt inherited from Piedmont-Sardinia; simply servicing this debt consumed a sizable proportion of the nation's revenue. Finally, the nature of Italian politics inspired little popular enthusiasm. In the south, this indifference reflected the absence of any sense of identity with all of Italy. When asked to cheer for Italy at the time of unification, many bystanders in Naples wondered, "Who is Italy?"

In spite of these feelings in the newly unified nation, the Italian parliament began to function, and Italy had all the trappings of a nineteenth century constitutional monarchy. Technically the king retained considerable political power; he could, if he wished, appoint ministers of his own choice, and he could rule by decree. Through the king, advisors at the court, especially the military advisors, were able to exercise an influence on Italian policies. But even with these sources of political power, the balance of strength rested with the Chamber of Deputies. After a series of confrontations, Cavour had managed to reduce the strength of the Senate, and prime ministers habitually assured themselves of a majority in the Chamber. The prime minister who could master a parliamentary majority became, in fact, an essential element in the political system.

Parliamentary Politics: Trasformismo

Initially parliamentary politics revolved around two political groupings, the "right" and "left," which roughly identified conservative and liberal tendencies. But by the late 1880's, as party differences became blurred, this distinction had little meaning. "Parties" tended to be factions with loyalty to a particular leader or individual rather than groups based on ideological principles. Ministries were coalitions drawn from a variety of groups representing the spectrum of liberal to conservative views. For many deputies the acquisition and use of political influence because more important than party discipline or doctrine. The absence of fixed party lines permitted the transformation of any group into a governmental party, a process that acquired the name *trasformismo*. Essentially the process involved the granting of political favors by a prime minister in return for parliamentary support; through an adroit use of his power a talented prime minister could gain support from any source, except the extremists.

Perhaps the most skilled practitioner of *trasformismo* was Agostino Depretis, who dominated the Italian Chamber from 1876 to his death in 1887. He supplied continuity and direction to a succession of cabinets, maintaining his balance by a careful distribution of political favors. A thoroughly pragmatic man, he believed politics to be the art of the possible, and preferred modest achievements to ambitious schemes. His pragmatic approach and conciliatory policies won him many political allies.

Depretis' tenure in office allowed him to manage elections easily for his own benefit. Given the limited electorate and the coercive powers of the local prefects, majorities were not hard to obtain, particularly in the south where political corruption was rampant. Moreover, prefects who seemed incapable of providing a majority of votes for government candidates often found themselves transferred to undesirable posts. Once elected, candidates became lobbyists for the economic interests of their constituencies—a new bridge, post office, or railway connection impressed the constituents more than speeches in the Chamber defending some abstract principle. By careful dealing, Depretis could arrange a sympathetic majority in the Chamber. Depretis exploited this self-reinforcing political system to muffle political discontent.

Critics of the practice have argued that *trasformismo* fatally weakened democracy in Italy at the outset by breeding cynicism. According to them, the absence of party or ideological distinctions prevented open debate on significant issues; moreover, problems tended to be simply ameliorated by temporary expedients rather than solved by well-conceived programs. Other critics, frequently nationalists, have observed that the high hopes of the *risorgimento* had given way to drab and sordid practices. Such comments reveal the underlying malaise that existed in the tenor of Italian politics, but they should not obscure the benefits that the system offered. Depretis was persuaded that Italy required a period of modest achievement that would not add further burdens to the taxed resources of the state. While he was in office he also tried to soften some of the antagonisms created by unification. He made modest attempts to satisfy southern politicians by launching a limited (ultimately inadequate) school-construction program, and he lifted a grist tax that weighed heavily on southern peasants.

The System in Crisis: Crispi's Second Ministry

The functioning of *trasformismo* depended on the methods and style of the prime minister who devised the political combinations for controlling parliament. The undemonstrative and persuasive Depretis made the system function smoothly. Francesco Crispi, who succeeded Depretis in 1887, possessed a totally different temperament, and his provocative behavior during the 1890's touched off a crisis that threatened to bring down the constitutional government in Italy.

A series of economic problems provided the background against which the political drama of the 1890's unfolded. Crispi bore some responsibility for these economic difficulties, for he had encouraged a tariff war with France that brought southern Italian winegrowers and those northerners engaged in the silk trade to the brink of ruin. The shock was most intensely felt in the south, particularly when compounded with the agrarian crisis caused by the dumping of cheap Russian and American grain on the European market. Violent peasant riots broke out in southern Italy and on the island of Sicily. When Crispi came to power in 1893 for the second and last time, these disturbances had been going on for over a year.

On the basis of his background Crispi might have been expected to conciliate the southerners. He was, after all, a Sicilian himself, a radical in his political philosophy, and he had passed a number of welfare measures during his first ministry. By 1894, however, he had changed. He considered himself a forceful leader who had been called to office to save the country from internal chaos and to lead it to great achievements abroad. His remedy for domestic chaos was to send fifty thousand troops to Sicily and to impose martial law wherever strikes or uprisings appeared likely. Proclaiming that socialists were responsible for all civic disturbances, he took steps to have the party's organizations outlawed. The radical element in Crispi had become thoroughly authoritarian in his later years; increasingly he looked on parliament as a nuisance, and even though he was able to obtain a parliamentary majority in the election of 1895, he entertained the possibility of ruling without parliament. Crispi's high-handed methods and soaring self-confidence soon won him enemies: the left disliked his authoritarian tendencies and many Catholics feared his unbridled anticlericism. Moreover, because economic conditions failed to improve, social unrest continued despite the repressive measures. Crispi became more intemperate in his behavior and public utterances.

Failing to secure a social truce at home, Crispi looked abroad for distractions, whereupon he was confronted by a dilemma. His hatred for France and his admiration for Germany had tied Italy firmly to the Triple Alliance with Austria and Germany. He therefore underplayed Italian irredentism in the Trentino (South Tyrol) and instead turned south toward Africa, specifically toward Ethiopia. In the 1880's Italy had established a foothold in East Africa with the control of two rather dreary ports on the Red Sea; shortly afterward the Italians began pressing toward Ethiopia. This expansionism was checked by a defeat of Italian troops at Dogali in 1887 and by the opposition of Ethiopia's rulers to further Italian advances. By the mid-1890's however, Crispi was ready to resume attempts at building an Italian empire in eastern Africa through the acquisition of Ethiopia. He believed, furthermore, that a little colonial war would bring glory and prestige to Italy and to himself.

In pursuing his colonial adventure Crispi underestimated the risks at almost every level. First, he did not have unified political support at home, even within his own cabinet. At a time when the budget was already strained and the country was in the midst of an economic crisis, a colonial conquest was one luxury that Italy could not afford. Few businessmen, other than arms-dealers, saw much profit in an Ethiopian empire, and irredentists resented any distraction from the question of Trentino. Thus an important segment of opinion was skeptical of Crispi's maneuver. Second, Crispi failed to prepare adequately for the campaign. He had promised to strengthen the Italian army, largely for the purpose of controlling domestic uprisings, but the economic crisis limited the funds available for this purpose. Much of the proposed new equipment was never purchased, and the army was far less prepared for a colonial war than Crispi imagined.

Third, Crispi failed to listen to his commanders in East Africa, who realistically assessed the difficulties that they faced. They asked that they either be allowed to withdraw to the coast or be sent enough men to conquer Ethiopia. Crispi followed neither course. Italy's financial plight imposed real limits on the number of reinforcements that could be sent to Africa. Rather than accept the consequences of this situation, however, Crispi goaded his generals into an aggressive policy by accusing them of cowardice. After an Italian setback in a minor skirmish, Crispi implied that the Italian commander General Baratieri lacked courage, and he sent another general to replace him. What Baratieri lacked was not courage but wisdom. Hearing of his impending replacement and Crispi's remarks, Baratieri decided to march on Adowa in Ethiopia with four columns of troops. The plan was complicated under any circumstances, but a lack of accurate maps made its execution extremely difficult. Confusion resulted when the four columns failed to meet at the appointed time. Instead of achieving a military triumph in Ethiopia, Baratieri led six thousand men to disaster. The Ethiopians cut the disorganized columns to pieces at Adowa in 1896, killing or capturing virtually the entire Italian force.

Dreams of an Italian empire came crashing down as did Crispi's political career. The temptations of an empire suddenly became liabilities. Italy was discredited as a colonial and military power in the eyes of Europe. "Italy has a big appetite but very poor teeth," Bismarck had once remarked, and Adowa seemed to confirm this harsh judgment. The defeat became a national disgrace. Italians rioted and tore up rail lines to prevent further troop shipments to Africa. Social unrest continued in the southern countryside as clashes began to break out in the northern industrial cities as well. The parliament attacked Crispi's policies, and both socialism and Catholicism, Crispi's sworn enemies, took on significance in Italian political life. Most important, Crispi's adventurism unleashed a political crisis that, like the Dreyfus affair in France, tested the viability of parliamentary politics.

Realizing that his unpopular colonial adventure placed him in an untenable position, Crispi resigned and left behind him an enraged Chamber of Deputies. His successors, conservative in outlook, had no success in restoring order and confidence in the country. Strikes, raids on granaries, and attacks on tax officials revealed the extent of disaffection. The government staggered through 1897 and then faced an intense wave of strikes in the spring of 1898 that culminated in a clash between workers and army units in Milan during a week of rioting in May. Some eighty people lost their lives in the fighting. The Milanese May days brought martial law to the city and provoked repression throughout the country. Universities were closed; radical and socialist politicians were arrested; a number of private associations, including Catholic societies and labor organizations, were disbanded by government decree; some one hundred newspapers were suppressed. The government's crackdown was extensive and severe. In the hands of the conservative Marquis de Rudini, the government ignored constitutional guarantees, suppressed all demonstrations, and arrested suspected demonstrators on the slightest evidence.

The Triumph of Parliament

Events reached a climax the following year when Rudini's successor as prime minister, General Pelloux, introduced legislation designed to control public meetings and the press, and to permit the exile of political offenders. When the parliament balked at these strictures, Pelloux threatened to rule by decree in defiance of parliament. He had the support of the king, and he was willing to rely on royal assistance in a showdown. Pelloux's stance presented a severe challenge to the Italian political system. There is evidence that conservative advisors to the king had encouraged Pelloux to replace parliamentary government with a more authoritarian royal rule.

The challenge galvanized the opposition on the left, ranging from liberal democrats to socialists. They engaged in filibustering and other obstructionist tactics to prevent a vote on the Pelloux legislation. At one point the government suspended parliament for three months until the courts decided that this action was unconstitutional. The coalition on the left finally decided to force the issue. They simply walked out of parliament as a group when Pelloux again expressed his intention of ruling by decree. This tactic was dangerous, for Pelloux might have seized the act as justification for a coup d'état against parliament (as did Mussolini later in the century). Pelloux hesitated to take this extreme action; instead he called for elections, with the expectation that his policy would be endorsed. His efforts to influence the election of 1900 failed, however. The left bloc displayed solidarity and increased its representation in parliament while government supporters lost. Pelloux bowed to the electoral verdict and resigned from office. The parliamentary crisis had been weathered.

It was a few days after these events that King Umberto was assassinated by an expatriate Italian anarchist who had returned to Italy for the purpose of avenging the May days in Milan. Although Umberto had shown a willingness to engage in politics, his son and successor, Victor Emmanuel, shunned a partisan role—at least for the time being—and consciously tried to return the monarchy to a more neutral position. He sensed that the country required a period of calm after the turbulence of the late 1890's. At the same time an upturn in the economy created a favorable atmosphere for a restoration of normal parliamentary politics. Giuseppe Zanardelli, a liberal, assumed responsibility for this task and was appointed prime minister in 1900. He selected as his minister of the interior a man who was to assume a dominant role in Italian politics before the First World War, Giovanni Giolitti. Under their guidance Italy embarked on an era that many hailed as a "liberal spring."

The new direction was perhaps most apparent in the handling of rural discontent and industrial strikes. Zanardelli declared that the state should remain neutral in quarrels between workers and their employers. He also eased certain food taxes that heavily burdened the poor. But these measures were merely a prelude to the policy of moderation pursued by Giolitti, who succeeded Zanardelli as prime minister in 1903. Although a series of strikes confronted him during his first year in office, Giolitti refused to interfere in most of them. As a result the workers made significant gains: wages improved and unions attracted new recruits. Giolitti's patience ended only when railwaymen and civil servants threatened to strike; these workers, he felt, were in a special category. He also defended the right of workers to cross picket lines if they wished to do so and provided protection for those who continued to work. Generally, however, the government policy seemed tolerant of, and even sympathetic to, workers' grievances.

Giolitti insisted that society's most important responsibility was to improve the condition of the poor; moreover, he recognized that prosperity contributed political stability. Under his auspices parliament passed legislation regulating factory employment for women and children, establishing legal holidays, providing medical assistance, reducing taxes on foodstuffs, and so on. None of these measures was spectacular, but taken together they marked a departure in government policy toward social responsibility. Giolitti had hoped that such a program of piecemeal reforms might entice moderate socialists into supporting, or perhaps participating in, the government. Socialist strength was on the increase, a development in part furthered by Giolitti's encouragement of trade unions. At one point Giolitti even invited a moderate socialist into the cabinet, but the offer was refused because the socialists thought acceptance would divide their party.

Giolitti's efforts to collaborate with the socialists elicited the hostility of the socialist party's revolutionary wing, which was adamantly opposed to compromise with bourgeois groups. Giolitti's handling of these more militant socialists exemplified his political technique. He allowed the revolutionaries to expend their energies struggling against the system; when their efforts failed, he offered the mediation and reforms of the government. This tactic served him in meeting the general strike of 1904. In the socialist party congress of that year the militants temporarily gained control of the party leadership. Under their inspiration a general strike erupted in September as a protest against the deaths of some strikers who had clashed with Italian police. Giolitti did nothing, and after four days the strike, which temporarily had halted services in many cities, simply collapsed. Giolitti then went ahead with his social reform program. The contrast between 1898 and 1904 is noteworthy.

But Giolitti did not look exclusively to the left for support. He also granted a share of the power to moderates and conservatives, and he tried to end the bitterness that had marked Church-state relations in Italy. Although he had been critical of the Church's influence in the past, Giolitti believed that what the radicals saw as the menace of clericism was a less important matter than the need for social reforms.

Giolitti's methods of obtaining support from a wide range of political factions marked a return to *trasformismo*. Certainly his pragmatic, undemonstrative approach was reminiscent of Depretis. Giolitti, like his predecessor, used bribes and political favors with great skill, particularly in southern constituencies, where he considered corruption a necessary evil in the absence of political sophistication on the part of the voter. Despite the artificiality of such practices, Giolitti defended parliament as the most important political instrument in Italy. Through parliament he hoped to lead Italy toward social and economic progress; equally important, he thought that parliament offered a prospect for a national reconciliation. Giolitti dangled before various factions the possibility of getting at least part—though perhaps not all—of what they wanted within the existing system. Deep cleavages still divided the booming north and the semi-feudal south, the socialists and the nationalists, but Giolitti was prepared to moderate them through his "sweet reasonableness" in parliament.

* * *

The assertion of parliamentary influence that could be seen in Britain, France, and Italy at the turn of the century did not mean that a totally satisfactory or successful political system prevailed in each state. In Britain, despite the liberals' willingness to embark on a reforming era, the old lines of social division, based on birth, education, and manner of speech, remained prominent features of the country's social development. In the years after 1906 these social distinctions provided the basis for political discontent; both political extremes became disenchanted with the middle-of-the-road stance adopted by the Liberals and toyed with the idea of violent opposition to parliamentary government. In France the radical republic proved to be insensitive to the demands of labor, and militancy spread among the working classes in the aftermath of the Dreyfus years. The French right also continued to nurse grievances against the republic. And in

Italy the moderation of Giolitti dismayed both the extreme nationalists and the revolutionists.

Political stability in each of the nations was subject to a wide set of imponderables, not the least of which was the confidence that people possessed in their government. What the transition from the nineteenth to the twentieth century showed in these three states of western Europe was that their citizens maintained their faith in representative institutions as satisfactory instruments for solving political differences. For all their imperfections, these institutions offered some prospect for tempering social conflicts and easing the strains associated with the emergence of mass politics.

SUGGESTED READING

The political history of the European states remains largely national rather than comparative in emphasis. *Imperialism and the Rise of Labour, 1895–1905* (New York: Barnes & Noble, 1961), the fifth volume of Elie Halévy's *History of the English People in the Nineteenth Century*, is the most detailed treatment of that decade in England. Halévy's sympathies lie with liberal England, and he is disturbed by trends of the period that threaten this liberal tradition. For a broad survey, Robert C. K. Ensor's *England, 1870–1914* (London: Oxford University Press, 1936) remains useful. The essays contained in Simon H. Nowell-Smith (ed.), *Edwardian England, 1901–1914* (London: Oxford University Press, 1964) offer insights into England before 1905, but the emphasis is on the prewar decade. For background, G. Kitson Clark's *The Making of Victorian England* (London: Metheun, 1962) is essential. George M. Young's earlier study, *Victorian England: Portrait of an Age* (London: Oxford University Press, 1953) is less interpretive but helpful in picturing the character of nineteenth century England. Several more specialized treatments of the changing social base of British politics are found in W. L. Guttsman's *The British Political Elite* (New York: Basic Books, 1964) and David C. Marsh's *The Changing Social Structure of England and Wales, 1871–1961* (New York: Humanities Press, 1965). Both authors use the techniques of sociology to enhance our understanding of poltical history.

A number of surveys are available for a study of French politics. A balanced, moderate approach characterizes the work of Jacques Chastenet, *Histoire de la Troisième République* (Paris: Hachette, 1953–). The first three volumes cover the period from 1870 to 1906. D. W. Brogan's *France under the Republic* (New York: Harper, 1940) is a detailed account of the republic's tribulations and is written in a vigorous style. A valuable survey of late nineteenth century France is Gordon Wright's *France in Modern Times* (Chicago: Rand McNally, 1960), which balances social, economic, and political developments. J. P. T. Bury's

France, 1814–1940 (New York: Barnes & Noble, 3rd ed. rev., 1954) and John B. Wolf's *France, 1814–1919* (New York: Harper & Row, 1963) stress political history, as does Guy Chapman's *The Third Republic of France: The First Phase, 1871–1894* (New York: St. Martin's Press, 1962). Among the specialized studies that analyze the nature of French politics under the Third Republic, David Thomson's *Democracy in France Since 1870* (London: Oxford University Press, 1958) makes a number of valuable observations that soberly assess the republic's difficulties in winning public acceptance. John A. Scott in *Republican Ideas and the Liberal Tradition in France, 1870–1914* (New York: Columbia University Press, 1951; Octagon Books, 1966), concentrates on doctrine rather than practice. The early chapters of Paul-Marie de la Gorce's *The French Army,* tr. by K. Douglas (New York: George Braziller, 1963) place military history within a political context. Intellectual opposition to the Third Republic is the basis for Michael Curtis' analysis in *Three Against the Third Republic: Sorel, Barrés, and Maurras* (Princeton: Princeton University Press, 1959). The Dreyfus affair has caught the attention of historians, although the social and economic dimensions of the affair are yet to be plumbed. Douglas Johnson's *France and the Dreyfus Affair* (New York: Walker & Co., 1967) is a balanced, recent account. A popular narrative, sympathetic to the Dreyfusards, is Nicholas Halasz' *Captain Dreyfus: the Story of a Mass Hysteria* (New York: Grove Press, 1955). In *The Dreyfus Case: a Reassessment* (London: Hart-Davis, 1955), Guy Chapman criticizes both sides.

A study of Italian history at the turn of the century may be approached by several general accounts, each reflecting a distinctive point of view. Benedetto Croce's *History of Italy, 1871–1915,* tr. by C. M. Ady (New York: Russell, 1929) reflects favorably on the Italian constitutional monarchy. Croce is sympathetic to Giolitti and others who attempted to make the system work. A more critical assessment may be found in Dennis Mack Smith's *Italy: A Modern History* (Ann Arbor: University of Michigan Press, 1959). Even more pessimistic about the prospects for the new Italian state is Margot Hentze in *Pre-Fascist Italy: the Rise and Fall of the Parliamentary Regime* (London: Allen and Unwin, 1939); she stresses the country's economic weakness and the artificiality of Italian institutions and practices after unification, which produced a cleavage between the government and the people. Richard Hostetter's *The Italian Socialist Movement* (Princeton: Van Nostrand, 1958) is a sound approach to an important topic, but the story is carried only to 1882; the promised sequel has not yet appeared. W. Hilton-Young's *The Italian Left: a Short History of Political Socialism in Italy* (New York: Longmans, Green, 1949) is a lively, brief survey covering the period from unification to Mussolini's consolidation of power. On the question of Catholic political movements, Richard Webster's first two chapters of *Christian Democracy in Italy* (London: Hollis & Carter, 1961) serve as an introduction to the topic at the turn of the century.

4

POLITICS AT THE TURN
OF THE CENTURY
IN EASTERN EUROPE

As in the West, the three empires that sprawled across eastern Europe and reached the edges of Asia experienced political conflicts at the end of the nineteenth century that were marked by sharp differences between conservatives and liberals. The balance of power rested with the traditional conservative executive authority in these empires—the emperor's court, the bureaucracy, and the military —rather than with more liberally inclined representative institutions. Much of the initiative for establishing laws was the prerogative of the emperor's government, often chosen without regard to the political composition of the representative institution. In Russia, of course, prior to 1905 there was no elected assembly to challenge imperial authority; in the other two empires the power of the national legislatures was carefully circumscribed. The objective of liberal groups in eastern Europe was to strengthen or extend the authority of representative institutions by reducing imperial prerogatives—or, in Russia before 1905, simply to obtain some elected assembly for the empire that would share in the exercise of political power.

In Germany the structure of imperial government gave considerable strength to conservative elements in German society. Although the Reichstag, the national assembly, was elected on the basis of universal suffrage, it lacked power to propose legislation and had little real control over the chancellor and his ministers, who were appointed by the emperor. Moreover, conservatives controlled the state government of Prussia because of the restrictive voting system that prevailed there and that favored landowners and wealthy businessmen. The conservatives used their position within Prussia, the largest state in the empire, to block any efforts at constitutional reform that would make the imperial government more responsive to the wishes of the Reichstag. Nevertheless, the Reichstag at least carried some influence; reports of its debates were widely circulated in the press and were avidly followed by a well-educated, politically-conscious population. The spectacular development of the German Social Democratic Party was further evidence of a growing political dynamism based on wide popular support. But in any confrontation between liberals and conservatives the Reichstag's power was limited and was less effective than representative institutions in western Europe as an instrument for political change.

In Austria-Hungary major political problems stemmed from the conflicts between nationalities. Austrian Germans and Hungarian Magyars steadfastly opposed any concessions to Slavic peoples within the empire. The elected parliament in Hungary became a forum for the defense of Magyar privileges, while the Austrian assembly frequently descended into chaos because of the irreconcilable attitudes of its German and Czech delegates. The emergence of parties espousing either revolutionary or racist doctrines further clouded Austrian politics. This seemingly insoluble political dilemma was avoided only by the emperor's ability to rule by decree and exercise his authority through a loyal bureaucracy. Despite internal political pressures, conservatives in both Germany and Austria-Hungary were able to maintain their hold on the critical sources of power. Both empires entered the twentieth century with only minor alterations in their political practices and with no fundamental changes in their political structures.

In Russia the Czar ruled unchecked by any representative institution throughout the nineteenth century. Liberals urged that such an assembly be granted, but the Czar remained deaf to their appeals. By the turn of the century, political pressures had increased to the point where the Czar faced widespread dissatisfaction with the status quo.

Rapid economic modernization had produced enormous social tensions in the Russian countryside and in the empire's emerging industrial centers. The political consequences of this rapid development surfaced dramatically in 1905 when a military defeat precipitated a revolutionary upheaval, and the Czar was forced to install an elected Duma to share responsibility for saving the Russian empire. Russian conservatives ultimately survived this shock, but the experience demonstrated that war and, above all, military disaster threatened their political control. Although Russia was the only eastern empire to experience revolution, conservatives in all three empires found it increasingly difficult to maintain the status quo against domestic political pressures in the form of reformist, revolutionary, or nationalistic political movements.

The German Empire: Bismarck's Legacy

The way in which political power was exercised in Germany was a matter of concern to all Europeans, not just the Germans themselves. By 1890 Germany had become the most powerful state on the Continent, and any irresponsible behavior on the part of the nation's political leadership would have grave consequences. The political mechanism for governing Germany at the end of the nineteenth century was hardly reassuring, for it represented an uneasy compromise among several political forces within Germany, Bismarck's legacy to the empire.

Bismarck devised a political system that was well suited to preserving the status quo and, above all, was designed to assure the unity and survival of an empire that had been forged only at great risk and with considerable struggle. But it was not equipped nor inclined to accommodate the social and economic changes that the rapid expansion of German industry and the equally dynamic growth of the population had produced. Bismarck as chancellor exercised decisive influence. With the accession of William II the locus of power shifted, but Bismarck's complex structure continued to favor those elements in Germany that wished to avoid the political consequences of the social and economic realignments taking place within the empire.

Political Structure of the Empire

In many ways Chancellor Otto von Bismarck's skill in forming the German empire for William I in 1871 was a triumph of diplomacy.

German military victories over France had swept away many obstacles to unification, but the rulers of the German states and principalities in the south, as well as the city fathers of the Free Cities (Lubeck, Bremen, and Hanover), were wary of an empire in which their importance and influence would be reduced. Bismarck tried to soothe their feelings by creating a political system that balanced centralist and federal principles.

Federalism: the Bundesrat ▪ Federalism was represented by the Bundesrat (Federal Council), which served as the upper house of the imperial legislature and was composed of delegates selected by each state legislature. Although sometimes overshadowed by the lower house, the Reichstag, the Bundesrat possessed considerable importance. All imperial laws had to be approved by it, and no change could be made in the imperial constitution if, for example, the seventeen members of the Prussian delegation happened to vote against it. Thus, through the upper house, a single state was able to determine Germany's constitutional development. In addition to allowing them representation in the Bundesrat, Bismarck permitted the separate states to retain control over education, the courts, police, and taxation.

Centralization: the Reichstag ▪ As a counterbalance to the federalism of the Bundesrat, the Reichstag functioned as a central political institution representing the entire empire. Reichstag delegates were selected in imperial elections on the basis of universal male suffrage. Although Bismarck had little sympathy for popular sovereignty and parliamentary government, he hoped that a popularly elected Reichstag would offset any particularist tendencies on the part of the individual German states. The Reichstag's political parties, organized on national lines rather than by states or regions, debated imperial matters that were laid before them by the chancellor acting on behalf of the emperor.

Political groups within the Reichstag represented a wide range of opinion. There were two parties of conservatives: the German Conservative party, which defended the prerogatives of the Prussian state and expressed the attitudes of the Junker landholders of East Prussia, and the Free Conservatives who loyally supported Bismarck. As the interests of these two parties increasingly pointed in the same direction, they eventually united in the German Conservative party.

Toward the center of the political spectrum were the National Liberals. Initially they had opposed Bismarck in the 1860's, demanding that he give the Reichstag greater power in the empire, but the right wing of the party became ardent enthusiasts of the empire when it became apparent that Bismarck had successfully unified Germany.

In the 1870's the left wing of the National Liberals broke away from the main party to set up their own organization, the Progressive party. Progressive leaders continued to call for liberal reforms; they were some of the most caustic critics of Bismarck and of the empire he had created. The influence of the Progressives dwindled, however, toward the end of the nineteenth century as their electoral strength dropped. The National Liberals came more and more to represent Germany's business and industrial interests; because they prospered under the empire, the National Liberals had little interest in upsetting the status quo.

Two parties steadily gained support after 1871—the socialists and the Catholic Center party; both were regarded by Bismarck as fundamentally disloyal to the empire. He considered the revolutionary doctrines of socialism a threat to the empire's precarious unity. In 1878 Bismarck attempted to curb socialism by outlawing the party's activities: socialists who presented themselves for election had to do so without support of a formal party organization. Despite this restriction, the number of German Social Democrats in the Reichstag increased as the socialists won the loyalty of workers in Germany's rapidly growing industrial centers. Many of these socialist votes came from new participants in German politics—between 1871 and 1912 the number of nonvoters in the eligible voting population declined from 48 to 16 percent. Bismarck had believed initially that universal male suffrage would undermine the liberals' reformist pose to the advantage of the conservatives. Universal suffrage perhaps did undermine the liberals, but its main beneficiary was the socalist party. Much to Bismarck's dismay universal suffrage strengthened what he considered to be revolutionary tendencies in Germany. Near the end of his career he contemplated imposing even harsher restrictions on the socialist party and replacing universal suffrage with a narrower franchise.

The Catholic Center party represented the political interests of the sizable Catholic minority in the German empire. Not all Catholics necessarily supported the party, but enough did so that the party gained a rather solid position in the 1870's and 1880's. Bismarck and other German Protestants feared that the party had external, and therefore anti-German, connections with the Pope and with Austrian and French Catholics. A desire to enforce Catholic loyalty inspired Bismarck's crusade, or *Kulturkampf*, against Catholicism in Germany during the 1870's. When by the end of the decade his campaign had failed to reduce the influence of the party and only left resentment among many Germans, Bismarck put aside his hostility. Eventually the Catholic Center party became a strong supporter of the empire and a party to which the government could turn in forming political coalitions. Both the Center party and the Social Democrats gained electoral strength at the expense of the Conservatives and National Liberals, whose proportional share of the popular vote declined. This gave the Center party increasing political leverage, for a political combination with the socialists was considered impossible.

The Executive Authority ▪ The national political parties of the Reichstag and the federal character of the empire represented only part of the political equation in Germany. Among the other important centers of political power was the monarchy itself. The imperial system was a compromise between the theoretical sovereignty of the people and royal absolutism. In practice there was little effective parliamentary control over executive authority in the German empire. Although and the chancellor. Important arms of the executive, such as the army obtain approval for his legislative program and for the budgets presented to the Reichstag, technically he could retain office for as long as he held the confidence of the emperor. The ministers also held office at the discretion of the emperor and were not responsible to the Reichstag. Resembling imperial secretaries more than cabinet officials, they were given the tasks of carrying out the policies of the emperor and the chancellor. Important arms of the executive, such as the army and the bureaucracy, were for all intents and purposes also outside parliamentary control. The army's budget, for example, was approved for a period of seven years; parliament had no opportunity in the meantime to review the army's activities. Finally, the deputies in the Reichstag lacked the authority to initiate legislation and could only vote on programs presented to them by the government.

The Dominance of Prussia ▪ Another element in the political equation, unique to the German experience, was the dominant position of the Prussian state within the federal system. Because Prussia possessed some five-eighths of the territory in the empire and more than half the population, its influence in the empire was perhaps inevitable. As we have seen, the structure of the Bundesrat permitted the Prussian delegation to veto undesirable legislation and to block any effort at constitutional revision that it did not favor. What is especially significant is that the conservatism within the Prussian state government was able to cast its shadow over the rest of Germany. The Prussian government was elected by a three-class voting system; qualification for voting in each class was based on property ownership and tax payments. The numerous poor were relegated to a single class while the landholding Junkers and the wealthy industrialists of the

Ruhr obtained disproportionate influence. This voting system enabled the two parties most committed to the status quo—the Conservatives and the National Liberals—to escape the political consequences of a declining electoral support at the turn of the century; from their position in the Prussian state government, these parties were able to exercise great influence throughout Germany.

Prussia left its stamp on imperial Germany in other ways. First, eighteen of the twenty-one army corps in the imperial army were supplied by Prussia. Second, Berlin, the capital of Prussia, served also as the capital of the empire. The imperial bureaucrats came under the influence and control of Prussian aristocrats who had a long tradition of service to the state. In fact, many of the imperial offices created after 1871 had simply been transferred from the Prussian government. Thus, the imperial chancellor also served as head of the state government in Prussia. The failure of attempts to separate these two offices testified to Prussia's importance; it was found that coordination of Prussian and imperial policy was crucial to the smooth functioning of the system. Finally, the German emperor was also king of Prussia. Technically an "equal" among other princes of German states, the king of Prussia clearly possessed far greater political influence than any of his fellow sovereigns.

Bismarck's Political Techniques

The complexity of Germany's political structure provided opportunities for a strong chancellor, such as Bismarck, to impose his policies by exploiting one element against another. Bismarck's technique was to play royal against parliamentary authority and vice-versa. Fortunately Bismarck had influence with both. In return for his part in unifying the empire and saving William I's throne, Bismarck was able to count on the emperor's support. As long as he retained this confidence, Bismarck had a solid political base for a contest with either the Reichstag or an anti-Bismarck faction at the court.

Furthermore, as long as he could command a majority in the Reichstag, Bismarck had a powerful argument to use against those advisors to the emperor who suggested that the chancellor be replaced. Bismarck regarded the Reichstag as an important element of German unity, and he was not above using cajolery and blunt pressure to secure majorities. Often his tactics left bitter memories, particularly when he severed connections with allies whose usefulness had ended. Bismarck did not actually participate in the electoral process; being a man of the nineteenth century, political campaigning was beneath him

—although the manipulation of events to produce a favorable Reichstag majority was not. The Reichstag elections frequently occurred amid alarms and scares of domestic or international crises that Bismarck himself had produced. With the empire in danger, Bismarck could discredit his opposition by accusing them of threatening to tear the nation apart.

Bismarck's policy after unification centered on the need to consolidate the empire. For this purpose he claimed, despite his sometimes abrupt methods, to be a man of peace at home and abroad. In foreign affairs he wished to avoid a European war that might lead to a destruction of the empire itself. Domestically his concern was to reconcile the German people to the empire. Although he eventually concluded that the Catholics represented less of a danger than he had imagined, he remained convinced that socialism was a foreign and subversive doctrine. This belief led to both the anti-socialist laws of 1878 and his welfare program of the 1880's, during which time a whole series of social assistance laws, including insurance for accidents, disability, old age, and sickness, were passed. He calculated that these measures would reconcile German workers to the empire and neutralize the revolutionary appeals of socialism. The socialist candidates continued to gain, however, and despite Bismarck's every effort to coerce unruly delegates, the Reichstag became less and less manageable toward the end of the 1880's. When the elections of 1890 left Bismarck without a majority in the Reichstag, he contemplated a coup d'état that would impose even stricter limits on the socialists and at the same time restrict the franchise in favor of conservative parties. The newly crowned emperor, William II, did not consider these drastic measures necessary, however, and this disagreement provided the background to the quarrel that brought Bismarck's dismissal from office.

Bismarck had regarded the position of chancellor as a necessary intermediary between the crown and the Reichstag, but the events of 1890 revealed that this office was less the "essential third" in any political combination than it was a position dependent on the emperor's support. No longer able to command a majority, Bismarck could no longer argue that he was indispensable for dealing with parliament. Moreover, although William II respected Bismarck, he lacked the loyal commitment that his grandfather, William I, had maintained. The old emperor's deference to Bismarck had enabled the chancellor to survive several crises. Their relationship created the impression that the office of the chancellor held great power, whereas this strength actually depended on the force of Bismarck's personality and his ties with the emperor. In any confrontation between chancellor and emperor, the latter was clearly in a commanding position. The loss of his mastery over the Reichstag and his disagreements with the emperor critically weakened the base of Bismarck's power in 1890.

The decisive element in Bismark's dismissal was William II's wish to be his own master and to escape Bismarck's tutelage. He was encouraged in this direction by his advisors and other officials who were alienated by Bismarck's overbearing manner. In their eyes the chancellor had become too powerful, and they felt that the only way to reduce the chancellor's influence was through the emperor's assertion of his own position. The struggle between the emperor and Bismarck centered on measures of social legislation. A serious strike campaign in the fall of 1889 and the victories of socialist candidates in the 1890 elections demonstrated that Bismarck's combination of social welfare and repression of the socialist party had failed to halt the drift toward socialism on the part of the German working class. Rather than grant further concessions, Bismarck decided to introduce stiffer anti-socialist laws. In addition, he was willing to call for repeated Reichstag elections until he had a manageable majority or, if necessary, to impose a restricted franchise. William II, desiring at this time to present himself as an "emperor of the people," found that he could not do so if he followed Bismarck's policies. Consequently, when Bismarck submitted his resignation over an apparently minor dispute with the emperor, it was accepted.

The Caprivi Era

General Leo von Caprivi, the man chosen by William II to succeed Bismarck, is reported to have once remarked, "What kind of jackass will dare to be Bismarck's successor?" Certainly he realized any chancellor following the founder of the German empire faced a difficult task, if for no other reason than the inevitability of being compared to Bismarck. Moreover, Caprivi knew that the emperor wished to take an active part in shaping policies for the empire. In spite of his reservations, Caprivi served his five years in office with remarkable independence and integrity. If in making his appointment William II thought he had found a pliable chancellor, he underrated Caprivi's stubborn spirit. A capable and conscientious administrator, Caprivi believed that he had not only a responsibility to the emperor but also an obligation to pursue measures that were in the best interests of the German nation, as he interpreted them. As chancellor, Caprivi made every effort to guide the empire, and even Prussia, toward a more progressive course than the one that Bismarck had followed.

Caprivi considered himself a conservative, but his policies conformed to the vaguely liberal sentiments that William II had expressed at the outset of his reign. In his first speech after assuming office Caprivi announced that he would welcome ideas from any source— a statement that was interpreted as a gesture of reconciliation toward the opposition. His mild, pacific manner was in marked contrast to Bismarck's overbearing style. One of Caprivi's early decisions was to allow the anti-socialist laws to lapse when they came up for renewal in 1890. With this decisive step, the Socialist party was permitted to bring a dynamic and disciplined force into the arena of German politics. The well-organized Socialist party impelled the other rather loosely constructed parties to achieve a greater degree of organization in the 1890's.

Caprivi also made changes in governmental procedure that were designed to remove some of the bitterness left from Bismarck's tenure. He granted a greater amount of autonomy to certain departments over which Bismarck had kept a tight rein. A loosening of controls was in fact necessary, for Bismarck's insistence on supervising many details had made the chancellor's tasks burdensome, and had frustrated the initiative of other officials. These measures won Caprivi temporary popularity, but he soon found himself in conflict with conservative elements in German society.

Even though Caprivi was an aristocrat and an army officer, his major problems stemmed from the hostility that he elicited in Junker and military circles. His difficulties with the Prussian landowners began when he proposed a reduction of agricultural duties. Caprivi decided that agricultural protection forced the average German to pay a higher price for his food than he would if grain and other foodstuffs could be imported without a high tax. With the support of moderate and liberal parties he pushed lower tariffs through the Reichstag. His success, however, produced a permanent enemy. A severe agricultural depression—not directly related to the tariff revision—provoked the Prussian landowners into forming an Agrarian League in 1893, and this organization began a relentless campaign for Caprivi's dismissal.

Caprivi encountered further difficulties when he proposed a bill that would expand the size of the army by increasing the number of draftees but would reduce the total length of service from three to two years. The opposition to this reform came from a variety of sources. On the left, the Socialists and Progressives simply rejected any change in the military system that would strengthen the army. In addition these parties had no intention of adding to the country's economic difficulties by granting funds for an enterprise they regarded as unnecessary. On the right, Caprivi encountered hostility of a different sort. Although willing to see additional reforms for the army, many generals balked at the reduction of service from three to two years; the shorter time, they maintained, was insufficient to mold a soldier.

The army bill was finally passed, but not before an election was held in 1893 that was not encouraging for the stability of Reichstag politics and for Caprivi's own position. The political extremes gained at the expense of the moderate center, and Caprivi lost his majority support in the Reichstag. The conservatives were alienated by his liberal tendencies while the moderates were irritated by his plans for military reform.

After the election, agitation against Caprivi by the Agrarian League intensified. Caprivi was blamed for the decline in agricultural prices and was berated for having followed a lenient policy toward the Polish peasantry in eastern Prussia. The discontent of the Conservatives increased when Caprivi at one point suggested a modest reform of the Prussian voting system. His proposal would not have granted universal male suffrage, but it would have reduced the inequities of the system somewhat. The response of the Conservatives was a flat refusal to yield even a small part of their power in Prussia. Caprivi found himself politically vulnerable. He had yielded his position as minister-president in Prussia because it had proved a burden to hold both offices. His enemies were able to mount an attack against him when they won over his successor.

By this time William II had abandoned his original intention of serving as an emperor of the people. He had, in fact, come around to Bismarck's view that only repression of the socialists and a limitation of the franchise would effectively curb revolutionary tendencies in Germany. In the fall of 1894 the emperor's public speeches indicated that he no longer saw eye to eye with his chancellor. The combination of the loss of majority support, the campaign of the agrarians, and the emperor's disfavor provoked Caprivi's resignation in 1894.

The Caprivi era amply demonstrated that without a strong, domineering chancellor, political power in the German empire tended to fragment. The Reichstag, the army, the monarchy, and the Prussian agrarian interests all exercised a powerful role, but none seemed strong enough to give firm direction to Germany. Perhaps the monarchy in the hands of a more stable individual might have dominated the scene. In the years after Caprivi's dismissal, the emperor reasserted his authority, but he failed to supply a constant direction to German affairs. The result was a power vacuum that was filled with such vague and heady proposals as a "world policy" that had no specific, readily defined goals.

The New Course: Toward a World Policy

Caprivi's successor, Prince Hohenlohe, was an agreeable and wealthy aristocrat who had given long years of service to the Prussian state and the German empire. As chancellor, his major objective appeared to be to cause the emperor little difficulty. In effacing himself before the royal will he permitted a resurgence of William II's influence on the course of German policy. Although the six Hohenlohe years seemed unspectacular and in fact accomplished little in the way of a legislative program, they marked a significant turning point in German history. In this brief period Germany embraced a world policy that asserted its impressive material strength.

Germany had first embarked on a world policy, in a limited way, when a number of adventurers placed portions of Africa under German control during the 1880's. But it was not until the 1890's that imperialism gained widespread popularity at home. Much of this popularity arose from the propaganda activities of pro-colonial leagues that demanded a great overseas empire for a great nation. One of the more influential of these leagues, the Pan-German Union, called for overseas expansion and a reunion of all German-speaking peoples into one vast association. These heady ideas inflamed national sentiment; the call for expansion of the entire German nation transcended the narrow particularism among the German states. In addition, Darwin's notion of the "survival of the fittest," which was popular then, seemed to require that a great nation expand in order to meet the challenges posed by national rivals. Britain, the leading industrial power of the nineteenth century, was the standard by which German achievement was to be measured. A strong navy would provide solid evidence of Germany's rise to comparable power.

The Influence of Navalism ■ The search for a world policy under William II became more and more marked with the growing influence of Admiral Tirpitz, Germany's advocate of a strong naval fleet. Tirpitz was brought to William's attention soon after he read Admiral Mahan's *Influence of Sea Power upon History,* a book that spoke to his love for the sea and that confirmed his own belief that a mighty navy was the key to world-wide power. Tirpitz' articles on naval power were in a similar vein and led to his appointment as secretary of state for the navy in 1897.

Admiral Tirpitz quickly displayed his political skill in lobbying for a bill that would provide credits for the construction of a modern navy. Experts testified before the Reichstag on the need for a navy, while the Navy League spread the doctrines of naval strength throughout the empire by means of a carefully organized propaganda campaign. The strategical argument maintained that Germany could not be secure as long as Britain dominated the oceans—and Great Britain had recently begun a new program of naval construction. A series of colonial disputes with Great Britain, which received wide publicity in the German press, already had exposed the relative weakness of the German navy in the mid–1890's and prepared the ground for the pro-naval propaganda. The propagandists held that although the German navy could not match the British navy throughout the world, the German fleet should be powerful enough, particularly on the North Sea, to make the risk of war too great for Britain. By a curious bit of reasoning the German people were told that Germany had to have a navy to defend the empire and that this empire had to be developed to provide coaling stations for a navy yet to be built. The paradox of this argument escaped the deputies who were persuaded by Tirpitz and his supporters. In March 1898 the Reichstag passed the first of Germany's naval bills. Two years later, taking advantage of widespread anti-British feeling generated by the Boer War in Africa, Tirpitz pushed through an even larger bill that called for a construction program to give Germany no less than thirty-six battleships by 1920.

Consequences of World Policy and Navalism ▪ The creation of a German battle fleet reflected the international pressures of an imperialist era. William II insisted that Germany was asking for no more than its share of the glory, but the other states regarded Germany's pursuit of a world policy as evidence of an overbearing ambition. German statesmen tried to have a voice in a wide range of international disputes. It was inevitable that the construction of a huge German navy would alter the balance of power in Europe and consequently affect Germany's relations with other states, particularly Great Britain. After the turn of the century British statesmen regarded the German naval program as a deliberate, aggressive challenge to British maritime predominance.

In domestic affairs, the navy had a wide appeal among the Germans and became a symbol of imperial strength. The most enthusiastic support for it came from the prosperous German middle class. Whereas the army continued to be predominantly aristocratic in outlook and values, the navy was oriented toward the middle classes and offered sons of the upper bourgeoisie access to the prestige of a military commission. This nationalistic exuberance on the part of the German bourgeoisie was occasionally displayed at the expense of balance, restraint, and a sense of limits in the exercise of power.

Within the Reichstag the campaign for a powerful navy cemented a political alliance between the Conservatives and the National Liberals, thus bringing together the Junker landed interests and the business and manufacturing classes. By supporting each other's programs, they both obtained what they wanted. At the turn of the century, the National Liberals very much favored the building of a navy, for it meant additional orders for steelplating, machinery, electrical equipment, and armaments. Krupp industries contributed heavily to the Navy League, and openly lobbied in favor of naval construction. Although the East Prussian landowners had little interest in a large navy, they agreed to support the naval bill in return for the National Liberals' support for a higher protective tariff on grains. With no real objections to a higher agrarian tariff, the industrialists joined with the agrarians to pass the Bülow Tariff of 1901, the highest tariff in the empire's history. The alliance of rye and steel became a fundamental characteristic of political life under William II.

The National Liberals and the Conservatives also united in their support of a world policy as a defensive measure, for they felt their strength in the Reichstag threatened by the growth of the socialist party. The industrial boom that brought wealth and confidence to the middle classes also resulted in an expansion of the labor force and a concentration of workers in the cities, factors that facilitated recruitment into unions and into the Social Democratic party. An aggressive imperialist policy seemed to offer moderates and conservatives a means to by-pass pressures for domestic political changes. They hoped that popular enthusiasm for a world policy would offset the growing revolutionary potential of political parties seeking to transform the German empire. Evidence of a social fear of revolution and a desire to substitute the distractions of empire could be found in such organizations as the Imperial League Against Social Democracy and the German Association of Eastern Marches. The emperor shared these hopes; when socialists won fifty-six Reichstag seats in the elections of 1898, William II, after briefly entertaining notions of a coup d'état that would dispense with the Reichstag altogether, turned with renewed efforts to a world policy.

The socialist party opposed imperialism, but it lacked allies that might have made its opposition effective. Only a few Progressives and a minority of the Catholic Center party also criticized the new direction in German foreign policy. Moreover, the socialists' rank and file were less immune to the appeals of imperialism than the party leadership suspected. A kind of popular wave of imperialist sentiment swept over Germany at the turn of the century, and moderate socialists even suggested that the German worker could profit from imperial expansion.

An Abortive Challenge: Bülow and the Empire

In 1900 the aging Prince Hohenlohe, under whose chancellorship Germany's world policy had been launched, made way for Prince Bernhard von Bülow, a career diplomat of considerable charm and wit who had caught William II's fancy. Bülow handled the Reichstag with great adroitness and aplomb—indeed, he liked nothing better than to display his oratorical skills in parliamentary debate. His tariff law of 1901 earned for him the loyalty of the Conservatives, and his dazzling style corresponded to the manners displayed by the newly rich industrialists and businessmen who set the rather gaudy tone of the emperor's court. Unlike the somewhat stiff Caprivi and the timid Hohenlohe, Bülow enjoyed the emperor's admiration and respect. Unfortunately, in the interests of preserving their relationship, Bülow refused to use his influence to curb William II's propensity for making ill-considered comments on foreign and domestic affairs.

For the first few years of his administration Bülow faced no real domestic crisis. But in 1906 a storm broke over the administration of German colonies in East and Southwest Africa, where native uprisings had led to bloody conflicts with German troops. The most serious of these uprisings took place in Southwest Africa as a result of the brutal policies employed by German colonists and merchants in the area. The Social Democrats and the Catholic Center party condemned these abuses. The Catholics maintained that the government had ignored the appeals of missionaries for more humane treatment. Bülow tried to avold a confrontation by reorganizing the colonial office and by appointing an enlightened businessman, Bernhard Dernburg, as a new head to initiate reform. Bülow's gesture was not enough, for the Socialists and the Center party continued attacks on the government. At the end of 1906 they combined to reject the government's request for funds to restore order in Southwest Africa. Bülow then dissolved the Reichstag and called for elections.

The issue of colonial reform in the electoral campaign of 1907 drew attention to some fundamental problems of German politics. The colonial office, like all imperial offices, was outside effective parliamentary control and supervision; unchecked by the Reichstag, colonial administrators had gone their own way. Opposition to the government came from those parties most committed to winning a greater voice for the Reichstag in German political life. For this part, Bülow openly appealed to those parties that wished to preserve the status quo and that accepted Germany's world-wide responsibilities. A Bülow bloc of National Liberals, Conservatives, and even some Progressives campaigned with a nationalistic appeal for approval of Germany's world policy. The socialists and the Center party found themselves on the defensive, caught amid a wave of chauvinistic, pro-colonial sentiment.

The election brought a triumphant majority for Bülow and was a clear victory for the alliance of rye and steel—or conservatism and liberalism—that had been formed to back Germany's world policy. Apparently few Germans were prepared to challenge the status quo at this point or over this particular issue. Although the Catholic Center party managed to hold its own, the Social Democrats lost seats, indicating that German labor could be won by an appeal to nationalism. The lesson of this election was not lost on the reform parties. The advocates of caution were vindicated by the results; in the future the leadership of the opposition parties would hesitate before engaging in a direct confrontation with the government.

Germany emerged from the 1890–1906 period with its political system intact, although important changes had occurred in the way German policy was directed. The restraint that Bismarck had displayed in the conduct of German policy had yielded to the assertion of a German desire for "world power" under William II. Because the chancellor ultimately depended on the emperor's favor to stay in office and because parliamentary control over imperial policy was weak, this exercise of power lacked proper political supervision. The critical need of the German empire was to discover a method for the responsible direction of authority, but the empire made its passage into the twentieth century without resolving this problem.

The Austro-Hungarian Dilemma:
Nationalism Versus the Empire

In an age marked by growing national self-consciousness among various European peoples, the Austro-Hungarian empire represented a curious anachronism. The dual monarchy encompassed a polyglot of minorities differing from one another in language, custom, religion, and historical tradition. The head of the Hapsburg dynasty, Emperor Francis-Joseph, exercised authority over these disparate groups by means of a rigid political system that worked, but just barely. By the end of the nineteenth century many European statesmen, including Bismarck, were predicting the eventual collapse of the empire. The nationalities living within the borders of the empire, if not desiring complete independence, at least wanted some form of self-government. Yet because few could agree on what the new order should be, a paralysis born of internal division assured the continuation of the empire. At the turn of the century the Austro-Hungarian dilemma—how to reconcile nationalism with the existence of a multi-national empire—appeared to be insoluble.

The Political System

The dynastic rule of the Hapsburgs in the Austrian empire was the product of a long period of amalgamation during which territory in southeastern Europe had fallen under the Hapsburg house. Until 1866 the control of the political system was effectively exercised by the Austrian Germans, a minority nationality in the empire. They justified their hegemony by the fact that Austria played an important role within the German Confederation. In 1866, however, Austria suffered a military defeat at the hands of the rising Prussian state that significantly altered the position of the Austrian Germans in the Hapsburg domain. By the peace terms signed with Prussia, Austria was excluded from the North German Confederation. Unable to count on support from allies to the north, the Austrian Germans could no longer ignore the demands of non-German groups within the empire. The Hungarian Magyars, in particular, took advantage of the 1866 defeat to demand autonomy in the eastern half of the empire. The Compromise of 1867 granted this autonomy; henceforth Francis-Joseph was emperor of Austria and king of Hungary. The dual monarchy was the basis for the government of Austria-Hungary until the empire collapsed in 1918.

The institutions common to both halves of the empire were limited to a war ministry, a finance ministry, and a ministry of foreign affairs. In all other matters each half of the dual monarchy enjoyed autonomy. Under the terms of the compromise each of the shared ministries was responsible to a single political body whose delegates were selected in equal proportion by the Austrian and the Hungarian parliaments. These imperial delegates met each year, their meeting place alternating between Vienna and Budapest. But even though they met in the same city, they did not meet as a single assembly; the delegations convened in separate chambers and communicated with each other by means of written messages. This curious system required a group of runners to carry notes between the delegations, and the imperial ministers shuttled back and forth explaining their policies to each assembly in turn. The yearly change in location of the meeting place required that a parade of secretaries and officials accompany the delegates on their annual treks up or down the Danube. Records and information had to be transported from Vienna to Budapest and back in a process that simply added to the confusion. Perhaps the most severe handicap to the functioning of the imperial delegations was the loyalty the delegates maintained to their separate parliaments; they were not unified in a commitment to the empire. Debates over renewal of the economic agreement between the two halves of the monarchy provided occasion each year for mutual recriminations.

In addition to the imperial delegation and the three common ministries, sources of unity within the dual system were to be found in the person of the emperor, in the bureaucracy, and in the army. The emperor gave his careful attention to all matters of state and was in many respects the supreme bureaucrat of the empire. Imperial policy was transmitted from the emperor's palace through the elaborate reaches of the Austro-Hungarian bureaucracy. Although the bureaucracy functioned at a maddeningly slow pace, it managed to serve the entire ramshackle empire. The officials of the bureaucracy were staunchly loyal to the emperors, although their devotion to duty often seemed to be no more than an elaborate concern for procedure and red tape to anyone who had official business with the state.

Another element that worked against particularism in the empire was the army. Composed of heterogeneous elements drawn from all parts of the empire, the army was nevertheless loyal to the emperor and symbolized his power. The predominantly aristocratic officer corps reflected a conservative outlook that opposed any possible changes in the status quo. Finally, the Church and most of the nobility joined the military and the bureaucracy as "state-preserving" elements within the Austro-Hungarian domain.

Austria-Hungary was unique among European states in the diversity of its population and in the absence of a numerical majority of any one ethnic group. The two dominant minorities—the Germans in Austria and the Magyars in Hungary—composed only 24 percent and 20 percent, respectively, of the population of the empire as a whole. The rest of the population was composed of Czechs (12.6 percent), Poles (10 percent), Ruthenes (8 percent), Rumanians (6.4 percent), Croats (5 percent), Serbs (4 percent), Slovenes (2.5 percent), Italians (2 percent), and others (comprising 5 percent). This diversity made any system based on national principles, however defined, a matter of intense disagreement. The Compromise of 1867 assured the Germans in Austria and the Magyars in Hungary pre-eminence in their respective spheres, but neither was a majority. In both halves the Slavs seethed in their discontent with the existing political structure. Neither half-hearted gestures toward reconciliation in Austria nor a rigid adherence to the status quo in Hungary offered a solution to the Austro-Hungarian dilemma.

The Failure of Appeasement in Austria

The Austrian half of the empire was the less compact of the two. Geographically it stretched from the borders of Switzerland and Italy in the southwest to the edges of Russia in the northeast, incorporating all of present day Austria, western Czechoslovakia, and territory that had been acquired during the partitioning of Poland in the eighteenth century. In the 1870's the German Liberal party, based on the Viennese middle-class professional groups, had played a dominant role in Austrian politics. The German Liberals constituted the largest single faction in the Austrian parliament, but they did not have a majority. They were anticlerical in outlook, which distinguished them from the pro-Catholic German Conservatives, and they promoted centralizing tendencies as opposed to the various minorities who favored a looser, federal structure for the Austrian half of the empire. In 1873 the Liberals sponsored an electoral reform that strengthened centralist tendencies in Austria. Delegates to parliament were no longer elected by provincial diets but were selected from districts drawn in Vienna to favor the German-speaking population as much as possible. Elections were based on a restrictive franchise that favored large land-owners and wealthier townsmen.

By 1879 the Liberals lost their control of parliament. In addition to having quarreled among themselves over matters of foreign policy in the Balkans, the party had been badly shaken by a series of financial scandals involving prominent party members. At this point Emperor Francis-Joseph became disgusted with the Liberals' factionalism and their reluctance to extend Hapsburg influence in the Balkans. He decided to call on his old school friend, Count Taaffe, to form a ministry that would have support from German Conservatives, Poles, and Czechs, and that would exclude the German Liberals.

Under Taaffe the government relaxed the anticlerical policies of the Liberals, to satisfy the Conservatives, and it tried to appease the Czechs, the most aggressive of the minorities in Austria. In 1871 Francis-Joseph had even contemplated traveling to Prague to be crowned king of Bohemia, a concession to Czech nationalism that might have converted the dual monarchy into a triple monarchy. Protests from German Liberals and the Magyars, however, forced him to abandon the scheme at that time. Taaffe's reliance on the support of the Czechs and Slavs marked a return to this policy. Through limited concessions it was hoped that the discontented Czechs would be reconciled to the empire. The German Liberals complained that an "iron ring" had been forged around them; in fact, their fall from power in 1879 marked the first step in the eclipse of the German Liberal party.

Taaffe's long tenure (1879–93) gave him a virtual monopoly of the prime minister's office at the end of the nineteenth century. His method, somewhat in the style of Italian ministers, was to grant concessions to his political allies. For example, Taaffe founded a second Czech university in Prague in 1892 that in time surpassed its German counterpart. He also proposed compromise solutions on schooling and language, two issues that had caused considerable agitation in Bohemia. But Taaffe eventually ran into political difficulties. His reliance on the "iron ring" of German Conservatives and non-German elements in parliament won him the hostility of German Liberals, and his concessions satisfied neither the militant young Czech nationalists, who objected to the moderate nature of his compromises, nor the Germans, who opposed any concession to the Czechs. Taaffe's proposals for the creation of separate Czech and German administrative districts in Bohemia, although favored by the moderate "old" Czech elements, provoked remarkable scenes in the Bohemian diet. Ink stands and books were flung across the parliamentary hall, which became an arena for a series of fistfights and brawls. By 1893 Czech nationalism had attained new heights under the influence of the young Czechs; at the same time the Germans in Bohemia vehemently opposed any conciliation. Near the close of his ministry Taaffe was forced to decree martial law in Prague.

Taaffe's fall from office came in the aftermath of an attempt to stem the obstructionist tactics of Czechs in Bohemia and of the young Czech delegation in Vienna. Taaffe calculated that the masses would be more interested in social and economic measures than in the futile demonstrations of nationalist zeal. The rise of Austrian socialism and the equally significant appearance of a Christian Socialist party, both of which claimed to have a sectarian rather than a national base, encouraged him in his belief that the average citizen was interested in meaningful reforms. He proposed that universal male suffrage be introduced into the Austrian half of the monarchy, thereby abolishing a complicated "curia" system that gave preponderant weight to the clerical, aristocratic, and landowning elements in Austrian society. His proposal proved his undoing, however, for it threatened the vested interests of the Germans, liberal and conservative alike, and the Poles, who realized that their influence would be limited by universal suffrage. The defection of the German Conservatives and the Poles broke Taaffe's "iron ring" and brought his resignation.

Taaffe's experience in office revealed the fundamental problem that plagued Austria. The demands of Slav nationalism appeared insatiable unless autonomy was granted to at least the Czech minority. This measure would require a fundamental change in the structure of the empire, which the Austrian Germans, supported by the Magyars in Hungary, refused to consider. Concessions to the Czechs, they argued, would open the way to similar demands by other minorities. Taaffe's appeal to popular opinion foundered against German hostility. The proposed universal male suffrage so alarmed many Germans that they flocked to the pan-German movement. According to the doctrines of this movement, only a militant German supremacy, backed by the weight of the German empire, could halt the rising Slavic tide within the Hapsburg empire. Such notions filtered into the political atmosphere of Vienna during the 1890's and placed another obstacle in the way of a compromise between the German and Slav populations. At the turn of the century tensions were increasing, not abating.

Other Dimensions In Austria: Socialism and Christian Socialists

New political movements that appeared during the 1890's brought about changes in the political climate of Austria that made prospects for domestic stability less likely. In 1888 Victor Adler, a doctor who had become converted to Marxism while ministering to the poor in Vienna, formed the Austrian Socialist party. The Austrian Socialists called for a set of reforms ranging from welfare legislation for workers to universal male suffrage. Revolutionary appeals were tempered by practical demands. During its first years the party displayed remarkable growth and an impressive discipline. The massive but orderly demonstration that filled the streets of Vienna on May 1, 1890, and frightened the wealthy Viennese revealed the potential strength of this movement. Yet the Socialists soon faced the same nationalist dilemmas that confronted other Austrian politicians. The Austrian Socialists believed that a sense of loyalty among the working classes would transcend national differences. Thus socialism would be a kind of cement for the empire. The appeal of class solidarity was not always successful, however: the Socialist congresses of the Austrian party were marked by sharp disagreements and quarrels between the German and Czech members, and Adler constantly struggled to maintain the unity of the movement. Still, socialism became a dynamic force in Austrian politics. The party's consistent demand for universal male suffrage influenced the government's decision to grant this concession in 1907.

The other major political movement with a broad mass appeal was the Christian Socialist party. This party also claimed an allegiance, based on religious affiliation, that cut across national lines, although its strongest appeal was to the Catholic German-speaking population of Austria. At first the Catholic hierarchy showed little enthusiasm for the Christian Socialist party, for they were alarmed by the anti-capitalist aspect of its doctrine. This attitude changed as Christian Socialists won support among the lower middle classes of Vienna and among the peasantry. The clergy, in fact, became an active force in recruiting followers in the Austrian countryside.

The Christian Socialists deplored the secularizing aspects of nineteenth century liberalism and attacked doctrines of individualism as detrimental to moral order. They looked on modern capitalism as an evil that drove many toward poverty and degradation. The role of the state was to protect the poor through welfare measures and to defend the small businessmen and artisans who found themselves threatened by the competition of large industrial and business combinations.

The Christian Socialist movement made its first impression in the Austrian rural areas, but the party scored its greatest success during the 1890's in Vienna where it capitalized on the grievances of small entrepreneurs. This success can be attributed to the demagogic flair of Karl Lueger, one of the more colorful figures in Austrian politics before the First World War. Lueger won an enthusiastic following among the people of Vienna, much to the annoyance of the city's patriciate. He attacked political corruption in high places and called for parks, public utilities, and other benefits for the citizens of the city.

Anti-Semitism had a part in the appeal of Christian Socialists in Vienna. Jews were accused of having prospered while others suffered during the economic difficulties of the 1880's and early 1890's. Jews had gained positions of influence in Vienna, particularly among the liberal professions, and the lifting of restrictions on the Jews in the early 1880's permitted some degree of assimilation for them. The relative liberality of Austrian laws attracted many Jews from Russia where persecutions had been intensified. The economic strains of the period, the presence of Jews in Austrian finance, business, and professions, and the immigration of eastern Jews fed anti-Semitism among the socially and economically threatened classes of Vienna. The Christian Socialist party exploited this sentiment to the full.

The strength of the Christian Socialist party became apparent with the election of their candidate, Karl Lueger, as mayor of Vienna in 1895. The German Liberal party, which had governed the capital for nearly fifty years, was thereby displaced. Both German Liberals and capitalists feared the triumph of Lueger, an outspoken critic of laissez-faire principles and of big business. Lueger also filled his speeches with attacks on "the foreigner" (an ominously vague label), whose investments in public utilities and control of the wheat market he blamed for the high cost of living in the city. After his election brought a slump to the Viennese stock market, a number of liberals requested that the emperor refuse to confirm his election. New elections were held, but Lueger, who was an extremely persuasive politician, again won. After the fifth election in 1897, Francis-Joseph finally accepted Lueger as mayor of Vienna.

During his tenure in office Lueger carried through his public works programs, and he expressed a foreign policy of staunch support for the German alliance. Indeed, the Christian Socialist party displayed a pronounced strain of German chauvinism, outbidding the German Liberals and equaling the pan-Germans in emotional appeal. But Lueger did nothing to broaden the appeal of his party. Lueger and his followers disliked the Jews, the Slavs, and the Hungarian Magyars. Their attitudes prevented the Christian Socialists from transcending the ethnic groupings within the empire to become a truly imperial party.

Further Attempts at Conciliation

Austrian politics began to be redefined in the 1890's as a result of the appearance of the Socialist and Christian Socialist parties, but the old issue of the Czech-German quarrel remained. The mass parties added a new dimension to the dispute. In the absence of any other alternative to continued disorders born of irreconcilable hatreds, Taaffe's successors were driven to consider the same expedient he did—universal male suffrage. In doing so, they could count on assistance from the socialists. In October, 1894, a giant workers' rally in Vienna was called for the purpose of demanding universal suffrage. Victor Adler threatened a general strike unless a truly democratic suffrage were granted, but the government refused to yield at this time. Instead, another effort at conciliation was attempted.

In 1897 the government decreed that beginning in 1901 officials at all levels in Bohemia and Moravia would be required to know both Czech and German. This decree was an obvious concession to the Czechs, most of whom were bilingual; they would have an advantage over the Germans, few of whom understood Czech. Once more parliament descended into chaos; on this occasion the German Liberals tried to block the language decrees by obstructionist tactics. Again the ink stands flew, fisticuffs erupted, and the air was punctuated with the sounds of whistles and trumpets, one of the latter sounded by a professor at the University of Vienna who had a seat in parliament. Controversy over the language decree went beyond the halls of parliament, for nationalist passions were unleashed throughout Austria.

Because civil war between Czechs and Germans appeared entirely possible, Francis-Joseph ruled by emergency decree until 1905, when he was finally forced by the continuing demands of the Czechs, Social Democrats, and Christian Socialists to abolish the restrictive curia in favor of a broad franchise. Apparently frightened by the Russian revolution of 1905, he hoped to avoid a similar experience by making an expedient concession. At the same time he expected, as had Taaffe, that the votes of Austria's masses would offset the particularist nationalisms. The elections of 1907, when universal male suffrage finally went into effect, did see a loss of strength for German extremists and the militant young Czechs. But the Liberals also continued their decline. The two parties with notable gains were the Socialists and the Christian Socialists, the latter having the largest bloc in the Austrian parliament. Had the two mass parties combined they would have controlled parliament between them, but cooperation was unthinkable. Their mutual dislike was too well established.

Diversity continued to prevail; no methods of remedying the situation seemed to work. German liberalism had failed, and Taaffe's system of concessions had failed. Now universal male suffrage had failed, for a government majority could not be found in a political assembly that mirrored the empire's fragmented image. Emergency powers were again resorted to for running the government. Projects for a reform of Austria and the empire were launched in an atmosphere of pessimism. The aging Francis-Joseph became a symbol for a fragile system, and many predicted that his death would bring the empire's disintegration.

Magyar Supremacy in Hungary

The contests for political influence in Hungary occurred within the ranks of a limited, Magyar elite. Although the Magyars represented slightly less than half the population of Hungary, a system of gerrymandered districts combined with a restricted franchise assured the Magyar landowners control of parliament. The most fertile black-soil districts of the predominantly rural country, representing about half of all the agricultural land, were in the hands of approximately two thousand Magyar families. Some of these latifundia were among the largest in Europe, and they provided the economic base for the country's political leadership.

But this concentration of landownership was also the source of a great land hunger that affected the peasantry, the bulk of which was without political influence. About ten million peasants were landless or possessed holdings that provided an insufficient livelihood. Their survival depended on the employment available on the large estates. Population pressures forced many to emigrate to America. Beneath the veneer of elite Magyar dominance a rising social and political conflict between landlord and peasant was taking shape at the turn of the century.

During the 1890's the Magyars were also facing difficulties arising from their own version of the nationalist passion that was sweeping through the empire. A significant element of the ruling Magyars nursed grievances over their connection with Austria; they recalled the brief period of Hungarian independence that the state had enjoyed during the revolutions of 1848–49, and they looked back fondly on the days when Hungary had dominated the lower Danube. The intense nationalism of the Magyars also represented a response to the growing disaffection of the other national groups within Hungary at the end of the ninteenth century. These groups wanted to share political power in Hungary, but the Magyars were determined that they should not.

Magyar supremacy was absolute in Hungary's political structure. According to the Magyar electoral law of 1874 only about 6 percent of the male population was eligible to vote. Other national minorities had representation but not in proportion to their population. In Transylvania, for example, some 5,000 Magyars elected twelve delegates to parliament while an equal number of Rumanians elected only one delegate. Furthermore, there was no secret ballot. Voting was conducted by declaration, and the Magyars who presided over electoral boards were in a strategic position to intimidate voters. In addition to thoroughly controlling the parliament, the Magyars provided the ministers that dominated the administration. National minorities were heard, but their views were drowned amid a heavy Magyar chorus.

The ruling Magyar elite replied to the nationalist claims of the Croats, the Serbs, the Rumanians, and the Slovaks by engaging in a kind of internal colonialization—or "Magyarization"—of these groups. Magyar language, history, and customs were imposed on the rest of the population through the educational system, even though this policy technically violated the agreement made in 1867 recognizing the rights of all groups living under Magyar rule. The Magyar language was used for all official business within the Hungarian half of the empire, and any deviation from strict Magyar customs was quickly suppressed. Instead of inducing tranquillity, "Magyarization" only excited hatred of the Magyars and intensified nationalism among the non-Magyar groups. The super-heated and ill-considered nationalism among certain elements of the Magyar elite that resulted from the struggle with the Slavs ultimately provoked a crisis within the dual monarchy.

Consequences of Magyar Nationalism

During the 1880's Hungary was under the political direction of Prime Minister Coloman Tisza, a man who ruled firmly and tried to encourage the economic prosperity of his homeland. Under his guidance Hungary began a policy of railway construction sponsored by the state. Much of this construction was in the interests of Magyar landowners, for it provided them with transportation for their grain to the Austrian market. Politically, Tisza was a moderate—at least within the context of Hungarian politics. The Liberal party that he headed was less a party in the modern sense than a faction loyal to him; "parties" in Hungary tended to be groups that rallied behind political families.

Tisza was a loyal supporter of the dual monarchy because he realized that dualism guaranteed Magyar supremacy; he therefore opposed any alteration of the Compromise of 1867. Although he promoted Magyarization and seemingly held the keys to political power in Hungary, toward the end of his rule Tisza encountered hostility from an ardent group of Magyar patriots who disliked his strict adherence to the spirit of dualism. These opponents rallied behind the scion of a rival political family, Francis Kossuth, whose father, Louis, had led the Hungarian independence movement in 1848. The elder Kossuth had gone into exile after the failure of the revolution and became a living symbol for those who desired full separation from Austria. His death in 1894 occasioned a massive procession in Budapest that led to clashes between nationalists and the police.

Francis Kossuth invoked his late father's name and the nationalist sentiments that it aroused to gain leadership of the independence movement. In the 1890's this group demanded as the first step toward full separation an end to Hungary's economic ties with Austria. Seizing every opportunity to demand separation, the impulsive Francis Kossuth began making a series of inflammatory speeches at banquets in Budapest and throughout the countryside. The movement reached a climax at the turn of the century when the Kossuthists insisted that Magyar replace German as the language of command among Hungarian regiments in the imperial army. Compliance with this demand would have weakened the army as an element of imperial unity and would have elicited similar requests from other national groups. Francis-Joseph's military advisors were appalled at the consequences that might result, and the emperor himself resented this intrusion into military affairs, which he regarded as his personal sphere. His refusal of the demand touched off an intense dispute between Hungarian nationalists and the crown.

Caught in the middle of this quarrel was Stephen Tisza, the eldest son and political heir of Coloman, who was called on to find a compromise that would satisfy some of the Magyar nationalists yet avoid a break with the emperor. He was able to obtain some concessions from the emperor; the Hungarian colors could be shown alongside the imperial standard and in certain correspondence the Magyar language could be used. But these reforms fell short of the nationalists' desires. The emperor refused to concede more, and Tisza had no interest in challenging him. Tisza believed that independence from Austria would be merely a prelude to either the breakup of Hungary or an invasion by a greater power.

Tisza's warnings appeared as no more than an apology for imperial rule in the eyes of militant Magyar nationalists. In 1904 the Hungarian parliament became the scene of violent disturbances directed against Tisza's government; they culminated in a destruction of furniture that made a shambles of the assembly hall and of orderly political discourse. Tisza dissolved the parliament. In the elections of 1905 Kossuth's Independence party led a coalition of anti-Tisza parties to victory. The Hungarian parliament increased their demands for independence when, later in the year, Norway's separation from Sweden provided the Kossuthists with an example. Meanwhile, normal government ground to a halt as towns and counties refused to pay royal taxes and declined to send recruits to the imperial army.

The Magyar dissidents represented a minor proportion of the Hungarian population—at best a vocal faction within the Magyar elite. The bulk of the population, although perhaps harboring few positive sentiments concerning the emperor and the dual monarchy, was not involved in this parliamentary squabble. The socialists, for example, claimed that the independence movement was merely a smoke screen intended to obscure the real social and economic problems of the workers and peasants. Nevertheless, the movement was sufficiently strong to cause alarm in Vienna. In order to restore the Magyars to their senses, Francis-Joseph threatened to introduce universal male suffrage into the Hungarian half of the realm. This reform would have seriously jeopardized both the Magyar dominance and their nationalist dreams. Chastened, the Kossuthists played down their independence propaganda and devoted their energies to blocking any meaningful suffrage reform. They accepted a token liberalization of voting laws that in no way threatened Magyar dominance. The Magyars, including the more ardent nationalists, recognized that any change in the existing arrangement would be to their own disadvantage. Nationalism was a two-edged sword for the Magyars, and for their own safety this weapon had to be sheathed.

The Hungarian impasse was typical of the political dilemma of Austria-Hungary. Few were satisfied with the empire's political structure, but few could see any change that would not have extensive disruptive consequences. The result was a stalemate, as political conflicts within the empire created a balanced state of tension. It was agreed that this balance was fragile, and any rash move would upset the equilibrium. Meanwhile, the cultural life of Vienna assumed a gaiety that seemingly belied the realities of imperial discord. Viennese coffee houses were filled with intelligent, charming people who seemed determined to enjoy themselves. They were living for the moment, for no one was certain how much longer the splendor of the Hapsburg empire would last. The dilemma of the empire was deplorable and insoluble but accepted as a fact of life. Inertia, made charming by an insouciance among the comfortable classes of the capitals, sustained the empire.

Russia Between Reform and Revolution

Of all the European states Russia had the fewest checks on the arbitrary exercise of royal authority at the end of the nineteenth century. Like Austria-Hungary, Russia was a dynastic state in an era in which nationalism and political liberalism were dynamic forces. Yet the Russian Czar governed without limitations beyond the cumbersome nature of his own bureaucracy. In many ways Russian institutions reflected the military demands that had long been part of Russian history. An absolute monarchy was an effective way of enforcing discipline in time of emergency, while the nobility supplied military or diplomatic service to the state. The Czar was far more powerful than the German emperor, for example; that he was not as dangerous, or appeared less awesome to the outside world, was a reflection of Russian economic backwardness and relative military weakness near the end of the nineteenth century.

The Russian state had been an expansionist power for several centuries. Forced to defend itself against a wide variety of enemies, including Mongols, Turks, Swedes, Lithuanians, and French, the state had nonetheless, and despite periodic reverses, pushed its borders toward the east, south, and west. By the eighteenth century Russia had emerged as a great European power, with wide holdings in eastern Europe. Russia's influence in Europe did not correspond to the size of its population or territory, for czarist absolutism had limits as an effective system; it could not adapt to changing conditions nor fulfill the potential of the state. The very size of the governing task and the inefficiency of the Czar's police made pure absolutism impossible. But as long as the bulk of the population accepted traditional ways, czarist rule seemed in little danger. In the nineteenth century, however, a series of external events joined with domestic crises provoked changes that ultimately transformed the state in a radical fashion.

First Reform Attempts: Emancipation of the Serfs, 1861

When Russia was defeated in 1854 by Britain and France in the Crimean War, Russia's status as a great power seemed threatened. The war had exposed Russia's military weakness. Advisors around the new Czar, Alexander II, argued that certain reforms were necessary if Russia were to catch up and compete with the states of western Europe. This consideration, rather than a deep-seated humanitarian concern, inspired the emancipation of the serfs in 1861. Because serf labor was inefficient, reformers argued that the institution acted as a drag on Russian society and inhibited realization of Russia's true potential. The liberation proclamation was designed to prepare the way for a greater strengthening of the state through social changes. Moreover, the dislocations caused by the Crimean War had produced peasant unrest, and liberation was seen as one possible way of forestalling more extensive disturbances.

The Russian state showed that it was aware of the danger of revolutionary upheaval that might arise as a domestic repercussion of an unsuccessful war. Alexander II believed that his reform would avert the greater danger of revolution. But the liberation of the serfs itself posed a threat to the old order to an extent that could not be accurately gauged then. From the start it created a new problem in the Russian empire: could changes be introduced into one sector of society without producing repercussions at all levels? Emancipation prepared the way for the economic modernization of the country, but it also disturbed the social, economic, and political equilibrium of the state. The social and economic changes that followed emancipation brought with them increasing political tension.

The full impact of emancipation was not felt for a generation, and in its early stages the liberation of the serfs did little to relieve the grievances and discontent of the peasantry. Serfs were to receive land from former masters in exchange for redemption payments, but often the nobles placed inordinately high prices on small plots of land. While payments were being made, the Russian peasant frequently continued to fulfill many of the old obligations owed his former master. Under these circumstances few peasants succeeded in truly liberating themselves. Moreover, the emancipation did not represent a general program that affected the entire Russian peasantry, for even before 1861 more than half the Russian peasants were technically outside the restrictions of serfdom.

Emancipation did not solve the problem of Russia's low agricultural production, which resulted in large measure from an inefficient land usage. Rather than passing into the hands of individual peasants, much of the land after 1861 was placed under the control of peasant communes or *mir*. The land was owned collectively but several plots were assigned to each family within the commune for cultivation. This practice of parceling out the land prevented any one family from monopolizing the best soil, but it created a highly fragmented and inefficient use of the land. In addition, the communes often perpetuated older, outmoded agricultural practices, use of the three-field system, for example, meant that one-third of all land was fallow at a given time. Communal leadership tended to resist modern innovations so that the yield from Russian farms remained much lower per acre than from modernized farms in central and western Europe.

The continuing poverty of most of Russia's population was compounded by the tremendous growth of population in Russia—from approximately sixty-three million to over ninety-two million inhabitants between 1867 and 1897. Pressure on the land increased, and, unhappily, productivity of agriculture failed to match the proliferation of the masses. Famines, which had disappeared in most of Europe, occurred in several regions of Russia during the last decades of the nineteenth century. Although rural conditions failed to show improvement, the Russian peasantry was not yet prepared for revolution. Hostility toward the landholding gentry, often accused of undermining the Czar's generous intentions, simmered through the 1870's and 1880's. The gentry also felt oppressed by economic hardship. Declining agricultural prices reduced profits for all except a few landholders who had converted to commercial farming and were able to export grain to western Europe. Many noblemen fell into debt; bankruptcy became common, and estates changed hands at a high rate. The amount of land held by the nobility declined during the last third of the nineteenth century so that in 1905 it is estimated that the nobility possessed only about one-fifth of all the land in Russia. The remainder was owned by the crown, the communes, some individual small farmers, and speculators and entrepreneurs who bought up bankrupt estates. The "cherry-orchard syndrome" was not rare by any means. But this shift in landholding did not bring a corresponding increase in productivity. Russia continued to lag behind the rest of Europe, and the country seemed caught in a descending spiral of rural impoverishment.

Some relief from rural overpopulation might have been possible if employment had been available in the cities, but here too Russia trailed the industrial states of western Europe. Methods and industrial equipment were primitive, and the country lacked ready capital to stimulate modernization. Intervention by the state appeared necessary to encourage industrial growth. The state did favor investment and the use of foreign capital, particularly in the construction of a railway network. Some 13,000 miles of rail lines were built between 1860 and 1880, yet this constituted only the very beginning of a modern transportation system. Generally, the agricultural and industrial policies of Alexander's era were simply the first steps on the path toward modernization.

Challenges to the State

In the realm of politics some efforts were made to liberalize the regime. In the 1860's, for example, Alexander permitted the election of provincial district councils (*zemstva*) that had some authority in such areas as education, transportation, and famine relief. Despite their carefully limited powers, these councils were considered by Russian liberals as an important step toward a measure of self-government outside the Czar's bureaucracy. The more progressive zemstva became centers of liberal opinion among the nobility; occasionally they even offered mild criticism of government policy. The peasantry elected representatives to the councils, but the meetings were dominated by the provincial landowners. Thus the zemstva provided at best a restricted outlet for political opinion.

A much more basic challenge to the political methods of czarist rule appeared in the 1860's and 1870's among intellectuals who sought not to reform but to destroy the old order and subsequently to construct a new social and economic system. A number of movements and doctrines emerged, and their adherents were pursued by the police. Among the more aggressive of these groups were the early populists, who argued that the basis for a new society in Russia could be found in the communal traditions of the Russian peasantry. In the summer of 1874 a number of young students, who embraced the ideas of Bakunin, actually "went to the people" preaching revolutionary doctrines. The peasantry proved unreceptive to such notions and, much to the dismay of the populists, distrusted the students' motives to the extent that they frequently turned them over to the authorities. The populist movement foundered on peasant suspicion, government repression, and its own internal disagreements. But it revealed evidence of continuing dissatisfaction with the government on the part of younger radicals, many of whom remained convinced that compromise with the existing order was impossible.

After the failure of "going to the people" many populists turned to direct action as a way to shock the government into recognizing the plight of its people and possibly touch off a surge of revolutionary sympathy. A number of anarchists joined the disparate revolutionary groups and in the late 1870's commenced a campaign of attacks on government officials. One of the most determined of the revolutionary societies was the "People's Will"; its ultimate objective was the assassination of Czar Alexander II. After narrowly escaping death in 1880, the Czar was killed the following year by a bomb explosion.

Instead of inspiring an uprising, this act only led to intensified government repression. Under the guidance of Konstantin Pobedonostsev, a man of thoroughly reactionary opinions and lay head of the Orthodox church, Alexander III inaugurated his reign with a suppression of all groups and organizations suspected of subversive tendencies. In the 1880's revolutionaries were hunted down and revolutionary societies were suppressed. Universities were closed; the press was censored; and opposition to the Czar, whether revolutionary, liberal, or even mildly reformist, went underground. For many the only escape was exile. The revolutionaries became discouraged in those years, for the exiles bickered among themselves and despaired of any chance to act while the zemstva movement lapsed into docility. No one around the Czar dared suggest concessions or liberal reforms.

Meanwhile the government embraced Slavophile views, which regarded western ideas with unmasked hostility and looked to the union of all Slavic peoples under Russian leadership. As part of this chauvinistic wave, it engaged in a policy of "Russification"; through education and propaganda Russian customs and practices were imposed on non-Russian territories, such as Poland, the Baltic states, and Finland. The government vigorously suppressed local and national tendencies within these regions. This chauvinistic surge was also directed against other "non-Russian" elements, notably the Jews. Limitations on Jewish activities were extended; education for Jews, types of occupation, and locations for Jewish residence were all restricted.

The Ferment of the 1890's

For nearly a decade the reactionary course of Pobedonostsev guided the Czar. There was some effort to assist peasants in purchasing land through a Peasant Bank that was established in 1882. Interest rates remained high, however, and as long as the mir retained its hold on the peasantry, agricultural overpopulation continued to depress rural Russia. Government measures proved inadequate to meet the severe problems of overpopulation and low productivity.

The failure of the government's agricultural program, as well as continued industrial backwardness and military weakness, forced the government to reconsider some of its policies, particularly in the economic sphere. Advisors to Alexander III feared that unless the economy showed a more dynamic growth revolutionary discontent would be furthered and the possibility of revolution would increase. It was hoped that an improvement in Russia's economic structure would strengthen the state against foreign threats as well. No less than his predecessors, Alexander III had to contemplate alternatives with undesirable features; he tried to choose the course that would be least disruptive to the state but that would undercut as much as possible the danger of revolutionary ferment. The government decided to give the economy a new direction by pressing for Russia's industrial development. In adopting this policy the Russian government faced formidable problems, including the need to obtain capital despite the country's lack of financial resources.

I. A. Vishnegradsky, Russia's finance minister, established the pattern of Russian development. He encouraged foreign investment in Russian enterprise by offering favorable terms and selling government bonds abroad. At the same time he raised tariffs to give protection to infant Russian industries. These measures created burdens for the average Russian, since protection entailed higher industrial and agricultural prices. Foreign investment added to the inflation, and the rising prices usually outdistanced salary increases. The reforming ministers were determined to push industrial development at all costs. Even during the great famine of 1891–92, which cost half a million Russian lives, grain was exported to western Europe as a means of obtaining foreign currency credits.

The economic crisis of 1891–92 brought Vishnegradsky's dismissal, but his work was continued by Count Sergei Witte. During the next ten years Witte forced a reluctant country to suffer the pangs of industrialization, but he brought about a spectacular industrial advance. Railway construction, much of it financed by French capital, accelerated. The amount of track put down in the 1890's was twice that of any previous decade. In 1891 construction was started on the trans-Siberian railway. New metallurgical industries, many located in the Donetz basin to the south, partially met the demand for rails and locomotives created by the railway boom. Other industries, particularly textiles and oil, also boomed during the 1890's. The Russian government played a crucial part in encouraging this initial effort to overcome economic backwardness. Many of the railways, for example, were either owned by the government or guaranteed by government bonds. Between 1894 and 1903 approximately two-thirds of the government's expenditure went toward the economic development of the country. The result was that at the turn of the century Russia's rate of economic growth, admittedly beginning from a low base, was the highest in Europe.

Worker Unrest ▪ The industrial process in Russia was accompanied by the same social and economic dislocations that had characterized the industrial revolution in western Europe. As industrialization progressed and communal restrictions on migration relaxed, the rural population began drifting into the cities. First-generation migrants composed perhaps one-half of Russia's industrial labor force in the 1890's. Some migrants could not abandon the customs associated with the village and returned to the commune after brief employment in the new industrial centers. As village ties loosened, however, many of the migrants acquired the attitudes of a working class and joined sporadic, uncoordinated but intense wildcat strikes in protest against the long hours, poor pay, and unhealthy conditions that prevailed in Russian industrial cities during the 1890's. These strikes rarely lasted for more than a few days and were quickly suppressed. Unions sprang up spontaneously, in spite of the fact that the government declared them illegal.

Organizers appeared in factories and working-class districts, often at great risk, to help form strike committees and to urge concerted action against oppressive employers. At first workers sought only immediate improvements in pay and working conditions, but gradually political objectives aiming at a revolutionary overturn of czarist institutions emerged as part of the labor movement. Often the government itself appeared as the oppressive employer, for many workers worked in state-controlled enterprises. Bans against workers' organizations and the government's willingness to use troops in breaking up strikes increased the alienation between the worker and the state. Toward the end of the 1890's revolutionary literature began to attract a wide audience among Russian workers.

The growing sense of common injustice and revolutionary temper were manifested in the St. Petersburg textile strikes of 1896–97. The first strike occurred in May 1896 when workers in certain St. Petersburg textile plants believed that their employers had deprived them of three days' pay during the holidays decreed at the time of the Czar's coronation ceremony. News of their walkouts quickly spread to other textile factories, and within two days the entire textile industry in St. Petersburg was halted by what amounted to a general, industry-wide strike. The movement collapsed after a week because of a lack of strike funds, but the solidarity displayed during the strike impressed workers and employers alike. In January 1897 workers demanding a reduction in working hours declared a second strike. Largely in response to the strike movement, the government made a major concession by lowering the minimum working day from thirteen and a half to eleven and a half hours. During the St. Petersburg strikes a number of revolutionary associations supported the workers, including the Union of Struggle for the Emancipation of the Working Class that had been formed by Lenin and others in 1895. These groups published tracts and supplied messengers to coordinate actions among the workers. Workers' committees also emerged during the strikes to formulate demands and to supply leadership for the movement.

Revolutionary organizations appeared in other industrial centers at the end of the 1890's, and a Bund, or association, of Jewish workers was formed in the mining and manufacturing regions of Poland and western Russia. Deprived of their rights by the Czar's anti-Semitic policies, many Jews turned to revolutionary groups for a redress of grievances. Although numerically weak and constantly harrassed by the police, these movements provided focus for the widespread discontent that swept across Russia. By the turn of the century a proletariat had been forged in Russia: some three million workers were involved in transportation and manufacturing in 1900. Evidence of the growing militancy of this class could be seen in the frequency with which the government had to call in troops to suppress strikes (on 33 occasions in 1900, 271 in 1901, and 522 in 1902). It was to this restive class that the small and often bickering Russian Social Democratic party, formed illegally in 1898, looked for a transformation of the Russian state.

Peasant Unrest ▪ While the Russian working class of the cities expanded with the expansion of industry in the 1890's, the Russian peasantry continued to be faced with a shortage of land and the threat of starvation. The annual consumption of foodstuffs by a Russian peasant continued to be far below that of a western European peasant. Signs of social despair could be detected in the high consumption rates of vodka and other spirits; revenues from the government liquor monopolies provided about one-fourth of all government income in 1903.

Many of the younger generation of peasants adopted revolutionary politics as a way out of miserable conditions. Improvements in literacy and communications permitted this new generation, which had not known serfdom but had abundant experience with rural poverty, to develop a militant political voice. When famine spread again in 1898–99, peasant uprisings broke out in many districts. In the peasant riots of 1901–02 a number of manor houses were put to the torch. Rural discontent provided the basis for a new revolutionary political party, the Socialist Revolutionaries. This group updated the populist notions of a previous generation and saw in the commune a unique foundation for the eventual development of Russia along socialist lines. The Socialist Revolutionaries predicted that the impulse to sweep away the old order would come from the countryside.

Middle-Class Unrest ▪ In the 1890's the relatively small group of Russian middle-class liberals regained the confidence it had had before the repressions of the 1880's. The zemstva movement recovered during this decade and became the major source for a liberal program. Another manifestation of the liberal reform movement was the Kadet, or Constitutional Democratic, party formed—illegally—in 1903. This middle-class group remained aloof from revolutionary movements but it insisted that the Czar grant certain concessions within the existing system. The most important of their demands was for a national assembly representing all of Russia that could debate issues, pass laws, and participate in the formation of foreign and domestic policies. The liberals eventually exploited the opportunity provided by the revolution of 1905 to press for this concession.

The industrialization program pursued by Witte in the 1890's not only produced great strains in Russian society; it also challenged the resources of the government itself. During this decade the Russian consumer market was too weak to provide adequate demand for industrial goods, and, at the same time, there was a shortage of investment capital. Faced with this dilemma the Russian government became both a supplier of capital and a customer, absorbing industrial goods in such projects as the construction of the trans-Siberian railway.

The state debt increased steadily in the decade from 1894 to 1903 as deficit financing became an important means for stimulating industrial growth. But the state finances also required continual infusions of new capital, and this demand tied the economy to Russia's main source of credit, France. In 1898 a series of international crises temporarily disrupted this connection.

The international tensions arising from these events, including the Fashoda crisis, the Spanish-American War, and the Boer War, which broke out in 1899, created an unstable international money market. French credit temporarily disappeared and other sources for loans were not readily available. The lack of foreign capital caused a sharp recession in Russia's economic boom at the turn of the century. This economic crisis was accompanied by extensive strikes and demonstrations against the Czar's government. In the next few years discontent spread to the countryside where peasant uprisings occurred with alarming regularity. Under these circumstances the liberals demanded in 1903 that the Czar convene a national assembly endowed with legislative authority to meet the crisis. Russia found itself in a state of revolutionary ferment.

Domestic agitation placed Witte in a difficult position. He had argued that prudent reforms would prevent disorders of this sort. At Witte's urging the Czar had allowed zemstva representatives to participate in a national conference on rural questions in 1902. The conference appointed some 600 local committees, which reported the conference's findings the following year. In addition to proposals for changes in Russian agriculture, the committees recommended other improvements, including an overhaul of judicial procedures, abolition of corporal punishment for peasants, and the convening of a parliamentary assembly. Even the calling of the conference was regarded by conservatives as a dangerous concession, and the recommendations of the reports shocked them.

Czarist ministers and advisors inflexibly opposed Witte's policies.

Any compromises with the modern world, they claimed, were in themselves revolutionary departures from conservative Russian traditions. In many ways these ministers were right. Perhaps failing to appreciate the full significance of his own reforms, Witte believed that economic modernization under government sponsorship was the only path to power and the only way to save the monarchy from even greater revolutionary conflicts. His opponents insisted that any change would undermine the Czar's authority.

Czar Nicholas II, who acceded to the throne in 1894 on his father's death, agreed with his cautious counselors. A man of limited intelligence, Nicholas II tended to cling to the rights of his office as an inviolable trust; he feared innovations that seemed to be radical deviations from past tradition. Although he recognized Witte's talents and kept him as finance minister, he showed little sympathy or understanding for Witte's reform-minded policy. When unrest spread throughout the country after the turn of the century, Nicholas inclined toward the advice of those who suggested that Witte should be sacrificed and domestic repression be stepped up as the only means for curbing internal disorder. An intensified campaign of anarchist terrorism, which claimed the life of the minister of the interior in 1902, lent weight to the arguments of the reactionaries for stern measures.

Against a background of terrorism, rural uprisings, and industrial strikes, a brief contest developed between Witte and the new minister of the interior, V. K. Plehve, a man devoted to reactionary policies. A series of strikes in southern Russia during the summer of 1903 provided Witte's opponents with the opportunity to point out the failure of his policy of conciliation. Plehve persuaded Nicholas II that Witte should be dismissed. Witte's fall from power opened the way for an era of intense repression under Plehve's guidance. Police attacks on strikers increased. Police spies infiltrated radical political movements, informing on their activities and acting as provocateurs. The police also began harrassing liberal zemstva politicians; the zemstva council in Tver province, considered particularly dangerous, was dismissed at the beginning of 1904. The government revived Russification campaigns in Finland, the Polish districts, and the Caucases to further tighten their control. In Bessarabia a new wave of anti-Semitic outrages took place with official sanction. Jews were regarded as particularly active in subversive movements, and Plehve countenanced attacks on them as measures that provided a salutary "anti-revolutionary counteraction."

War with Japan, 1904–05 ▪ When he realized that agitation against the government was diminishing very little after months of repression, Plehve began to be persuaded that an aggressive foreign policy would silence domestic discontent. At the beginning of 1904 he remarked, "In order to hold back the revolution, we need a small victorious war." In choosing this path he allied himself with the ambitions of men who favored an active Russian policy in the Far East, particularly in northern China and Korea. This group, led by a clique of adventuresome businessmen and army officers who had gained influence with the Czar, looked on Japan's strength in the Far East with dismay. For over a decade Russia and Japan had been on a collision course in that part of the world, because both countries coveted the untapped resources of Manchuria. Japan had taken an important step toward advancing its influence in Manchuria by defeating China in 1895 and gaining virtual control over Korea. One year later Russia pressed the Chinese to agree to the construction of a railway across Manchuria that would shorten the trans-Siberian route to the seaport of Vladivostok by 600 miles, and in 1898 the Russians obtained a lease on an ice-free naval base at Port Arthur, the port for Peking. The Japanese had demanded this port from the Chinese in 1895, but three European powers, including Russia, exerted diplomatic pressure that forced them to abandon the claim at the time. Anti-Russian feelings ran high in Japan, while Russian imperialists considered Japan as their major opponent in the Far East.

The occasion for an open conflict emerged from a joint expedition of European and Japanese troops to Peking in 1900 to relieve the foreign embassies from attacks by the nationalistic Chinese "Boxer" society. After the rebellion had been suppressed the Russians delayed withdrawal of their troops from Manchuria, despite pressures from Japan, the United States, and other powers. Negotiations between Russia and Japan over withdrawal of troops dragged along, since the Russians believed that the Japanese would eventually yield and recognize Russian supremacy in Manchuria. Japan, however, was in a strong position which the Russians underestimated. The Japanese had modernized their army and navy, and in 1902 they had signed an alliance with Great Britain. When conversations with the Russians appeared to have reached an impasse, the Japanese recalled their ambassador to Russia and on February 9, 1904, attacked and severely damaged the Russian fleet at Port Arthur.

This attack was the first of a series of unrelieved military disasters for the Russians. After a ten-month siege the Japanese forced the Russian garrison at Port Arthur to capitulate. Meanwhile, the Japanese pushed north into Manchuria, winning a series of victories over the Russians through superior generalship, military organization, and equipment. In February 1905, one year after the first attack, a land battle was fought in Manchuria at Mukden in which the Japanese army decisively defeated its Russian opponent. Russia's only hope for salvaging something from a disastrous war rested with the archaic Baltic fleet, which had been sent on a fantastic around-the-world voyage from St. Petersburg to the Pacific. This fleet of naval museum pieces arrived in Japanese waters in the spring of 1905 and tried to reach Vladivostok. A modern Japanese navy under the command of Admiral Togo awaited them at the Straits of Tsushima. In two days' fighting all but two ships in the Baltic fleet were either sunk or captured. Exhausted by the struggle, both sides accepted American mediation. The peace treaty ended Russian hopes in Manchuria and confirmed Japan's victory.

Revolution, 1905 ▪ The Russians had to face the domestic consequences of a war that had become highly unpopular. News of Russian defeats exacerbated the revolutionary temper of the country. Strikes broke out in a number of cities, and in St. Petersburg word of Port Arthur's capitulation became the occasion for a massive demonstration in January 1905. A delegation of workers, led by Father Gapon, marched on the Winter Palace to place their grievances before the Czar himself. They were met by a detachment of excited soldiers who fired on the crowd; some one hundred people lost their lives in the ensuing turmoil. "Bloody Sunday," the first major event in the 1905 revolution, served to discredit the Czar in the eyes of the people.

During the spring and summer of 1905 revolutionary disturbances swept across Russia. Several peasant revolts erupted in the Volga and northern black-soil districts. In some of these uprisings land was seized and crops were burned; many peasants refused to pay rent or taxes. By autumn at least one-half of the provinces of western Russia had experienced some form of violence. In certain northwestern districts revolutionary committees of peasants came into being, prepared to assume governing power. Disaffection spread also to the military. In June of 1905 sailors of the battleship Potemkin on the Black Sea mutinied, while along the trans-Siberian railway a number of troops staged brief revolts. A strike of railway workers brought much of the Russian rail network to a standstill. Internal order simply collapsed.

The response of the Czar was hesitant. He appointed a new minister of the interior, who proved ineffective, and he gave General Trepov, a ruthless military leader, dictatorial powers in St. Petersburg. But these gestures failed to turn back the wave of revolution. The assassination of his uncle, Grand Duke Sergei, shocked Nicholas and forced him to realize the seriousness of the situation. Somewhat in panic, he promised that a consultative assembly would be called in the near future. This modest concession lagged far behind the heated temper of the country and was considered inadequate by the moderates. In June delegates from the zemstva and town councils met and urged the Czar to summon a legislative assembly for all of Russia. He indicated a willingness to do so, but the vague tone of his response left even his supporters dissatisfied. Already a more radical and insistent liberalism had appeared with the organization of a League of Unions headed by Paul Miliukov, a highly regarded historian and a pamphleteer for a liberal political system in Russia. This group also called for a constituent assembly empowered to draft a document that would reorganize the state into a constitutional monarchy. By the end of the summer this demand, as well as an extensive program of social reforms, became the basis for pressure on the Czar.

At the end of October workers' councils, or soviets, appeared in St. Petersburg, Moscow, and other cities. They raised a series of political demands of their own and issued calls for strikes against the government. By this time transportation had completely halted; schools were closed; many government offices were shut down; and a number of cities had already been paralyzed by general strikes. A thoroughly frightened Czar turned to Witte for advice. Witte, who had just returned from the peace conference ending the ill-fated Japanese war, was unequivocal in his response: either the Czar must impose a military dictatorship or he must grant the people a constitution. Nicholas yielded and issued a manifesto that promised civil liberties and a Duma with legislative authority. The Duma was to be chosen on the basis of a wide franchise. Witte became prime minister with the task of guiding Russia through the difficult period of transition.

The granting of the October Manifesto marked the climax of the revolution, although revolutionary spirit ran high in the country for the next few weeks as strikes and peasant agitation persisted. The soviets, particularly the St. Petersburg soviet, maintained a strong influence among the working classes. The liberals, many of whom rallied to the Constitutional Democratic party, were heartened by the manifesto but were awaiting fulfillment of the Czar's promises. By the end of the year, however, the revolution saw its momentum deflected. Insistence on exclusively working-class demands by the St. Petersburg soviet, for example, caused a rift between the workers and middle-class liberals. Other moderates proclaimed themselves satisfied with the October Manifesto and lost their revolutionary zeal. Finally, in the fall of 1905 the conservatives recovered their nerve. Bands of reactionary vigilantes roamed the countryside terrorizing the peasants and attacking suspected revolutionaries. Behind them stood a number of ultra-nationalistic organizations that encouraged attacks against "enemies of the state." Ultra-nationalists stimulated anti-Jewish pogroms in several cities, and intellectuals and students suffered abuse and physical violence at their hands.

The authorities overlooked such behavior, and Nicholas gave every indication that he approved of it. Repression was increased as discipline began to be restored to the army. The end of the revolution came in December when a general strike in Moscow led to clashes between workers and police. The fighting turned into a pitched battle that lasted nearly two weeks; it ended only after the army was called in and some thousand dead were left on the streets. The government had triumphed, and the Czar's power, although badly shaken, remained intact as the events of the next few years were to reveal.

The rapid recovery of the conservatives placed Witte in a difficult position. Instead of presiding over a liberal revolution when the Duma convened, Witte found himself faced with the hostility of the conservatives and of Nicholas II, who now regretted the October Manifesto and blamed Witte for advising that it be granted. Before the Duma could meet, the Czar had promulgated a series of fundamental laws that contradicted the spirit of his earlier promises. These laws assured that many of the Czar's prerogatives would remain. They stipulated, for example, that the Czar had authority in declaring war or making peace, that he could dismiss the Duma at will, and that he would appoint all ministers, who therefore would not be responsible to the Duma but to the Czar. On the same day in April 1906 that the fundamental laws were published, Nicholas asked for and received Witte's resignation. Never a popular man, he had been nevertheless one of Nicholas' best ministers. With his resignation it became clear that the revolution had passed. Many celebrated its accomplishments, but whether or not it would lead to a new era depended on the outcome of the contest between Czar and Duma that was already taking shape as the Duma assembled for its first session in May 1906.

Significance of the Revolution ▪ Russia was the only state in Europe that entered the twentieth century with a revolution that produced what appeared to be significant modifications in the nation's political structure. The political changes that had occurred in western Europe represented shifts in the balance of power within existing institutions, and in Germany and Austria-Hungary the effects of new political pressures had not upset the predominance of existing groups or altered their political systems—although in Austria the emperor had been driven to rule almost exclusively by decree. The granting of a

Duma even with the limitations later imposed on it was a major departure from Russian ruling traditions. The revolution also marked the first popular uprising in Europe since the Paris commune of 1871, and, as was the case for the commune, a military defeat supplied the crucial impetus for revolutionary upheaval.

Undoubtedly the accelerated pace of social and economic change throughout Europe intensified political conflict at the turn of the century, but most states appeared to be adjusting, perhaps somewhat awkwardly, to the new conditions. Yet many conservatives throughout Europe shared 'Plehve's fear of revolutionary change or even moderate reform and believed that war would generate patriotic enthusiasm and thereby solidify the existing social order. Perhaps their argument had something to recommend it in the short run. But war was also a gamble, for it could unleash disruptive forces and produce unexpected results; certainly defeat—which no statesman anticipated —carried the risks of discrediting the ruling authority until the existing society stood in danger of disintegration. The lesson of 1905 in Russia was that the political risks of war were great indeed, but this was a lesson that few European statesmen fully grasped.

SUGGESTED READING

Golo Mann's *The History of Germany*, tr. by Marian Jackson (London: Chatto & Windus, 1968) provides a lofty perspective of German history that at once criticizes the shortcomings and recognizes the merits of William II's Germany. Rather critical of the empire is Arthur Rosenberg's *Imperial Germany* (Boston: Beacon Press, 1964), one of the best introductions to the topic. For views of Bismarck as chancellor, there are a number of biographies, including Erich Eyck's *Bismarck and the German Empire* (New York: Macmillan, 1950), A. J. P. Taylor's *Bismarck: the Man and the Statesman* (London: Hamish Hamilton, 1955), and Otto Pflanze's second volume of his Bismarck biography, *Bismarck and the Development of Germany: the Period of Consolidation, 1871–1890* (Princeton: Princeton University Press, forthcoming).

The Wilhelmian era has been subjected to harsh scrutiny. An excellent guide to the military influence in Germany may be found in the appropriate sections of Gordon A. Craig's *Politics of the Prussian Army, 1640–1945* (London: Oxford University Press, 1955). The emperor's impact on his country and on Europe supplies the basis for Michael Balfour's perceptive volume, *The Kaiser and His Times* (Boston: Houghton, Mifflin, 1964). An older critique may be found in Erich Eyck's *Das Personliche Regiment Wilhelms II* (Zurich: Eugen Rentsch, 1948). The problem of finding a locus for political power after Bismarck's fall is the subject of J. C. G. Roll's stimulating *Germany Without Bismarck: the Crisis of Government in the Second Reich, 1890–1900* (Berkeley: University of California Press, 1967). J. Alden Nichols in *Germany After Bismarck: the Caprivi Era, 1890–1894* (Cambridge, Mass.: Harvard University Press, 1958) sympathizes with Caprivi's efforts to cope with the various contending interests and factions of the early 1890's. Eckhardt Kehr in *Schlachtflottenbau und Partei Politik, 1894–1901* (Berlin: E. Ebering; New York: Kraus Reprint, 1930) may be credited with exposing the political alliance of "rye and steel" that emerged in Wilhelmian politics. Another critical view of the politics of economic interest is given by Alexander Gerschenkron in his *Bread and Democracy in Germany* (Berkeley: University of California Press, 1943).

Surveys of Austria-Hungary are less abundant than those of Germany, but they are of a high quality. One of the most reliable is Arthur J. May's *The Hapsburg Monarchy, 1867–1914* (Cambridge, Mass.: Harvard University Press, 1951). More recently, R. A. Macartney has provided a broad, balanced view of the development of the Hapsburg domains in his *The Hapsburg Empire 1790–1918* (London: Macmillan, 1968). Robert A. Kann's *The Multi-National Empire*, 2 vols. (New York: Columbia University Press, 1950) is a detailed survey. An entertaining history is Edward Crankshaw's *The Fall of the House of Hapsburg* (New York: Viking, 1963), and A. J. P. Taylor has passed a harsh judgment on the Hapsburgs and their monarchy in his *Hapsburg Monarchy, 1809–1918* (London: Hamish Hamilton, 1948). Treatments of more specialized topics include Peter Pulzer's *The Rise of Political Anti-Semitism in Germany and Austria* (New York: Wiley & Sons, 1966), and Andrew Whiteside's *Austrian National Socialism before 1918* (The Hague: Martinus Nijhoff, 1962).

Several important studies deal with Russia's social and political development before the Revolution of 1917. Behind each of them is the unanswerable question whether the monarchy might have adapted to changing conditions or was incapable of doing so. Hugh Seton-Watson in *The Decline of Imperial Russia* (New York: Praeger, 1956) tries to strike a balance between pessimism and optimism concerning the demise of the imperial regime. Richard Charques in *The Twilight of Imperial Russia* (London: Oxford University Press, 1958) sees nothing inevitable in the eventual triumph of the Soviets. Although less overtly stated, much the same assumption lies behind Sergei Pushkarev's *The Emergence of Modern Russia, 1801–1917*, tr. by R. H. McNeal and T. Yedlin (New York: Holt, 1963), a valuable survey that treats a wide range of topics and stresses the dynamic aspects of Russian society. In *Russia in Revolution, 1890–1918* (New York: New American Library, 1967), Lionel Kochan treats social and economic trends in depth to emphasize the strains associated with rapid change in Russian society. A revolutionary situation was at hand, Kochan argues, although this did not necessarily point to the Bolshevik triumph. Other views, which also stress change but are not necessarily pessimistic about the outcome, appear in Cyril Black (ed.), *The Transformation of Russian Society* (Cambridge, Mass.: Harvard University Press, 1960). Eight scholars have used recent research in their varying assessments of the late empire in Theofanis Stavrou (ed.), *Russia under the Last Czar* (Minneapolis: University of Minnesota Press, 1969).

In addition to the above general approaches, there are specialized studies of this complex era. Theodore H. von Laue's *Sergei Witte and the Industrialization of Russia* (New York: Columbia University Press, 1963) is the basic work on the reform minister. Von Laue sees both czardom and liberal constitutionalism as incompatible with Russia's rapid economic development; he has developed this thesis in several articles as well as in his *Why Lenin? Why Stalin? A Reappraisal of the Russian Revolution, 1900–1930* (Philadelphia: Lippincott, 1964). Jacob Walkin in *The Rise of Democracy in Pre-Revolutionary Russia* (New York: Praeger, 1962) is much more sanguine about prospects of a liberal political evolution in Russia. A number of studies consider the early growth of Marxism in Russia, including Leopold H. Haimson's *The Russian Marxists and the Origins of Bolshevism* (Cambridge, Mass.: Harvard University Press, 1955), Richard Pipes's *Social Democracy and the St. Petersburg Labor Movement, 1885–1887* (Cambridge, Mass.: Harvard University Press, 1963), and Samuel H. Baron's *Plenkhanov: the Father of Russian Marxism* (Stanford, Calif.: Stanford University Press, 1963).

5

EUROPEAN DIPLOMACY IN TRANSITION, 1890–1907

By the turn of the century it was clear that any war on an international scale would mobilize unprecedented numbers of men and women and touch the lives of nearly every citizen. It is not surprising that in an age tending toward mass politics a popular concern about the fundamental issue of war and peace should emerge. The average male European's life was at some point likely to be affected by this issue, for most of the European major powers and many minor states maintained large standing armies, usually supported by a draft and reserve system. Mass circulation newspapers devoted a significant portion of their space to international questions, particularly during diplomatic crises. The issue of war and peace also received attention from the socialist movement as socialist leaders sought ways of international cooperation to prevent war. They were hopeful that their mass movement was a guarantee for peace. They assumed that the common man was peace-loving and immune to the appeals of chauvinism.

Yet the basic decisions on matters of war and

◀ "Dropping the Pilot," 1890 *Punch* cartoon depicting Bismarck's fall from power.

peace were the responsibility of a limited elite that directed foreign policy in Europe. Although aware of the political pressures exerted by the population-at-large, these men pursued their countries' interests as they interpreted them. Usually the men who composed this elite had basically conservative views, and they looked on diplomacy and the securing of allies as both means for maintaining peace and ways of strengthening the state in the event of war. Diplomats did not seek war, but national interests required constant vigilance and preparation. Above all, they had responsibility for adapting their nations' foreign policies to shifts in the relative material strength of the European states.

In 1890 the basis for the balance of power in Europe—and for the stability of the European state system—was a series of alliances that had been signed as a result of Bismarck's diplomacy. This "Bismarckian system" represented a distinctive attempt to regulate international affairs in Europe during the nineteenth century.

The Development of the Bismarckian System

During the first half of the nineteenth century the statesmen of Europe believed that revolution led to wars of conquest; at least this was the lesson the conservative powers—Russia, Austria, and Prussia—learned from the struggles against Napoleon that finally ended in 1815. The underlying assumption of European diplomacy during the next forty years was that peace could be maintained by preserving the status quo as it had been fixed by the Congress of Vienna in 1815, and any revolutionary impulses had to be contained through cooperation among the great European powers. At first these powers established a formal "concert" with regular meetings to discuss international issues and to assure that the status quo was maintained. This formal concert broke down in the 1820's when Great Britain, objecting to the conservative powers' ideological interpretation of the concert's function, refused to support intervention in the internal affairs of another state. But European interest in maintaining peace through international cooperation lasted on an informal basis until 1854. On at least two occasions the informal concert prevented revolution from leading to a general European war. In 1830 the powers cooperated to contain the revolutionary fervor that had appeared in France and had led to the formation of an independent state in Belgium. The insurrections of 1848 throughout Europe again brought the European powers into an informal alliance to check the spread of revolutionary sentiment;

Russia even went to the aid of Austria in helping to suppress the Hungarian uprising.

The outbreak of the Crimean War in 1854 brought Russia, Britain, and France into conflict and shattered the informal concert. Between the Crimean War of 1854–56 and 1871 no less than five wars erupted on the continent, including the wars fought for the unification of Germany and Italy. After this rash of warfare a return to the confident era of the European concert seemed difficult if not impossible. One further attempt was made, however, to use a European concert for the prevention of general European conflict. The concert was called when a Russian victory in southeastern Europe grew to have international implications.

In 1878 Russia defeated Turkey after an unexpectedly difficult campaign. The Treaty of San Stefano, which the Russians imposed, represented a triumph for Russian ambitions and, more particularly, a success for the pan-Slavists who fancied themselves the protectors of their Slav brothers in southeastern Europe. A large Bulgarian state was created out of former Turkish territory in the Balkans. The treaty greatly increased Russian influence in southeastern Europe, but it had been drawn with little concern for the reaction of other European powers, who in fact were annoyed at Russia's success. Diplomats in Vienna spoke of war with Russia and Great Britain sent its fleet into the straits to protect the Turks and Constantinople from further Russian menace. As Europe was veering toward conflict, Bismarck reluctantly assumed the role of mediator.

Bismarck had little desire to become involved in Balkan quarrels which, as he put it, were not worth the bones of a Pomeranian grenadier. The Balkans were particularly troublesome to him since he did not want to commit Germany to supporting either Russia or Austria-Hungary in southeastern Europe, and he made every effort to escape taking a hand in the conflict. But he realized that an international war might have dangerous repercussions within the recently formed German empire. It might stimulate separatism and resentment at Prussian domination, which were still very much alive in Germany. Therefore he intervened in the dispute by suggesting that the powers meet in Berlin to resolve the problems arising from the eastern conflict. Given Bismarck's talents and Germany's powerful position in Europe, it was perhaps unavoidable that the German chancellor should undertake such a crucial role in European diplomacy.

The Berlin Congress of 1878 was at once a success and a disappointment. War between Russia, Britain, and Austria-Hungary was prevented, and an uneasy balance of influence in southeastern Europe was retained. But when the Russians left Berlin they were bitterly disillusioned. They had been forced to give up many of the spoils that they had forced out of the Ottomans; at the same time they saw their rival in the Balkans, Austria-Hungary, secure administrative control over the Turkish provinces of Bosnia and Herzegovina. Moreover, the Congress did little to resolve the question of Balkan nationalism; resentment simmered, particularly in Serbia where nationalists dreamed of a greater Serbia that would include Bosnia-Herzegovina.

The Dual Alliance

The resentment stirred by the Berlin Congress convinced Bismarck that he had to continue taking an active role in maintaining Europe's equilibrium. He feared that a hostile coalition might be formed against Germany because of his part in presiding over the congress. In his later years he claimed to have nightmares on the subject. In order to place Germany in an advantageous position, he decided to build the country's diplomatic strength on the foundation of a solid alliance in central Europe, for which purpose he turned to Austria. In October 1879 an agreement was reached whereby each state pledged to aid the other if attacked by a third power. In embarking on this alliance Bismarck believed that he had found a more realistic approach to international peace than could be found in vague talk about a European concert. For Bismarck "Europe" was only a "geographical expression." The Dual Alliance became the first step in the construction of Bismarck's system; by the time he was through, he had brought most of the major powers into some connection with Berlin. The exceptions were France and Britain, but Bismarck counted on Anglo-French imperial rivalry to keep them from forming a mutual alliance.

Critics of Bismarck's diplomacy have pointed out that his practice of making military commitments during peacetime only made the European state system more rigid. Such obligations became part of subsequent treaties signed between other powers; with a military commitment in writing, it became difficult to back out of an alliance. But it must also be recognized that Bismarck's system was less "systematic" than it appears in retrospect. He had certain general aims that he pursued consistently—for example, he was sincerely concerned about preserving peace, and he wanted to keep France isolated —although he carried out his general policies by seizing whatever opportunities were at hand. Moving from one situation to the next, he succeeded in building a complex diplomatic network.

Evidence of Bismarck's pragmatic approach could be seen in the next alliance he formed—with Russia. Fearing that the Austrian-German alliance might harm their interests in southeastern Europe, the Russian statesmen decided to come to terms with Bismarck. The Russian ambassador in Berlin formally proposed an agreement between Germany and Russia in January 1880. Bismarck suggested that Austria be included in the arrangement and argued for a revival of the "Three Emperors' League," which had first appeared in 1873 but had fallen by the wayside during the Russo-Turkish War. At first the Austrians resisted joining an alliance with their Balkan rival, but they finally signed the treaty in 1881. Under its terms any two of the signatories would remain neutral if the third state were attacked by an outside power.

The Three Emperors' League offered Russia a Balkan détente, but it also confirmed Austria's recent gains in Bosnia and Herzegovina. Implied, but not specified, in the agreement was a division of the Balkan peninsula into spheres of influence, with Russia dominant in the east and Austria in the west. Germany profited from the arrangement. Technically, Germany was still committed to support Austria in the event of a Russian attack, but Bismarck calculated that the Russians would have the sense to avoid war against both Germany and Austria. On the other hand, Germany was not required to support any unprovoked Austrian aggression. Thus the two agreements—the Dual Alliance and the Three Emperors' League—made Germany the key element in a triangular arrangement. As long as Germany was an "indispensable third," Bismarck could keep Austria and Russia in check.

Completion of the System

By 1881 the foundation of the Bismarckian system had been laid, and in the next six years a superstructure was added. In 1882 Italy joined Germany and Austria in a triple alliance. The Italians were driven to this agreement by the French occupation of Tunisia in 1881; Italy had had designs of its own on Tunisia because of the great number of Italians living there. Without allies, Italy could do little to dislodge the French from their newly acquired protectorate across the Mediterranean. When Italians turned to Bismarck, he informed them that the road to Berlin ran through Vienna—German friendship could not be obtained without including Austria. Thus the Italian government found that the price for an alliance was a reduction of their claims on Italian-speaking portions of the Austro-Hungarian empire. The price was paid; the Italians had a guarantee of protection against a French attack and no longer found themselves in diplomatic isolation. For the Austrians and Germans, Italy was now neutralized.

The final additions to this complex set of relationships came in 1887. In the first half of that year a series of "Mediterranean agreements" were signed among Italy, Austria-Hungary, Spain, and Great Britain. Couched in very general terms, these agreements pledged the signatories to a preservation of the status quo in the Mediterranean. Bismarck gave his blessing to the Mediterranean accords because they conveniently warned Russia against pressing into the eastern Mediterranean and at the same time drew Britain into a connection with continental powers. Bismarck did not, however, *sign* the agreements because he was unwilling to compromise Germany's position vis-à-vis Russia, which was somewhat precarious at that time.

The Three Emperors' League had fallen apart over a Balkan quarrel occasioned by Bulgarian rulers who had decided to escape Russia's tutelage. In 1885 Bulgaria and Serbia had gone to war, and for a while it appeared as if Russia and Austria might come to blows over the Balkans. Although the Bulgarian crisis was eventually settled peacefully, the Three Emperors' League was a major casualty. In the aftermath Bismarck sought desperately to keep the Russians from turning to France for diplomatic aid. His solution was to offer the Russian government a reinsurance treaty. By the terms of this agreement each state would promise neutrality if the other were attacked by a third power. The neutrality provision did not apply in case of a "war of aggression" against either France or Austria-Hungary. The reinsurance treaty raised obvious problems in the event of a Russian-Austrian war, but Germany had the option of deciding who was the aggressor and acting accordingly. After some debate, the Russian government signed the treaty in June 1887.

The reinsurance treaty completed Bismarck's system. A diplomatic web had been stretched across Europe with its center in Berlin. Directly or indirectly Germany had a part in all the international agreements signed since 1879. The most salient feature of the system was the diplomatic isolation of France. As long as France could not find allies, the possibility of a war of revenge against Germany could be discounted; the German army was simply too powerful. Even if France reached an agreement with Britain, there was no immediate threat to Bismarck's system, for the British army was small, much of it committed to the empire, and the British navy, as Bismarck noted, could not reach Berlin. In any event, Lord Salisbury's government was more favorably disposed toward Germany than toward France at the end of the 1880's

Bismarck's system was imperiled in eastern Europe by the Austro-Russian rivalry, which troubled the German foreign office. War over the Balkans was precisely what the system sought to prevent. The crucial element in this area was Germany's assessment of aggression. In any crisis, a German warning would be sufficient to impose restraint, for it was unlikely that either Austria or Russia would go to war without assurance of either German support or neutrality. The arrangement was a delicate one and required constant attention, but as long as German policy restrained Austria and Russia, the system was able to preserve peace in the troubled Balkans.

Whether or not peace in Europe resulted from the static tension engendered by the Bismarckian alliances is a question that cannot be answered decisively. Certainly Bismarck had devised a novel international system that was neither a return to a classic balance of power nor a restoration of the European concert. It was a system that was conceived within a European framework in which Germany, by reason of its geographical position and growing material resources, had a central role, shaped by Bismarck's concern for peace in Europe. Bismarck's perspective was fundamentally that of a Prussian nobleman. He had gone about the task of shaping the German empire in a way that would preserve the essential features of Prussia, and his diplomacy was guided by a belief that peace in Europe would assure the survival of the German empire and those Prussian elements embodied within it. At any event, his diplomatic system offered some stability to the European states before 1890. After Bismarck's retirement that year, his system was to be radically altered.

The Collapse of the Bismarckian System

The process of unraveling Bismarck's legacy began within weeks of his departure from the German chancellery and the foreign office. Enemies that he had made in the German foreign office by his dictatorial ways saw an opportunity to strike out on an independent course. One means of asserting this independence was to reject the reinsurance treaty that was due to be renewed in 1890. This course was favored by Baron Friedrich von Holstein, an important figure in the foreign ministry who had a deep distrust for Russia and had chafed under Bismarck's tutelage. Historians in the 1930's and 1940's blamed Holstein for all that went astray in German foreign policy after Bismarck's fall. Recent studies have corrected this exaggerated view, but it is still evident that in the rejection of the reinsurance treaty Holstein's role was significant. He argued that Germany's alliances with Austria and Russia were incompatible. The new chancellor, Caprivi, and the new foreign minister, Marschall, accepted Holstein's assessment. They persuaded William II, despite his sentimental fondness for Russia, to drop the reinsurance treaty.

When Russian negotiators arrived in Berlin, they were told that although Germany retained its friendship for Russia it could not renew the treaty. This news stunned the delegation, and the Russian foreign minister Nicholas Giers tried unsuccessfully to make some sort of agreement with Germany. A decade of Bismarckian diplomacy had accustomed diplomats to having friends in writing; Giers, who was pro-German, feared that Russia would be isolated. The German foreign office refused to heed his pleas.

The Franco-Russian Alliance

The lapse of the reinsurance treaty prepared the way for Bismarck's nightmare, a Franco-Russian alliance. An alliance between these two states was not a simple affair, however, for both sides had reservations. The Czar balked at an association with an unstable republic, and republican politicians, although delighted to escape twenty years of diplomatic isolation, had their own distaste for reactionary czardom.

A period of preliminary conversation and cautious negotiation preceded the final signing of the alliance. In 1890 General Boisdeffre, chief of the French general staff, attended Russian military maneuvers, and the following year the French fleet stopped at Krondstadt, the Russian port on the Baltic. These military visits led to an accord signed in 1891, whereby the two governments pledged mutual consultation on all questions that might threaten European peace. In 1892 this connection was further strengthened when Boisdeffre signed a formal military convention that committed both states to mobilization if either were attacked by a member of the Triple Alliance—Germany, Austria-Hungary, or Italy. The agreement was to last as long as the Triple Alliance was in effect. Final ratification of the alliance was delayed when the Panama scandal in France rekindled the Czar's belief in the Third Republic's instability, but a visit of the Russian fleet to Toulon in 1893 was taken as a sign that such ideological concerns would not obstruct diplomacy. In January 1894 the accord was finally ratified.

The German government did not display undue alarm at the prospect of a Franco-Russian alliance. Britain remained outside any strong European connection. Moreover, British policy appeared more favorably disposed toward the Triple Alliance than toward Russia and France, Britain's traditional rivals. Britain continually found France in the way in Africa and Asia, and Anglo-Russian rivalry at Constantinople, in the Near East, and on the borders of India was long standing. Germany, by contrast, presented no obstacles to British interests overseas; instead, the two countries had reached an agreement in the summer of 1890 whereby Britain gave Germany Heligoland, an island off Germany's northern coast that had been acquired during the Napoleonic wars, in exchange for a reduction of German claims in eastern Africa. There was even talk of an Anglo-German alliance. Meanwhile, Germany, still dominating the Triple Alliance that stretched across central Europe, assumed that it was in a strong position diplomatically.

The Franco-Russian cooperation did create problems for German military planners however. In 1892 General Schlieffen became chief of the German general staff at the moment when the Franco-Russian military convention was about to be signed. Because this accord confronted the German army with the prospect of a two-front war, Schlieffen immediately turned his attention to preparing a strategy that would be able to meet this threat. Schlieffen's plan called for a rapid mobilization and an attack against France that was to come through the Vosges and overwhelm the French army assembled along the border. The Germans would then take advantage of their superior rail network to reassemble in the east and defeat the Russian forces, which were presumed to be slow in mobilizing. An important variation of this plan, calling for a rapid attack against France across Belgium rather than through the Vosges, was not added until 1904, but the main assumption of German military strategy came into existence while the Franco-Russian alliance was taking shape. Henceforth, war in Europe meant a two-front war for the German army .

Near the end of the century Europe appeared to be divided. But the alliance systems were not entirely rigid, and for the next decade Europe experienced a fluid diplomacy in which many possible combinations were considered. In the mid-1890's, for example, the possibility of a continental league embracing Russia, Germany, and France, was discussed, but a basic agreement among the three countries remained beyond reach. European diplomacy gave the appearance of fluidity simply because major conflicts did not arise. The attention devoted by individual nations to problems outside Europe, notably those arising in their colonies, permitted a diversion from traditional European conflicts.

An End to Britain's Isolation

The rumors of a continental combination indicated the widespread resentment that Russia, France, and Germany felt toward Great Britain in the 1890's. This attitude became even more pronounced during the Boer War at the turn of the century; without exception European opinion favored the Boers in their struggle against British domination. Although the antagonism toward Britain failed to produce a continental league, the hostility of the continental states had a significant impact on the direction of British policy. British statesmen were forced to reconsider Britain's "splendid isolation" of the nineteenth century; in the 1890's this isolation seemed less splendid than it had in the past. The navy, which was regarded as indispensable for securing Britain's food supply from overseas, was the first object to which British political leaders turned their attention. They discovered that it had been neglected for over a generation and required an extensive program of modernization.

The Naval Race

Although later couched in terms of an Anglo-German rivalry, the naval race that affected Europe at the turn of the century had its origins not in the German naval bills of 1898 and 1900 but in the prospect of a growing cooperation between France and Russia in the early 1890's. By that time British military planners had already taken alarm at increases in Russian naval expenditure; in 1889 the admiralty established a "two-nation standard" whereby the British navy was to be sufficiently powerful to hold off the combined navies of any two powers. With France and Russia, however, the British admiralty faced the combined strength of the second and fourth strongest fleets in the world. The visit of the Russian squadron to the French base at Toulon in 1893 dramatically illustrated the threat that the French and Russian fleets could pose to Britain's Mediterranean link with India.

When the Franco-Russian alliance was made formal in 1894, the British government embarked on a crash naval construction program designed to bring the navy up to the two-power standard. Almost immediately, however, British politicians called this effort inadequate and urged in 1897 that a three-power standard be established. The prospects of a continental alliance including France, Russia, and Germany seemed to justify the demand for increased naval credits. In the 1890's the navy budget doubled, from thirteen million pounds to twenty-six and a half million. British leaders were determined, given Britain's dependence on imports, to maintain the country's naval supremacy, even though the costs of naval construction were soaring and the number of competitors was increasing.

It is within the context of a possible continental league, which would array three major powers against Britain, that the German decision to build a North Sea fleet must be considered. The addition of a powerful German navy would make this combination formidable for the British fleet. Even so, the British were not at first unduly alarmed by German naval building activity. Although a virulent anti-German campaign had been launched in some chauvinistic British journals, the London *Times* indicated that the proposal for a German fleet was a relatively modest and necessary adjunct to Germany's expanding commerce. Even Germany's advocate of naval strength, Admiral Tirpitz, underplayed the significance of the navy, hoping to mollify London and to allay certain Reichstag deputies who were critical of the expense of a fleet. He planned to seek further expansion once the initial program had been completed, but the outbreak of the Boer War accelerated his timetable. The anti-British sentiments that the Boer War evoked in Germany provided Tirpitz with an opportunity to get higher naval credits past the Reichstag. He pushed through a program that called for the construction of thirty-eight battleships in the next twenty years, accompanied by a corresponding increase in other types of warships.

During the debates on this bill the notion of a "risk fleet" was publicly advanced as the basis for German naval strategy. The German fleet was to be sufficiently powerful to discourage any other state, including the greatest naval power, from risking war with Germany. Britain was obviously the standard measure for this strategy. The "risk" theory had unfortunate effects on the course of Anglo-German relations, for it created an irreconcilable disagreement over the extent of naval preparations. Germany wanted a navy that would deter any single power from attacking, yet Britain wanted a navy that could defeat any two, or possibly three, opponents. The two objectives could not be squared. As one naval ministry raised its requirements, the other followed suit or went higher, and the naval race was on.

Accompanying the military build-up, a wave of chauvinism, expressed as hatred for the rival power, swept across Germany and Britain. In Britain a number of journals played on the theme of a German peril. Uneasiness developed over what Germany intended with its new world policy, and Germany was accused of fomenting projects for a hostile coalition against Britain. Meanwhile German merchants appeared in markets that British traders had taken for granted. Britain, it was argued, had to trade for survival, and now the German merchant, seldom described in very flattering terms, became a menace to Britain's existence. On the other side, popular hatred of Britain, perhaps stemming from envy, appeared in the German press. In the pamphlets and speeches turned out by German colonial associations, England became the villain, an obstacle to Germany's legitimate ambitions. Without a strong fleet, the plea ran, German merchants and German industry were at the mercy of the British navy.

Attempts at an Anglo-German Agreement

Although the naval rivalry has assumed great significance in retrospect, there was another side to relations between Britain and Germany. Even as the rivalry was taking shape, diplomats in the two countries tried to find the basis for some understanding. The men who initiated the naval building program in Germany did not believe that the policy would necessarily produce conflict with Great Britain. Instead, they argued that a navy would make Germany a more desirable ally and cause other states, including Britain, to seek German friendship. Closer ties with other powers might take the form of a continental league, or an alliance with Great Britain. At the end of the 1890's, just as the naval race was getting under way, there were discussions of such an agreement between Britain and Germany. In 1898, for example, British concern at Russian advances in Manchuria led the British cabinet to consider the need for closer cooperation with Germany, and preliminary soundings were made with the German foreign ministry.

Even during the Boer War, there were efforts to improve relations between the two countries on the diplomatic level. At the end of 1900 Bülow and the emperor made a visit to England where discussions on a wide range of topics were held, although neither side was prepared to enter a firm alliance. Shortly after this visit, the British colonial secretary, Joseph Chamberlain, suggested a grandiose alliance of Teuton and Anglo-Saxon that would join Germany, Britain, and the

United States. Chamberlain's proposal found little favor at the time it was made, but it indicated a willingness to seek accommodation with Germany, particularly if such an alliance were to serve as a warning to Russia in the Far East.

In 1901 another occasion arose for discussion of an Anglo-German agreement. During the fatal illness of Queen Victoria that year, Emperor William II demonstrated great personal consideration and tenderness toward his grandmother, a gesture that won him unaccustomed popularity in England. If any understanding were to be achieved, the climate of popular opinion could not have been more receptive. Conversations again took place among the diplomats. At one point the German first secretary in London, apparently hoping to win credit for achieving an agreement, indicated that Lord Lansdowne, who had taken over the foreign office from Salisbury, had suggested an alliance designed to keep France and Russia in check. This deliberate misrepresentation of the discussions unfortunately heightened the already existing opinion in Berlin that sooner or later Britain would seek an alliance with Germany on German terms. This was not Britain's intention. After weeks of discussions, the project was dropped, although it appears that Lansdowne was prepared to make an agreement if the Germans made proposals first. Neither side seemed willing to take the initiative.

The 1901 discussions revealed some of the basic misconceptions that plagued German-British relations at the turn of the century. For British statesmen, an alliance with Germany offered practical benefits in one area, that of curbing Russia in the Near or Far East. Berlin, however, considered this an inordinately high price to pay for British friendship. Basic to German calculations was the conviction that sooner or later Britain would have need of allies and that it was impossible for Britain to reach an understanding with either France or Russia. Officials in the German foreign office complacently assumed that they were in a strong bargaining position. The navy, they believed, gave Germany additional strength. These officials did not consider that Britain might look elsewhere to counter the threat that the German navy presented to British interests.

The Anglo-Japanese Alliance

With Salisbury's retirement from the direction of foreign affairs, influence passed to younger men who were less tied to splendid isolation. Chamberlain had already dangled the prospect of some form of foreign alliance before the nation, but that Britain's first major step away from isolation should be an agreement with Japan was somewhat startling to European powers. Britain saw definite advantages to an association with this rising Asian power. The most important was the possibility of Japanese assistance in curbing Russian advances into Manchuria and China; in fact common opposition to Russian ambition provided the basis for agreement. Serious discussion on the alliance began in the summer of 1901, although the final signing of the treaty was delayed by reservations on both sides. An influential group within the Japanese government preferred reaching an understanding with Russia to forming an alliance obviously directed against Russian aims. And Lansdowne did not abandon Britain's splendid isolation easily. Those who favored an alliance finally prevailed in London and Tokyo, however, and the treaty was signed on January 30, 1902.

The signing of the treaty with Britain was hailed by the Japanese as a triumph and a confirmation of Japan's arrival as a major power. Japanese pride received a great boost, and grateful crowds in the streets of Tokyo cheered Britain. Japanese officials now counted on an ally—perhaps the greatest of the European powers—to back them in any struggle with Russia. As the prospect of a war with Russia increased, these officials remained firm in their demands. Having been recognized as an equal by Britain, Japan felt prepared to challenge a major European power.

Britain also counted gains from the alliance. British statesmen hoped that the clear warning given by the alliance would induce the Russians to adopt a more reasonable attitude concerning the Far East. Moreover, support for continued access to the China market had been affirmed in the treaty. Although a guarantee for India was not included in the 1902 treaty, India was nevertheless a bit further removed from any Russian threat. The signing of the treaty eased some of Britain's burdens in Asia, but it was at the same time a confession that British power was not universal. Britain was forced to turn to alliances for assistance in maintaining its world-wide interests.

The Anglo-Japanese alliance marked a crucial turning point within the realm of international politics. In seeking some way to check Russia, Lansdowne reached halfway around the globe; a "new world" had been called on to help redress the balance of the old. Britain's alliance with Japan signified the acceptance of an Asian power as being of political and military importance and no longer considered a declining society ripe for European exploitation. The alliance anticipated the enormous rise in Japanese prestige that was to occur throughout the world in the aftermath of the Russo-Japanese War some three years later.

The Anglo-French Rivalry and Entente

The signing of the Japanese alliance was the beginning of the end for "splendid isolation," and it signaled the advent of an age in which major powers outside Europe were to be included in the calculations of European diplomats. Nevertheless, the alliance did not put an end to Britain's search for allies within Europe. The settlement of British and French colonial differences between 1898 and 1904 prepared the way for a diplomatic alignment that in the 1890's had been difficult to imagine.

Imperial Conflicts

For over twenty years the two imperialist nations of Britain and France found themselves disputing territory and concessions throughout Africa and Asia. The quarrel began over Egypt and Suez in 1882. That year an anti-European riot in Alexandria led to the deaths of some fifty Europeans in the city; a retaliation by a joint British-French force was proposed by Great Britain, but the French government under pressure from the Chamber of Deputies declined to take part in the expedition. Britain, therefore, proceeded unilaterally. British warships bombarded Alexandria itself, and an expeditionary force defeated the Egyptian army at Tel-el-Khebir, opening the way to Cairo. From this moment Britain replaced France as the dominant European power in Egypt.

The British government had no thoughts as to what they hoped to accomplish in Egypt. Undoubtedly the Liberal cabinet under Gladstone would have preferred that the Ottomans continue to exercise control over Egyptian affairs from Constantinople, while local rulers drifted along in amiable corruption. But the rise of an Egyptian nationalist movement, the virtual bankruptcy of the Egyptian state, caused by the exactions of European moneylenders, and, above all, the Suez Canal, which provided a vital link to India, drew Great Britain into greater involvement in Egypt. The British were concerned that no other power be in a position to control it. Although the canal had been planned, built, and largely financed by Frenchmen, it was of greater importance to Britain than to France. After 1882 successive French governments resented France's eclipse in Egypt and hoped to force Britain either to leave Egypt or to grant compensation to France for having stood aside in 1882. The hope remained ephemeral, and Egypt served to antagonize British-French relations.

In the years following the Egyptian affair, Britain and France crossed swords in several other areas. As the scramble for African territory commenced, these two powers set their sights on many of the same regions. Expanding from previously established bases along the West African coast, French and British colonial officers and explorers began encountering one another in the interior. The process of marking boundaries almost always brought diplomatic maneuvering and tension between the two states.

Tension also arose from territorial rivalries in the Far East. Shortly after the Egyptian episode the French government, urged on by naval officers and colonial administrators on the spot, decided to expand holdings on the Indo-China peninsula by moving north from Cochin-China to annex the territories of Annam and Tonkin. All of Vietnam fell under French rule. In 1893 Laos was added to the French Union of Indo-China. But the annexation of Laos once more brought Britain and France into conflict, for the French occupation of Laos threatened the British colony of Burma. The two powers ultimately agreed to maintain Siam as an independent buffer between their respective colonies; still, suspicion of each other's intentions in the Far East lingered.

The British-French colonial rivalry reached a climax in Africa at the end of the 1890's. The scramble for African territory, in the decade after 1885, occurred in a haphazard fashion, but as land fell under European domination certain patterns of colonization materialized. One pattern consisted of a chain of British holdings stretching from the Cape to Cairo. The French in less coherent fashion seemed to be building an empire that would reach from the Atlantic to the Red Sea. By the mid–1890's the ambitions of both imperial powers centered on the Upper Nile Valley in the heart of the African continent. French officials believed that whoever controlled the waters of the Upper Nile controlled Egypt's destiny. They began toying with the idea of sending an expedition into the region to see if Britain could not be blackmailed into making some negotiation over Egypt that would compensate for French losses there.

At the end of 1895 Captain Marchand began preparing a French expeditionary force that was to travel up the Congo and then make an overland portage to the headwaters of the Nile and to Fashoda. The expedition was a remarkable feat of perseverance on the part of Marchand, the French colonial officers who accompanied him, and the natives who were pressed into service. But the French military force did not amount to more than one hundred and fifty men. This band carried with it the quixotic hope of forcing Britain to recognize French interests in Egypt by gaining control of the Nile water.

Meanwhile, Britain made plans to counter this move. The most direct way to do so was to conquer the Sudan and secure British interests there. In the spring of 1898 Lord Kitchener mounted an impressive expedition to march toward the Upper Nile. A decisive battle took place outside Khartoum on September 2, 1898, when the Anglo-Egyptian army broke the resistance of the anti-European natives. From this moment Britain and Egypt assumed joint control of the Sudan, and Kitchener was prepared to deny the influence of any other power in the Upper Nile Valley.

After the Khartoum victory Kitchener immediately set out for Fashoda with a sizable contingent of native troops and a detachment of British officers and troops. His resources were clearly far superior to Marchand's, whose small group was virtually isolated. Marchand, realizing that he had little prospect for success, went aboard Kitchener's steamer to discuss what was to be done. Despite the overwhelming superiority of Kitchener's forces, Marchand declined Kitchener's suggestion that the French withdraw, but he did agree that the Egyptian flag would be raised over the post. Further negotiations, they decided, would be conducted in London and Paris. Meanwhile, Kitchener courteously offered Marchand a whisky and soda and the two colonial officers settled down to let diplomacy take its course.

The repercussions in Europe did not reflect the polite atmosphere of the colonial station. The British press denounced the French for their presumption in sending Marchand to the Nile and expressed a willingness to go to war. Lord Salisbury, normally a damper for such heated emotion, decided that the French bluff had to be called. He issued an ultimatum: there would be no negotiation until Marchand withdrew. The French press indulged in violently anti-British tirades, and nationalists called on the government to remain firm in its opposition to British pressure. But the new French foreign minister, Théophile Delcassé, realized that his country was in a weak position. Marchand was at the mercy of Kitchener on the Nile, and the French navy could not match the British fleet. France's ally, Russia, showed no inclination to become entangled in this dispute. Finally, France was at the time internally divided over the Dreyfus affair. Delcassé decided to end the crisis as gracefully as possible by recalling Marchand.

This conflict brought Britain and France to the brink of war and marked a low point in their relations. Antagonism remained intense on both sides of the channel even as the Fashoda issue receded. Throughout the crisis, Delcassé had tried to be conciliatory, but he had found the British government unwilling to make any concessions to the French.

After the Fashoda incident, Delcassé studiously made efforts to strengthen French ties with Russia. The renewal of their treaty in 1899 committed both states to common action not only to preserve peace in Europe, but also to maintain the balance of power. By this subtle shift in terminology, the alliance between Russia and France became even more firm and applied to a much wider range of eventualities. Germany and France also engaged in some discussion of a possible accord. In London, too, gestures were made toward reconciliation with Germany. In this climate of international negotiations, France and Britain were as far apart as they had ever been and the prospect of an Anglo-French accord seemed out of the question. Colonial problems continued to give direction to the oscillations of European diplomacy.

Resolution of Colonial Conflicts

It is not surprising that the resolution of outstanding colonial conflicts between Britain and France only six years after the Fashoda crisis should have produced a decisive realignment of European diplomacy. For twenty years differences over Egypt had been a major source for discord; the resolution of these differences supplied the impetus for an entente. The two countries began the process of rapprochement in 1902. By this time, Delcassé had reached the conclusion that an agreement with Germany was impossible, but an understanding with Britain could be reached that would offer France a number of benefits, not the least of these being the opportunity of gaining decisive influence in Morocco. Being next to Algeria, Morocco had considerable strategic importance for France in addition to having economic interest, but because Britain had prior claims there British approval was requisite for any French move. Delcassé realized that a colonial agreement with Britain would also benefit France within the context of European diplomacy; it would warn Germany that it could no longer take an Anglo-French rivalry for granted. Delcassé was always careful in his negotiations to keep both colonial and continental interests in mind.

On Britain's part, Joseph Chamberlain had been disappointed by his country's failure to reach an understanding with Germany. Because isolation was no longer a desirable policy for Britain to follow, he decided that Britain should turn to France. Lansdowne, the foreign secretary, at first was unenthusiastic about a French alliance, but he gradually came to share the pro-French sympathies of several influential members of the British foreign office. Britain could enjoy many advantages from an end to imperial conflicts with France.

Agreements on Egypt and Morocco would permit the admiralty to shift some of the Mediterranean fleet to Atlantic or home waters. An entente with France would lessen the possibility of a continental alliance and therefore relieve pressure on the British navy. The French navy was still the second largest fleet in the world, although soon to be surpassed by Germany and the United States. Above all, an accord with Britain's colonial rival would permit some reduction in the military burdens of maintaining Britain's imperial responsibilities, the high costs of which had been painfully demonstrated in the Boer War.

The suggestions for an agreement made by the French ambassador, Paul Cambon, in 1902 received a favorable response in Great Britain. In July 1903, serious negotiations began and the final entente was signed on April 8, 1904. Nothing was said in the treaty about Europe. Settlement of minor disputes over Siam and fishing rights in Newfoundland were part of the agreement, but the two most important provisions dealt with Egypt and Morocco. Essentially, France recognized Britain's predominance in Egypt in exchange for an acknowledgment that Britain would not oppose any French action deemed necessary to preserve order in Morocco. Although both sides gained by the treaty, Delcassé was blamed for having yielded too much. One of his critics accused him of having paid Britain with hard currency in exchange for a promissory note that could be cashed only at some unspecified future date.

Yet this date was sooner at hand than either side could have realized at the time of the treaty. Delcassé had signed an agreement with Italy in which, anticipating later bargaining with Britain, France was freed from Italian interference in Morocco in return for a recognition of Italian ambitions in Tripoli. A further clearing of possible opposition from other powers came after the entente with Great Britain had been signed. In October 1904, France and Spain defined their respective spheres of influence in Morocco, with by far the larger portion falling to France. At the end of that year, the French representative at Tangier was scheduled to go to Fez, the Moroccan capital, to discuss plans for a reorganization of the Moroccan army under French supervision. The impecunious ruler of Morocco, Abd-al-Aziz, had already been forced to accept a French loan that was guaranteed by French administration of his customs receipts. Morocco appeared to be falling under French sway.

The only uncertainty as far as Delcassé's diplomacy was concerned was Germany, but at the time of the Anglo-French entente Delcassé assured the German ambassador in Paris that German commercial interests in Morocco would be respected. Either deliberately or by oversight Delcassé did not pursue the Moroccan question any further with the Germans; perhaps he was confident that his policy was about to produce another colony for France. The German government, however, decided to interfere with the diplomatic agreements concerning Morocco; in so doing they precipitated a major diplomatic crisis in 1905–06.

The Moroccan Crisis of 1905

In the first months after the signing of the Anglo-French entente, the German foreign office gave little evidence of contemplating any dramatic stroke. The German chancellor, Bülow, minimized the agreement in a speech before the Reichstag in which he pointed out that as long as German commercial interests in Morocco continued to be unhindered, the agreement need not cause alarm. In reality, however, the German foreign office found the agreement irritating and began considering action that would test the strength of the new accord.

An opportunity came at the beginning of 1905. The Moroccan Sultan, Abd-al-Aziz had become alarmed at French military advances into Morocco from Algeria, and he looked to Germany for support against growing French pressure. The German government decided to assume the role of protector of Moroccan independence. The moment seemed favorable for challenging French pretensions. The French army had been demoralized by the Dreyfus affair and the controversies surrounding attempts to impose republican political preferences on the officer corps. Furthermore the French army could not count on any support from Russia if a showdown with Germany came about. The Russian army was being defeated in the Far East by the Japanese, while the state itself was plunging into revolution. Moreover, British-Russian relations were strained at that time because the Russian fleet had fired on British fishing vessels off Dogger Bank in the North Sea, mistaking them for Japanese torpedo boats. The French government, to its embarrassment, found itself in the middle and did not want to have to choose between the two sides. Bülow decided to exploit the French predicament and, at the same time, demonstrate that Germany could not be ignored in Morocco.

A scheme was proposed by Baron Holstein of the foreign ministry, and it had the full endorsement of Bülow. An international incident was to be deliberately provoked when the German emperor visited Tangier during his winter cruise in the Mediterranean. William II was far from enthusiastic about the proposed visit and tried to get out of it. At last he was persuaded that in a conference over Morocco, France would find no diplomatic support, and a German triumph was assured. At the end of March 1905, he went ashore at Tangier and made a strong speech in which he promised that Germany was prepared to guarantee the freedom and independence of Morocco. His own visit, he announced, was in itself evidence of Germany's willingness. The emperor's performance demonstrated a lack of diplomacy evident whenever he took a hand in foreign affairs. Whatever his doubts and reservations may have been about provoking a crisis over Morocco, they did not appear in the belligerent stand that he took in Tangier. The German pressure on France was intense, and Germany quickly had the crisis that Holstein wanted. The prospect of war with France loomed in the spring of 1905 as Bülow hinted to the German general staff that an attack on France might be necessary if the French government ignored German demands.

In France the general staff informed the government that they could not guarantee a successful defense if Germany should attack. The German foreign office set its terms: Delcassé, the architect of French policy since 1898, was to be dismissed as French foreign minister and an international conference was to be called on Morocco. Both conditions were met. In June 1905, Delcassé resigned his office, yielding in part to German pressure and in part to the political opposition to him within the newly formed cabinet. In September the French agreed to the conference proposal. This meeting was to be held at the Spanish town of Algeciras, directly across the Mediterranean from Tangier. The Germans looked forward to a diplomatic triumph in the Moroccan issue and an undermining of the French foreign policy that Delcassé had constructed.

The Algeciras Conference

From the German viewpoint Algeciras was a failure. An agreement was reached on Morocco, presumably the main issue. France would assume responsibility for strengthening Moroccan border security forces, assisted in a minor way by Spanish officers. This was scarcely to Germany's advantage, although the independence of Morocco and right of free trade for Europeans were solemnly endorsed. In the debates over the Moroccan question the German delegation found to their dismay that of the twelve countries attending the conference only Austria-Hungary and Morocco supported the German arguments; instead of being in a position of bringing France to terms the Germans found themselves on the defensive. Forcing an international conference turned out to have been a mistake, and the architect of Germany's ploy in Morocco, Baron Holstein, was forced to resign from office shortly after the conclusion of the conference.

Instead of dividing Britain and France, German behavior during the Moroccan crisis strengthened their entente. On the eve of the Algeciras Conference, Britain and France began military-staff talks on plans for cooperation between the two armies in the event of a war in Europe. Joint military planning created what amounted to a moral commitment for Britain to aid France if war broke out on the Continent. The conversations evidenced increasing British suspicions of German diplomatic aims; a clear opposition to Germany's world policy and to German efforts to establish a continental hegemony became a prominent characterisstic of British policy after 1905. Britain's suspicion had the effect of further cementing the entente. If the balance of power on the Continent were to tip in favor of Germany, Britain was prepared to intervene in support of France. This policy continued Britain's traditional interest in maintaining a balance of power on the European continent, but it required a much more active commitment than had been necessary in the nineteenth century.

Algeciras also revealed that the Triple Alliance between Germany, Austria, and Italy was not what it had been in Bismarck's day. Italy's failure to support the German position confirmed the Italian disaffection from the alliance that had been increasingly apparent since the turn of the century. In 1898 the Italians had ended their economic rivalry with France by signing lower tariff accords. In 1900 the two countries struck a bargain over Tripoli and Morocco, thereby terminating their Mediterranean disputes. In 1902 the Triple Alliance came up for renewal. Italy again signed, and its obligations, including an agreement to aid Germany if attacked by France, remained in effect. But at the same time the Italian foreign minister exchanged letters with the French ambassador in Rome in which he declared that Italy was in no way obliged to engage in a war against France. This letter violated Italian promises to Germany and Austria, for the Italians indicated that they would be neutral even if France were provoked into an attack on Germany. Rumors of Italian wavering spread in diplomatic circles, and the Germans tried to joke about it. Bülow commented that a marriage did not break up if a man's wife danced with another partner. But after Algeciras, Italian faithlessness seemed less amusing. The Germans henceforth lamented that Austria was their only friend in Europe, and the German foreign office sounded the alarm—Germany was in danger of having a hostile coalition drawn around it.

Implications of the Moroccan Crisis

The Moroccan crisis brought sober thoughts to Europeans of every country. They had experienced the most serious war scare since 1878, and the foreboding produced by it touched both diplomatic and public opinion. William II's visit to Tangier and the subsequent pressures put on France revealed the menace that hung over France. From that time any thought of reconciliation with the overbearing German state seemed impossible. A wave of nationalist emotion and anti-German sentiment gathered momentum in France and Britain after 1905. From the German point of view, however, France and Britain were wrongfully and stubbornly opposed to rightful German ambitions; these two states were "encircling" Germany and denying all Germans a share of world power.

The Moroccan crisis signaled a crucial shift in the diplomacy of imperialism that had dominated European international relations during the 1890's. Morocco represented a colonial spoil, but the competition for dominance in Morocco was less serious than the conflicts within the European state system that were revealed. Although European imperialism was at its zenith and expansion was still under way in many parts of the world, the limits of this expansion were in sight. As the heady era of imperialism approached these limits, European powers had to grapple with problems that arose, quite literally, closer to home.

The Anglo-Russian Entente

Throughout the nineteenth century relations between Great Britain and Russia had followed a rocky course; in 1854 the two states had even gone to war in the Crimea. After the settlement of the Crimean War, relations did not improve very much, and Britain and Russia found themselves competing for influence in the Ottoman empire, Persia, and China by the end of the century. The Dogger Bank incident in 1904 threatened to bring about another armed conflict, but the crisis was resolved peacefully by an international tribunal; the Russian state had more than it could handle in fighting Japan at the time. Even so, resentment against Britain ran high in St. Petersburg, for, after all, Britain was Japan's ally.

It was the Russian defeat in Manchuria in 1905 that cleared the way for an accommodation with Great Britain. Exhausted by the effects of defeat and revolution, the Russian state required a period of domestic reconstruction, accompanied by a restricted foreign policy. This meant, above all, limiting Far Eastern ambitions, which the war with Japan had destroyed in any case. In 1907 Russia signed an agreement with Japan that defined their respective spheres of influence in Manchuria. With Russia contained in Asia Britain no longer needed to be anxious about a possible Russian advance toward India or further into the China market.

Both sides saw advantages to an entente. Reconciliation was desirable for Russia because the shaky state of Russian finances required that loans be sought in London as well as in Paris. In addition, diplomats in the Russian foreign office realized that disagreement with Great Britain complicated relations with their ally, France. The British were concerned, as usual, about preserving an equilibrium in Europe. It seemed to the British foreign office that an alliance of France, Britain, and Russia might be necessary to check German ambitions and to prevent the possibility of a continental league. Britain was also alarmed by the acceleration of Germany's naval program.

Prospects for an understanding between Britain and Russia became brighter when Alexander Isvolsky became Russian foreign minister in April 1906. Izvolsky had the reputation of being something of a liberal, and he favored closer ties with England. Discussions commenced in the summer of 1907, touching on Far-Eastern and Middle-Eastern questions. It was decided that Tibet would be neutral ground under the nominal suzerainty of China, and Afghanistan was acknowledged to be within Britain's sphere of interest. Agreement on these points removed the Russian threat to India's northwestern frontier. To the west, India touched Persia, a state in which Britain and Russia had been actively competing for influence. The compromise that they reached over Persia became the cornerstone for the entente. While endorsing Persian independence, the entente delimited zones of influence for the two countries. Roughly the northern third fell within Russia's area of interest and the southeastern third was open to British penetration. The two zones were to be separated by a neutral band. At first, it appeared as if the Russians had the better bargain in Persia, for their zone included the capital, Teheran; however, it was later discovered that the British zone gave access to the important oil reserves of the Persian gulf. The entente said nothing about European affairs directly. Like the Anglo-French accord of 1904, it was designed to end disputes arising out of imperial rivalries. Both agreements, it was hoped, had reduced potential areas of conflict, not increased them.

Effects of the Diplomatic Realignment of Europe

Although neither entente was specifically designed against Germany, both came to be interpreted in this fashion. Europe seemed to have become divided diplomatically according to two alliance systems, and Germany was convinced that a grouping of hostile powers was being forged around her. As the idea of "encirclement" gained currency in Berlin, Germany's foreign policy became more assertive and blunt, a pattern that simply confirmed apprehensions and increased anti-German sentiments. There was no reason why the grouping of the European powers into two camps should be more likely to produce war than the Bismarckian system, or the diplomacy of the 1890's. But the impression that emerged in Europe after 1905 was that there was less room for compromise than there had been in the past.

Perhaps the psychological impact of the diplomatic division was as important for the diplomats and for public opinion as the precise terms of the accords that had been signed. Popular opinion looked on international crises not only as a matter of national interest but also as an occasion to support one's "friends" or to call on them for support. As each state sought to maintain its security and prestige, allies became crucially important, and the "moral" obligation of sticking by one's allies was by no means a negligible factor in the calculations of diplomats after 1905. This desire to maintain allies added rigidity to the system that had emerged in Europe. A kind of static equilibrium had been achieved, and peace could be maintained as long as the weights on the balance remained roughly the same. If one state appeared to gain strength—through a sudden increase in military power or by the addition of territory—or if one state began to weaken as the result of a domestic crisis, then the balance would begin to oscillate. What made this situation alarming was the simultaneous growth of military power within the European states and, as part of this growth, the need to assemble mass armies rapidly in accordance with fixed schedules whenever war threatened. This was a system based on fear and suspicion. There were provisions for aid in the event of war but not for concerted action to prevent it.

The realignment of European diplomacy reflected a changing relationship between Europe and the non-European world that was becoming apparent after 1905. The years right after the turn of the century provided the first glimpse, as Hajo Holborn noted in his *Political Collapse of Europe*, of "global" politics. The most dramatic example of the interaction of three continents, as Holborn has put it, came in the Far East with the Russo-Japanese War, a conflict between a European and an Asian power of the first rank that was resolved by the mediation of the United States. Already the American defeat of Spain in 1898 and the Japanese alliance with Britain in 1902 had served as preludes to an era in which events and forces arising outside Europe were to intrude on European history.

The "global" crisis of 1905 produced a turning point in Europe's relationship to the non-European world in yet another way. Japan's victory over Russia that year inspired a wave of opposition to European dominance that reached across the Middle East and Asia. This resistance was admittedly feeble in some areas, and in many regions European states were still expanding their imperial domains and extending their overseas investments. Nevertheless, the European powers, although they had achieved an unprecedented material strength, found their hegemony challenged after 1905 by the rise of non-European industrial nations, notably Japan and the United States, and by the stirrings of resistance to European control in many parts of the non-European world.

SUGGESTED READING

Sound general discussions of European diplomacy are plentiful. Generations of historians have dissected the diplomatic record to discover how the Europeans maintained a peaceful balance in the last half of the nineteenth century and to find out why this state of affairs was not preserved. Among these surveys, Raymond J. Sontag's *European Diplomatic History, 1871–1932* (New York: Appleton-Century-Crofts, 1933) shows a remarkably balanced viewpoint. The enormously well-informed volumes by William L. Langer, *European Alliances and Alignments, 1871–1890* (New York: Knopf, 1931) and *The Diplomacy of Imperialism, 1890–1902* (New York: Knopf, 1935), are indispensable to the student of the period. Langer's major articles, many of them related to prewar diplomacy, have been collected and republished in *Explorations in Crisis: Papers on International History,* edited by Carl E. and Elizabeth Schorske (Cambridge, Mass: Harvard University Belknap Press, 1969). A lucid, balanced discussion of late nineteenth century diplomacy emerges from Pierre Renouvin's *Histoire des Relations Internationales,* Vol. 6, *Le xixe siècle II: de 1871 à 1914: L'Apogée de l'Europe* (Paris:

Hachette, 1955). A. J. P. Taylor's *The Struggle for Mastery in Europe, 1848–1918* (London: Oxford University Press, 1954) reveals a masterful command of sources and a zestful style, although Taylor's search for originality in interpretation sometimes confuses the beginning student. Less colorful, but informative, is René Albrecht-Carrié's, *A Diplomatic History of Europe since the Congress of Vienna* (New York: Harper, 1958).

The antagonism between Britain and Germany has provoked a number of studies, including Raymond J. Sontag's *Germany and England: the Background of Conflict, 1848–1894* (New York: Russell, 1964), Ernest L. Woodward's *Great Britain and the German Navy* (London: Oxford University Press, 1935), and Ross J. S. Hoffman's *Great Britain and the German Trade Rivalry* (New York: Russell, 1964). The breakdown of the Bismarckian system provides the subject for William L. Langer's *The Franco-Russian Alliance, 1890–1894* (Cambridge, Mass.: Harvard University Press, 1929). Some of the mysteries associated with the role of Baron Holstein in the German Foreign Office have been removed by Norman Rich in his *Friedrich von Holstein: Politics and Diplomacy in the Era of Bismarck and Wilhelm II,* 2 vols. (Cambridge: Cambridge University Press, 1965). Britain's decision to abandon its traditional role of splendid isolation had a decisive and not entirely salutary effect on European diplomacy in the opinion of George Monger; his volume, *The End of Isolation* (London: Thomas Nelson & Sons, 1963), is critical of the new men in the British foreign office who were responsible for this policy after 1900. A perceptive, important analysis of French policy is Christopher Andrew's *Théophile Delcassé and the Making of the Entente Cordiale* (London: Macmillan, 1968), based on a wide range of unpublished sources.

Ian H. Nish's *The Anglo-Japanese Alliance: the Diplomacy of Two Island Empires, 1894–1907* (New York: Oxford University Press, 1966) is a carefully researched investigation of this important relationship. John A. White analyzes the strains on European diplomacy produced by an Asian war in *The Diplomacy of the Russo-Japanese War* (Princeton: Princeton University Press, 1964). Although its accuracy has been qualified since its publication by some of the findings of Christopher Andrew, cited above, Eugene N. Anderson's *The First Moroccan Crisis, 1904–1906* (Hamden, Conn.: Shoe String Press, 1966) remains the basic study of that episode.

6

EUROPE'S IMPERIAL SURGE, 1890–1914

At the end of the nineteenth century several European states rapidly extended their political and economic influence in Africa, Asia, and the western hemisphere. This "new imperialism" was the latest, and perhaps the most impressive, chapter in the long history of European overseas expansion that began with the crusades. The Europeans had always shown a remarkable propensity for sending their ships, traders, soldiers, explorers, and colonists to distant lands. From time to time, however, there had been pauses in this expansionism, and the first three quarters of the nineteenth century appeared to be one of those intervals. By the first decade of the nineteenth century, Spain and France had lost most of their overseas possessions; even in Britain, the greatest of colonial powers, there was some discussion of possibly shedding the burdens of empire.

In spite of a diminishing enthusiasm for empire building, however, the trend toward overseas expansion remained very much alive. In the first half of the nineteenth century France conquered

Algeria, established a foothold in Cochin China, and made a modest enlargement of its holdings in Senegal on the West African coast. Great Britain increased the areas under effective British rule in India and consolidated its hold there. Moreover, European trade with the non-European world expanded steadily; in many areas the Europeans exercised an "informal imperialism" in which trade was pursued without requiring the security of direct political control of the overseas country.

What set the new imperialism of the late nineteenth century apart from all earlier expansion was its enormous scale, backed by Europe's formidable material development, and a tendency toward direct political domination, particularly in Africa. Before considering the nature and impact of this late nineteenth century imperial surge, let us examine briefly some of the theories that have been advanced as explanations of this phenomenon.

The Causes of Imperialism

The search for an explanation of imperialism has generated a variety of interpretations without, unfortunately, producing a wholly satisfactory thesis. Formation of such a comprehensive analysis has been made difficult by the complexity and variety of imperialist tendencies within Europe and by the great differences that existed among the societies that came into contact with European expansion. Ideological rhetoric has further clouded the issue, for imperialism remains a highly charged term.

The "Economic Argument"

One of the most durable of the theories advanced to explain imperialism is the "economic argument," which has been most consistently advocated by Marxist and neo-Marxist historians and theorists, although others have also subscribed to it. One of the first expressions of the view that imperialism emerged from economic pressures came at the turn of the century with the publication of J. A. Hobson's *Imperialism, a Study* (1902). Hobson was a liberal, rather than a doctrinaire Marxist, but he made what remains a classic formulation of the economic thesis. Many of his arguments were subsequently used by Lenin in his pamphlet, *Imperialism, the Highest Stage of Capitalism,* published in 1915. Other European Marxists, including Otto Bauer, Rudolf Hilferding, and Rosa Luxemburg, had taken up the argument before the First World War.

The economic argument maintains that industrialists faced declining prices in Europe at the end of the nineteenth century as a result of overproduction, and therefore searched abroad for new customers who could absorb surplus goods. At the same time, industrial Europe required increasing quantities of raw materials that could only be found overseas. In order to pay for these imports, the industrial nations had to sell abroad. Hence, both the search for markets and the need for essential raw materials pushed European capitalism toward imperial expansion. In addition, the accumulation of wealth among the European middle and upper middle classes created a glut of capital within Europe that drove down interest rates; the bourgeoisie was willing to export capital to foreign lands and imperial territories to obtain a better return for investments than could be found in Europe. Finally, cheap labor costs overseas encouraged the investment in and exploitation of colonial territory.

For Lenin these tendencies indicated a fundamental crisis within capitalism; imperialism represented a desperate attempt to escape the contradictions of a capitalist economy, which could not balance profits, prices, and labor costs at home. Hobson also saw imperialism as evidence of a crisis in capitalism, but one in which a few capitalists profited by taking advantage of the government's willingness to underwrite the administrative and military expenses of empire. Hobson believed that imperialism did not pay on the balance sheet; he insisted that surplus capital and government funds used to maintain empires would be more wisely spent in raising wages so that workers could purchase the produce of the industrial system.

At first glance there appears to be a plausible connection between imperialism and a crisis of capitalist evolution. The new imperialism coincided with the late nineteenth century price decline that, beginning in the late 1870's, certainly caused apprehension among European manufacturers. The anxieties among businesses that depended on export trade were heightened by the trend toward protection, which placed obstacles in the way of selling products to other industrial nations. Thus the financial difficulties of the late nineteenth century encouraged nations to seek secure markets by imperial expansion.

Yet critics have pointed to certain difficulties with a purely economic explanation. For one thing, empires were not essential to provide markets. Despite the effects of protectionism, trade continued to increase among the industrial states throughout this period, and the most profitable trade tended to be outside the imperial domains. Only about one-tenth of all French trade was with the empire, for example. Germany, whose industrial capacity and exports boomed during this period, had a relatively modest empire compared with France, whose industry grew at a much slower rate. Nor was there any necessary connection between overseas investment and imperial domination. The United States became an important area for British investment in the nineteenth century without becoming an imperial territory.

Finally, the great expansion of the late nineteenth century cannot be attributed to a crisis whose source was capitalism. The European economy did suffer a setback at the end of the century, in part because of overproduction, but this was not yet the era of monopoly and finance capitalism. Finance capitalism developed in response to the crisis and reached its apogee long after imperialism had begun. The upswing in the European economic cycle after 1900 had little to do with the success of imperialism.

The Influence of Politics

Imperial expansion could not be ascribed exclusively to economic motives; the politics of diplomacy must be counted as a source for imperialism. For example, Bismarck encouraged French overseas ambitions at the expense of British ambitions in order to divide the two western liberal states. Although interested primarily in the European balance of power, Bismarck also took an active role in African affairs, giving sanctions to German adventurers and eventually calling a colonial congress to establish ground rules for the partition of Africa. Whatever his intentions were, the effect was to draw the imperial powers deeper into Africa than perhaps they would have gone otherwise.

A significant part of the diplomacy of imperialism centered on strategic problems. When financial instability led to a political crisis in Egypt, the desire to protect British investments was not the only nor the most important reason for Britain's occupation of that territory. The Suez Canal was not only an economic asset but a strategic one. To keep open the Mediterranean-Suez link with India Britain had to make sure that no other European power occupied an area that might threaten this link. The tendency of every nation was to occupy a region, particularly in Africa, simply to keep another power out. Although the interplay of European power politics had an influence on imperialism, again this was not the sole motive force.

The Force of Nationalism

Instead of looking to the politics of diplomacy, some historians have interpreted imperialism in more general terms—as a manifestation of nationalism: a great nation had to have colonies to demonstrate national strength and even superiority. According to these historians, France sought an empire as a way of recovering prestige after the humiliating defeat by Prussia in 1871, and Britain and Germany considered the expansion and defense of imperial holdings to be necessary for the exercise of world power. If it were not for nationalism, the proponents of this theory argue, how else could one explain the great wave of popular enthusiasm in Britain for the Boer War, or popular support for Germany's naval construction program? These historians have pointed out that apologists for the empire found lively sales for novels and pamphlets that extolled an imperial mission.

National pride was an intense sentiment among Europeans in the nineteenth century and was used by a number of governments to deflect revolutionary aspirations among the populace. There is reason to believe that imperialist programs were encouraged by these governments as a part of efforts to increase nationalism. But the attempt to see imperialism as simply a further manifestation of nationalism encounters some difficulty. The great wave of popularity for imperialism came in the 1890's, after the race for colonies had been started; the emotional popularity of imperial adventures seems to have been a product rather than a cause of imperialism. Moreover, some sincere patriots objected to imperial commitments on the ground that they weakened rather than strengthened the state. In France during the 1880's this view was held by conservatives who feared that colonial enthusiasts played Bismarck's game and distracted the country from more important issues. Finally, the effort to use imperialism as a means of unifying society came largely after the fact of imperial expansion.

Certainly a sense of national greatness was an important element in the climate that produced imperialism, and undoubtedly, as the economic historian Joseph Schumpeter has argued, human aggressiveness had an influence. The imperialists were proud men; even religious missionaries had little doubt that they brought superior beliefs to benighted people. But all imperialism of the late nineteenth century cannot be attributed to the Europeans' sense of their cultural and national superiority.

Non-European Developments

More recently, a group of historians have suggested that in the search for the causes of imperialism too much attention has been devoted to developments in Europe. These men believe that political conditions in the non-European countries played a large role in determining European intervention. The European states were led into Africa, for instance, not as the result of deliberate calculations but as the consequence of a series of crises that forced the Europeans to choose between withdrawal or taking an active part in governing territories in which they already had some interest. Once started, the pursuit of African possessions had a snowballing effect. This thesis has much to recommend it, and it is a useful balance to European-centered notions about the causes of imperialism. There are instances and types of imperialism, however, for which the thesis is not wholly valid. It does not take into account, for example, economic penetration into areas that did not fall directly under European imperial rule.

All the forces mentioned, and perhaps others, contributed to European imperialist expansion. Economic drives, diplomatic maneuvers, nationalism, and an unanticipated interaction between Europe and the non-European world undoubtedly had some influence in each instance of overseas expansion. Imperialism was too complex a phenomenon to be explained by a single causal factor, and an understanding of imperialism should recognize the many forces at work that drove the Europeans toward a rapid extension of their power in the non-European world. It is clear that the precipitate increase in European power throughout the world had profound repercussions for world history in the twentieth century. The speed with which this extension of European power occurred was perhaps the most surprising aspect of the phenomenon, but equally impressive was the resistance to the imperial powers that developed in its wake.

The Scramble for Africa

France was in some ways the most ambitious of the European powers that participated in the partitioning of Africa during the last two decades of the nineteenth century, despite the objections of deputies to imperialism and its attendant expense. The revival of French imperialism began with the invasion of Tunisia in 1881.

The Tunisian Affair

The colonization of Tunisia demonstrates a pattern that was subsequently to become common in the scramble for Africa. A combination of rival European interests, financial weakness, and internal rebellion would bring European intervention; the occupying power would then be faced with the task of securing its gain through effective occupation and administration. The Tunisian affair also demonstrates the combination of motives that operated in imperial expansion.

When the Bey of Tunis' preference for high living brought his country to the brink of bankruptcy, an international commission of French, Italian, and English bankers assumed supervision of Tunisia's financial affairs. Not long afterward, Italy and France began competing for railway and telegraph concessions within Tunisia. But these economic considerations mixed with political rivalries and diplomatic maneuvers. Because large numbers of Italians had settled in Tunisia, Italy felt it might some day claim a protectorate over the area. France was strongly opposed to this prospect, for the control of Tunisia by another European power would threaten French Algeria. Therefore, during the Congress of Berlin in 1878 the French were gratified to receive the encouragement of Germany and Great Britain for any measures that they might take to secure their influence in Tunisia. The French government delayed taking up this option, however, because the domestic political climate did not appear favorable. It was not until the spring of 1881, when rumors of a possible Italian maneuver coincided with a more favorable parliamentary opinion, that the government decided to send a military expedition into Tunisia.

The expedition appeared to be a punitive one, a chastisement for one of the periodic raids that had occurred across the Tunisian-Algerian border, but its true purpose was the founding of a French protectorate. The French government believed that this goal could be quickly achieved. Within three weeks the army had reached Tunis, whereupon the Bey signed a treaty that recognized a French protectorate over his country. Following this rapid success the French government withdrew most of its military force, an action that proved to be hasty. By the end of the summer a violent, anti-French rebellion swept through the tribes of southern Tunisia, and the French army was recalled from Algeria. The pacification proved much more costly and protracted than the original military conquest. As a result, many deputies reacted against imperial adventures. This anti-colonial mood, although temporary, was to have an effect on French behavior during the next African crisis, which occurred over Egypt.

The Occupation of Egypt

Britain had remained benevolently neutral in the Tunisian affair, estimating that France at this point represented no danger to British interests in the Mediterranean. The crisis over Egypt, however, not only led to a further partitioning of territory but also served to divide

Britain and France. Again, it was the combination of an internal rebellion, financial weakness, and rival European interests that provided the vital ingredients for the occupation of an African state by a European power.

The financial disorders of Egypt stemmed from the exorbitant interest rates that European lenders charged Ismail, the Khedive of Egypt, when he sought to finance a series of public works. He was driven to borrow more simply to meet the charges on his debts. In 1875 he was forced to sell his shares in the Suez Canal Company in order to meet his financial obligations; these shares were promptly purchased by Disraeli, on behalf of the British government. But the sale of Ismail's interest in the canal failed to end the country's financial plight, and Ismail's debts continued to soar. In 1876 to forestall the bankruptcy of the country the Khedive agreed to a joint British and French commission that would assume control of Egyptian finances.

Egypt's internal troubles continued and reached a climax in 1882. In an effort to satisfy creditors, the Khedive imposed heavy tax burdens on the peasantry, which created widespread discontent. At the same time a group of Egyptian nationalists began agitating for the expulsion of foreigners whose influence they felt was strangling Egypt. The nationalist movement gained support within the Egyptian army, and its leader, Colonel Arabi, forced the dismissal of ministers who were considered too subservient to British and French interests. Early in 1882 a nationalist ministry was formed that showed every intention of taking a tough line against European encroachments on Egyptian sovereignty. But their intentions were compromised by a riot against foreigners that erupted in Alexandria in June 1882, taking the lives of some fifty Europeans. In retaliation the British naval squadron in the eastern Mediterranean bombarded Alexandria, and an expedition went ashore to protect the lives and interests of Europeans in Egypt. Colonel Arabi was chased from the office of war minister. From this moment the British in effect ruled Egypt.

Although France had traditionally shown a strong interest in Egyptian affairs, the French Chamber at the last moment declined to vote credits that would have permitted joint occupation with Great Britain. The mood of the Chamber was temporarily against further overseas entanglements. Thus Britain went into Egypt alone, and the consequence for European diplomacy, as already noted, was an alienation between Britain and France that lasted for twenty years. This Anglo-French rivalry served as a major catalyst for the partitioning of sub-Saharan African territory during these same years.

Africa was well on the way to subdivision by the middle of the 1880's, in large measure as a result of Bismarckian diplomacy. The mounting conflicts over the Congo River basin provided Bismarck with an entrée into African problems. In 1876 King Leopold of Belgium had installed the International African Association, a business concern, along the left bank of the Congo River, claiming rights to much of the Congo basin. Subsequently, a French explorer, Savorgnan de Brazza, signed treaties on behalf of the French government with African rulers inhabiting the right bank of the Congo. But Portugal made claims to the same region, and the British government backed Portugal. Out of this complex dealing, the prospect of a major European quarrel loomed. Bismarck proposed a conference in Berlin to settle the Congo question and thereby remove the danger of a European war arising out of African rivalries.

Prior to the convening of the Colonial Congress of Berlin in 1884 Bismarck had established Germany's position as an "African power" by announcing Germany's protectorate over the desert coasts of Southwest Africa; he sent a German explorer to raise the German flag in the Cameroons and Togo. Then, as the congress was meeting, Bismarck assumed a protectorate in eastern Africa that had been claimed by a German trading company headed by Karl Peters. Germany thus had a double interest in African questions, and Bismarck, not a disinterested chairman of the congress, wished to find a basis for agreement on the rapidly developing partition of Africa.

The Colonial Congress of Berlin had far-reaching implications for Africa. The delegates laid down certain rules for making claims to African territory, which they believed would neutralize Africa as a potential source of danger. According to the agreement reached in Berlin, existing coastal possessions gave an occupying European power the right to a "sphere of influence" extending up to another power's possessions. To claim the territory, however, effective occupation—that is, a trading post or military station—had to be established in the interior and notification given to the other powers. This provision actually encouraged advances toward the interior. After the congress the colonial officials, explorers, and officers used these agreements to justify the assumption of considerable initiative. They argued that if they did not advance toward the interior, representatives of a rival power would.

Beginning of the Scramble for Territory ▪ During the last half of the 1880's tentative gestures were made toward defining European

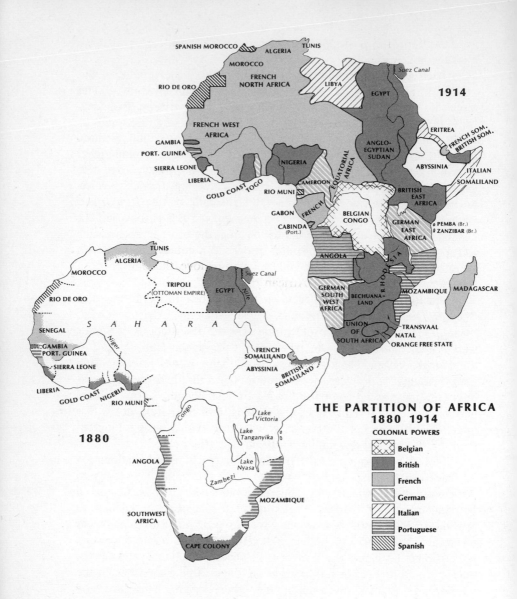

THE PARTITION OF AFRICA
1880 1914

COLONIAL POWERS

- Belgian
- British
- French
- German
- Italian
- Portuguese
- Spanish

possessions on the African continent without actual commitment on the part of the governments. In western Africa, French officers and British traders signed a few treaties with tribes in the hinterlands of their existing possessions. The treaties were preliminary maneuvers aimed at gaining influence along the Niger River. By 1890 not much progress had been made by either nation toward effective occupation. French officers pressed forward from Senegal, but they found themselves hampered by a reluctant government in Paris. From England, Salisbury hoped that the traders in the Royal Niger Company would watch after British interests in western Africa without unduly disturbing the colonial office in London.

In eastern Africa, Britain and Germany jockeyed for position behind the trading activities of William Mackinnon's Imperial East Africa Company and Karl Peters' East African Company, hoping to extend spheres of influence through these intermediaries. Neither nation profited from its possession, and both trading companies found themselves in financial straits by the end of the 1880's. By 1890 the two states reached an agreement on their respective interests in eastern Africa; Britain secured the section of the coast north of Zanzibar, while Germany occupied the adjacent region to the south. Both countries anticipated further gains in the interior, but at that time the hinterlands were virtually unknown to any Europeans save a few explorers and missionaries.

In the 1880's South Africa also became the scene of a preliminary scramble for territory. British colonists at the Cape feared that Germany might block access to the interior by linking its possessions in the southwest with the autonomous Afrikaans-speaking republics of Transvaal and the Orange Free State. In 1884 Cecil Rhodes formed the British South Africa Company, which became the vehicle for creating a British protectorate in Bechuanaland, separating German Southwest Africa from the Boer states. The immediate danger of a link between the Boers and the Germans avoided, Rhodes continued to push farther north. In 1889 his company received a charter from London that permitted the exploration of a vast region north of Bechuanaland. Rhodes began dreaming of a north-south axis of British colonies that would connect the Cape with Cairo through the heart of Africa.

Effective Occupation ▪ It was one thing to draw spheres of influence on paper and another to make them valid. The process of effective occupation took place in the decade of the nineties. In the late 1880's French officers in West Africa had urged the government in Paris to provide credits that would permit a campaign against the Moslem tribal rulers who blocked the French advance toward the Upper Niger. Constrained by the reluctance of a parsimonious Chamber, the colonial ministry in Paris could give only limited encouragement to the expansionist ambitions of the officers. But the strength of the African rulers, who preached a holy war against the infidel invader, rendered ineffective any compromise or effort to advance by treaty-making. Colonial officers claimed that they could not successfully police trade routes to the interior until the power of the African chiefs was broken. A retreat to coastal enclaves, which was the only alternative to fighting the chiefs, was unacceptable even to Paris. Although the Chamber continued to be concerned over military ambitions, the officers gained support among the pro-colonial party and were able to pursue their adversaries. In 1893 the legendary city of Timbuktoo drew them into the light soils of the Upper Niger basin. The city fell to French troops, and the following year the Sudan became a French colony. Meanwhile, French and British explorers and soldiers had carved out slices of territory running north from the Bay of Benin toward the interior of western Africa, but by this time France clearly controlled the interior, including states on the Upper and Middle Niger.

The success of French expansion in West Africa presented an opportunity to fulfill dreams of an empire stretching from Algeria to the Atlantic coast. West Africa might become the base for a final push east so that a band of French possessions girding the African continent and reaching north to Algeria might be created. Moreover, if the western territories could be linked to French holdings on the Congo, the British and German possessions in Nigeria, Togo, and the Cameroons would be encapsuled within French domains. The key to these plans was Lake Chad, the junction for French western and equatorial Africa. When French officers and explorers began pushing toward Chad, they discovered another black Moslem tribal chief blocking their path—Rabah, a former slave trader. Rabah had moved into the region in 1893 and established a personal empire that was hostile to any European encroachment. At first French officials tried to come to terms with Rabah, but when negotiations failed, an expedition was planned to destroy him. In 1900 three columns from the Sudan, Algeria, and the Congo converged on Lake Chad and defeated Rabah; France then established claims to Chad. The interaction of European strategic aims and the anti-European resistance of a local ruler had produced a further partitioning of Africa. The French army completed the conquest of the Sahara and the deserts of Mauretania in the next few years. In 1912 the northwest corner of Africa fell to France when the army began the pacification of Morocco.

In reaching farther afield, toward the Upper Nile, France challenged Great Britain directly. In the early 1890's French reconnaissance missions sought routes from the Congo to the Nile waters, and the French made plans for an expedition to the basin of the Nile.

These Nile projects had two objectives—to force Britain to negotiate over Egypt and to obstruct British hopes for a Cape-to-Cairo empire. In 1898 Major Marchand's intrepid band of 150 French and native troops was confronted by Lord Kitchener's superior forces at Fashoda in the Nile basin. As noted in the preceding chapter, Marchand and Kitchener met and decided to leave the matter of victory to the diplomats at the conference table. France subsequently withdrew its expedition from the Upper Nile.

The Fashoda crisis represented the climax of the scramble for territory in black Africa. The appetite for expansion had grown with the conquests, until there was no more territory left. By 1900 tropical Africa was in European hands, after a frantic decade in which French and British soldiers had broken the power of recalcitrant chiefs and raced to plant the flag ahead of their rivals. The process of partitioning was haphazard; boundaries had been drawn on the basis of conquest or agreement without much respect for tribal differences. Often several native tribes, some with long records of mutual antagonism, became part of the same political unit. The responsibilities of empire required that order be imposed, but this order was determined by the requirements of European occupation and administration.

Government of the African Colonies

Order was generally imposed from above; a small European minority, backed by military power and by an efficient, centralized organization, ruled uncounted millions of black Africans. In some areas, an elite among the black population was permitted a small role in the administration of their lands, but this practice was not widespread. The attitudes of European colonial officials ranged from a benevolent paternalism to outright contempt and exploitation. Some officials hoped to lead black Africa into the twentieth century through gradual reforms, but there were limits as to how radical any of these changes would be. A major reorganization of traditional societies in Africa might produce unforeseen, violent reactions. For the most part European administrators wished to rule with as little turmoil as possible and were principally concerned with maintaining the domination of a white minority. There were, in short, formidable obstacles to modernization under paternalistic auspices.

As the European governments weighed the costs of imperialism, there was some attempt to make the colonies profitable. Often this required limiting outlays for schooling, roads, medical facilities, and other benefits of European rule. The improvements that the European governments introduced, however well intended, were largely designed for European convenience. Although the European presence in Africa left much of the traditional society intact, it planted the seeds of social change that were to cause turmoil later in the twentieth century. A conflict between cultures was imperialism's legacy for black Africa.

The Boer War

While the scramble for tropical Africa was in progress, a conflict of a different sort developed in the temperate tip of the continent. Here the antagonism was neither between rival European powers nor between European invaders and black Africans. Instead, the quarrel centered on differences between British colonists at the Cape and the Boers, the Afrikaans-speaking descendants of Dutch settlers in the Transvaal and the Orange Free State; the black Africans were only bystanders.

The discovery of gold in the Transvaal and the Boers' determination to resist British encroachments on their independence were at the bottom of the dispute. In 1881 the Boers had rebelled against British efforts to incorporate the Transvaal and the Orange Free State into a Union of South Africa. They preferred their impoverished independence to a connection with the more prosperous Cape Colony. A modus vivendi might have been reached in South Africa if gold had not been discovered in the Transvaal. This discovery shifted the economic balance in South Africa from the Cape, which no longer served as a strategic way station on the route to India, to the Boer lands. Foreign capital and immigrants poured into the Transvaal.

As tension between the Boers and the newly arrived foreigners, or Uitlanders, mounted, President Kruger of the Transvaal Republic looked to Germany for assistance in resisting pressure from British colonists at the Cape. The independence of the Boer states became more precarious as their wealth increased. Cecil Rhodes, prime minister of the Cape Colony, thought that the only way to forestall German advances toward the Boer republics was to annex them, a move that would add a golden link to Britain's Cape-to-Cairo chain. Rhodes himself had a major investment in the Transvaal goldfields, so his imperial vision neatly coincided with personal interest. As a way of pressuring the Boers, Rhodes signed treaties to bring first Bechuanaland and then what was to become Rhodesia into the British empire, thus surrounding the Boer republics. But Kruger escaped dependency on the British ports at the Cape by building a railway to Delgoa Bay in Portuguese Mozambique. Frustrated by Kruger's maneuvers,

Rhodes unwisely attempted to unseat him by sponsoring the ill-fated Jameson raid into the Transvaal. When this maneuver backfired, Rhodes was forced to resign as prime minister. His successors were also unable to come to terms with Kruger, who refused to compromise either his republicanism or his Boer nationalism. He accurately sensed that most Afrikaaners, both in the Transvaal and in the Cape Colony, stood behind him in his struggle with Great Britain.

In 1899, fresh from its diplomatic triumph over France at Fashoda, the British government decided to end the bickering with Kruger by going to war. Fighting broke out in October 1899, but the British were not victorious until the beginning of 1902, for the Boers put up a surprisingly stubborn resistance. With its victory Britain obtained a valuable addition to its territories, which now stretched continuously, with the exception of German East Africa, from Egypt to the tip of the continent. Rhodes's dream had nearly been fulfilled. The victory was costly, however, because it left Britain with an insoluble problem. The addition of the Boer republics to the Union of South Africa brought with it a population that deeply resented the British conquest and remained hostile to British rule and customs. In 1909 the formation of the Union of South Africa by the Liberal cabinet opened the way to a measure of self-government; this step permitted Afrikaaner nationalists to gain important influence within the Union. The Boers refused to become reconciled to British rule and in the immediate aftermath of the Boer War their nationalism pointed the way to eventual independence.

The Scramble for China

In the Far East, European expansion revived at the time Britain and France were quarreling over Egypt. The great prize was China, whose reputed riches and great potential market tempted European traders. The quest for China intensified largely as the result of French initiatives in Vietnam. (In recent times it has become customary to refer to three of the states of what became French Indo-China—that is, Tonkin, Annam, and Cochin China—as Vietnam.)

French Indo-China

The French possession of Cochin China became the base for expansion into Tonkin and Annam in the north. Although Cochin China offered a fueling station for French ships in the Pacific and support for Catholic missions in Vietnam, it was unsuitable as a starting point for a route into southern China because the Mekong River was not navigable. In the early 1880's French merchants suggested that a direct and relatively easy route into China could be found through the Red River Valley in Tonkin.

France had already made claims in the north by signing a treaty in 1874 whereby the court at Hué, which ruled over Annam and Tonkin, would make no agreements with other foreign powers without French approval. In 1880–81 China was trying to maintain its tributary rights in Annam, although the French foreign ministry believed that the 1874 treaty had broken this connection. The search for a trade route into China and alarm at anti-French maneuvers in Annam and Tonkin brought a French military expedition to Hanoi in 1882.

When the commander of this expedition met his death outside the gates of Hanoi the next year, the French Chamber voted credits for a larger expedition to restore French prestige in Tonkin. Soon France and China found themselves in an undeclared war; French warships menaced Chinese ports while bands of Chinese clashed with French marines in Tonkin. Eventually, the French military power wore down Chinese and Annamite resistance, and in 1885 a treaty was signed in Peking that recognized a French protectorate over Annam and Tonkin and effectively ended Chinese claims to tributary rights in Vietnam.

By the time the treaty was signed, the French Chamber had grown weary of continued demands for credits to meet the military expenses of the Tonkinese venture. Anti-colonial critics unseated Jules Ferry, the author of the Tonkin policy, as premier in 1885; later in the same year the Chamber agreed to stay in occupation of Tonkin—by a narrow majority of four votes, which was obtained after the government promised no more military adventures. But the French could not pacify Tonkin. During the rest of the decade continuing skirmishes between French and local forces took place throughout Tonkin. Not until a thorough military campaign had been waged in the 1890's did the French administration succeed in bringing Tonkin under effective control. The demands of pacification were much greater than the government had anticipated in the 1880's.

French Indo-China, formed into a union in 1887, was further expanded with the addition of Laos in 1893. This annexation touched off a brief crisis with Great Britain, whose position in Burma appeared threatened by the French advance. The crisis passed when Britain and France agreed to recognize and maintain Siam as an independent buffer between their possessions. But the extension of British and French holdings in Burma and Indo-China suggested that these two states were preparing to press northward toward South China to further add to their possessions.

Russian and Japanese Ambitions

By the end of the 1890's the struggle for China reached an acute phase. While Britain and France were knocking at the southern door, Russia and Japan were both eyeing Manchuria in the north. The expansion of Russia across the steppes toward China had taken place throughout the last half of the nineteenth century, but the commencement of the trans-Siberian railway gave new impetus to Russia's eastward migration. The timber and mining resources of Manchuria and Korea added luster to Russian ambitions in the East.

Meanwhile, Japan displayed expansionist tendencies toward China. The source of conflict between Japan and the Chinese empire was Korea, a natural bridge for Japan's entry onto the Asian continent. By the 1890's Chinese influence in Korea had weakened, although the Chinese still claimed a nominal suzerainty over the Korean peninsula. In 1893 the Korean king, faced with an uprising of militant, anti-Japanese nationalists, called for Chinese troops to help quell the uprising. The Japanese government, urged on by military advisors, decided to intervene before the arrival of Chinese troops, and the Japanese army restored order in Korea. After China protested Japan's action the two states attempted to reach a compromise, but the negotiations broke down and war was declared in 1894. The outcome was a clear victory for the Japanese army; it signaled Japan's position as a serious competitor for the riches of China.

Foreign Demands on China

The Sino-Japanese War exposed the weakness of the Chinese empire, which was obviously in a state of internal decay after two and a half centuries of Manchu rule. At the end of the 1890's, the European powers raced to claim a share of the spoils. The Manchu dynasty was bombarded with demands from them for concessions. In the south France received the right to trade through three frontier stations along the Tonkin border and won important mining and railway concessions. Britain immediately countered by procuring the right to construct a railway into southern China from Burma. In 1896 Russia received authorization to build a railway connection to Vladi-

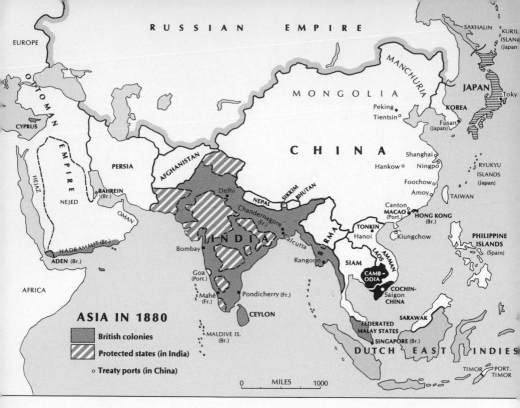

ASIA IN 1880

- British colonies
- Protected states (in India)
- o Treaty ports (in China)

vostok across northern Manchuria, a route that shortened the trans-Siberian railway by some 600 miles. Two years later the Russians returned to Peking and demanded a lease on a naval station at Port Arthur; despite the anger of the British government and the irritation of the Japanese, who had given up this port three years earlier, the lease was granted. Finally, Germany also gained a foothold in China by using the assassination of two German missionaries as the occasion for insisting on a naval station at Kiao-Chow.

The dismemberment of China appeared to be at hand, much to the consternation of American businessmen who feared that Chinese trade as well as Chinese rail and mining concessions would fall into European hands. In 1899 John Hay, the American secretary of state, requested that the right of access to the China market for all businessmen be respected. This first suggestion of an "open door" for China was temporarily put aside, but it revealed the concern at that time that China might be headed for the fate Africa experienced. There was good reason for concern; the expansionist ambitions of most of the major powers suddenly and dramatically converged on China at the end of the 1890's.

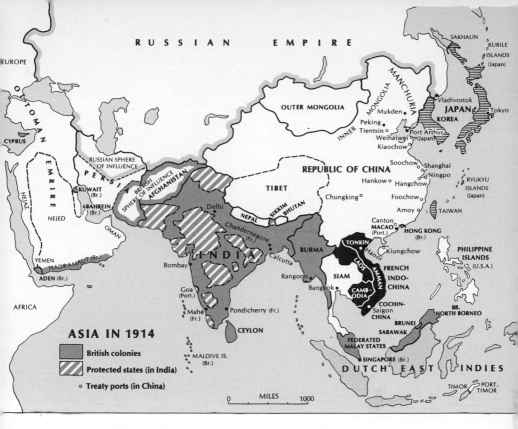

Map labels:

RUSSIAN EMPIRE
SAKHALIN
KURILE ISLANDS (Japan)
EUROPE
MANCHURIA
OUTER MONGOLIA
INNER MONGOLIA
Vladivostok
JAPAN
Tokyo
KOREA
Mukden
Peking
Tientsin
Port Arthur (Japan)
Weihaiwei (Japan)
Kiaochow
RUSSIAN SPHERE OF INFLUENCE
PERSIA
Soochow
Shanghai
REPUBLIC OF CHINA
Ningpo
RYUKYU ISLANDS (Japan)
CYPRUS
OTTOMAN EMPIRE
Hankow
Hangchow
AFGHANISTAN
BRITISH SPHERE OF INFLUENCE
TIBET
Chungking
Foochow
KUWAIT (Br.)
BAHREIN (Br.)
Delhi
Amoy
TAIWAN
NEJED
EMPIRE
NEPAL
SIKKIM
BHUTAN
Canton
MACAO (Port.)
HONG KONG (Br.)
OMAN
Chandernagore (Fr.)
BURMA
TONKIN
Kiungchow
PHILIPPINE ISLANDS (U.S.A.)
YEMEN
HADRAMAUT (Br.)
INDIA
Calcutta
Hanoi
LAOS
ANNAM
FRENCH INDO-CHINA
ADEN (Br.)
Bombay
Rangoon
SIAM
Goa (Port.)
Bangkok
CAMB-ODIA
AFRICA
Mahé (Fr.)
Pondicherry (Fr.)
COCHIN-Saigon CHINA
BR. NORTH BORNEO
CEYLON
BRUNEI
SARAWAK
ASIA IN 1914
FEDERATED MALAY STATES
British colonies
MALDIVE IS. (Br.)
SINGAPORE (Br.)
Protected states (in India)
DUTCH EAST INDIES
Treaty ports (in China)
TIMOR
PORT. TIMOR
MILES 1000

Chinese Reactions: The Boxer Rebellion

While the Europeans, Japanese, and Americans contemplated future profits in China, the government in Peking debated measures that would enable them to escape further submission. Reformers argued that a cautious policy of modernization, including a stream-lining of the archaic bureaucracy and its traditional practices, might save China from more humiliation. This was a risky course, for it threatened the conservative Chinese bureaucracy, the main support for Manchu power; the Mandarins would resist any reforms that threatened their privileges. Reform proposals thus presented the court with a dilemma: the government's weakness invited foreign intervention, but reforms threatened domestic upheaval.

For a brief time in the summer of 1898 the emperor appeared to have chosen a reformist course. Encouraged by reformers at his court, most of them from southern China, he published a series of decrees that called for a reorganization of the army, a westernization of Chinese schooling, and institution of economic policies designed to strengthen the state. What these reforms might have accomplished, had they been allowed to take effect, is difficult to judge; perhaps they would simply have accelerated the process of internal disintegration instead of providing the means to oppose foreign domination. In any event the reforms lasted only one hundred days; the dowager empress, a powerful figure despite her nominal retirement from Chinese politics, returned to an active role at court and effectively undermined the decrees.

The reformist impulse was succeeded by an entirely different movement that drew on Chinese xenophobia. Just as the emperor published his reform decrees, a Society of the Harmonious Fists was founded with the stated purpose of driving the foreigner and all foreign influences from the Celestial Empire. The "Boxers," as members of this society were called, appeared to have the approval of the court and the dowager empress as they attacked foreign missionaries and engineers in southern China. The Boxers also won a following among Chinese peasants who were suffering from a series of floods and crop failures that had ravaged the countryside in the fall of 1898. Some of the more moderate provincial rulers in southern China disliked the movement and pushed the Boxers out of their districts toward the north. As the Boxer movement approached Peking, the government vacillated in its policies. Fearing the extremism of the movement, moderates urged the government to disband the Boxers, but the reactionaries at court definitely favored the Boxers and their militant hostility to foreigners. At one point, the government sent a delegation to negotiate with the Boxers. The reactionary composition of this delegation made the outcome a foregone conclusion; in the spring of 1900 government troops were withdrawn from the district between Peking and the Boxer stronghold.

The foreign delegations in the capital realized the danger they were in should the Boxers decide to invade Peking. Foreigners had already been advised to leave the interior of China, and at the end of May many of them were fleeing the capital. Nevertheless, the delegations decided to remain in Peking, believing that they were in less danger there than if they attempted to reach the coast. On June 13 the Boxers entered the city and began attacking all foreigners. The legations quickly became besieged, as the capital was cut off from all contact with the outside world. Although the Boxers controlled the capital for two months, the legations were able to hold out, partly because for some unknown reason the Chinese did not use artillery against them. By August 15 an international army, assembled from European and American troops stationed in Asia and greatly bolstered by a sizable Japanese contingent, reached the capital and chased the

Boxers out. The emperor and dowager empress fled from the capital disguised as Chinese peasants. They took up residence in a western province and opened negotiations with the invaders. The Boxer policy had produced disaster, and the court broke with its pro-Boxer advisors, who were exiled or executed, or else committed suicide.

The Aftermath of the Boxer Rebellion

The climax of imperialism in China was symbolized by the presence of European, American, and Japanese troops in the capital while the Manchu dynasty nursed its wounds in a distant province. In the south, moderate provincial rulers had ignored the nationalism that seized Peking. During the uprising, many southern rulers compromised with the imperialist powers by guaranteeing the lives and property of Europeans in exchange for promises that the Europeans would not send gunboats up the rivers. China appeared to be breaking into two, or perhaps into many, pieces. Manchu authority had been greatly discredited by the Boxer episode, and China lay prostrate before the foreigners who controlled most of China's trade, railways, and mines.

Once more a conflict between the imperialism of the industrial states and a nationalistic resistance to this expansion had produced a crisis in the non-European world. This particular crisis occurred in an empire that had long taken the superiority of its civilization for granted. For this reason the shock of the 1900 invasion was the more severe. In the decade after the Boxer uprising it became clear that the Manchu dynasty was incapable of adjusting to the twentieth century. It seemed that a radical change might be necessary to escape foreign domination. Imperialism in Asia touched off a new Chinese nationalism that was modernist—even revolutionary—rather than traditionalist in outlook.

For all of its internal weakness, the Chinese empire escaped partitioning. Having asserted their authority in 1900, the imperialist powers drew back from taking this final step. Perhaps they sensed that any attempt to divide the Chinese treasure would provoke conflicts among them. As it was, Russia and Japan were already headed for war over Manchuria. The prospect of providing a government for populous China was in itself another cause for the imperial powers to have second thoughts about a partition. Despite their formidable military and administrative skills, there were limits to the capacity of expansionist states for overseas rule. When spheres of influence in China were being considered, a member of the British government expressed his country's unwillingness to undertake "the immense responsibility of governing what is practically a third of China." The American proposal for an "open door" offered an alternative to such risks.

Informal Imperialism: the Economic Expansion of Europe

In the short space of two decades the European imperial powers had won impressive domination over large sectors of the Asian and African continents. Most Africans responded to European administration and laws while China had no choice other than to accede to European demands for rights and concessions. But the pressure of European expansion could also be seen in parts of the world that fell neither under the control of a European government nor within a self-proclaimed sphere of influence. European financial expansion overseas represented an extension of "informal imperialism," particularly after 1900, when the rate of Europe's overseas investments increased rapidly. Although these investments did not lead to direct imperialism, they created interests that often brought political pressures.

In the Levant

European capital was particularly active in the Ottoman empire, an area in which Europeans had a long tradition of trade and commerce. The Ottoman rulers granted Europeans exemptions from any special taxes. This agreement assured the Europeans access to the Turkish market. Economic competition among Europeans within the Ottoman empire became intense at the turn of the century. By investing heavily in government bonds, French capitalists controlled some 60 percent of the Ottoman state debt. Britain also had investments in the Ottoman empire at the end of the nineteenth century, but the European state that was gaining an important interest in the Turkish lands was Germany, whose investments were nearly as heavy as those of France. In 1903 the Deutsche Bank obtained a concession to build a railway network across Asia Minor that would eventually link Baghdad and Constantinople. Evidence of German economic penetration into the Ottoman empire and the Middle East alarmed Britain and France. For a while the London and Paris stock exchanges were closed to the sale of Baghdad railway bonds, and French bankers feared that Germany might replace France as the Sultan's principal creditor.

European economic penetration brought political intervention in Ottoman affairs. In 1881 the Sultan, finding himself bankrupt, had been forced to accept the presence of a European Debt Commission, which began supervising his finances and collecting his customs. So efficient were the Europeans at squeezing revenue out of his state that the Sultan allowed them to collect taxes, a percentage of which went into the Sultan's personal treasury. Europeans enjoyed other sorts of privileges. In disputes among themselves they were not tried by Turkish law courts, but were judged by European consular officials. In any quarrel between a Turk and a European, the trial was held before a Turkish magistrate, but the European had the right to have a representative from his embassy in court; the intimidating presence of this observer usually persuaded Ottoman justice to be lenient toward the Europeans. Thus European subjects enjoyed what amounted to extraterritorial privileges within Ottoman domains. The European states dominated Turkey, albeit indirectly; whatever independence the Ottoman government possessed amounted to playing off one European power against another.

Elsewhere in the Levant, European economic penetration became pronounced at the turn of the century. In Persia and along the Persian Gulf British geologists and engineers prospected for oil reserves, while in northern Persia Russian engineers were engaged in the same activity. Both Britain and Russia gained important mining concessions from the Shah. The 1907 entente between Russia and Britain divided Persia into spheres of influence, and the independence of the Shah's government was, in practice, quite limited. For example, when the Shah tried to escape the pressure of Britain and Russia, by turning to Germany for loans or to an American financier, Morgan Shuster, for advice, Britain and Russia combined to force him to abandon these plans.

With the growing importance of oil and petroleum to run internal-combustion engines in Europe's industry, it was unlikely that Britain would be disinterested in the Middle East. If anything, the Suez Canal was more important than ever for providing transportation for these crucial raw materials, which were available only in limited quantities within Europe itself.

In Latin America

In Latin America Europeans found outlets for their capital and markets for their industrial wares, as well as food and raw materials for importation. By treaty agreement several Latin-American states assured European investors and businessmen that they would not be subjected to special taxes if they invested in their countries. Among the European powers Britain had the largest stake in Latin America. British capital was particularly active in promoting railway construction throughout the continent. In Argentina, five-sixths of the railway mileage was built by British companies or with British money, and British equipment and coal were imported to run the railroads. In Peru, Uruguay, Paraguay, and Brazil British capital and engineers were responsible for financing and laying much of the railway mileage. British companies played an important part in early railway construction in Mexico, but by the end of the nineteenth century the United States had come to replace Britain there. The other European states also invested heavily in Latin-American railway construction. French capital underwrote the railway building around Bahia in Brazil, and Belgian investors were responsible for most of the rail lines in the southern provinces. Germany financed some railway systems, particularly in areas that had experienced a German migration, such as southern Brazil and Venezuela.

The construction of railways in Latin America gave the continent an impressive transportation system after the turn of the century, but most of this network served European needs. The rail lines were closely tied to the mining industries and to the development of Argentine meat and grain production. The lines ran from the interior to the shipping ports instead of serving to establish effective connections among the Latin states. This pattern clearly demonstrated the European influence in the economic structure of Latin America.

European investments promoted the mining of tin, manganese, silver, and copper in Latin America, and European companies controlled the valuable Chilean nitrate industry. On the eve of the First World War, the initial explorations by European companies were made in rich Venezuelan oil fields. The impact of European investments was also felt in Latin-American agriculture, particularly in Brazilian coffee production and in the Argentinean meat industry.

Another lucrative investment was in government bonds. Because of the political instability that plagued several Latin-American states, the governments had to offer the enticement of high interest rates. Returns of 6 to 20 percent were relatively common in Latin America whereas the maximum return on capital in European banks was less than 3 percent. To supervise the flow of capital, European banks established branches throughout the continent. Buenos Aires, perhaps the most European of Latin-American cities, had six foreign banks.

The pattern of European investments generally reflected tendencies within the European economy. That is, Britain placed capital in the traditional, heavy industries—such as railways and mines—that were characteristic of the early industrial revolution; French investors preferred government securities because of the guaranteed return that they promised; German enterprise, rapidly increasing in scale, turned to newer industries, such as optics, electrical equipment, and chemicals.

Capital was not the only resource that Europe exported to Latin America. European engineers, many seeking their fortunes in a more adventuresome and exotic climate, supplied the skills to build and run the railways and mines. European firms preferred to hire technicians trained in Europe, for the curricula of Latin-American universities did not provide opportunities for gaining knowledge in scientific and technical fields.

A migration of European labor accompanied the influx of capital and technicians. Most of the immigrants settled in the southern, temperate tier of Latin-American states. Argentina absorbed the largest number of Europeans, the majority being from Spain and Italy. Chile acquired a considerable number of Irish, Germans, and other northern Europeans as well as immigrants from Latin Europe. This influx from Europe gave a pronounced European cast to the Latin-American states. For instance, Rio Grande do Sul in southern Brazil became a kind of German province, reflecting the customs and language of the home country.

Many of the immigrants found employment on the railways and as farm laborers; others settled on their own farms, pushing into the pampas in a last wave of colonization; still others settled in the growing cities, such as Rio, Buenos Aires, and Montevideo. Not all the immigrants stayed in Latin America however; the turn of the century witnessed the appearance of a kind of "floating" proletariat that periodically crossed and recrossed the Atlantic in cheap steerage passages. Conditions of labor for this proletariat were harsh; often the contracts signed in Europe were less rewarding when fulfilled than the promises of labor recruiters had led the immigrants to believe. By severe economizing many of them were able to save enough to either escape their contracts and purchase return passage, or send their savings to their families in the homelands.

The "informal imperialism" in Latin America and the Levant testified to the enormous expansionist energy that existed within European society at the outset of the twentieth century. Backed by their material power, Europeans pressed into nearly every corner of the globe. The technological innovations in transport and communications produced by the end of the nineteenth century played a large part in this expansion. As a result many parts of the world found themselves economically and technologically dependent on Europe to a much greater extent than at any time in the past. Perhaps the impact of Europe's expansion only scratched the surface of many non-European societies; but there is little doubt that the contact between the European and non-European worlds provided the impetus for change. The need for modernization could no longer be avoided by those societies that felt the full impact of European expansion.

The Rise of the United States and Japan

With the shrinking of the world the European powers were confronted with two non-European states that had successfully equipped themselves with industrial systems. The material strength of the United States and Japan enabled these two countries to pursue their own policies, independent of European wishes, and their emergence helped define the limits of European expansionism at the turn of the century.

The United States' Challenge to Europe

Economic Growth ■ The construction of a transcontinental railway system kindled an era of dynamic economic growth in the United States. The transcontinentals gave the American farmer access to the markets of the urban eastern seaboard and of Europe itself. In the decades after the Civil War, American agricultural produce flooded into Europe. For a while it looked as if the United States would serve as a vast European granary, but the same years also witnessed an industrial boom in the United States. In addition to connecting the agricultural and mining regions of the west to the industrial northeast the transcontinentals and the water routes made accessible an enormous domestic market that was potentially much greater than that of any European state. Protected by high tariffs, American industry began expanding as the domestic economy boomed.

By 1900 the United States was well on the way toward shedding its economic dependency on European capital (such as Britain supplied in financing the transcontinentals) and could take advantage of growing domestic financial resources to underwrite further expansion. In fact, the economic balance in the world was beginning to shift away from Europe, as some European observers realized. In 1902 the French ambassador in London, Paul Cambon, warned of a growing American economic penetration of Europe. To illustrate his argument he cited the competition of two American financial companies for control of the London underground transportation system. He also noted that British capital seemed unable to finance "the enormous American enterprises" and was employed elsewhere. Britain, he predicted, was going to be challenged for financial leadership of the world, a clear foreshadowing of future trends.

The Spanish-American War ▪ The Spanish-American War of 1898 is the event most commonly cited as evidence for the emergence of the United States as a world power. In the last decades of the nineteenth century, the expansionist energies of the United States had been consumed in fulfilling the nation's "manifest destiny"—that is, the construction of a federal state that stretched from the Atlantic to the Pacific. Following the last settlement of frontier territory in 1890 American expansionists continued to seek outlets for their energies and ambitions overseas. At this moment the cause of Cuban revolutionaries struggling to gain independence from Spain caught the attention of the American public, largely as the result of sensational newspaper stories that publicized Spanish atrocities committed in suppressing the rebellion. Indignation over Cuba reached a fever pitch in February 1898 when the American battleship *Maine* exploded and sank in the Havana harbor. Although the cause of this tragedy has not been established, press and public opinion in the United States immediately blamed Spain. President McKinley, responding to the outcry raised by the Maine affair, sent an ultimatum to the Spanish government. Even though most of the American government's demands were met by Spain, Congress, in a belligerent mood, declared war.

Within three months the American forces had won a complete victory in Cuba and also in the Philippines, where Spanish weakness in the Pacific was exploited. The peace treaty created an independent Cuba, but the United States subsequently insisted on special rights there, including the lease on a naval base and a provision in the Cuban constitution giving the United States authority to intervene in Cuban affairs for the purposes of preserving order. This provision made Cuba in effect a dependency of the United States. In addition, by the treaty with Spain the United States acquired other imperial holdings, notably Puerto Rico, Guam, and the Philippines. American imperialism in the Caribbean and the Pacific had clearly begun.

The New Imperialism Under Theodore Roosevelt ▪ President McKinley presided over America's entry into world politics, but it remained for Theodore Roosevelt, who became president on McKinley's assassination in 1901, to give vigorous expression to this new role. Roosevelt embodied a paradox to be found among many American—and European—imperialists. In domestic affairs Roosevelt won a reputation as a reformer for his programs to curb the power of American trusts and to preserve American wilderness areas from despoilation. Many of his fellow Republicans found him a bit too radical for their conservative tastes. Yet in foreign affairs Roosevelt sponsored an active policy of intervention and readily supported American business and financial interests in the Caribbean and in Latin America. Roosevelt may have pursued "dollar diplomacy" out of concern for the interests of the American investor, or he may have used investments as an excuse for intervention, but the effect was the same—a close alliance of American economic and political interests. This alliance came to characterize United States policy in the Caribbean after the turn of the century.

Interest in the Caribbean was further heightened by the decision of the United States to build a canal across the Isthmus of Panama. Some rather blunt behavior on the part of Roosevelt and the American government was necessary to implement this decision. In 1850 the United States and Britain had signed a treaty in which each country pledged not to construct a canal without the participation of the other power. This obstacle to an American canal under purely American control was removed in 1901 when Great Britain, anxious to maintain good relations with the United States during the Boer War, renounced its interest in a joint canal project. Roosevelt then turned his attention to Colombia, the government that controlled Panama. The Colombian Congress refused to ratify a treaty granting the United States the right to build and operate a canal, and American threats failed to change this stand. At that moment, however, a rebellion broke out in Panama that conveniently served American plans for the canal. Forewarned of the uprising, the United States promptly recognized the independence of Panama and sent a cruiser to discourage any Colombian attempt to suppress the revolt. Within two weeks the Republic of Panama signed a treaty that gave the United States the right to build a canal across the Isthmus and guaranteed the United States administration of the canal zone.

The construction of the Panama Canal increased the strategic importance of the Caribbean and led Roosevelt to redefine American intentions to keep European powers away from the area. The occasion for his pronouncement of a "Roosevelt corollary" to the Monroe Doctrine came in 1904, when the financial weakness of the Dominican Republic threatened to bring intervention of European powers concerned about protecting the investments of their citizens. To forestall this possibility, the United States stepped into the Dominican Republic and forced the government to sign an agreement that established an American economic protectorate over the country.

At the time Roosevelt declared that the United States would intervene whenever the difficulties of a Latin-American state required supervision by "an international police power." With this declaration Roosevelt warned the Europeans that the western hemisphere was a sphere of American interest.

In subsequent years the United States employed economic, military, and political pressure to extend its influence in the Caribbean and elsewhere in Latin America. Despite their heavy investments on this continent, European governments were inclined to respect American claims to political pre-eminence in the western hemisphere. This attitude was amply demonstrated by the behavior of Great Britain. As a sign of British respect and confidence in American policy, the British squadron was withdrawn from the Caribbean. The British government consistently deferred to American claims, justifying its policy on the basis of a special relationship—unacknowledged by any treaty—between Britain and the United States.

Elsewhere in the world the United States took an active part in international affairs after the turn of the century. The American suggestion of an open-door policy in China was accepted as the basis for the dealings of the imperial powers with the empire. In 1905 the United States used its good offices to help bring the war between Japan and Russia to an end. Meanwhile, President Roosevelt, whose style was in some ways reminiscent of William II, began a crash naval construction program and in 1908 and 1909 sent a "white fleet" on a voyage around the world to demonstrate the potential power of the American navy.

The assertion of American interests in Asia and Latin America revealed the presence of another power in international politics, which the European states were compelled to acknowledge. But prior to the First World War, European observers, while recognizing the country's potential power, chose to emphasize the fact that this power was still potential rather than actual. European ambassadors, for example, reported an American distrust of the military that kept the American army small and relatively weak. The growing importance of the United States was recognized in the realm of economic relations but not in diplomacy or power politics, and was considered to be significant in Latin America and in the Pacific but not in Europe itself.

Japan's Challenge to Europe

The rise of the United States to the status of a great power was not necessarily astonishing to the Europeans, for many of them looked on the United States as a derivative culture, still rather crude and in the process of formation, but perfectly capable of mastering the technological power of the industrial revolution. Much more startling was the appearance of a modern society in Asia that was capable of meeting the European powers on their own terms. Yet the rise of Japan as a military state with imperialist ambitions of its own provided further evidence that European hegemony could not be taken for granted throughout the world.

The Modernization of Japan ▪ Japan successfully modernized its economy and escaped domination at the end of the nineteenth century while other Oriental civilizations, such as China, lay prostrate before foreign invaders. How Japan was able to do this is a puzzle that has caught the attention of many social scientists who are concerned with finding a theory to explain the process of modernization. The search for this theory is still going on and will probably continue for several years; certainly the problem cannot be resolved here, but a brief description of Japan's leap into the modern world should be given.

From the middle of the seventeenth century to the middle of the nineteenth, Japan experienced a period of isolation and domestic peace under the Tokugawa family shogunate, a dictatorial military regime, with the emperor as titular and spiritual head. This long era of internal stability had two major consequences that assumed significance for the course of Japanese political and economic modernization. Peace brought about a decline in the warrior class, or samurai, within Japan. This class still retained its identity, but its importance was greatly reduced and many samurai became impoverished. At the same time, the stability imposed by the Tokugawas encouraged the development of vigorous commercial activity based on domestic handicrafts. Toward the end of the eighteenth century, a number of city merchants prospered and rose to new prominence. But this commercial enterprise eroded the economic foundation of the Tokugawa system. Tokugawa power was based on traditional relations between local lords and the court of Edo (Tokyo). This meant power rested on birth and prescribed position rather than commercial wealth. The rise of a prosperous merchant class threatened to disturb the traditional pre-eminence of the lords. Behind a façade of stability, Tokugawa power was beginning to crumble in the nineteenth century.

When Admiral Perry and his fleet arrived in 1853 to open Japan to trade, Tokugawa officials sensed Japan's relatively weak position. As a result the shogunate agreed to Perry's demands to open two ports to American trade and allow an American consular official to reside in Japan. Not long afterward the British, Russians, and Dutch pressed their own demands on the Japanese, including an insistence on trading concessions and on extraterritorial rights that placed their citizens beyond the reach of Japanese law. By the 1860's Japan faced the humiliating prospect of passing from isolation to subservience within a short space of time.

In responding to this danger Japan moved toward modernization. The Tokugawa rulers were discredited for their concessions to foreigners, and a group of Japanese nationalists, rallying under the slogan, "Revere the emperor and expel the barbarian," began working against the shogunate. These ultra-conservatives succeeded in assassinating the councilor who had signed the treaties with the western powers. A period of domestic political anarchy ensued that ended with the "Meiji restoration" of 1868 by which effective political power returned to the emperor. In this struggle the emperor served as a rallying point for those who wished to eliminate the Tokugawa system. They justified their action by claiming that the restoration was a return to older Japanese political traditions.

The Meiji restoration did not, however, produce a chauvinistic hostility to foreign ways of the sort that inspired the Boxer uprising in China a generation later. The oligarchy of powerful families that now ruled Japan determined that their salvation lay in catching up with western technological achievements as rapidly as possible. Foreign technicians were hired by the government, and thousands of Japanese students were sent abroad to the universities of western Europe and the United States to study the new science and technology. Meanwhile, after a period of internal conflict, the government successfully imposed its will on the country and demanded sacrifices in the struggle to overtake the West.

The intention of the new rulers was to preserve as much of Japanese tradition and independence—and their own privileges—as possible, but in the pursuit of these aims they did not shrink from dispensing with those traditions or practices that stood in the way of Japan modernization and eventual rise to the status of a world power. Feudalism, for example, was abolished. In the nineteenth century European liberals tended to praise Japan for its quaint skill in imitating the West. What this evaluation missed was that Japan modernized its economic life not out of any desire to become "westernized" but, on the contrary, for the defensive purpose of avoiding falling under the sway of western political power. The major impetus for Japanese modernization was national pride.

Because the Meiji government decided to rely as little as possible on outside financial assistance in the pursuit of its goals, enormous sacrifices were required of the Japanese people. Those who paid most heavily for the costs of modernization were the peasants, who were squeezed by taxes to raise revenue for industrial investment. Despite these burdens, they succeeded in introducing simultaneously more intensive agrarian methods. The output of rice per acre and per man-hour increased at an impressive rate at the end of the nineteenth century, thereby mitigating some of the hardship that the peasants suffered from the squeeze in prices brought on by the industrial revolution.

The government also gave subsidies to nascent industries in a further effort to spur modernization. These policies favored a few families who gained a dominant role in the Japanese economy, but these families rationalized their activities and profits as a means of strengthening the state and enabling the emperor and the government to resist the foreigner.

Japan's Assertion as a World Power ▪ With the expansion of Japanese industrialization, the government began making overtures to the western powers for the elimination of the extraterritorial rights that had been granted in the 1860's. The government and the Japanese nationalists regarded the abolition of these treaties as an essential step in the recovery of Japan's full independence and self-respect. Agitation for treaty revision began in the 1880's, but it was not until Japan had defeated China in the war of 1894–95 that substantial progress was made. In 1894 Britain agreed to abandon the special privilege clauses in its treaty with Japan; within a few years other nations followed suit.

The war with China also brought a humiliation of a different sort, however. Japan's victory so stunned the Europeans, who had under-estimated Japan's military capacity, that Germany, Russia, and France felt constrained to force Japan to abandon some of its war spoils. A surge of anger subsequently engulfed the Japanese nation, and the incident was not forgotten. Both the victory over China and the ultimatum from the European powers impressed on Japanese military and political leaders the conviction that the decisive element in power politics was military strength. The government embarked on a further strengthening of the Japanese army in preparation for the next conflict.

This conflict came within a decade with the Russo-Japanese War in 1904–05. The victory over Russia confirmed Japan's arrival as a world power; not only Russia but all Europe realized that Japanese interests in Asia could not be trifled with. The triumph was, of course, highly popular within Japan. It had been a just war in the eyes of the Japanese people, and the victory was a fitting reward for years of sacrifice and preparation. A number of nationalistic societies were founded, some of which succeeded in gaining an important following within the military. In the aftermath of victory Japanese expansionist aims became more pronounced: Japan looked to China as an area for further penetration, and enthusiastic Japanese imperialists began to argue for the extension of Japanese leadership throughout Asia.

Japan's triumph sent a thunderclap across Asia. Asian nationalists, underestimating the extent of Japan's own imperial ambitions, were encouraged by the Japanese example in their struggles against European domination. By exploiting European industrial and military techniques, Japan had defeated a European power on equal terms and had preserved its independence. In the next decade, this lesson, derived from the events of 1905, had a great impact on the opposition to European rule that was taking shape in Asia in the form of nationalist movements.

The Rise of Nationalist Movements

In the decade after 1905 many exiled Asian nationalists took refuge in Tokyo and other Japanese cities to plot ways of chasing the Europeans from Asia. When the Japanese government realized that the revolutionary doctrines of these exiles encouraged revolutionary sentiments within Japan itself, the government expelled them. Japanese nationalists had no intention of promoting social revolution in Asia. Nevertheless, they could not prevent the example of what Japan had accomplished from making its impression and giving encouragement to the nationalist movements.

Nationalism in India

Repercussions of the Japanese triumph had an influence in India on a conflict that was taking shape between the British administration and the nationalist movement within the Indian National Congress. The congress, which had been formed in 1885 by middle-class Indians, met annually for the purposes of debating reforms that would be passed on to the British administrative officials. The congress had no formal power within the British system, but it provided a forum where middle-class Indians could practice parliamentary debates and press for greater Indian participation in ruling the country. The congress was by no means a radical organization; its proposals were moderate in tone, but the British rulers looked with some concern on the emergence of an Indian middle class that was interested in reform and skilled in political debate.

The British civil service in particular disliked the new Indian middle class, which seemed to be complaining constantly. Although the average British civil servant in India was conscientious and hard-working—perhaps the best of all colonial administrators—he preferred ruling with benevolent paternalism to trying to find ways to satisfy difficult people whose competence he distrusted anyway. The attempts at reform that Britain did make often produced misunderstanding and disillusionment. In 1883, for example, the viceroy of India proposed that Indian judges in Bengal should be on a par with Europeans, a reform that would have allowed Indian judges to try cases among Europeans. When the British civil service threatened to strike if this reform were enacted, the viceroy compromised, much to the disappointment of those members of the Indian middle class who had foreseen an opportunity to put their English legal training into more effective practice. British promises for a wider participation in local government for Indians also remained largely unfulfilled or seemed inadequate when carried out.

The gap between the aspirations of the Indian middle classes and the paternalism of British rule became clear during Lord Curzon's tenure as viceroy (1898–1905). Curzon was a highly effective administrator who sought to run India efficiently; he introduced improvements in transportation, streamlined the government, and extended the frontiers of India to the northwest. But he was also an autocrat who had little sympathy for the new Indian middle classes. During the last years of his tenure his behavior showed great insensitivity to Indian aspirations. His proposals for a reform of Calcutta University, for example, struck Indian educators as a high-handed invasion of one area in which they enjoyed some autonomy. Even more serious was his decision to divide the state of Bengal in order to streamline its administration.

This proposal only served to unite all classes in Bengal in opposition. Commercial groups organized a boycott of British goods and riots broke out in several parts of Bengal. The boycott movement received support from the National Congress, whose more militant members called for a tax strike and urged that the congress seek self-government for India. Even moderates condemned the partition of Bengal and fully supported measures of resistance. More extreme nationalists began a terrorism campaign against British rule. Growing

Indian nationalism, already fed by Curzon's autocratic policies, reached new heights as news of Japan's victory over Russia swept across the country.

When the Liberals came to power in Great Britain at the end of 1905, they responded to the nationalist sentiment with a mixture of reform and firmness that henceforth marked British rule in India under Curzon's successors, Earl Minto and Lord Hardinge. Under reforms introduced by Minto, Indians were given wider participation in running Indian affairs, and were allowed to sit with the viceroy's council. The Liberal imperialists, however, for all their reform programs, had no intention of releasing power in India. Progress toward further measures of autonomy came to an end, for the Liberals believed that they had gone quite far in satisfying Indian political complaints. At the same time, the Liberals took severe measures to repress the terrorist faction of the Indian nationalist movement.

The decade before the First World War revealed the dilemmas of liberal imperialism, which permitted gradual change but under strict British control. Whether such measures would satisfy Indian nationalists was still uncertain on the eve of war, although some of the agitation of the previous decade had died down. Only when the First World War reached India did the Congress realize that the reforms had produced little real change, and the Indian nationalists resumed their campaign against British rule.

Nationalism in Indo-China

French rule in Indo-China encountered a similar opposition after 1905; here too, liberal imperialism could not resolve the conflicts. By the turn of the century Tonkin had at last been pacified by the French army, and the civilian French government turned toward a program of public works designed to make Indo-China prosper. As capital began to flow into the country, the government tightened its hold on the administration. The important posts were in the hands of the numerous French bureaucracy sent out to run Indo-China, but at the local level the French government tended to rely on village and regional chiefs, or mandarins, for administrative support. For a few years French paternalistic rule gave an appearance of stability to the country.

Some of the French reforms, however, especially those in education, created hostility to French rule. In the villages the French administration introduced various measures, including a westernization of Chinese script and the teaching of French, that undermined traditional Vietnamese schooling and brought an actual decline in Vietnamese literacy levels. Many of those involved in the education process disliked these changes. These intellectuals became leaders of a resistance to French rule after 1905. A secret society of teachers and translators was formed that was anti-French in its attitude, and other secret societies emerged in Hanoi and Saigon. Informal schools and doctrination centers equipped with books and pamphlets critical of French rule spread into many villages. By 1908 French colonists were complaining that the Indo-Chinese college in Hanoi had become a center for anti-French propaganda.

The presence of a militant anti-French movement became dramatically apparent in 1908 when an attempt was made by a group of conspirators to poison the French garrison in Hanoi. Investigation revealed that this attempt was part of a wider plot backed by revolutionary exiles who had their headquarters in Japan and southern China. The plot was forcefully suppressed within Indo-China. The conspirators who were caught were sentenced to death or lengthy prison terms. Meanwhile, acts of revolutionary terrorism erupted throughout Indo-China. In 1912 two French officers were killed by a bomb thrown into a Hanoi restaurant frequented by Europeans; only two weeks before a pro-French mandarin had been assassinated in Tonkin. In 1913 bomb plots were discovered in Saigon. In each instance French investigators established a connection between the conspirators and the revolutionary exiles.

The French response to these disturbances utilized the same mixture of force and liberal concessions that Britain employed in India. Successive governor-generals urged that liberal policies be continued, including educational measures designed to introduce an elite of the Vietnamese to western knowledge, a greater use of Vietnamese in the administrative bureaucracy, and the calling of an elected, consultative assembly. These measures, it was hoped, would gain the loyalty of the majority of the Vietnamese people. At the same time French military strength was increased, for it was believed that the reforms would be successful only if the French government showed its determination to resist all terrorist activity. The security provided by French military power would permit the inhabitants of Indo-China to find the way to progress under French guidance, or so the liberal imperialists believed.

The combination of force and reform failed to silence the opposition to French rule in Indo-China, although a temporary lull in nationalist agitation descended just before the First World War. The governor-general of Indo-China, Albert Sarraut, recognized the problem that European governments faced throughout Asia. Agitation in Persia, the Philippines, India, Indo-China, and China, he wrote in a 1913 report, "is like a vast fire covering all of Asia." What did these revolutionaries seek? Sarraut answered his own question: an elimination of all foreign domination and a new social condition for their countries. Sarraut's recommendation was that a combination of force and liberalism would convince the Asians that Europe offered the way to modernization.

Nationalism in China

The Asian ferment was not confined to areas in which the Europeans ruled directly. In China, for example, revolutionary movements began to gain a following after the turn of the century. The Manchu dynasty, at last recognizing its weakness, introduced a series of reforms that it hoped would bolster its position in the countryside. The army was reorganized, and the education system was revamped along western lines. In 1908 the emperor presented a constitution, which included a provision for a legislative assembly, to go into effect in 1917. On paper, these reforms signaled extensive and even revolutionary changes for Chinese society. Unfortunately the deaths of the emperor and venerable dowager empress in 1908 eliminated the two figures with enough determination to see the reforms through to realization.

After 1908 Chinese domestic politics quickly descended into disorder as effective power fragmented in the hands of provincial rulers. A series of local strong men appeared who became the de facto rulers of the country. Meanwhile, Chinese revolutionary and reformist groups in Japan and other places of exile began calling for a variety of changes in Chinese political life. The reformists believed that the imperial form of government should be retained although under a different dynasty. Republicans within China, headed by Sun Yat-sen, favored a democratic republic as a way to recovery and eventual escape from foreign domination. Sun Yat-sen's supporters formed a political party called the Koumintang and began to recruit a following in southern China. The Koumintang was clearly revolutionary in its opposition to the Manchu dynasty and in its preference for a republic. The Koumintang also exploited widespread discontent in the countryside, particularly after a crop failure in 1910.

The occasion for revolt came in 1911 when the imperial government tried to nationalize the railway in Szechwan province, a move that provoked strong local opposition. A general strike broke out in the province, and the Koumintang quickly began promoting resistance to the imperial government. The decisive break came when a provincial garrison mutinied and proclaimed itself the People's Army. By November much of southern China, including the ancient capital at Nanking, was in republican hands.

The dynasty turned to General Yuan Shih-K'ai and asked him to march south and repress the rebellion. Yuan Shih-K'ai agreed, but, seeing himself as master of the situation, he began playing one side off against the other. He first came to terms with the Koumintang and signed an armistice. Then he returned to Peking and persuaded the new dowager empress, who ruled in the name of her infant son, that only abdication would save China from further disorders. In February 1912 China became a republic—but in name only. Sun Yat-sen, recognizing that Yuan Shih-K'ai commanded the only effective military force in the country, stepped aside and allowed the general to be elected president of the republic. Once elected, Yuan Shih-K'ai promptly undermined the republic. He transferred the capital from Nanking to Peking, thereby escaping republican pressures in the south. Two years later he dissolved the Koumintang. The era of the generals was at hand as China plunged into a period of renewed internal strife. The Chinese revolution had succeeded in overthrowing the Manchu dynasty, but it had not yet been able to throw off the pressure of foreign domination.

Other Nationalist Movements

Elsewhere in the world nationalist movements also succeeded in overturning the old order and taking preliminary steps toward a national reawakening. In the Ottoman empire a group of young officers staged a mutiny in 1908 that forced the Sultan to convene a parliamentary assembly and restore the suspended 1876 constitution. When the Sultan tried a counter-coup the following year, these young officers, or "Young Turks," thwarted his plans and deposed him. In addition, they made certain that his successor's powers were clearly limited. The Young Turks saw themselves as both modernizers and patriots. Taking heed from the Japanese example, they favored the adoption of western practices as a necessary step toward regaining Turkish strength and escaping the subservience to European pressure that the Sultan had not been able to avoid.

In Persia a nationalist revolution, also inspired by events in the Far East, succeeded in expelling the Shah in 1906. Liberal reforms, including the introduction of parliamentary government based on a written constitution, followed the next year. As in the Ottoman empire, these reforms adhered more to the letter than to the spirit of liberal western practices. The economic influence of Britain and Russia continued unabated, despite efforts of the nationalist government to escape these pressures. The Persian nationalist revolution, like the Young Turk movement, had made only limited progress toward the goal of a national reawakening by 1914.

Finally, in Mexico a revolution erupted in 1910 that was at once an expression of peasant grievances and a rejection of foreign influence, particularly that of the United States. The local causes for the Mexican upheaval were quite distinct from those that operated in Asia and the Levant, but the Mexican revolution was also an expression of the desire to escape the humiliation of national weakness that had been exposed by contact with western expansionism.

Many nationalist movements remained weak beside European power in 1914, and in many areas, such as tropical Africa, there was no resistance to European domination. After the First World War the imperial states added even more territory to their domains. Nevertheless, there was evidence before the war that the dynamic expansion of Europe had brought resistance and the beginnings of a national awakening throughout the non-European world. The unsettling impact of the contact between European civilization and other cultures was to last well into the twentieth century.

SUGGESTED READING

There are a few general accounts of late nineteenth century imperialism. A recent survey by D. K. Fieldhouse, *The Colonial Empires: a Comparative Survey from the Eighteenth Century* (London: Weidenfeld & Nicolson, 1966), is more descriptive than comparative. Heinz Gollwitzer's *Europe in the Age of Imperialism, 1880–1914* (London: Thames & Hudson, 1969) is a brief, stimulating account of the imperlalist phenomenon and its many ramifications. Articles by F. C. Langdon, A. P. Thornton, R. E. Robinson, and J. Gallagher in *The New Cambridge Modern History*, Vol. XI, *Material Progress and World-Wide Problems, 1870–1898* (Cambridge: Cambridge University Press, 1962) consider overseas expansion in the Levant, Asia, and Africa.

Highly personal and contrasting interpretations may be found in G. W. F. Hallgarten's *Imperialismus vor 1914* (Munich: Beck, 1963) and Parker T. Moon's *Imperialism and World Politics* (New York: Macmillan, 1926). Other interpretations of the phenomenon include Joseph A. Schumpeter's "The Sociology of Imperialism" in *Imperialism and Social Classes: Two Essays*, tr. by H. Norden (New York: Meridian Books, 1965), and in the section on imperialism in Hannah Arendt's *The Origins of Totalitarianism* (New York: Harcourt, Brace & World, 1966). A lively account of theories of imperialism is given in Archibald P. Thornton's *Doctrines of Imperialism* (New York: Wiley & Sons, 1965). The economic impact of imperialism is weighed and found to constitute an overall deficit by Grover Clark in *The Balance Sheets of Imperialism* (New York: Russell, 1936). The classic accounts of economic imperialism are J. A. Hobson's *Imperialism, a Study* (Ann Arbor: University of Michigan Press, 1965 ed.) and V. I. Lenin's *Imperialism* (New York: International Publishers, 1939, rev. ed.). The semantic roots of the word "imperialism" are the subject of a study by R. Koebner and H. D. Schmidt, *Imperialism: the Story and Significance of a Political Word, 1840–1960* (Cambridge: Cambridge University Press, 1964).

Imperialism within the European states has inspired a variety of special studies. Bernard Semmel's *Imperialism and Social Reform: English Social-Imperialist Thought, 1895–1914* (Cambridge, Mass.: Harvard University Press, 1960) traces the connection between the imperialist urge for expansion and belief in social progress among certain British writers and politicians at the turn of the century. Another valuable attempt to assess the motives and causes for British imperialism is R. Robinson and J. Gallagher's *Africa and the Victorians* (New York: St. Martin's Press, 1961), which stresses the response in London to unanticipated developments throughout Africa that led to partition. The high tide of imperialism's popularity and its subsequent decline in Great Britain form the subject of A. P. Thornton's *The Imperial Idea and Its Enemies* (New York: St. Martin's Press, 1959). *The Empire-Commonwealth, 1870–1919* (Cambridge: Cambridge University Press, 1959), Vol. III of *The Cambridge History of the British Empire,* is a standard, straightforward account.

For France, one of the best surveys is Jean Ganiage's *L'Expansion coloniale de la France sous la troisième république, 1870–1914* (Paris: Payot, 1968). Earlier accounts include Herbert I. Priestley's *France Overseas* (New York: Appleton-Century-Crofts, 1938; Octagon Books, 1966) and C. Southworth's *The French Colonial Venture* (London: P. S. King, 1931). Henri Brunschwig has emphasized the political and patriotic motives behind French imperialism in his *French Colonialism, 1871–1914: Myths and Realities* (New York: Praeger, 1966). Thomas F. Power, Jr., also underplays economic motives in his *Jules Ferry and the Renaissance of French Imperialism* (New York: Columbia University Press, 1944; Octagon Books, 1966). An excellent recent monograph by A. S. Kanya-Forstner, *The Conquest of the Western Sudan* (Cambridge: Cambridge University Press, 1969), provides insight into the military role in French expansion.

The German imperialist drive is discussed in Mary E. Townsend's *The Rise and Fall of Germany's Colonial Empire, 1884–1918* (New York:

Macmillan, 1930). Bismarck was more than a disinterested bystander during the beginnings of the scramble for overseas territory, according to A. J. P. Taylor in his *Germany's First Bid for Colonies, 1884-1885* (London: Macmillan, 1938). Further insights into German imperialism may be found in W. O. Henderson's *Studies in German Colonial History* (Chicago: Quadrangle Books, 1962).

The impact of European imperialism on non-European cultures is just beginning to be investigated, although a sketch of the spreading post–1905 revolutionary surge in Asia may be found in Ivar Spector's *The First Russian Revolution: Its Impact on Asia* (Englewod Cliffs, N.J.: Prentice-Hall, 1962). Several surveys of Asian countries consider the forces that opposed European rule and influence: Kenneth S. Latourette's *A History of Modern China* (London: Penguin, 1954), Li Chien-nung's *The Political History of China, 1840–1928* (New York: Van Nostrand, 1956), and Teng Ssu-yu and John K. Fairbank's *China's Response to the West: a Documentary Survey, 1839–1923* (Cambridge, Mass.: Harvard University Press, 1954). Surveys of Japanese history include William G. Beasley's *A Modern History of Japan* (New York: Praeger, 1963) and Richard Storry's *A History of Modern Japan* (New York: Barnes & Noble, 1962). General accounts of India are given in K. M. Panikkar's *A Survey of Indian History* (New York: Taplinger [Asia Publishing House], 1963, 4th ed.) and Volume 2 of T. G. P. Spear's *A History of India* (London: Penguin, 1966).

7

NEW PERCEPTIONS:
THE RISE OF MODERNISM
IN EUROPE

European expansion at the end of the nineteenth century produced a tremendous increase in knowledge in both the arts and sciences. Exploration and experimentation prevailed. Modernism in the arts and sciences brought about a growing specialization and subsequent expertise in various fields within each realm, for as the depth of knowledge increased, the range that one man could master necessarily became limited. The humanistic ideal, dating from the Renaissance, had maintained that the mark of the cultured individual was his ability to be conversant with the whole range of human knowledge. The nineteenth century expression of this ideal synthesis was a faith in progress based on a belief in natural law, the mechanistic science of Newton, the evolutionary theories of Darwin, and a confidence in reason as the foundation of politics and the arts. As Europe entered the twentieth century this synthesis was shaken by the pressure of the cultural upheaval. Each area of endeavor—the visual arts, literature, the natural, physical, and social sciences—proceeded to establish its own rules and to assert the validity of its own perception. Not even the most gifted and talented of individuals would hope to become expert in all fields.

The Cultural Consequences of a Wider World

European culture was greatly enriched by expansion into the non-European world. For one thing, knowledge of the physical world increased rapidly. As accurate information about the physical characteristics of the globe came to light, a final charting of the world's continents became possible. In the two decades that preceded 1914 explorers pushed across the Sahara, climbed the mountains of Tibet, and made their way across frozen ice caps toward the northern and southern poles.

Much of this exploration was undertaken by adventurers and military officers, but it happened to create a reservoir of information for geographers and geologists. Often private geographical societies contributed heavily to these exploratory missions. A strong faith in the scientific value of explorations was the primary motivation, although there was a hope that such missions might turn up valuable mineral deposits or open new markets, and improvement in European technology often arose from the process of exploration. Mining techniques were refined in an effort to reduce wastage; the geologists' search for mineral and oil resources led to improved methods of excavation and of classification and description of the earth's crust, which aided the work of archeologists.

Contact with the non-European world also opened perspectives on other civilizations and "exotic" cultures. Archaeological investigations provided new insight into the character and development of earlier civilizations. Many of the archaeological treasures found in excavations were shipped back to Europe where they graced the museums of the Continent and Great Britain. The older civilizations of the Levant and Asia attracted European scholars; centers for the study of eastern civilizations emerged as features of European university life. Anthropologists embarked on a process of classification of the customs and social institutions of a wide variety of peoples. Comparative studies even served as a way of evaluating European cultural standards, although assumptions of cultural superiority sometimes biased the studies of non-European peoples.

In the visual arts, European painters and sculptors derived inspiration from African art forms that appeared in primitive art exhibits held in Paris and elsewhere. Many painters, including the impressionists and the fauves in France, were profoundly influenced by oriental art, especially Japanese silk screens and prints, with their distortion of perspectives and imaginative use of color.

New modes of perception opened up as European scientists and artists pursued their exploration and experimentation. Men gained deeper insight into the physical world and more sophisticated views of political and social structures. Meanwhile the arts moved toward a greater abstraction or a heightened emotionalism. These modernist trends represented a wholesale onslaught against conventional views of reality.

Attendant on the new perceptions, however, were anxieties and a seeming flux of cultural values that produced doubt and self-questioning within European intellectual circles. The feeling was prevalent, particularly among conservatives, that older standards had been abandoned with nothing to take their place. On the eve of the First World War some intellectuals called for a return to traditional values and praised institutions, such as the church, the army, and the state, that stood for stability, continuity, and order. An excessive emphasis on diversity and cultural permissiveness, they feared, would lead to chaos and anarchy.

Even intellectuals who were not conservatively inclined expressed the need for a reassessment of values. In their reaction against bourgeois materialism and their search for spiritual values, they showed their concern at the direction European history had taken. To these critics, it seemed as if Europe had lost its bearings and had poured its goods, wealth, and power into the world without any clear purpose. Behind the façade of Europe's material success they sensed a spiritual void.

It is ironic that just when Europe had attained an unprecedented material power, when its science promised abundance, and when Jules Verne was drawing fantastic visions of the near future in his science fiction, European culture became marked by uncertainty, even pessimism, about that future. Some historians looking back on European culture at the turn of the century have emphasized that this pessimistic assessment was an accurate anticipation of subsequent atrocities. This foreboding was imporant as part of the atmosphere of the period and as a divination of things to come, but it can be exaggerated. Alongside the internal doubts were the excitement and optimism of cultural ferment, and the creativity they engendered. The spirit of experimentation was manifested in the radical innovations introduced by European artists and architects at the turn of the century.

Revolutionary Trends in Art

Although certain artists in the early nineteenth century, like Turner, Delacroix, Constable, and Courbet, experimented with composition or color, most artists remained attached to conventional principles. Art academies and schools, which commanded decisive authority in forming public tastes, established relatively rigid rules of painting; art critics reinforced these traditional tastes. Academic painters were praised insofar as they adhered to official standards, and differences among them in technique or subject matter varied only slightly.

The Impressionists

In the 1860's and 1870's a major break with past tradition occurred in France when a group of artists evolved a radically new approach to many of the problems of painting. Originally used by critics as an epithet, "impressionism" describes their school and indicates one of its fundamental characteristics—the attempt to capture impressions of light and color.

The impressionists rejected many sacred principles of academic art. Fascinated by the effects of sunlight, they fled the confines of the studio to paint directly in the open air of the countryside. In so doing, they abandoned the practice of laboriously preparing canvases and toning down their colors with browns and grays. Instead, they applied paint directly to the canvas, using pure colors for the most part and only a minimum of mixing. Their light palettes created brighter effects than were achieved in the murky landscapes painted by early nineteenth century artists.

The decision to go outdoors had other consequences as well. Because the impressionists had to work quickly outside, they used rapid brushstrokes that appeared crude and unpolished to the academically trained eye. In Claude Monet's "Regatta at Argenteuil" the broken reflection of the sails on the water is indicated by single, vertical brushstrokes of white against the blue Seine. Monet deliberately sought to capture the fleeting, momentary impressions of light, color, and movement; what was lost in refinement of detail was more than compensated by a sense of immediacy.

Impressionists also abandoned the gradual shading from light to dark that Renaissance painters had adopted to give volume to objects in space. The impressionists discovered that objects seen in direct sunlight showed distinct contrasts of light and dark, not a gradual blending of light and shadow. Sharply defined patches of light, created by

Women in the Garden by Claude Monet. Louvre. Bulloz photo. Permission SPADEM 1970 by French Reproduction Rights, Inc.

sunlight streaming through trees, spangle the Sunday crowd portrayed in Auguste Renoir's "La Moulin de la Galette" and the dresses of the ladies in Monet's "Women in the Garden."

Not only in their concern for light and color effects, but also in their choice of subject matter and composition the impressionists seemed unorthodox by nineteenth century standards. Gone were the heroic subjects and the mythological or religious allegories of earlier periods. The everyday scenes of middle-class life caught the attention of the impressionists—Sunday crowds relaxing at Montmartre, street scenes in Paris, ladies in the garden. Above all, the impressionists discovered the charm of the small towns and rural villages of the Parisian basin and the beauty of the ordinary seascapes of the Normandy coast. Only Degas' preoccupation with the theater and ballet and Renoir's studies of the human figure offered variations to the themes of open-air painting. Rarely did the industrial world intrude, as it happened to in Monet's "Gare St.-Lazare." Although many impressionists suffered economic hardship and some of them leaned toward revolutionary political movements—Pissarro, for example, was an anarchist—they did not use painting as an instrument for political action. Their main concern was with technique, and in this domain the influence of impressionism was revolutionary.

Although roundly condemned by academic painters and critics at the time, the impressionists actually may be seen as at once the last of the "representative" painters and the pioneers of modern trends in painting. Their critics complained that impressionists left off whole parts of the body and made men look like blobs of paint. The impressionists insisted that they painted reality, that is, what the eye actually saw and not what it had been trained or conditioned to see. The details of figures at a distance—girls in poppyfields or strollers on Parisian boulevards—cannot actually be discerned by the eye, although the beholder knows that these figures have legs, arms, and fingers. The impressionists maintained that a few brushstrokes were enough to capture the highlights, or impressions, of people at a distance. To the objection that their paintings were blurred and out of focus, the impressionists replied by pointing out that the study of optics had demonstrated that the eye was capable of providing its own mixing of color; by placing patches of complementary colors on the canvas next to each other they left the integration of forms up to the eye of the viewer.

Armed with the scientific knowledge derived from optics, the impressionists saw themselves advancing the Renaissance tradition that required the artist to reproduce nature as faithfully and accurately as possible. Critics pointed out that technical improvements in photography made this task superfluous, for the camera could accomplish in an instant what the artist could achieve only after hours of painstaking work. Impressionism, however, found a way out of this dilemma. Instead of simply reproducing nature on canvas, the impressionists claimed to analyze nature into its component parts of light and color. If the beholder could "pop" a picture into focus by stepping back from it, so much the better, but the real subject of impressionist art was the abstract qualities of light and color seen in nature and expressed through the medium of paint. The observer was called on to look at the arrangement of color on canvas as much as to contemplate a landscape. This concern with the effects of light and color can be seen in Monet's contrasting studies of the façade of the Rouen Cathedral under varying conditions of light—full sunlight, morning, evening, fog. He made similar studies of other subjects. Monet's preoccupation with color became even more pronounced in his later career with an extensive study of water lilies that amounted to an essay in pure color. Impressionism was at the same time an attempt to represent light and color accurately in the tradition of representational art and a break away from tradition toward abstraction. The process of abstraction was carried to much more radical lengths by artists who succeeded the impressionists.

Post-Impressionists

By 1886, when the impressionists held their last group show, the movement had lost the solidarity of the 1870's. A small measure of critical appreciation had been won, but more significant was the acceptance of the impressionists' innovations by the young artists who flocked to Paris during these years. These younger innovators were anxious to go beyond impressionism, and in the late 1880's and early 1890's impressionism was regarded as a point of departure for the avant-garde.

One of the most original of the post-impressionists was Georges Seurat who took one aspect of impressionism to a logical extreme. Toward the end of the 1880's Seurat evolved a "pointillist" manner in which paint was applied to the canvas in dots of primary colors arranged in a mosaic-like pattern according to a formula of mathematical precision. Seurat retained conventional forms in his paintings, but they became highly stylized and static. Any attempt at duplicating reality was abandoned in favor of creating patterns through building up of dots of paint. Figures in his canvases, such as "Sunday Afternoon on Grande Jatte Island" or "The Circus," show very little motion. Pointillism took painting one further step toward abstraction.

The trend toward abstraction was advanced in a radically different direction by two men who went through an impressionist phase in the 1880's—Paul Gauguin and Vincent Van Gogh. Gauguin had been a successful Parisian stockbroker before renouncing his financial security and his family in favor of art. Behind his personal odyssey was a deep contempt for the glib superficiality that he detected in Euro-

Ia Orana Maria by Paul Gauguin. The Metropolitan Museum of Art, bequest of Samuel A. Lewisohn, 1951.

pean civilized society at the end of the nineteenth century. Seeking to portray a more potent existence found among simpler people who had not yet been spoiled by civilization, he first went to Brittany and then to the South Pacific.

Gauguin believed that conventional manners stifled true sentiment, and he tried to paint in a manner that would express a more primitive emotionalism. The awkwardness of Gauguin's painting was a deliberate attempt to recover a naive simplicity. Figures were drawn in awkward poses on the canvas with little regard for perspective, and the guiding principle in the use of color was not whether it corresponded to the color in nature but whether it provided a strong emotional response. According to Gauguin, the impressionists, for all their daring, had "kept the shackles of representation"; their concern with technique was indicative of rather shallow emotions. Painting was not a representation of reality for Gauguin—it was an intense emotional experience that tried to recapture some of the mysterious strength found among less sophisticated people.

Van Gogh also used brilliant color and exaggerated drawing for strong emotional effect. Indeed, Van Gogh used painting as an outlet

The Starry Night by Vincent Van Gogh. Collection of the Museum of Modern Art, New York. Acquired through the Lillie P. Bliss bequest.

for his intense, overwhelming moral passion. After an unsuccessful attempt to become a pastor among the poor in his native Holland, Van Gogh decided to devote himself to painting, but he retained a strong sympathy for the downtrodden throughout his life. In the mid-1880's Van Gogh arrived in Paris and went through a brief impressionist phase. In 1888 he traveled to the south of France where his talent burst forth in two years of activity under the intense southern sun.

Van Gogh's exaggerated shapes created by broad brushstrokes and his vivid palette gave his paintings an explosive quality. Cypresses became twisted columns writhing in the Mediterranean heat, and his skies often had an unnatural cobalt hue. In a letter to his brother Theo, who encouraged him in his artistic quest, Van Gogh wrote, "I use color more arbitrarily so as to express myself forcibly." The subject matter of Van Gogh's art became less and less the object represented on the canvas and more and more Van Gogh's own

The Cry by Edvard Munch.
The National Gallery, Oslo.

passion. An outdoor café in the south of France, seen under a summer, starry sky, became in Van Gogh's words, "a place where one can run mad, or commit a crime." After struggling with successive periods of mental disturbance, Van Gogh committed suicide. But he left a permanent mark on modern art as his paintings gained a posthumous frame for this lonely and extremely sensitive figure.

The Norwegian artist Edvard Munch shared Van Gogh's interest in the emotional quality of art, but his use of color was far more subdued. In a series of eerie woodcuts and paintings Munch greatly accentuated lines to the point of caricature and distortion to achieve emotional impact. He reduced the objects in his work to stark simplicity and subordinated them to the single emotional state that he wished to express. In his most famous painting, "The Cry," the lines incorporating a sketchily outlined landscape, a bridge, and a harbor vibrate around the open mouth of a girl shrieking on the bridge. The distortions that Munch and Van Gogh employed for emotional impact greatly influenced avant-garde art in Germany, particularly that of the German expressionists.

The Expressionists

German expressionism centered on two groups that, despite some differences, shared many of the same artistic goals. One was The Bridge (*Die Brücke*), which was founded in Dresden in 1905 and later moved to Berlin; the other, The Blue Rider (*Der blaue Reiter*), appeared in Munich in the prewar decade. Both movements reacted strongly against the monumental art that characterized official taste in the Germany of Kaiser William II. The saccharine sentimentality and inflated heroism of the conventional art seemed false and superficial to the expressionists. They also disliked the crass materialism that vulgar art and statuary evidenced. Although both schools of German expressionism shared many goals, the Bridge group tended more toward social commentary and the use of primitive modes in their work while the Blue Rider artists placed emphasis on achieving an inward, psychological depth through abstract color and forms.

In searching for a spiritual, poetic meaning to replace the stifling conventions of the period, the expressionists found inspiration in Gauguin, Van Gogh, and Munch. Members of the Blue Rider group admired Gauguin's use of color to give nature a symbolic, poetic quality. Both groups sympathized with his flight from an ultra-rationalistic, materialistic society. Munch's preoccupation with a terrifying fantasy and his morbid suggestions of death provided a welcome contrast to be sentimental optimism of Wihelmian culture. Van Gogh's vibrant colors and his tremendous capacity and need for personal expression had a particularly profound influence on the two groups. His sympathy for the oppressed and the disinherited appealed to the expressionists of the Bridge group, who proclaimed their compassion for the working classes' struggles against the hardship and brutality of the industrial world. As one German expressionist confessed, "Van Gogh was a father to us all."

Painting (Winter) by Vasily Kandinsky. The Solomon R. Guggenheim Museum.

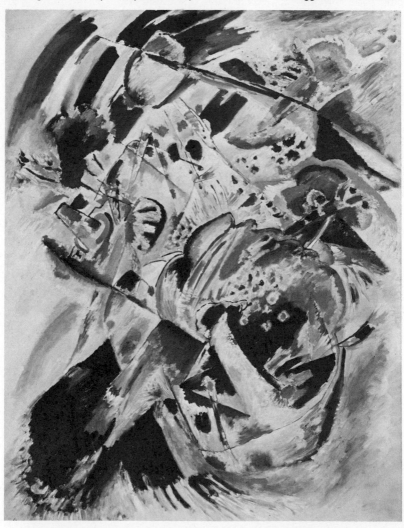

In technique the expressionists relied on a deliberately childlike drawing of human figures to convey a sense of simplicity and directness. The intentional crudeness of expressionist paintings and woodcuts was highly effective. Emil Nolde's paintings depict the harshness of rural life along the marshlands of the North Sea coast. Nolde's crude, sometimes grotesque drawing and his deep colors evoke a sympathy for the peasant and his environment, without sentimentalizing the subject. In landscapes by Nolde and other expressionists identifiable objects are submerged in patterns and eddies of pure color. The trend away from representation among the expressionists reached a culmination in the work of Wassily Kandinsky, a Russian-born artist associated with the Blue Rider group before the war. Kandinsky believed that painting could become as abstract and detached from external reference as music. He painted what he called "compositions of color," and the "pure abstraction" of musical expression continued to influence his work throughout his career. Kandinsky's abstraction was not without emotional meaning—quite the contrary; he was deeply concerned with painting as a means for communicating inner spiritual truths. The relationship of colors and forms on canvas could, in his words, "create a spiritual atmosphere" determined by the artist's own emotional direction at the time of painting.

While the German expressionists were engaged in their experiments, a group of French artists pursued similar goals. In 1905 these young artists held an exhibition of paintings in which every attempt to create volume or the illusion of perspective was abandoned. The colors employed were "wild," and for this reason the painters won the name *les fauves*, or "wild beasts," from hostile critics.

The best known of the fauves was Henri Matisse. Influenced by the decorative patterns of North African art, Matisse saw the painter's task as that of creating a design without perspective. The subject matter was used as a framework for a pattern of color, the essential element in the work. By this time the accurate reproduction of nature had become irrelevant to the artist. When once reproached for drawing a woman's arm too long, Matisse replied, "This is not a woman, this is a picture."

Matisse and the fauves made a further advance in the use of Oriental techniques and styles, particularly in their emphasis on large areas of contrasting color in their compositions. Other fauves, such as Georges Roualt, turned to Medieval art and the color patterns of stained glass windows for inspiration. Whatever the source, inventiveness in the use of color in an interesting design was the distinctive mark of the fauve group; their style showed them to be heirs of Van

Mont Sainte-Victoire by Paul Cézanne. The Metropolitan Museum of Art, bequest of Mrs. H. O. Havemeyer, 1929, The H. O. Havemeyer Collection.

Gogh and Gauguin. The fauves shared with the contemporary German expressionists a high regard for the emotional expressiveness of pure color, but they seemed more restrained than the Germans in the spiritual significance that they attached to their work.

Paul Cézanne: Precursor to Cubism

At the time that Gauguin and Van Gogh were experimenting with pure color, Paul Cézanne began to move beyond the boundaries of impressionism in another direction. After a period in Paris in which he participated in impressionist shows, Cézanne retired to the south of France where, supported by a modest income, he had the leisure to go his own way without feeling the pressure of critics.

Complaining that there was something insubstantial about impressionism, Cézanne set out to give structure and order to impressionist subjects—"to make," as he said, "impressionism into something more solid and enduring, like the art of museums." Returning again and again to a single subject, such as Mont Sainte-Victoire, Cézanne eventually found his solution by constructing his paintings in planes of color. Although reluctant to theorize about his work, he once remarked that he saw nature in terms of a geometric ordering of cones, cylinders, and spheres. Brushstrokes were carefully made to emphasize these geometrical shapes and planes on the canvas. The paintings of his later years, in which this trend became more pronounced, opened the way to one of the most potent of the modernist movements—cubism.

The Cubists

After Cézanne's death in 1906 an impressive retrospective held in Paris revealed the full extent of the artist's achievement. His work had already begun to have an impression on younger painters, but the retrospective came as a thunderclap. Among those who were affected were the two artists who launched cubism—Pablo Picasso, a Spaniard then living in Paris, and Georges Braque, a French artist. The two men worked together and shared many views on painting. They dissected whatever happened to be the subject of their paintings into its component parts and then reassembled the objects on the canvas as disjointed planes. These objects overlapped on the canvas with utter disregard for traditional perspective or depth. Rather than one perspective, there were many, and geometry itself became the "subject" of the painting.

A Dutch painter, Piet Mondrian, carried this geometrical abstraction to even more severe extremes. Mondrian began his career under the influence of late impressionism, and subsequently went through an expressionist phase. When he arrived in Paris in 1912, Mondrian experienced a revelation on seeing the work of Picasso and Braque. He rapidly evolved a style in which identifiable shapes dissolved into numerous small blocks of pastel colors. By 1914 he was well on the way toward the analysis of reality into large blocks of primary colors divided only by black lines and white spaces. His "Composition No. 6," of that year, showed Mondrian moving toward the geometrical rectangles of pure color that characterized his postwar work.

With expressionism and cubism, European painting had arrived at almost complete abstraction. In describing the trends of the period, the art historian Nikolaus Pevsner has observed that in twentieth century art, "Not closeness to reality but expressiveness of pattern is what matters; not quick observation of natural facts but their perfect translation into a plane of abstract significance." In the short space of a generation, European artists, liberated by the impressionists' experiments, had radically and decisively broken the confines of post-Renaissance art. Cubism and expressionism, although seemingly quite different from one another—the former being geometric and intellectual, and the latter emotional and turbulent—both brought European art to a point where the artist's concept of "reality" was reduced to the form and color presented on the plane of the canvas. Indeed, occasionally the movements overlapped: painters such as Ernst Ludwig Kirchner, Franz Marc, August Macke, and Lionel Feininger, who began as expressionists, eventually adopted cubist techniques.

Expressionism and cubism were only two among several artistic schools that sprang up in Europe in the decade preceding the First World War, but they were perhaps the most important and influential in the development of modernism in European painting. Futurism, an Italian artistic development that stressed the speed and dynamism of the contemporary world, showed definite evidence of cubist influence, as did vorticism, an offshoot of futurism in Great Britain designed to relate all art forms to industrial civilization. Even distant Russia, experiencing its own cultural upheaval in arts and literature during the prewar decade, felt the impact of cubism, as seen in the paintings of Kasimir Malvich. Although Paris remained Europe's leading center of artistic innovation, the effervescence could be found throughout Europe. Rapid communications assured that the latest development in Paris would spread quickly to other art capitals. Centers such as Berlin and Munich had a momentum of their own.

New Forms of Architecture

Throughout most of the nineteenth century European architecture displayed a pronounced historicism—architects and builders produced buildings in a variety of styles from previous centuries. Rules were formulated for the styles that were suitable to different types of buildings. By the end of the century, however, the best architects and engineers had tired of this eclectic borrowing from the past and decided to find an architectural form that would express the true spirit of the age by making imaginative use of the materials that technology could provide. An early indication of this dissatisfaction with historicism could be seen is the Art Nouveau movement of the 1890's.

Art Nouveau

Art Nouveau was characterized by long, sweeping lines incorporating irregular areas of space or color. It had an impact in a variety of arts, including painting such as that of the English artist Aubrey Beardsley, but was largely confined to the design and decoration of books, furniture, and other everyday objects, and ornamentation for buildings. In the realm of architecture, the swirling lines and exaggerations of Art Nouveau could be seen in the curved grillwork used to decorate stairways, in the façades of buildings covered with fantastic patterns, and in the twisted pillars and drooping lamps of the Parisian metro entrances. The most remarkable examples of Art Nouveau in architecture are the churches and residences designed by Antoni Gaudi in Barcelona. His preference for elaborate detail and intricate lines found expression in a series of fantastic, almost grotesque, buildings that are unique in European architecture; the undulating curves and irregularities reveal a delight in the unexpected and create a fairyland impression. In the wide range of unorthodox materials Gaudi used in the construction and decoration of his structures he showed a strong sense of the possibilities of concrete and an irrepressible taste for pure decorative effect.

The short-lived, mercurial fashion of Art Nouveau recalled the Baroque preference for movement and curved lines; at the same time it was a self-consciously modern style. But the fantasy of Art Nouveau was superseded after the turn of the century by a balanced, severe functional style that was more akin to the geometric proportions of cubism.

Functionalism

Buildings designed in the functional style made unabashed use of new materials and extensive use of glass. At the turn of the century two French architects, Tony Garnier and Auguste Perret, sensed the possibilities of reinforced concrete and began to design buildings that made no attempt to disguise the sinews of their construction. Emphasis was placed on simple, straight lines with a clearly delineated geometric organization of space. Some lingering influence of Art Nouveau could be seen in the floral pattern impressed in the façade of Perret's pioneering apartment building in Paris completed in 1903, but the main lines of the building were determined by the concrete beams and girders that created rectangular patterns largely filled with plate glass windows. Unencumbered by elaborate decorative embellishments, the

Perret's Théâtre des Champs Elysées. Photo by Eileen Michels.

stark, concrete lines of Perret's building seemed cold and naked to critics of the period; in retrospect, however, the building may be seen as the harbinger of an era that would make even more radical use of glass, concrete, and geometric design. Similarly, Garnier's plans for a modern city, drawn up between 1901 and 1904, anticipated later developments in its organization of space and in the cubist shapes that characterized public buildings and private dwellings. He also foresaw that the use of steel for cantilevered support would permit the opening up of wide areas of internal space.

Reinforced concrete and steel girders enabled engineers to construct buildings of unprecedented height without relying on heavy masonry walls for support. Architects could then design "lighter" structures with more glass or open space between supports. Above all, functional architecture emphasized utility. The way in which space was to be organized depended on the materials available and on the function of the building or group of buildings being designed. Throughout much of the nineteenth century, the roles of architect and engineer had been distinct, the former being called in to add decoration to buildings after the engineers had devised the layout. The new architects showed a clear understanding of engineering principles, but they also insisted that functional buildings, even factories, could be well designed and aesthetically pleasing. In the United States Frank Lloyd Wright began championing such ideas at the turn of the century. He worked in a climate that was less encumbered with historical traditions, and a number of his patrons in the Chicago area were willing to accept his unorthodox designs for private residences. These homes, characterized by simple, direct lines, were placed as unobtrusively as possible into their natural surroundings (although they still managed to shock conventional opinion). An even more modern style appeared in Wright's office buildings and skyscrapers of the same epoch. By 1910 Wright's ideas had found a favorable reception in Holland, Scandinavia, and especially Germany.

German architects and engineers took the lead in promoting the modern style in Europe. At the turn of the century German architecture was dominated by a ponderous official style, but in the following decade and a half the streamlined, functional modern style gained enthusiastic converts among progressive German architects. One of the most significant pioneers, Peter Behrens, designed a series of factories for a German electrical combine that demonstrated an imaginative use of steel structure, glass, and concrete. His turbine factory in Berlin (1909), despite its gigantic proportion, managed to convey a sense of balance and even lightness as a result of his bold use of large glass areas divided by vertical steel girders. The simplicity of the design produced a gracefulness that simply could not have been achieved by the heavy, ornamental style then employed in German public buildings.

Among Behrens' many students was Walter Gropius. In his design for the Fagus Works in Alfeld, Gropius surpassed his master in the use of steel and glass in a harmonious, geometrical design that was at once simple and open. The Fagus factory and Gropius' model factory exhibited in Cologne in 1914 anticipated his enormous influence on the glass-and-steel architecture of the twentieth century through the postwar Bauhaus movement.

Despite the pioneering work of Wright, Gropius, the young Mies van der Rohe, and others, the modern style had by no means triumphed by 1914. But in several countries of western Europe innovating architects had emerged whose designs spoke for an age of mechanization, industrial growth, and scientific achievement. Moreover, the modern architect, with his interest in utility, tried to adapt his principles of design to social needs. Everyday objects such as teapots, light fixtures, and furniture were created with sparse, streamlined features that emphasized the utility of the objects themselves. The bric-a-brac of nineteenth century household objects was abandoned. On a broader level, architects such as Garnier in France turned their attention to problems of town planning. This type of planning was minimal in the prewar years, but at least the possibility of creating towns that would be at once places of business and pleasant environments was being explored.

Even with the concern for utility, the aesthetic principle that guided the modern movement in architecture was abstraction. The removal of decorative clutter by the introduction of streamlined, geometrical shapes corresponded to the cubist principles of Cézanne and his successors. The modern design in architecture was another analysis of reality—this time the organization of space—in terms of geometrical form.

Innovations in Music

Neo-Romanticism

In the last decades of the nineteenth century European music was dominated by the full sounds of neo-romanticism and by the towering figure of Richard Wagner. In 1878 Wagner had established a festival for the production of his vast musical dramas at Bayreuth in southern Germany, which rapidly became a Mecca for ardent admirers from all over Europe. Wagner tried to fuse the visual arts, drama, and music in mammoth operas that were marked by elaborate stage presentation and heavy orchestration. The effect was impressive, even overwhelming. Long, sweeping, slightly dissonant phrases prolonged musical tension and created a sense of longing that was fulfilled only after a thorough exposure to musical emotionalism. The lush, erotic sonorities of Wagner impressed a generation that nurtured his principles after the master's death in 1883.

During the same years, and in conflict with Wagnerians, the more academic romantic tradition of Brahms commanded a rival following. Full-blown neo-romanticism reached fulfillment in the music of the Viennese composer Anton Bruckner and his pupil Gustav Mahler, who carried the rich sound and full orchestration of late nineteenth century music to its highest expression and, some would say, its exhaustion. By the turn of the century a reaction against the heaviness of late and neo-romantic music had appeared in the diverse works of Debussy, Stravinsky, and Schoenberg. With the latter two composers, a distinctively modernist trend in music made its appearance in Europe.

Modernism

Claude Debussy sought an alternative to the heavy strains of Wagner in the subtle effects and more fluid harmonies of musical impressionism. Poetic evocations replaced the heavy drama of the Wagnerian mode. Debussy's ballet "Afternoon of a faun" combined the poetry of Mallarmé, the brilliant dancing of Nijinski and the Ballets Russes, and the Art Nouveau sets of Leon Bakst in a light and charming performance that was in sharp contrast to the dramatics of Wagnerian opera. Yet the refinements and finesse of Debussy's musical impressionism did not represent a dramatic overturning of musical convention. Far more radical were the rhythmic experiments and harsh dissonances devised by Stravinsky and the atonality adopted by Arnold Schoenberg in the prewar decade.

After studying under Rimsky-Korsakov in St. Petersburg Stravinsky came to Paris where he gained fame and notoriety as the composer of ballet scores for the Ballets Russes troupe, which was winning enthusiastic acclaim. His first ballet, "Petrushka," had caused a sensation in 1911, but his ballet of 1913, "The Rite of Spring," created a scandal. When it was presented in the Théâtre des Champs Elysées under the direction of Pierre Monteux, a riot erupted in the theater. Stravinsky's sharp dissonances and heavy, primitive rhythms evoked hoots from his critics and equally vociferous defense from his supporters. After the first few minutes, little could be heard in the uproar, and Monteux finished the evening with great difficulty. The Théâtre des Champs Elysées, designed by Perret and one of the first public buildings constructed of reinforced concrete in the modern style, became a battleground between the adherents of modernism and its opponents. Stravinsky went through a succession of styles in his career, but his early use of dissonance and primitive rhythm or American jazz beat put a decisive stamp on contemporary music. The bounds of conventional nineteenth century rhythm and harmonics had been broken.

Even more radical in his revolt against nineteenth century music was Arnold Schoenberg, who began his career as a romantic very much under the influence of his Viennese teacher, Gustav Mahler. Vienna was perhaps the most musical of the European capitals at the turn of the century; great performances could be heard at the State Opera and the Vienna Philharmonic, over which Mahler presided. Despite his traditionalism and the neo-romantic tendencies in his own compositions, Mahler showed an understanding of those younger pupils, including Schoenberg, who were dissatisfied with traditionalism.

Reacting against the massive orchestration of romanticism, Schoenberg wrote for small chamber groups. In 1905 he composed a series of works, including his "Chamber Symphony," which revealed his evolution toward greater clarity and simplicity—or, as Schoenberg stated, "a tendency to condense." His contact with the expressionists provided him with an aesthetic justification for refuting many accepted musical conventions. Schoenberg had been associated with the Blue Rider group in Munich and had even exhibited some of his own paintings with them. Expressionism in music meant for him abandoning traditional tonal structure in favor of an "atonal" music that permitted expression of his inner feelings. Schoenberg argued that dissonance was just as valid for musical expression as consonance based on established harmonic structure—and perhaps more effective. He once wrote: "In composing I decide only in accordance with feeling, with a feeling for form."

Defying conventional musical opinion, Schoenberg presented his first clearly atonal works in 1908 and 1909 with his "Book of the Hanging Garden" and "Three Piano Pieces." Subsequent compositions carried through on the atonality and continued to reject the thematic repetitions that had been a characteristic of European music for over two hundred years. By 1912 Schoenberg had sensed that the sheer atonality of his expressionist period was leading toward chaos, and he composed a "Serenade" that marked his first essay in the twelve tone system that he was to refine in the postwar years. Schoenberg had already launched contemporary music on an uncharted, experimental course toward abstraction of form and sound.

New Directions in Literature

Developments in Drama

Expressionism in music and painting had a parallel in the drama at the turn of the century, especially in the work of the Swedish playwright, August Strindberg, and in the avant-garde German theater. These dramatists broke with the melodramatic and sentimental styles of early nineteenth century drama as well as with the naturalism of those who portrayed a "slice of life" on the stage. The departure point for modernism in drama may be found in the plays of the Norwegian poet and dramatist Henrik Ibsen, who carried naturalism to a high art but also employed symbolism to heighten the impact of his plays.

Ibsen was highly critical of middle-class conventions, which he considered to be filled with hypocrisy, and it was the expression of this belief in his plays, rather than any radical innovations in dramatic form, that gained Ibsen a reputation as a revolutionary. Ibsen's plots usually followed the classic, conventional formula of the "well-made play" with a beginning, middle, and end organized around three acts, but audiences of the time were stunned by his discussion of taboo subjects on the Victorian stage—syphilis, the hypocrisy of the family's double standard, sanctimonious religious practices, and so on. To the critics who labeled his plays sordid Ibsen replied that he simply exposed the truth beneath the mask of bourgeois respectability.

There was a strong moral strain to Ibsen's iconoclasm. Usually his plays presented a hero struggling for high ideals only to be misunderstood and defeated by a narrow society. From *Peer Gynt* to his later symbolic plays Ibsen's characters struggled to achieve self-fulfillment and freedom; they were apostles, as was Ibsen himself, of freedom and openness for the individual. Under Ibsen the drama no longer offered the audience a "catharsis" or purging of emotions; instead, the spectator was presented with social or moral problems of immediate importance.

Quite different in purpose and method was the Swedish playwright August Strindberg. Strindberg shared Ibsen's hostility to stuffy middle-class conventions and saw through them with equal clarity, but whereas Ibsen implied that the destruction of false conventions could liberate the artist, Strindberg held little hope of this sort. His characters, when stripped of their illusions and conventions, revealed themselves to be mean souls inhabiting a hell from which there was no escape. Strindberg's pessimism is clearly revealed in his *Dance of*

Death (1902) in which a couple, already far along the path of mutual hatred and destruction, are stranded on an island. They psychologically destroy one another. Fatally united, they have no possible salvation.

Behind the naturalistic setting of Strindberg's drama lies a deeper reality of emotional and psychological horror. By the conclusion of his plays the setting is subordinated to the emotional force of the protagonists' despair; reality and his characters' perception of that reality become blended into a single nightmare. The unrelieved emotionalism of Strindberg's drama broke away from the tradition of the naturalistic theater of the nineteenth century and prepared the way for the expressionist theater of the twentieth century.

German Expressionists ▪ Strindberg had a particularly deep influence on the German expressionist theater. In the decade before 1914 many of his plays were produced throughout Germany in translation. The German expressionists admired Strindberg's psychological intensity and found his pessimism an antidote to the culture of Wilhelmian Germany. The expressionist playwrights and poets shared with painters a belief that Germany had become spiritually impoverished; the artist's task was to release the spiritual energies contained within the individual. Among the expressionist dramas that had an impact on the prewar generation were Rheinhard Sorge's *The Beggar,* Paul Kornfeld's *Seduction,* and Walter Hasenclever's *The Son,* which was a kind of manifesto for the expressionists.

German expressionist drama approached the emotional abstraction that could be found in painting during the same years. Naturalistic stage devices and dramatic techniques were rejected in favor of exaggerated effects that would heighten the emotional impact of the play. Inarticulate shouts occasionally replaced intelligible language as a method for indicating deep feeling; unorthodox, vivid colors and sharp lighting contrasts characterized the productions. Expressionism on the stage was at once a repudiation of conventional techniques of a middle-class culture and a messianic appeal. According to the expressionist playwrights, a "new man," spiritually and emotionally liberated from a materialistic society, would appear to open the way to a new era.

Anton Chekhov ▪ The malaise of the late nineteenth century, reflected in Ibsen, Strindberg, and the expressionists, was also central to the dramatic works of the Russian writer Anton Chekhov. In its subtle, ironic tone, however, Chekhov's style was quite different from the intensity of the expressionists or even the pessimism of Strindberg. Before embarking on a literary career, Chekhov had studied to be a doctor, and his writing was characterized by the human compassion and ironical detachment associated with that profession.

As a dramatist—and as a short story writer—Chekhov created moods and atmosphere rather than tightly constructed plots. Characters often talked *at* one another, without real communication, and they often responded to events without fully realizing what was happening to them. His greatest play, *The Cherry Orchard,* chronicles the demise of a Russian gentry family, a demise that represents the disintegration of a social class. A sense of tragedy emerges through seemingly disconnected remarks, snatches of conversation, and the musings of characters on stage. Chekhov believed that his dramatic technique accurately reflected the fragmentary and disconnected character of everyday existence. Chekhov seemed to be within the naturalist school, a detached recorder of events who lacked the exaggerated passion of the expressionists, but his oblique technique and use of symbols carried him beyond mere reporting of the specific into the realm of universal values and a poetic evocation of melancholy and foreboding.

Developments in the Novel

The break with naturalism, seen in the diverse styles of European dramatists, became even more apparent in the European novel in the years preceding the First World War. The late nineteenth century had witnessed an extraordinary proliferation of novels that described customs and conditions of life within a wide range of European social classes. The panorama included Charles Dickens' London slum dwellers, Leo Tolstoy's aristocrats, Theodore Fontane's ironically sketched upper middle class Germans, and Emile Zola's oppressed miners. The naturalist principle that inspired much of this literature had been current in Europe since the Renaissance: the writer held a mirror up to nature—perhaps some of the more bizarre characteristics of nature—to reproduce accurately what he saw. This tendency was reinforced by nineteenth century scientific theory, which maintained that minute attention to observed fact offered the surest path to truth. Novelists shared the principle behind this theory of science as they strove for objectivity in their description of society.

At the turn of the century a deviation from the naturalist tradition set in. A psychological dimension appeared in the novels that was descriptive of the anxieties behind the manners and conventions of the age. Often the novelist explored his own internal world, allowing his imagination to carry him where it would and to elaborate on a private reality that did not necessarily correspond to appearances. Above all, the novelist experimented. The novel took on the qualities of abstraction, ambiguity, and depth of perception that marked the other arts at the turn of the century; in so doing the novel—in many ways the most "middle class" of art forms—became less and less accessible and offered little reassurance to middle-class readers.

Thomas Mann ▪ One of the most impressive chronicles of bourgeois life in the nineteenth century was Thomas Mann's *Büddenbrooks* (1901), a history of the decay and decline of an apparently secure, stolid merchant family of Hamburg. The early generations of Büddenbrooks were practical, hard-headed merchants who had little time and less inclination to ponder the meanings of their lives. The pursuit of wealth and the enjoyment of material comfort were taken for granted; such unreflective confidence was in fact the source of much Büddenbrook strength. When a member of a later generation lost this confidence and began questioning himself about "deeper" meanings, the house began to slip until ultimately the Büddenbrook firm was liquidated. Although Mann was only twenty-six when *Büddenbrooks* was published, the novel showed remarkable psychological penetration of the uncertainty that lay behind the seemingly unshakable confidence of the bourgeoisie. The Büddenbrook family cycle was symbolic of the self-doubts that could menace a social class. Out of the decreasing vigor of the Büddenbrook patriarchs, Mann predicted the emergence of an artistic sensitivity among later generations, a theme that was to become a leitmotif of much of Mann's writing.

In technique Mann did not bring a radical innovation to the European novel; his achievement lay in giving a psychological dimension to the bourgeois chronicle. Mann was, as he confessed, "a bourgeois gone astray," able to sense the doubts of the class and the possibility of its decline. Far more unorthodox in their approach to the novel were three writers of the same generation who, like Mann, were concerned with achieving a greater psychological profundity and were interested in problems of change through time—Proust, Joyce, and Kafka. These novelists shaped the modern novel.

Marcel Proust ▪ The possibility that a work of art might triumph over the decay and change inflicted by the passing of time served the French writer, Marcel Proust, as the central theme and inspiration for his vast, rambling novel, *Remembrance of Things Past*. Although Proust began writing the novel shortly after the turn of the century the first volume did not appear until 1913, and the entire work was not completed until just before his death in 1922. In his work Proust portrayed French upper-class society at the turn of the century, including its foibles and self-isolation, but his method and purpose were not those of a social chronicler. Against the social background he examined the mechanism of the artist's conscious and unconscious memory as it sought to regain past experience. He rejected the objective reporting of events in favor of an internal monologue in which recall occurred in an apparently random manner. One must view Proust's work as one would view an impressionist painting: the seemingly accidental quality of his art comes into focus only as the reader gains some perspective on the "dabs" that Proust placed on his canvas. The principle that the novel had to make sense through logically developed narrative had been deliberately overthrown—or altered beyond recognition. A novel of more than two thousand pages on the memory of an introspective, sensitive man was far removed from the social panoramas of the nineteenth century middle-class novel.

James Joyce ■ A high sense of artistic purpose also inspired James Joyce, whose *Portrait of the Artist as a Young Man* was an imaginative recapitulation of the author's decision to exile himself from his native Ireland in order to pursue his art on the Continent. If the *Portrait* showed Joyce turning away from his homeland, his masterpiece, *Ulysses,* revealed that he had retained a vivid memory of Ireland and that he possessed an eminently Irish trait, a remarkable sense of the music of language. Although *Ulysses* was not completed until after the war, Joyce began work on it long before 1914.

Ulysses is the account of a day in Dublin in 1904 that focuses on the ramblings of the two principal characters through the city and their brief encounter toward the end of the day. Joyce deliberately explodes the form of the naturalistic novel for psychological depth. He employs internal monologues to explore his characters' unexpressed musings about the meetings, conversation, and trivial action of their daily activities. Many critics see in his stream-of-consciousness technique the ultimate expression of subjectivity. Yet *Ulysses* has a carefully elaborated structure that brings the ancient Greek tale of the Odyssey into the modern world. Both heroes of *Ulysses,* the young Stephen Daedalus and Leopold Bloom, are modern men who have become wanderers in search of themselves—and in search of each other—equipped only with their own resources of wit and cunning amid hostile elements. In the course of his novel Joyce manages to capture and parody every major prose style in English. The novel holds up to view a multiple perspective on English literature as well as a multiple perspective on the protagonists.

Franz Kafka ■ Like Proust and Joyce, Franz Kafka had his greatest impact on modern European literature in the 1920's although much of his most creative work came before and during the First World War. A resident of Prague, Kafka observed firsthand the political and psychological tensions that troubled the Austro-Hungarian empire.

Kafka's prose is remarkably lucid; there are none of Joyce's puns, obscure references, and reconstructions of language and syntax. The style is straightforward, but the substance of his stories and novels is a psychological nightmare in a surrealistic world; his principal characters struggle to comprehend and do their duty in an incomprehensible universe. The Kafka hero as seen in *The Trial* or *The Castle* seems burdened with an overwhelming guilt, as if he understands the responsibility he bears for his behavior but is unable to grasp the reasons for his actions. The search of the individual for meaning, or his concern about the riddle of the universe, is defeated by universal indifference. The answers for the actors in Kafka's parables either never arrive or are not properly understood when they appear. This nightmare world of uncertainty and guilt has acquired an awesome meaning in the twentieth century. Kafka was among the most "modern" of the avant-garde novelists in his elusive, unsettling simplicity; his ambiguous message has inspired a multiplicity of interpretations.

Other Trends in Literature ▪ Set beside the bold experiments with form were other trends in literature that have had a significant influence on twentieth century culture. Even writers who did not experiment radically with form often showed dissatisfaction with the conventions of the age. In Germany the poet Stefan George called for a rediscovery of spiritual values and noble ideals, which seemed to be lacking in the crass materialism of Wilhelmian society. George and his circle glorified leaders of the past, cultural and political figures who embodied and fulfilled a Nietzschean ideal of heroic vitalism through their great deeds and protean writings. George's heady teaching affected a generation of German youth who turned their backs on a banal, bourgeois culture and sought a more natural, vigorous, and emotionally satisfying way of life.

In France a group of conservative writers, including Charles Maurras, Paul Bourget, and Maurice Barrès, grew alarmed at the possibility that trustworthy moral signals had become obscured in the materialistic, scientifically oriented culture of their generation. As an answer to "sterile rationalism" they urged a return to the older traditions—the Church, the army, love of country—that provided security amid the confusions of the modern world. Their position was narrowly French, but their alarm was symptomatic of dissatisfactions that could be found elsewhere in Europe's cultural ferment.

In Italy, for example, Gabriele d'Annunzio set the virtues of a heroic existence against the banalities of his time. In Great Britain D. H. Lawrence railed against the philistinism of the industrial world in his novel *Sons and Lovers*. Later he advocated sexual vitalism as a romantic antidote to the inhibitions of conventional society. Joseph Conrad sensed that modern man was living precariously on the edge of a moral abyss; he feared that liberal freedom might easily become engulfed in either anarchistic chaos or authoritarian oppression. Exiled from his native Poland, Conrad had wandered the globe as a merchant seaman before settling down in England to write, and he understood the moral disorientation that could result from being uprooted. This theme, combined with a search for a standard of personal honor, filled Conrad's best novels. Thus, a major theme in the modernist trend in European literature was the attempt to find an emotionally satisfying place for the individual in modern society, a task that often called for the assertion of individual will or of a personal code against the leveling tendencies of a mass age.

The European novel and drama at the turn of the century showed much the same concern for discovering a deeper meaning in everyday experience that could be found in the visual arts. At the same time, European literature was marked by the unsettling suspicion that a deeper meaning, or fixed values, did not exist, and that men really drifted through their lives without any direction. For some writers the pattern of artistic creation or the call to a new, noble mission brought a measure of coherence amid confusion. The avant-garde reveled in their new-found artistic freedom to experiment. Others, however, looked on in fascination and bewilderment. Some either tried to build a new rigid order on the new principles or urged a return to older traditions as alternatives to what was seen as the potential anarchy of free expression. European culture became divided in almost schizophrenic fashion between the limitless diversity of experimentation and the demands for order and coherence.

The New Mass Culture

While the avant-garde experimented with new modes of expression in art and literature, the majority of the European people remained indifferent to or unaware of these trends. Only in architecture were some of the new ideas immediately apparent, but changes in architectural style were barely under way. The German expressionists, particularly the artists associated with The Bridge, consciously tried to find an audience among the working classes in Berlin. They set up their studios in working-class districts and held local exhibits in an effort to make their art more accessible to the masses. But their efforts often met with bewildered shrugs from their audience. Outlets for a mass culture, reflecting the rise in literacy levels at the end of the century, were to be found elsewhere.

The great popularity of the inexpensive press showed that a mass audience existed, but the content of this "yellow journalism" (so named because of the cheap quality of the paper used) ran toward the sensational or the sentimental. The London *Daily Mail* and *Daily Express,* which each had a circulation of one million readers, emphasized crimes and scandals to hold or increase their circulation. Often serialized novels, romances, or melodramas, aimed at unsophisticated readers, were included in popular journals. The mass press and the feuilleton novel testified to the existence of a mass audience but also indicated its lack of cultural sophistication.

Other forms of amusement were available to the average working man in Europe. Music halls and popular plays or skits provided relatively inexpensive entertainment, and popular concert halls proliferated in the major European cities. In Germany a number of municipalities established peoples' theaters and supported either resident or touring repertory companies for fairly lengthy seasons. These theaters proved enormously popular and were regarded with considerable civic pride by the local citizens. Although the bulk of their production consisted of melodrama or romantic comedy, classics were frequently produced, and occasionally a play by Ibsen, Strindberg, or even one of the expressionists was ventured.

Sports also offered popular entertainment and became an important feature of Europe's mass culture at the turn of the century. As attendance at sporting events increased, many sports became professional operations under the aegis of businessmen and promoters. Clubs appeared and cultivated a loyal following within a given metropolitan area. Both working and middle classes were caught up in the excitement generated by athletic competition. Europeans also had greater opportunities for participating in sports through local associations such as gymnastic clubs. Perhaps the clearest sign of a rising interest in sports could be seen in the popular development of international competition at the end of the nineteenth century, patterned after the ancient Greek Olympiad. The Olympic events were followed with great enthusiasm in the mass circulation press.

The Popularity of Film

The appearance of an entirely new cultural form—the film—and its immediate success best symbolize the style of the new mass culture. For one thing, the film was representative of the period in which it emerged, inasmuch as it was made possible by technological innovation and was a by-product of the industrial era. The final product—the film itself—was even "produced" by a kind of industrial organization that required cooperation among various specialists—cameramen, actors, directors, film editors, and the like—and this end product could be widely distributed and marketed at a relatively low price, much as consumer goods. Local theaters depended on a high attendance for their profits. The film was thus adapted to, and in fact was dependent on, mass consumption.

At first the film was considered merely a curiosity, even by Thomas Edison, one of the early pioneers in filmmaking. Early movies lasted barely a minute and were considered for this reason "peep shows." At first the novelty of recapturing movement on film was sufficiently strong to attract an audience, and early experimenters with the motion picture photographed anything that moved. Trick camera shots that showed trains rushing at audiences from the screen created frightening effects that lured crowds into movie theaters. But the fascination of such sensations quickly faded, and filmmakers were forced to find other subjects and extend their shows in order to retain their audiences.

One of the most inventive of the early filmmakers was the Frenchman Georges Méliès. Méliès introduced narrative into the movies and produced a number of traditional stories at the turn of the century, including "Cinderella" (1900) and "Red Riding Hood" (1901). As a former magician, Méliès delighted in creating fantastic effects and illusions with the camera. Trick shots that caused sudden disappearances and reappearances of people and objects embellished his narrative. He constructed fabulous sets, such as for "Trip to the Moon" (1902), which gave the spectator the illusion that he was participating in a space voyage. Méliès also reconstructed actual events in films such as "The Dreyfus Affair" (1899) and "The Coronation of Edward VII" (1902). By producing these pseudo-documentaries almost immediately after the events described, Méliès recognized the news value of the film medium—the sense it could give the viewer of being a witness to the world's happenings.

After the turn of the century more complex stories began to be filmed, and the length of film presentations increased. Filmmakers turned to literature and drama for their stories. At first, motion pictures seemed to follow the techniques of stage presentation, offering dramas on film, but film directors soon realized that the new medium required and permitted different techniques. They were not confined to a given set, for example, since they could go outdoors in search of more natural and varied settings for their presentation. Even relatively short films could include a large number of scenes and do so more economically than a stage presentation. As filmmakers became more skilled with the camera, they began exploiting its special characteristics. It was found that continuity could be broken by rapid shifts of scenes, or cuts, that enabled the director to present the audience with what appeared to be simultaneous action. Drama could be heightened by moving quickly from one thread of action to another. Devices such as flashbacks permitted directors to escape the limitations of strict chronology. The audience's imagination was allowed to fill in the gaps between such shifts and reconstruct continuity on several levels.

Within the short space of a decade and a half, the infant film industry began to acquire its own kind of artistic sophistication and open up a new realm of perception to a wide audience. Pushed on by a search for new cinematic devices—and spurred by the desire to find new ways of entertaining a mass audience—Italian, French, British, and American filmmakers quickly learned from one another, giving the art of movie-making an international dimension from the outset. Apart from this international exchange of ideas, certain national tastes were evident in filmmaking. The Italians excelled in the epic (a 1912 production of "Quo Vadis?" required an unprecedented eight reels and lasted two hours); the French favored chases, such as "The Great Pumpkin Race" (1907); British producers inclined toward adventures; and American filmmakers preferred westerns.

Whatever the theme, by 1914 the popularity of the motion picture had been clearly established among the masses throughout Europe and in the United States. Even the middle and upper classes, who at first regarded movies as cheap and low-class entertainment offered in dimly lighted, disreputable theaters, began to be attracted to the new medium by the presentation of somewhat self-conscious and stiff "art films" of classical drama. And movies were given a status as art by famous stage personalities who began making films. The great French actress Sarah Bernhardt, who made movies of "Camille" and "Queen Elizabeth" at the end of her career, declared that only the film assured her of immortality by capturing her performance for posterity. In any event, by reason of its distinctive techniques, its mode of production, its wide appeal, and the technological innovations that made it possible, the film industry may be taken as the art form most closely identified with the emerging mass culture of Europe and the United States.

Advances in the Social Sciences

During the same period that artists were experimenting in the fine arts, literature, and the film, innovative psychological and social theses were advancing the study of man both as an individual and as a social animal. No less than in the arts, the emphasis in the social sciences was on analyzing behavior beyond the recording of external appearances. Nineteenth century social theorists of the positivist school assumed that laws of social behavior operated in the same mechanical fashion as laws of science, and that a science of society could be established through the empirical study of events without any a priori hypotheses to guide or confuse research. After the turn of the century, however, social theorists abandoned the optimistic belief that scientific laws of human behavior could be produced through the mere accumulation of data. They formed a view of psychological and social development that was far more complex than nineteenth century positivists had assumed. Freudian psychology plumbed the uncertain depths of the subconscious while social theorists demonstrated that the development of hypotheses was essential to an understanding of social and political behavior.

The Influence of Freud

The way that men look at themselves and relate to their environment in the twentieth century owes more to Sigmund Freud than to any other figure who emerged in Europe at the turn of the century. The popularization of Freudianism has come closer to establishing a "world view" for the present century than any other doctrine; only Marxism has had a similar impact on the European consciousness.

Freud began his career as a medical practitioner with a strong interest in neurology. Financial circumstances compelled him to maintain a regular practice in Vienna, but his real interest was in medical research. Investigating the causes of hysteria in a young Viennese— "Anna O."—Freud concluded that the roots of psychological disorders lay in memories of earlier experiences of a sexual nature that had been repressed into the subconscious because such urges conflicted with accepted moral standards and were, therefore, considered shameful. Freud discovered that these deep-seated conflicts could be revealed through a process of free association of conscious memories that would lead back to the repressed event. The method proved successful in the therapeutic treatment of neuroses, and Freud subjected himself to analysis in the hands of a colleague in an effort to unlock his own unconscious mind.

Freud's theories and techniques provoked a hostile response from his colleagues in Vienna. His emphasis on sexual drives opened a taboo subject and offended many, while his insistence on infant sexuality seemed incredible and conflicted with Victorian notions of childhood. His assertion that the unconscious was primary to the conscious proved equally disturbing; according to this view rational behavior was simply an attempt to divert unconscious, primitive drives into socially approved channels. Reason thus seemed, if not the plaything of unconscious will, then no more than a kind of buffer between unconscious wish and reality. If Freud were correct, man was much more an animal of passion, and reason was far more fragile and tentative, than conventional opinion in the nineteenth century wished to acknowledge.

With the publication of his *Interpretation of Dreams* in 1899 and his *Psychopathology of Everyday Life* in 1904, Freud gained a following, despite professional resistance in conservative medical circles. By 1910 a professional association of psychologists had been formed that looked to Freud for inspiration. A Freudian school of psychiatry took root when younger psychologists came to Vienna to study under Freud, although some of his more illustrious pupils later broke with his teaching.

Freud did not limit his analyses to the psychology of the individual. Even before the war he had begun to extend his insights to the workings of the social order. Just as a person's "id," which in Freudian terminology stood for instinctual passions, had to be contained by his "super-ego," his social consciousness, civilization and culture checked the more primitive and aggressive tendencies in society. In *Totem and Taboo,* published in 1912, Freud proposed that institutions of social control derived from tribal rituals. One of his most controversial suggestions was that religion had its origin in some primitive era in which the tribal sons, jealous of a father-leader who dominated the women of the tribe, assassinated him and then imposed self-restraints to prevent a repetition of this act. From a tribal Oedipus complex had come the worship of a divine father figure, and an accompanying moral code. From the time that Freud constructed this elaborate and unprovable hypothesis, he showed a penchant for social analysis as well as psychological inquiry; Freudian social theory emphasized the primitive roots and thin veneer of civilization.

Although his discoveries pointed to the importance of man's instinctual drives, Freud did not assume that his work would encourage a regression toward primitivism or unrestrained sexual gratification for the individual. Nor was the thrust of his research a deliberate attempt to denigrate reason. Freud remained, as a biographer, Philip Rieff, emphasizes, a moralist, and he firmly believed in personal and social restraints. In his methods, Freud remained faithful to a scientific, rational approach to solving problems of the unconscious mind, despite the leaps of perception that sometimes outdistanced his evidence and a tendency toward hasty generalization. He realized that science and reason were the only possible guides in attempting to chart the depths of the mind and that this pursuit would extend man's understanding of himself. Freud was thus clearly within the enlightenment tradition, but he also showed a desire to push analysis beyond surface appearances and facile conceptions, however disturbing for conventional wisdom the pursuit might be. After the First World War exposed the aggressive and barbaric side of European civilization, Freud gained a wider renown, but much of his seminal work dates from the prewar years and expresses many of the preoccupations of the prewar generation.

Theories of Society and Politics

The behavior of the masses—or "the crowd"—as a social phenomenon commanded significant interest. One of the first to explore this realm was the French scholar Gustave Le Bon whose *The Crowd, a Study of the Popular Mind* was published in 1895. Le Bon sought the sources for irrationalist behavior in large groups, and he opened the way to a study of social psychology. His concern for discovering the roots of social behavior was even more apparent in his less well-known *Psychological Laws of Human Evolution*, in which he sketched an approach to explaining historical development that went beyond surface description of phenomena.

Equally anxious to form laws of social behavior was the French sociologist Emile Durkheim. Durkheim was not interested in establishing a system of metaphysical abstractions; he wished to place the study of social phenomena on a firm scientific foundation. In this respect he seemed to be a close follower of the French positivists, but he soon discovered that the "hard facts" of social science included phenomena that did not seem, from the perspective of his own beliefs, to be rational. Durkheim was a religious skeptic, yet he came to the realization that religion satisfied some social need for many people. He was forced to recognize religion as an important social force—a kind of persistent myth that was strong enough to provide social cohesion to many societies. The pursuit of social reality and the causes of social behavior proved to be a more complex task than Durkheim had originally assumed.

Another social theorist who recognized the importance of myths as motivating factors in history was Georges Sorel, also a Frenchman. Abandoning an earlier career as an engineer in the French civil service, Sorel devoted his later years to extensive reading and writing on problems of social evolution. He developed an original doctrine that urged a radical transformation of society. Sorel disagreed profoundly with reformist socialists who believed that existing social and economic systems could be gradually altered. Only some powerful force, such as an upheaval of the working classes, could bring about fundamental changes in the social order, and in his *Reflections on Violence* (1908) he made it clear that this path would be a violent one. But Sorel was cynical enough to believe that only some myth—not the logical evolution of historical forces or the well-intentioned reforms of liberals— would be capable of inspiring a revolutionary upheaval. Hence he proposed that the greatest myth of all, that of the "general strike," had to be advanced to elicit and sustain revolutionary fervor among the working masses. In his insistence on the need for violence and his advocacy of political myth as a device for manipulating and inspiring mass movements, Sorel's social theory was distinctly representative of the twentieth century.

While debates on man's social nature were continuing, political theorists were seeking a more profound analysis of the way in which the political order operated, a quest that led to some pessimistic conclusions. Liberal confidence in representative institutions as the best safeguard against an abuse of power and as a means of providing popular participation in the exercise of power came under attack by two Italians, Vilfredo Pareto and Gaetano Mosca, who sought to unmask the dominance of elites behind the democratic process. Pareto argued that a parliamentary state such as Italy was run not by popular will but by a clique that maintained its control by manipulating electorates through propaganda directed to irrational impulses. From time to time particular elites might lose their grip and be replaced by other rulers who would then control society by employing similar methods. Pareto showed himself to be conservative by his cynical assessment of revolutionary upheavals, which he claimed produced only a circulation of elites; he discounted parliamentary institutions as devices whereby elites exploited power. Mosca also examined the ruling class that operated behind the façade of democratic, representative institutions. Mosca insisted that the only difference between democracy and other forms of government, such as oligarchal or monarchal rule, was that democracy required a demagogic talent to exploit popular sentiment for those who wished to maintain their dominance.

Meanwhile, a German political and social theorist, Max Weber, was working out an equally hard-headed but much more sophisticated approach to the sociology of politics. According to Weber, the ruling class in any state was that which had gained control over the legitimate use of violence or coercion within that state. In making this assertion, Weber went beyond Marxian doctrine, which emphasized economic power as the foundation for the ruling class's strength. He respected Marx's insight into the importance of the economic system as the basis for class rule, but he insisted that the problem of political power was broader and more complex than Marx had allowed; it included military strength and administrative arrangements as equally important elements. Above all, he anticipated the growing importance of bureaucratic organizations as a way of structuring power in modern societies; such forms, he argued, were "rational" and assured continuity and stability. But he also predicted the occasional appearance of charismatic individuals who would be able to cut across bureaucratic institutions that had already become ossified and inflexible. In the resulting upheaval, new structures would emerge and a new equilibrium would be reached in the balance of political forces. Whatever the regenerating effects of a charismatic force, power would have to be reordered and reinstitutionalized to be effective.

Weber was prepared to advance theories—or hypotheses—about political and social behavior, but he always insisted that such generalizations had to rest on careful research and were subject to revision or modification as further information was gained and knowledge was refined. According to Weber, social science should rest on an analysis of a limited segment of reality; he hesitated to propose a general theory of social science. There was a certain ambiguity in Weber's attempt to give a scientific basis to the study of society, for he sensed that social science was in its infancy and capable of advancing only tentative hypotheses. In any event, Weber's work carried the analysis of social behavior toward a greater sophistication than could be found in the rather simplistic approach of the nineteenth century positivists.

Some Philosophical Viewpoints

A less scientific but more deliberately provocative attack on middle-class complacency found expression in the writings of the German philosopher Friedrich Nietzsche, which gained popularity among European intellectuals in the 1890's. Before his final mental breakdown in 1889, Nietzsche produced a collection of writings that was at once an impassioned condemnation of his own time and an exhortation for a new, more heroic age to rise from the rubble of European civilization. He believed that European culture had lost its bearings and had arrived at a spiritual abyss. For all practical purposes traditional religion had lost its currency ("God is dead!" Nietzsche announced). The European middle classes persisted in hypocritical religiosity in an attempt to disguise their own spiritual poverty. He railed against the mediocrity and falseness of a prosaic mass age that mindlessly followed values that no longer had any meaning. As a remedy, Nietzsche demanded the revival of a Dionysian spirit capable of lifting the Europeans toward new heights; in a series of aphoristic statements in *Thus Spake Zarathustra* he prophesied the appearance of a superman who would point the way to this new age.

In retrospect Nietzsche has been cited as a seer who anticipated Naziism, although Nietzsche scholars have tirelessly pointed out that resemblances between Nietzsche's superman or his "will to power" and Nazi doctrine were superficial at best, and, in fact, much of Nietzsche's writing ran counter to Nazi theory and practice. His importance, then, is less as a questionable precursor of later developments than as a representative of his time. His works won recognition at the turn of the century because they expressed much of the anxiety that accompanied the transition from the Victorian age to the modern era at that time. Old standards seemed hollow to the prewar generation, but the shape of the new era was still undefined. Nietzsche was less a prophet than a critic who saw through the pretenses of European society.

The French philosopher Henri Bergson gained popularity after the turn of the century through a series of speeches and writings in which he emphasized intuition and creative will as essential elements of the human mind. Bergson grew dissatisfied with rationalistic philosophies that failed to give an adequate account of the process of change through time. What was required was an intuitive understanding of this process, which could not be perceived by purely rational, logical methods. For Bergson intelligence was a combination of reason and intuition, but he placed decisive emphasis on the latter.

Moreover, Bergson insisted that existence could not be explained in mechanistic, materialistic terms. Life was basically spiritual, carried forward by what he described as *élan vital*, and man's accomplishments testified to the triumph of mind, or human spirit, over matter. Bergson's views gained him renown in France; fashionable Parisian ladies sent their footmen to hold seats for them whenever he lectured at the Sorbonne. Although Bergson and Nietzsche differed radically in temperament—Nietzsche was filled with apocalyptic visions while Bergson advanced modestly optimistic views—both spoke to a generation that sought escape from a purely materialistic interpretation of the universe.

The Revolution in Physics

Throughout the nineteenth century the study of science had been suffused with great optimism and confidence, despite occasional jabs from romantics who deplored the narrowness of mere reason and the shallowness of scientific materialism. Many expected that within the near future science would uncover all the secrets of nature and man would at last gain complete mastery of his environment. The French scientist Ferdinand Laplace boasted that for a man who grasped the laws of science, "nothing would be uncertain, both past and future would be present in his eyes." Such confidence shocked the devout, who bemoaned man's presumption in making this divine boast, but increasingly science won converts by its aura of absolute truth.

One of the basic assumptions behind nineteenth century science, seemingly confirmed by numerous experiments, was that the universe was composed of "matter" and that the atom represented the hard core, or building block, for all material substance. The world of matter responded to certain fixed laws governing motion that had first been expressed in mathematical form by Isaac Newton in the latter half of the seventeenth century.

In the last decade of the nineteenth century a series of discoveries in physics forced a radical revision of these basic assumptions by uncovering the complex world of sub-atomic physics, a world that has had profound repercussions in the present century. The structure of nature was seen to be far more complex than had been assumed. Although only dimly perceived by men at the time, the challenge presented by this new perception in physical science was as exciting and unsettling as any innovations in other areas of European culture.

The break with Newtonian physics began with experiments in electromagnetism conducted by James Maxwell, a Scottish physicist. Building on earlier experiments in electricity, Maxwell discovered that light traveled in waves much in the same fashion that electric impulses traveled, differing only in wave length. He supplied a mathematical explanation for this phenomenon, and at first his work seemed to conform to Newton's laws. But certain problems appeared in Maxwell's formulas; to resolve them other physicists were forced to abandon Newtonian concepts.

A proposal that light waves traveled through an "ether" that had no gravity proved unreasonable when Wilhelm Roentgen discovered X-rays, which could penetrate presumedly solid substances. The ether hypothesis could not adequately account for this phenomenon. The problem of explaining radiation was further complicated by the discovery of radioactivity: that is, the apparently spontaneous emission of rays from certain substances without external stimulation. This discovery was first made by Henri Becquerel when he found that photographic plates placed in a drawer containing a package of uranium salts became exposed. The implications of this phenomenon were investigated further by two other French physicists, Pierre and Marie Curie, who found other elements with a far greater radioactivity than uranium.

The radiation effect indicated that substances previously assumed to be solid could be easily penetrated by miniscule, as yet undiscovered particles. Confirmation of this suspicion came in 1897 when a British physicist, J. J. Thomson, discovered that atoms were really composed of smaller particles, or electrons. Thomson's discovery of the electron, which was identified as a negatively charged particle, suggested the electrical nature of matter itself. A few years later Ernest Rutherford proposed a structure of the atom that resembled a miniature solar system with a positively charged nucleus at the center balancing negative electron satellites. By this point Newtonian concepts of the structure of matter had been radically altered.

A step was made toward linking matter and energy when the German scientist Max Planck published a paper in 1900 explaining discontinuities that he had discovered in radiation. Planck proposed that energy from radiation did not emanate in a steady, continuous stream but came in bursts that he called quanta. Although seemingly unsteady and erratic in behavior, quanta could be determined and, in fact, conformed to a mathematical constant. To arrive at this conclusion Planck had to conclude that energy was not only discontinuous, contrary to expectations based on the wave theory, but was also atomic in character. The quantum theory, as Planck himself reluctantly acknowledged, simply did not conform to Newtonian mechanical laws. Albert Einstein's special theory of relativity, published in 1905, further undermined these laws. Einstein suggested that all energy traveled through space in discontinuous quanta. The one constant was the speed of light, and other measurements were relative to the position and motion of the observer, whereas Newtonian views had taken the constancy of space, time and motion for granted.

In 1913 Niels Bohr, a Danish physicist, reconciled Rutherford's atomic model with Planck's quantum theory by demonstrating that the energy produced by the "jump" of an electron from one orbit to another could be expressed as a quantum. By bombarding the atom with sufficient energy to produce such changes it became theoretically possible to achieve an age-old dream: the transmutation of one substance to another by altering its electrical arrangement within the atom. Although further decisive breakthroughs were not to occur until after the First World War, the pioneering theoretical work, which upset Newtonian laws of physical behavior, had appeared in the two decades before the war.

For the average educated European who was not trained in physics or mathematics, this new leap seemed bewildering. Newton's laws could be understood and accepted readily by the layman, but the laws of atomic physics seemed to defy sense. According to these laws, space and time became relative, and matter itself seemed to dissolve into a void of uncertainty where, it was later shown, physical behavior could be predicted only on the basis of statistical probability, not absolute certainty. Few men were equipped to follow the physicists in their technical realm. The new physics worked and produced remarkable results, as millions would discover in the twentieth century, but why this was so had to be accepted as a matter of faith. Science could offer very little spiritual comfort to those who were seeking absolutes.

The revolution in physics, the probing studies of social behavior, and the great imaginative freedom of the creative arts gave Europe one of its most dynamic ages in a wide range of disciplines, equaling or surpassing the artistic accomplishments of the Renaissance and the successes of the seventeenth century scientific revolution. Within the space of a generation wholly unexpected perceptions arose that transformed European cultural life.

New paths appeared, but where did they lead? The absence of reassuring answers to this question suggested that for all its dynamism there were gaps within European culture, as for instance between the high culture of the intellectuals and the burgeoning culture of the masses. Despite increases in literacy, communication between the elite and popular culture was not easy. The German expressionists discovered this when their efforts to establish rapport with Berlin workers met with indifference or ridicule. Among the avant-garde, modernism was moving toward what Harold Rosenberg has described as a "tradition of the new," in which critics would chase after the latest innovation for fear of being surpassed by events, but their modernism still evoked suspicion in many quarters.

Discontinuities could also be found within the realm of high culture itself. Modernism described tendencies—toward diversity, abstraction, experimentation, or analysis—but could not be seen as a coherent synthesis. Science was becoming a world in itself, although its technological by-products could excite wonder; and an older, humanistic ideal of individual fulfillment found itself menaced by an age of specialized knowledge. Europe at the height of its material and political power found itself in a cultural upheaval that was at once a movement of great achievement and of considerable self-doubt.

SUGGESTED READING

Perhaps the best introduction to the cultural upheaval at the turn of the century might be obtained by reading a sample of the literature and looking at some of the paintings produced at the time. But a great number of studies on the subject have been made. Gerhard Masur offers a sweeping survey in *Prophets of Yesterday* (New York: Macmillan, 1961). H. Stuart Hughes's *Consciousness and Society* (New York: Knopf, 1958) discusses the social theories and some of the novelists who criticized and revised positivism and Marxism at the turn of the century. A series of essays on special topics may be found in John Weiss (ed.), *The Origins of Modern Consciousness* (Detroit: Wayne State University Press, 1965).

A brief and clear survey of painting is given by Ernst H. Gombrich in *The Story of Art* (London: Oxford University Press, 1966, 11th ed.), and the same author's *Art and Illusion* (London: Phaidon, 1968) is a sure guide to the aesthetic problems posed by art. Art as an expression of social and class interest is the basis for Arnold Hauser's *The Social History of Art* (New York: Vintage Books, 1958), of which the fourth volume, *Naturalism, Impressionism and the Film Age*, pertains to the period under consideration. Among the many fine studies of impressionism, John Rewald's *The History of Impressionism* (New York: Doubleday [Museum of Modern Art], 1962, rev. ed.) should be noted. Robert Rosenblum provides a general introduction to cubism in his well-illustrated *Cubism in the Twentieth Century* (New York: Abrams, 1966), which relates the cubist movement to other contemporary trends. Two books on the expressionists are noteworthy: Bernard S. Myers' *German Expressionists, a Generation in Revolt* (New York: McGraw-Hill, 1963) and Peter Selz's *German Expressionist Painting* (Berkeley: University of California Press, 1957). A recent revival of interest in art nouveau has produced a number of illustrated books, including Robert Schmutzler's *Art Nouveau* (New York: Abrams, 1964). The connection between trends in painting and architectural style is observed in Dennis Sharp's *Modern Architecture and Expressionism* (New York: Braziller, 1966); Sharp concentrates, however, on the postwar period. A sound introduction to changes taking place in painting and architecture may be obtained from Nikolaus Pevsner's *Pioneers of Modern Design* (London: Penguin, 1964). Pevsner also discusses architectural changes in the later chapters of his *An Outline of European Architecture* (London: Penguin, 1960). Siegfried Giedion is concerned with the impact of technology on art in his *Mechanization Takes Command: A Contribution to Anonymous History* (London: Oxford University Press, 1948).

Edmund Wilson gives his appreciation of certain writers identified with the modernist movement in *Axel's Castle: A Study of the Imaginative Literature of 1870–1930* (New York: Scribner's, 1931). Expressionist writings are the basis for Walter Sokel's *The Writer in Extremis*

(Stanford: Stanford University Press, 1959) and for an earlier study by Richard Samuel and R. H. Thomas, *Expressionism in German Life, Literature, and the Theatre* (Cambridge: W. Heffer & Sons, 1939). The French literary scene is the basis for Micheline Tison-Braun's analysis in *La Crise de l'humanisme, 1890–1914*, Vol. I (Paris: Nizet, 1958), and Richard M. Griffiths' *The Reactionary Revolution: the Catholic Revival in French Literature, 1870–1914* (New York: Ungar, 1965). Raymond Williams in *Culture and Society* (New York: Doubleday, 1960) studies the effect of rapid social change on nineteenth and twentieth century English writers.

There are many biographies of artistic and intellectual figures of the period. George D. Painter has provided a masterly two-volume biography, *Proust* (Boston: Little, Brown [Atlantic Monthly Press], 1959, 1965). Interpretive studies are given by Roger Shattuck in *Proust's Binoculars* (New York: Random House, 1963) and by Germaine Brée in *Marcel Proust and Deliverance from Time*, tr. by C. J. Richards & A. D. Truitt (New Brunswick, N.J.: Rutgers University Press, 1955). A balanced evaluation of Thomas Mann emerges from Henry Hatfield's *Thomas Mann* (New York: New Directions, 1952). Richard Ellmann has provided a definitive, detailed study of Joyce's life in *James Joyce* (New York: Oxford University Press, 1959). Another massive, detailed biography of an important figure is Ernest Simmons' *Chekhov: A Biography* (Boston: Little, Brown [Atlantic Monthly Press], 1962). Robert L. Jackson has compiled a useful collection of critical articles in *Chekhov* (Englewood Cliffs, N.J.: Prentice-Hall, 1967). Freud is treated in Philip Rieff's biographical study, *Freud: the Mind of the Moralist* (New York: Doubleday, 1961).

Modernist trends in music have been studied by Joseph Machlis in *Introduction to Contemporary Music* (New York: W. W. Norton, 1961) and by William W. Austin in *Music in the Twentieth Century* (New York: W. W. Norton, 1966). A broader survey is Richard L. Crocker's *A History of Musical Style* (New York: McGraw-Hill, 1966). The movies are beginning to be studied as a serious art form with a history. Arthur Knight's *The Liveliest Art* (New York: The New American Library, 1959) is an early effort in this direction.

D. L. Hurd and J. J. Kipling (eds.) in *The Origins and Growth of Physical Science*, Vol. II (London: Penguin, 1963), give a glimpse of the men and the writings that were influential in altering the direction of science. Other valuable introductions for the lay reader include Sir James Jeans's *The Growth of Physical Science* (Cambridge: Cambridge University Press, 1948) and Albert Einstein and Leopold Infeld's *The Evolution of Physics* (New York: Simon & Schuster, 1938). A more detailed treatment may be found in *A General History of the Sciences*, Vols. 3 & 4 (covering the nineteenth and twentieth centuries), edited by René Taton and A. J. Pomerans (London: Thames & Hudson, 1965).

8

THE POLITICS OF DOMESTIC CONFLICT, 1906–14

In 1906 the states of western Europe appeared headed for an era of political and social progress under liberal auspices. The republicans had triumphed in France; the emergence of Giovanni Giolitti in Italy promised a period of modest social reforms; while in Britain the victory of the Liberal party presaged a new era after a generation of conservative dominance. The men in power in these countries were committed to peaceful change through parliamentary procedures. They favored a broadening of political participation, and, except in France, vigorously promoted social legislation. The underlying assumption common to British Liberals, French radicals, and the followers of Giolitti was a faith in gradual progress; there were few utopias on the horizon, for most of these men were pragmatists accustomed to political struggles and compromises. Yet the course of moderation proved difficult as political movements on both the left and right adopted a new militancy to accelerate or retard the pace of social and political change. A period that promised progress bogged

◀ Strike of French coal miners in the Pas de Calais.

down under domestic tensions produced by workers' demands, a surge of nationalism, the mass politics of a broader electorate, and a conservative reaction to these tendencies.

In eastern Europe the prewar decade opened with only qualified promise. Revolution had brought a new parliamentary institution to Russia, but the powers of the Duma remained untested. In Austria-Hungary the stubborn nationalism of the Hungarian Magyars posed difficulties for the imperial government, while the perennial Czech-German dispute paralyzed representative institutions in the Austrian sector. And in Germany hopes for political reform ran up against the intransigence of Prussian conservatives. A political deadlock occurred in eastern Europe, produced by irreconcilable conflicts of interest among the inhabitants of the empires.

In both eastern and western Europe political leaders experienced frustration before 1914. Neither liberal concessions nor control from above seemed to be effective in containing the ferment that marked domestic politics in Europe during the prewar years.

The Dilemmas of Liberalism in Great Britain

When the Liberals entered Commons after their impressive victory in the 1906 elections, they were filled with enthusiasm, but uncertain as to what to do with their majority. Their triumph had resulted from resistance to the protectionist views of Joseph Chamberlain; the party had offered little in the way of a program. Nevertheless, the vote for the Liberals had been a vote against the Conservatives for their failure to address themselves to domestic problems, and the Liberals rightly assumed that they had received a mandate for social reform.

Legislation and measures for reorganization of administrative services were quickly produced by the cabinet formed under Sir Henry Campbell-Bannerman, who was able to unite the many factions within his own party. His cabinet included both Liberal imperialists and "little Englanders" of the Gladstonian school; the brilliant Welsh commoner David Lloyd George found himself in the company of such distinguished Whig aristocrats as Sir Edward Grey, who became foreign secretary. Within this gifted cabinet, those who favored a strong foreign and imperial policy held positions at the war and foreign ministries while Lloyd George and other radicals addressed themselves to domestic reform. A concern for maintaining Britain's overseas obligations combined with a search for solutions to domestic conflicts became the pattern for Liberal rule.

One of the most important bills passed by the Liberal government during its first year in office was the Trades Disputes Act, which relieved labor unions from the threat of prosecution for actions committed during strikes. This decision reversed the Taff Vale Decision of 1902, which had held unions responsible for damages suffered by companies in the course of strike activities. Hesitating to give blanket immunity, the Liberals had at first proposed a limited liability for the unions, but under pressure from the unions and from Labor members of Parliament the act was amended to provide full immunity. The bill passed both houses with an almost unanimous vote; the Conservatives and the Lords evidently wished to avoid further alienating the working-class voters. Meanwhile, Lloyd George used his position as head of the Board of Trade to mediate several labor disputes on terms that were favorable to the workers. Liberal government was showing itself responsive to the emerging strength of the working class in British political life.

At the same time, the Liberal war minister, Richard B. Haldane, embarked on an extensive and overdue reorganization of the British army. He introduced a staff system patterned after the German model, created a territorial reserve army, and, most significant, formed six divisions into an expeditionary force ready for rapid mobilization and deployment on the continent. Haldane's reforms might have encountered objections from radicals within the cabinet, who disliked strengthening the army, had he not carried them out with a simultaneous reduction in estimates for the army's budget. This reduction was achieved by clearing the army administration of deadwood, an act that irritated many hide-bound officers but further streamlined Britain's military organization.

Commons Versus Lords: Constitutional Conflict

The labor and military reforms represented the Liberal government's major achievements under Campbell-Bannerman. In other proposed legislation the Liberals encountered determined opposition from the House of Lords, which rejected a series of Liberal measures, the most important being the Education Bill of 1906. The Liberals discovered that their important bills were either rejected outright by the Lords or returned to Commons in a totally altered form. By 1907 a political struggle between the houses had reached serious proportions; the Liberals simply permitted the rejected bills to accumulate, thereby compiling a list of grievances against the House of Lords. Campbell-Bannerman accused the Lords of obstructing the will of the British people by their actions, and a resolution calling for a reduction of the veto powers of the Lords was passed by the House of Commons. The Lords were defended in Commons by Arthur Balfour, who returned as leader of the Conservatives after winning a by-election. He argued that the Lords had a responsibility to check the Commons to insure that the interests of the nation were not transgressed by ill-considered measures. To this Lloyd George retorted that the Lords were not the watchdogs of the constitution, but simply served as "Mr. Balfour's poodle." There was much truth to his accusation, for the House of Lords had done nothing to block Conservative bills passed before 1906, but had vetoed most of the Liberals' legislation. The Liberals pointed out that the Lords could not be considered a disinterested body when they acted in a partisan fashion.

The issue dragged on without being resolved. In the spring of 1908 Campbell-Bannerman, whose health was failing, resigned as prime minister, and was replaced by H. H. Asquith. Lloyd George then became chancellor of the exchequer and Winston Churchill succeeded him at the Board of Trade. Both of these men were committed to carrying through social legislation, and they successfully sponsored bills that provided old-age pensions, labor-exchange boards, minimum-wage scales in certain non-union industries, and protection against child labor. Despite these successes, the Liberals continued to feel frustrated. None of their measures had passed without negotiation with the Conservative opposition in order to assure acceptance in the House of Lords; other bills were blocked. Labor was growing restive at the slow pace of reform, and the electorate showed its disenchantment with liberalism by returning Conservatives to Parliament at by-elections.

On top of this, the social legislation that had been passed required financing; the budget, however, was already strained by the demands of Britain's naval construction program. Lloyd George proposed a budget for 1909 that would meet these needs, but it included a number of innovations, notably sharply increased inheritance taxes for the wealthy estates, a graduated income tax, and a tax for unearned increases in land values. The budget was designed to reduce economic inequality and, as Lloyd George put it, "to wage implacable warfare against poverty and squalidness." This "People's Budget" was at once an economic and a political measure that would give substance to Liberal reforms and challenge the Conservative opposition in the House of Lords. This opposition denounced the budget as a piece of socialism.

By proposing a controversial budget Lloyd George had chosen his ground well, for under British constitutional practice financial measures were the prerogative of the House of Commons. But Conservatives in the House of Lords became so inflamed over the radical implications of the budget that they decided to veto it and thus defy constitutional tradition. Nothing could have suited Lloyd George better. He immediately denounced the Lords as a group of privileged men more interested in defending their own wealth than in advancing the common good of the country. The ensuing controversy was tumultuous; by late summer it became clear that the House of Lords would reject the budget. When this step came in November, the House of Commons promptly passed a resolution that censured the House of Lords for having breached the constitution and usurped the Commons' rights in money matters.

Since the two houses of Parliament had reached a deadlock, a general election was called in January of 1910 to place the isssue before the people. The constitutional question may have been too abstract for the average voter, but the Liberals had no difficulty in presenting the matter as a contest between the democratic process and the privileges of a wealthy elite. Had the Conservatives awaited the next election, instead of forcing the issue, they undoubtedly would have turned the Liberals out. The pendulum of opinion was swinging in the Conservatives' direction prior to the budget controversy. As it was, they increased their representation in Commons by over 100 seats, but the Liberals in alliance with the Irish delegation retained control of the House of Commons. As soon as the Irish found themselves the arbiters of a Liberal majority, home rule again returned to the front of British politics. When Parliament reconvened, Asquith was able to gain Irish support in passing the "People's Budget" only by promising to satisfy at last their demands for home rule. Home rule was, however, a difficult demand to meet. The peers had reluctantly yielded on the budget after the election, but they set themselves against granting home rule to Ireland. If the Liberals were to fulfill their promise, the veto power of the Lords had to be broken. The Liberals decided to use the Lords' "revolt" over the budget as a way of reducing their power.

The Parliament Act

In March 1910 Asquith introduced three resolutions into the House of Commons: one required all financial measures to become law within a month of being sent to the Lords, a second limited the Lords' veto power on any legislation to three sessions (two years), and a third required elections to be held for Commons every five years. Together these formed what was to be known as the Parliament Act and marked the beginning of a constitutional struggle that was to last a year and a half.

The resolutions passed Commons in April, but before they could be considered by the House of Lords King Edward VII died after a brief illness. During his funeral and the subsequent coronation of George V a truce was declared in the political conflict; by autumn the controversy had revived. Determined to get the Parliament Bill through the House of Lords, in November Asquith obtained assurances from King George that, if necessary, enough Liberal peers would be created to assure its passage. A second election for the year was held on the constitutional question. By this time the electorate had tired of the issue, and the turnout was light. But the results repeated the January election, for the Liberals and the Irish delegation still controlled Commons. In February the Parliament Bill passed the Commons once more and went to the House of Lords where a sizable group of die-hard members were preparing to block it. The issue remained in doubt until the final debate in the House of Lords on August 10, held in the midst of an intense heat wave that added further tension to the scene. Under the king's threat to create new peers, enough Lords abstained from voting to assure passage of the Parliament Act by a narrow majority. The Lords had yielded, and the constitutional crisis passed.

The events of 1910 and 1911 marked a significant point in British constitutional history. The Parliament Act confirmed the supremacy of Commons and reduced the Lords to largely ceremonial functions. In a sense, the Liberals simply put into law what had been constitutional tradition until the Lords rebelled against Lloyd George's budget. After 1911 there was no doubt where the center of power lay within the British political system.

The Parliament Act cleared the way for a major piece of social legislation, the National Insurance Act, which gave comprehensive disability and sickness protection to all workers in Britain and provided unemployment payments in several industries. Additional legislation that year established salaries for members of Parliament, a measure that enabled those who enjoyed no outside income to afford parliamentary office. These measures brought a significant democratization to British political life, and they marked the high point in the Liberal party's achievement before 1914. After 1911, however, a change occurred in the temper of British politics that was far less encouraging for the future.

Labor Militancy

Despite the tangible gains earned by the Liberal government, the Labor party had become increasingly restive in harness with the Liberals. To some extent this dissatisfaction stemmed from a feeling that the upper-class Liberals within the party leadership regarded labor with a condescending *noblesse oblige* and lacked real understanding of the workers' problems; but equally important were differences within the labor movement itself. Disagreements between party and union leaders undermined the movement's unity and sense of purpose.

The most serious division within the British labor movement was between the older union leadership and the younger members of the trade unions who had lost patience with gradualist tactics and inclined toward the syndicalist doctrines of direct action. They inspired a series of strikes in Britain in 1910 that reflected syndicalist ideas and discontent with actual economic conditions. After 1905 Britain had experienced an upturn in economic activity. Industrial production and exports and imports all rose steadily, but so did prices; wage rates failed to match, or at best barely matched, increased costs of living. The earlier improvements in living standards had raised expectations that only turned to frustration when British workers found themselves scarcely holding their own. In these conditions syndicalist activity had an impact, particularly among workers in the less skilled occupations.

The militant syndicalist leaders had no faith in Parliament as a means of obtaining measures of assistance. An early sign of labor's new mood appeared in 1910 when Welsh miners went on strike and troops finally were called in to preserve order. The following year extensive strikes broke out among railway workers, dockers, and seamen, many of them without union sanction. In 1912 nearly a million miners struck for five weeks, affecting another million workers in related industries, and later that year a national strike brought the transport industry to a halt. Moderate union leaders seemed to be losing control of the movement, and the strikes were characterized by an unaccustomed bitterness.

The Liberals were incapable of curbing this labor militancy. Asquith, the party's leader, seemed reluctant to press for far-reaching reforms that might have tempered some of labor's discontent. He and other members of the party believed that Lloyd George's earlier program had gone far enough in the direction of social-welfare legislation. A half-hearted attempt to gain a minimum wage failed because of the

Liberal leadership's hesitancy. Labor discontent continued to mount and reached a climax in the spring of 1914 when three of the most militant unions—the transport workers, the railwaymen, and the miners—formed a "triple industrial alliance" for the purpose of engaging in common action against employers. Although the triple alliance did not explicitly propose such a strike, the threat of a coordinated strike that would involve some two million workers directly, and indirectly affect nearly all of Britain's industrial system, hung over the country in the summer of 1914.

Suffragette Militancy

While British labor was turning toward direct and militant action, a parallel trend appeared in an unexpected place, the women's suffrage movement. In 1903 Mrs. Pankhurst and her daughter Cristabel founded the Women's Social and Political Union, which was devoted to obtaining the vote for women and was prepared to use any means to publicize the inequalities that arose from the inferior status of women in Edwardian England. At first the suffragettes confined themselves to peaceful demonstrations, issuing pamphlets and heckling Liberal speakers. After a few years in which little progress had been made toward female suffrage or other forms of emancipation, the more militant suffragettes began chaining themselves to the railing in the visitors' gallery of the House of Commons to draw further attention to the cause. When suffragettes were imprisoned, they promptly went on hunger strikes; whereupon the desperate authorities resorted to force feeding, an action that only served to give the suffragettes more publicity.

After 1910 suffragette violence increased as bombs were placed in churches, manor houses were burned, trains were fired on by snipers, presumably suffragettes, and paintings in museums were slashed. The government, however, refused to yield to pressure, and a proposal for extending the vote to women was dropped. The suffragettes represented another militant movement whose grievances remained unresolved in 1914.

Conservative Militancy: the Home Rule Issue

The temptations of violence were not confined to the political left or the more ardent suffragettes. Within the ranks of British conservatism advocates of violence appeared, and a traditional sense of moderation seemed to have become a thing of the past. Conservative intransigence first emerged during the debates over Lloyd George's budget and over the Parliament Act, but conservative militancy became feverish over the proposal for Irish home rule.

At the beginning of 1912 Asquith fulfilled his obligation to the Irish delegation by introducing a bill that provided legislative autonomy for Ireland on most internal affairs. A separate parliament was to be formed, although the Parliament in Westminster was still to decide certain issues, notably those arising from foreign affairs, and a reduced Irish delegation was to continue sitting in the Commons. Not all the Irish welcomed this proposal for home rule. The northern provinces, known as Ulster, were Protestant and industrial; the northern Irish rebelled at the idea of being a minority group tied to rural, Catholic southern Ireland. As the Home Rule Bill entered Parliament, the Ulstermen had already organized themselves into a volunteer army. In their speeches in the Commons, the opponents of home rule openly counseled resistance and defiance of the law if it were passed. At one point Bonar Law, the leader of the Conservative opposition in Parliament, threatened civil war. This threat was not an inaccurate description of the danger in Ireland, for in the south an Irish nationalist volunteer force had been formed, but it was scarcely responsible behavior for a politician.

Had Asquith acted with determination, a compromise, however uneasy, might have been achieved on the basis of a separation of Ulster from the rest of Ireland. In deciding instead to "wait and see" Asquith allowed opposition to home rule to mount in Conservative circles. In March 1914 a home rule bill was introduced into Commons for the third time, after having been rejected twice, in 1912 and 1913, by the House of Lords. Under the Parliament Act, the bill would automatically become law if it passed the Commons a third time, and it was assumed that home rule would be introduced in Ireland some time that year.

In a desperate effort to halt the institution of home rule, several prominent Englishmen, including Lord Roberts, the hero of the Boer War, and Rudyard Kipling, issued a proclamation that the law should be disobeyed until a public referendum could be held on the issue. The opponents of home rule were strongly opposed to ending the hundred-year-old union of the two countries and thereby eliminating direct British control over what they regarded as an essential part of Britain's possessions. The army rallied to the cause of the Conservatives. High-ranking officers revealed their sympathy for the unionists; Sir Henry Wilson, Asquith's director of military administration, gave covert advice to the Ulster volunteers; and at the end of March, fifty-seven of the seventy officers stationed at Curragh in Ireland threatened to resign rather than carry out orders to march north to Ulster and enforce the home rule decision, which was to go into effect in September. Although opinion in England ran against this "mutiny" at Curragh, J. E. B. Seely, the war minister, assured the officers that they would not be called on to impose home rule. When news of this leaked out, Asquith forced the war minister's resignation, but did nothing to punish either the officers or their sympathizers within the upper ranks of the government. Asquith glossed over the whole episode. Meanwhile, both sides in Ireland had armed themselves and civil war loomed.

Confronted with labor and suffragette militancy alongside the Conservative insurgence, moderate liberalism found itself on the defensive in Great Britain. The spirit of compromise, which many considered the essence of the British system of government, had disappeared when confronted with this three-pronged crisis. Britain had entered a period that has been described as "domestic anarchy." The dangers were apparent at the time. In July 1914, three weeks before the outbreak of war in Europe, Lloyd George admitted that the nation faced a difficult trial. Should a rebellion over the Irish question accompany a general strike that year, "the situation will be the gravest with which any government has had to deal for centuries."

When the war broke out, a temporary political truce prevailed. Labor called off its proposals for a general strike; suffragette agitation quieted as more and more women became engaged in the war effort; the Irish Home Rule Act was suspended for the duration of hostilities. A sense of patriotic duty restored unity to the country, at least for the first two years of the war. This phenomenon has led some historians to speculate that a desire to escape a domestic crisis by rallying the country behind a common cause may have inclined cabinet members toward accepting a declaration of war. In any event the war did not solve Britain's domestic disputes; it simply postponed them.

Giolitti's Middle Way in Italy

In Italy the prewar decade brought the ascendancy of Giovanni Giolitti, in many ways an untypical Italian politician. His prosaic style and pragmatic approach to politics contrasted with the flamboyance of Crispi, but his mastery of parliamentary maneuver enabled him to carry through a modest though promising program of social reforms.

Ultimately he led Italy into an era of mass politics with a wholesale extension of the franchise in 1912. Yet, even with his talent for manipulating parliamentary combinations, Giolitti encountered difficulties in charting a moderate course between the extreme left and the ultra-nationalist right.

One of Giolitti's tactics was to give up the office of prime minister during brief periods, allowing others to assume responsibility for unpopular measures. He remained the arbiter of parliamentary politics by preserving a solid bloc of delegates who were loyal to him in return for the political favors that he gave them whenever he was in power; the other prime ministers held power at his discretion. As soon as Giolitti judged the moment favorable for a "return," he would provoke a governmental crisis and reappear as prime minister. Between the end of 1903 and the outbreak of the war Giolitti formed three ministries that totaled seven years and seven months.

Social Reform Under Giolitti

In May 1906, Giolitti returned to power after one of his temporary retirements. During his absence the Italian rail lines had been nationalized, a highly controversial measure that Giolitti favored but that he wished to have someone else guide through parliament. The Italian economy was beginning a surge that was to continue throughout this ministry, which lasted until 1909. In those years Giolitti produced reforms that seemed to confirm the hopes that had been placed in the "liberal spring" following the political strains at the turn of the century. Such reforms included stricter controls over factory working conditions and the promotion of workers' cooperatives. Giolitti also managed to reduce the interest rates paid on government bonds, thereby easing the state's financial burdens.

Attention was directed toward the long-neglected south. After several parliamentary studies exposed the misery of this region, the government adopted measures to provide better credit and introduce more effective agricultural techniques to increase productivity. Yet the south continued to lag behind northern Italy. Parliament lacked funds for the wholesale reforms that were necessary to overcome both the natural and social obstacles to the region's development. Many southern Italians continued to protest against their poverty by emigrating to North or South America.

The elections of 1909 showed a strengthening of the parliamentary left. At first Giolitti tried to satisfy this political faction by proposing an increase in inheritance and income taxes. But this project created an uproar among conservatives; during one debate a duke pitched an inkwell at the prime minister. Giolitti took this as the signal for another exit. When a succession of ministers failed to weld a durable majority out of the various factions within the Chamber, Giolitti returned in 1911 with more proposals for social legislation. Under this ministry life insurance became a government monopoly; this measure at once reduced abuses and produced revenue for the state; estimates indicated that annual profits from life insurance amounted to 100 percent for some companies before nationalization. Giolitti also launched a campaign to enforce compulsory education and thus reduce the rate of illiteracy, which characterized nearly 50 percent of the population according to the 1910 census. There was also an attempt to shift the emphasis in higher education from humanistic studies, which had created a glut of lawyers, to the sciences and technical fields. But Giolitti's capstone to an era of reform came in 1912 when he extended the franchise to nearly all males so that the electorate jumped from 3.5 to 8 million voters.

Giolitti's System

Giolitti's social reforms and franchise bill brought Italy into a democratic era. Paradoxically, Giolitti has been criticized by historians for having fatally weakened Italian democracy. The criticism rests on two counts: first, the sudden increase in the electorate brought unsophisticated voters into the political process who were amenable to demagogic appeals, a development that subsequently facilitated the rise of fascism; and, second, Giolitti's methods of gaining parliamentary support by the use of political bribes created a cynical disillusionment and indifference toward parliamentary practices. Certainly the sudden increase in the electorate altered political life. Many who went to the polls were illiterate, so that signs indicating parties had to be printed on the ballots; others of the newly enfranchised showed their indifference by abstaining from voting. Giolitti's corrupt political practices did little to encourage political morality on the part of others. The Italian electorate passively accepted the manipulations of government power plays and shrugged off political scandals; as a result there seemed to be only a light commitment to the "system" of government as such.

On the other hand, Giolitti's system of government showed some positive achievements. Wishing to broaden the consensus favorable to democratic practices in Italy, Giolitti was willing to turn toward the left and the right. He sought the advice of reform socialists and hoped that someday they might be induced to enter the government. On the right, Giolitti made overtures to Catholic deputies, seeking to mitigate the Church-state antagonism. The Vatican had relaxed its ban on Catholic participation in the political life of the secular Italian state, and Giolitti accepted this gesture as an encouraging sign. In the elections of 1913 he signed a pact with the Catholic leader, Count Gentiloni, whereby Giolitti's Constitutional Liberals would receive Catholic support if they declared their opposition to a divorce law. The Gentiloni Pact subsequently cost Giolitti the support of the anticlerical radicals, and he found himself in one of his temporary retirements when war erupted in 1914. The pact was evidence of Giolitti's "sweet reasonableness," his effort to find accommodation for a broad spectrum of political tendencies. His franchise reform may be interpreted in the same light; it was a means for opening channels of political expression to those who had been excluded from politics in Italy and were showing their dissatisfaction by joining anti-parliamentary movements, such as syndicalism.

Giolitti understood Italy's limitations. Although an industrial boom had developed in northern Italy by the turn of the century, the country still lagged behind other industrial states and the state debt remained high. Giolitti estimated that such difficulties could be overcome if the country avoided the strains and pitfalls of a policy that ventured beyond the nation's resources. Admirers of Giolitti, including the philosopher, Benedetto Croce, praised him for a pragmatic realism that brought Italy considerable benefits by 1914. His detractors lamented his sordid, prosaic approach to politics, which blurred ideological distinctions and sapped parliament of its vigor.

Italian political difficulties may have stemmed in part from the Giolittian system, but more alarming were movements that openly declared themselves against parliamentary methods. Italy, like other European countries, experienced a growing militancy of the extreme left and right during the years immediately preceding the First World War.

Militancy on the Left and Right

The Italian Socialist party showed many of the internal divisions that plagued other European socialist movements during these years. In 1906 the moderate reformists had scored a notable success at the party congress in Rome. As the syndicalists and others on the extreme left found themselves outnumbered, the leadership of the party and the editorship of its newspaper, *Avanti,* passed into the hands of the reformist wing. Democracy was favored by the moderates as a preliminary step toward socialism, and the party gave tacit support to Giolitti on welfare legislation, although they refused to join the government for fear of alienating the revolutionary wing. This wing, which had found a spokesman in the young Mussolini, comprised no more than one-fourth of the party. At the 1911 party congress the secretary of the Confederation of Labor pointed out that the workers had more to lose than simply their chains by pursuing a blindly revolutionary course. In practice, the moderate members of the movement, particularly leaders such as Bissolati and Bonomi, were moving close to Giolitti in their views.

The apparent triumph of reformism did not heal the rifts within Italian socialism; after 1911 a revival of militant, revolutionary sentiments split the movement. Disagreements first appeared over the Italian conquest of Tripoli. The Socialist party condemned the war as a wasteful, imperialist adventure, but some Socialists, including Bissolati and Bonomi, voted for the war against Turkey. Reformist opponents of the war, including Turati, temporarily joined Mussolini's supporters and expelled Bissolati and Bonomi from the party during the 1912 Socialist Party Congress. This congress brought a radical shift within the movement, for the militants gained control of the party. Mussolini became editor of *Avanti,* and he used the pages of the party's newspaper to condemn all cooperation with bourgeois elements for any purpose. Such sentiments spelled an eclipse of reformism within Italian socialism. The revolutionary trend was apparent in the elections of 1913: some seventy-eight Socialists were elected to parliament, but only twenty-six of them were reformists; the remaining fifty-two condemned parliamentary practice as a bourgeois sham.

Although the failure of syndicalist-sponsored agrarian strikes discredited syndicalism at the time, the movement staged a revival in 1914. Several strikes broke out in which police and strikers clashed. In May 1914 an intensive strike developed on the state-owned railways that threatened to become a general strike. But the most serious outburst of violence occurred during the "red week" in June in Romagna, when anti-draft demonstrations led to fighting between the demonstrators and police. To protest this action a general strike was called for the province; it ultimately turned into a revolutionary uprising. Republicans removed symbols of royal authority from public buildings; syndicalists raised the red flag over the town hall in Bologna; train tracks were torn up and shops were looted by surging crowds; and at one point Romagna was proclaimed an independent republic. Mussolini praised the revolutionaries in the pages of *Avanti* and participated in some of the events. Nearly 100,000 troops were called in to suppress the uprising at considerable expense and strain for the country's military reserves.

A tendency toward violence and a marked distrust of parliamentary methods also emerged among conservative and ultra-nationalist groups in the immediate prewar years. Nationalist intellectuals published tracts that glorified war and called on Italians to demonstrate the nation's virility through their martial qualities. In 1911 Enrico Corradini began publishing *L'Idea Nazionale,* a journal that provided an outlet for the opinions of the Nationalist party, formed the preceding year. The Nationalists called for a vigorous foreign policy and demanded an authoritarian state in which obedience and discipline would replace the disorder of democratic rule. Similar views could be found among the "futurists," artists and intellectuals who praised action for its own sake and promoted a cult of violence in which war was the highest virtue.

This extremism might be dismissed as the expression of a limited intellectual elite, except that a tendency toward violence could be found elsewhere in Italy. Within parliament itself were advocates of larger military budgets despite the urgent needs of the impoverished south. Landowners began arming themselves and forming motorized private armies to intimidate peasants who joined socialist or syndicalist organizations or who dared to form their own cooperatives. The activities of these landowners in breaking strikes and attempting to destroy cooperatives had been partly responsible for provoking riots in Romagna in 1914. At the same time industrialists subsidized nationalist publications and pressured the government for contracts for steel plating and armaments. The close connection between government and industry was an important characteristic of Italy's economic growth, and this connection gave industrial groups important political leverage.

The clearest demonstration of Italy's nationalism was the Libyan War, which broke out in September 1911. For several years the Italians had believed that they would have the approval of the other European powers if they should establish a colony across the Mediterranean in Tripoli. Nationalists who were calling for an exploit that would demonstrate Italian greatness pressured the government to take up the Tripoli option. Initially, Giolitti resisted such pressures, for he doubted the value of the Libyan Desert, and he hesitated to use Italy's resources for such limited gains. In the summer of 1911 he reversed his stand and decided that Italy should embark on a colonial conquest; he hoped to take away some of the nationalists' thunder by satisfying their claims to Tripoli. An expedition to Africa would, as the nationalist propaganda ran, give the descendants of Roman legionnaires an opportunity to reaffirm their martial prowess. Moreover, the international climate at that time appeared favorable, as Britain, France, and Germany were preoccupied with the Moroccan question.

On a pretext, war was declared against Turkey, which exercised nominal suzerainty over the region. The campaign, although ultimately victorious, proved more difficult and far more expensive that Giolitti had calculated. In the aftermath of the costly war Giolitti soberly reassessed Italy's capacity for military ventures and concluded that Italy's international ambitions had to be contained. The government had to shoulder the additional costs of administering Tripoli and ruling a hostile population. Unfortunately, a sponsor of the colonial expedition, Giolitti could not be entirely candid about how much the war had cost the Italian people.

Counsels of moderation arose from several quarters. The Socialists, for example, remained critical of any adventurous overseas exploits; they argued that Italy had to tailor its foreign policy to its capacity. But nationalists regarded the Libyan conquest with enthusiasm, and parliament, swept along by the patriotic sentiment, enthusiastically voted the credits—or, rather, approved the debts—that had been rung up by the expedition. The prudent positions of the Socialists and of Giolitti made little impression on those who saw Italy as a great power destined to have a leading role in European affairs.

When the European war broke out in 1914, Giolitti was out of office but he urged that Italy remain neutral. The prime minister, Antonio Salandra, at first followed this careful policy and merely watched the developments on the battlefields. Meanwhile, a debate broke out in Italy over what policy should be followed with respect to the war. The nationalists insisted that Italy had to be allied with the winning side in order to be present at the conference table when the spoils of war were distributed. Salandra became converted to this view, and he agreed to enter the war on the side of Britain and France in exchange for their promises of territory at the war's conclusion. In taking this step, he broke with Giolittian moderation. Giolitti was unable to get back into power and prevent a war that he feared would be harmful for Italy. Under Salandra's leadership, Italy declared war in May 1915 against its former allies and entered a conflict that was to aggravate many of the state's internal difficulties.

The Radical Era in France

In 1906 the French Radicals emerged triumphant from the Dreyfus crisis and from the struggles over the separation of Church and state.

A radical ethos, marked by an anticlerical bias and a strong republican faith, seemed to be the prevailing strain within French political culture. In countless small towns throughout the provinces the local schoolmaster, frequently a radical or radical socialist, waged a relentless and usually successful campaign against the influence of the local curé. As a result a generation of electors came of age in the prewar decade endowed with anticlerical views and a strong commitment, heavily laced with nationalism, to republican values. The anniversary of the fall of the Bastille, July 14, became a national holiday in the 1880's, and its celebration was a festival for republicans. Streets and squares in provincial prefects and sub-prefects were renamed to honor republican heroes who had been instrumental in founding the Third Republic. Radicalism seemed firmly entrenched.

The elections of 1906 returned the Radical party with the largest representation, almost constituting a majority, of the parties in parliament. Georges Clemenceau formed a Radical cabinet that also included two former Socialists, Aristide Briand and René Viviani. His ministry lasted until 1909, a durable one by Third Republic standards.

The 1906 election was the last occasion of the cooperation between Socialists and Radicals that had first emerged during the Dreyfus crisis. In the runoff elections Radicals and Socialists supported the party whose candidate had the best chance, thereby concentrating their votes effectively, but the cooperation did not extend beyond the electoral pact. The Socialists remained loyal to their promise given at the Socialist Congress in Amsterdam in 1904 to refuse to participate in, or support, a bourgeois ministry. Clemenceau thus had to count on support from the Radicals for his government, and obtain support from other groups as needed on particular issues.

Worker Unrest

At the Amiens congress of the General Labor Confederation (C.G.T.) in 1906 a charter was passed that embraced many syndicalist views. The charter repudiated official connections with political parties and advocated using a general strike to provoke a crisis within the bourgeois order and precipitate capitalism's collapse. The uncompromising doctrine contained in the Charter of Amiens denoted labor's deep skepticism toward politics and encouraged a new militancy among the unions after 1906.

In 1907 and 1908 workers in building trades, electrical industries, and coal mines struck against their employers in a series of labor disputes marked by sharp clashes between the workers and the police and soldiers called in to preserve order. In southern France during the same period peasant disturbances erupted in the aftermath of a price slump; the government's decision to call in the troops simply led to more bloodshed. Union leaders, including the head of the C.G.T., Victor Griffuelhes, urged soldiers to disobey orders when the government called on them to break strikes. In return the government jailed Griffuelhes and other union leaders for incitement to disobedience.

Discontent spread to public services despite a government ban on union organizations among state employees. A primary-school teachers association was formed, and in 1909 postal employees went on strike. After initially promising—or seeming to promise—some satisfaction to the postal workers, Clemenceau retaliated with mass dismissals of strike leaders and their supporters. The C.G.T. called in vain on other unions to engage in a sympathy strike that would have amounted to a general strike. The failure of this appeal was a setback for the French unions, and the government gained the upper hand.

Labor dissatisfaction seethed on, however; the following year, 1910, workers on the northern railway lines went on strike. Clemenceau's successor, Aristide Briand, who only a decade earlier had been a spokesman for the left wing of the Socialist party, showed no more patience than Clemenceau with labor strikes. Briand called the striking railway workers back into the army as reservists and then sent troops to break the strike.

Strike action died down after the collapse of the northern railway strike, but the conflict left deep scars on French social and political history. The government's triumph over labor militants failed to eradicate syndicalist tendencies within the French working class. Many workers nursed a deep distrust for political parties whose leadership was predominantly bourgeois, and they remained skeptical of using legislation to ameliorate working conditions or provide social benefits, because they feared that such action would "domesticate" the labor movement and blunt its revolutionary zeal. For much the same reason the workers' syndicates showed little interest in direct negotiations with employers; such activity, according to syndicalist doctrine, would bind the unions to capitalism. Even collective bargaining was rejected. The only acceptable means of protest was the strike, or demonstration in the street, culminating in a general strike. This meant that the possibility of cooperation between worker and employer was reduced. The fact that employers refused to recognize unions as workers' organizations in salary negotiations placed the worker at a definite disadvantage, and industrial relations became marked by a paternalism that tended to exacerbate the gulf between workers and employers.

Because unions could not act as bargaining agents, few workers could see any merit in joining them and paying dues; only about

14 percent of France's industrial labor force were actually union members. The unity of French labor came from a kind of mystique, from a sense of participation in a movement that was ready to engage in revolutionary protest, rather than from membership in an organization that watched out for workers' interests on a day-to-day basis. The syndicalist struggle left a sizable segment of the French working class with a sense of alienation from bourgeois society and the state.

The syndicalist struggle also had an impact on the French political left. The Socialist party's parliamentary leader, Jean Jaurès, tried to minimize disagreements between reformists and the militant syndicalists. In an effort to preserve working-class unity, Jaurès couched his political formulas in broad terms, and he maintained that the Socialist party and the C.G.T. had distinct but complementary roles to play in advancing workers' interests. Jaurès retained his belief in parliamentary action and persistently attacked the government for its neglect of social problems. Perhaps his efforts might have healed some of the suspicion that existed between the French Socialist party and the syndicalists. In the years after 1910 moderate voices gained influence within the C.G.T., and Jaurès' humanitarian socialism might have provided the basis for a greater unity on the French left. But Jaurès was assassinated early in 1914, on the eve of the First World War; during the war the divisions within the French left did not heal.

Radicalism's Turn to the Right

In the prewar years French Radicals, as well as other republican groups, embarked on a "sliding to the right." The collapse of the Dreyfusard bloc of Socialists and Radicals caused the Radicals to turn more and more to parties of the center or to moderate conservatism for parliamentary alliances. Their reluctance to pass social legislation was one symptom of this tendency to the right. Although Clemenceau included two former Socialists in his ministry, he refused to pass social-welfare laws under pressure. He was, as he confessed, the nation's "number one cop"; law and order had to be restored before any thought could be given to social reforms. A law providing for workers' pensions was not passed until 1910, when Clemenceau was out of office. Clemenceau's finance minister introduced a progressive income tax, but it was vetoed in the Senate. Negligible achievements in social legislation angered Jaurès; he accused Clemenceau of betraying his own early ideals, to which Clemenceau sardonically replied that he had no intention of sanctioning revolution and anarchy.

The reaction to the right was also prompted by a growing alarm over the international tensions of the period; Germany once more appeared as a threat to the French nation. In an atmosphere of growing nationalism the government turned its attention to the army, which had been neglected since the Dreyfus affair. The army command was reorganized with a generalissimo, Joseph Joffre, who was to give overall direction to French military planning. The most prominent advocate of French military preparedness was Raymond Poincaré whose 1912 ministry proposed the legislation that culminated in a draft law. This law, passed in 1913, extended obligatory military service from two to three years in an effort to counterbalance the numerical superiority of the German army. The new law proved unpopular with the voters, however, and the elections of 1914 returned a majority committed to revoking it. Poincaré, who had been elected president of the republic the year before, appointed the ex-Socialist Viviani as premier. Viviani delayed taking action on rescinding the three-year law; whether he could have done so depended on some imponderables, including cooperation from both the Radicals and Socialists. The war engulfed France before any action could be taken by the government.

The Anti-Parliamentary Right: the Action Française

In the arena of French politics an organization that was strongly nationalistic and anti-parliamentarian in its attitude gained a vocal following before the First World War. This was the *Action Française,* which had been formed at the time of the Dreyfus crisis and gained wider support after the turn of the century. The *Action Française,* led by the royalist Charles Maurras, displayed marked authoritarian tendencies; according to its doctrine, France needed a return to strong rule that would restore unity to the fragmented state. Emphasis was placed on those institutions, particularly the monarchy, the Church, and the army, that symbolized French greatness. Those who wrote in behalf of the *Action Française* claimed that true France had become decadent under republican misrule; they delighted in exposing parliamentary scandals. What France required was a purging of corrupt, foreign (which meant "Jewish") influences in high places and the abolishment of parliament. Order and discipline, which were absent in French society, had to be imposed from above.

The State of the Republic in 1914

Early in 1914 the Third Republic found itself in what was only an apparent calm. The Radicals, who commanded the center of French politics, represented the dominant tendency of French political life, but they had to contend with a large segment of the working class that felt itself alienated from the political and social life of the nation, and with the increasing numbers of the *Action Française,* who proved that French anti-parliamentarianism had by no means lost its voice with the Dreyfus affair.

The structure of the Third Republic displayed certain weaknesses that exposed it to criticism at this time. Divisions within parliament often led to paralysis, for the multi-party system favored political compromises that offended as few interests as possible. Moreover, parliament served as a forum for provincial and special interests. Deputies showed more concern for the favorite projects of their constituents, particularly on the eve of elections, than for planning for national development. A fear of appearing dictatorial prevented either the premier or the president from exercising decisive executive authority. Meanwhile, the bureaucracy supplied a centralized administration that was often rigid in its function and, in its own way, as negative as other features of French politics under the Third Republic.

The Third Republic remained a remarkable system for perpetuating the status quo. Indeed, the basic hesitation within the republic came from a fear of disturbing the social order. Behind the nationalist revival of the prewar years was not only a fear of Germany but also a fear of social revolution. Men of the extreme left fell under the suspicion of moderate republicans, not just members of the *Action Française.* The government kept dossiers on left-wing leaders and was prepared to jail them. Socialist contacts with German Social Democrats, discussions of general strikes to maintain peace, and declarations of class allegiance across national borders added further alarm.

Had closer attention been paid to Jaurès and other Socialists, the government would have detected a strong element of patriotism in a majority of the members of the left. Fears of Socialist disloyalty proved unfounded when the French Socialists voted war credits, and the order for the arrest of Socialist leaders was shelved in the summer of 1914. The enthusiasm that greeted the decision to go to war to defend the country against German invasion temporarily postponed domestic conflicts; these conflicts reappeared under the exhausting strain of the war effort.

The Political Stalemate in Germany

The Locus of Power

Perhaps the most important problem for the German state lay in determining the effective locus of power within the political system.

The static nature of Bismarck's constitution became increasingly apparent in the years immediately preceding the war. The Prussian state, controlled by Junker Conservatives, blocked even mild attempts at political reform. The Reichstag freely criticized government policies and could block legislation, but it could not initiate measures. Moreover, internal disagreements among the parties limited the Reichstag's ability to force changes on the imperial government. The parties often seemed content to remain critics; at crucial moments they showed a reluctance to try to secure greater responsibility for themselves. The chancellor had responsibility for presenting the government's programs, and a strong chancellor could make the German system dynamic. But Bismarck's successors increasingly saw their function as that of an intermediary between the emperor and the Reichstag, and they were satisfied just to keep the cumbersome structure going. The emperor retained considerable initiative, but the unstable character of William II made his influence erratic. In addition to the emperor other sources of power outside parliamentary review—the army, the bureaucracy, the court—influenced German policy. Meanwhile, the German state grew more powerful, propelled by the energy generated through a continued industrial growth.

Against the static and cumbersome Bismarckian constitution, new pressures, many of them the by-products of Germany's social and economic transformation, continued to develop. Many members of the Reichstag were inclined toward democratic reforms of the imperial constitution. Because the Reichstag reflected the diverse tendencies and competing interests at work in German society, it was more representative of the political views current in the German empire than was the army or the monarchy. Parties such as the Social Democrats and the Catholic Center, opposed to the status quo maintained by the Bismarckian system, gained adherents and increased their representation in the Reichstag. Perhaps a triumph of these groups would have given greater cohesion to German politics by enabling a body representative of the people to control the government. In any event, constitutional revision was never attempted, although these parties gave promise of introducing reforms.

Progressive Tendencies Within the Reichstag

In the prewar years the Social Democrats recruited followers with impressive success, and the elections of 1912 brought a dramatic surge in votes for Socialist candidates. One-third of the electors voted for the Socialist party, giving the Social Democrats 110 seats and the largest single representation in the Reichstag. This success raised awkward problems since the Socialists were pledged to a thorough alteration of Germany's political institutions and the party refused to participate in the affairs of government. This meant that a sizable bloc of Reichstag delegates were hostile to any government.

But moderates within the party, including trade union leaders and a younger generation of party officials, felt that the practice of abstaining from any bourgeois combinations was self-defeating. The 1912 election had seen an informal cooperation between the Socialists and the Progressives in which Socialists supported Progressives in runoff elections to avoid splitting votes on the left. Moderates also tempered the party's revolutionary statements in the hope of winning electoral support outside the working class among artisan and professional groups. The 1912 victory was attributable to the party's moderate stance during the campaign; once elected the delegates were strongly tempted to use the party's position within the Reichstag—within the system they theoretically opposed—for tangible gains. This meant, of course, some cooperation with other parties.

In addition to giving evidence of Socialist strength, the 1912 election showed that the Catholic Center party retained support among a sizable proportion of the electorate. The Catholics had long complained of a second-class status within the predominantly Protestant German empire. At least the progressive wing of the party favored a change in the Bismarckian system. The Progressive party and a faction of the National Liberals also seemed inclined toward democratic reforms. Had these parties combined with the Socialists, a constitutional crisis might have been forced. But these parties of change continued to show a reluctance to press forward. They displayed largely negative tendencies, voting together to censure the government but failing to go further.

Progressive tendencies were additionally offset by the reactions of the political right. When in 1910 a reform was attempted in the Prussian state legislature that would have reduced, but not eliminated, some of the inequalities of the three-class electoral system in the state government, the proposal was flatly rejected by the Prussian Junkers. They refused to yield even a small measure of their privileged position; instead, German Conservatives gave support to such reactionary and nationalistic groups as the Agrarian League and the Pan-German Association. The alarms of the right grew in proportion to the gains registered by the Socialist movement, and political fear confirmed resistance to political change. The Reichstag reflected the divisions and uncertainties of German politics.

The uncertainty that afflicted the Reichstag could be seen in two political crises that marked German politics between 1908 and 1914. The first crisis erupted as the result of an interview with Kaiser William II published by the London *Daily Telegraph* on October 28, 1908. In the course of this interview the emperor committed a succession of gaffes that irritated the British public, embarrassed the German government, and reflected ill on his own judgment. He maintained that he was a true friend of Britain, but he also claimed, perhaps to prove his point, that he had to constantly struggle against the anti-British sentiments of his own subjects. He mused that it was a curious coincidence that the plan of battle used by Lord Roberts in defeating the Boers resembled a military plan that he had once sent to his grandmother, Queen Victoria—a claim that was both inaccurate and insolent in view of William's openly expressed sympathy for the Boers. Finally, he made the preposterous suggestion that German naval construction was directed against Japan rather than Great Britain.

The interview raised a storm of protest in the German press and within the Reichstag. All parties, including the Conservatives, deplored the emperor's remarks and demanded that in the future he be restrained in his public commentaries, especially in matters that affected Germany's foreign relations. Some of the parties insisted that a greater exercise of control over foreign and imperial affairs be granted to the Reichstag, a demand that implied basic changes in Germany's political structure. The psychological moment seemed favorable for such changes, for the popularity of the emperor had reached its nadir. The Social Democrat, George Ledebour, made a speech in which he called on the Reichstag to press for ministerial responsibility: "You, gentlemen, have the opportunity, because of the general discontent of the people, to achieve really democratic parliamentary government, and since you have the opportunity you must use it."

After he surveyed the excitement caused by the *Daily Telegraph* episode, the chancellor, Bülow, decided to save what he could. He appeared before the Reichstag and promised, without having obtained William's approval, that the emperor would exercise greater self-restraint in the future. The emperor was highly irritated at the chancellor's behavior, for Bülow shared responsibility for the interview. A draft of the interview had been sent to him for approval before publication, and Bülow negligently authorized it without reading the contents. But in the midst of a political storm the chancellor sided at least temporarily with the Reichstag, hoping to calm the wave of anti-imperialist sentiment and minimizing his own part in the incident. The tactic worked. William II withdrew from public view, nursing his grievance at Bülow for "betraying" him before the Reichstag, but he was sufficiently chastened by the affair to sign a document in which he promised to observe his constitutional responsibilities.

The storm raised by the *Daily Telegraph* interview blew over without producing any significant change in German political life. The dilettantish Bülow was not one to lead a revolt or even sponsor a reform of the constitutional system, although he did take refuge in the Reichstag when the storm broke. This maneuver ultimately cost him the chancellorship, for the emperor took his revenge in 1909 by dismissing Bülow when he was defeated on a tax reform issue. The behavior of the parliamentary parties also enabled the *Daily Telegraph* affair to pass. The Conservatives contented themselves with the emperor's pledge of good behavior, and other parties were reluctant to use the crisis to force political concessions from the emperor. The Social Democrats were not reluctant, but without political allies they were unable to press the issue.

The second political crisis that the Reichstag showed a reluctance to use to political advantage was the Zabern affair of 1913. That Bülow's successor, Bethmann-Hollweg, should face a crisis arising in the Alsatian town of Zabern was ironic, for his policy toward the former French provinces of Alsace-Lorraine had been liberal. Although the inhabitants of Alsace-Lorraine had disliked being severed from France in 1871, some of their early bitterness had apparently diminished under German rule. In 1911 they had been granted a constitution that placed them on equal footing with other German states. It was hoped that this gesture would make the inhabitants better integrated, or at least reconciled to their inclusion in the German empire.

In the fall of 1913, a dispute developed between the civilian residents and the military garrison stationed in Zabern. The provocative behavior of some hot-headed young officers had led to a demonstration by the civilians. The commander of the garrison retaliated by illegally jailing a few prominent citizens in the military prison for an evening. News of the episode reached the Reichstag, where deputies began questioning the government about the high-handed behavior of the army. When Bethmann made an ineffectual defense of the garrison commander, he was severely criticized for trying to exonerate an injustice perpetuated by military authorities. Perhaps Bethmann considered the incident trivial, but it united moderates and socialists in an impressive opposition. A vote of "no confidence" on his handling of the affair passed the Reichstag by an overwhelming majority. Under customary constitutional practice in other countries this vote would have compelled the government's resignation; in Germany, nothing happened. The government remained because several parties retreated from their position and decided that the vote simply referred to the incident and was not a wholesale vote of no confidence in the government. Politics continued as before, and the military commander at Zabern received a decoration within a few months of the incident.

On two occasions—in the *Daily Telegraph* affair and the Zabern episode—the Reichstag leveled criticism at the government, and at the crown and the army, respectively. Yet in each case an impotence or at least an indecisiveness within the Reichstag prevented it from using the crisis to extend its authority within Germany. The parties most critical of the existing system proved unable—or unwilling—to co-operate in a manner that might have forced constitutional changes in the Bismarckian system. The political deadlock reflected a deep social conflict within Germany. The parties of the left and right—notably the Social Democrats and the Junker Conservatives—regarded each other with a deadly enmity born of class hatred and mistrust. In this climate the prospects of gradual reform through compromise were not encouraging.

Nationalism: the Common Bond

Perhaps, as the German historian Golo Mann has suggested, Germany in 1914 was not one nation but a conglomeration of separate entities—workers, industrialists, peasants, landlords, officers, bureaucrats—having little in common to bind them together. Yet there was one element that held the German nation together and later would sustain it through four years of war: national pride. Nationalism found expression not only in the expansionist dreams of the pan-Germanists but within the ranks of the Social Democratic party. The crisis of war in 1914 revealed the ambivalence within German social democracy. The Social Democrats wanted fundamental changes and an end to capitalist control of industry, but they also had a pride in Germany's industrial power, which they had helped forge. Moreover, they were fearful of destroying their own organization, which all socialists regarded as the most impressive workers' movement in Europe. When war came, it came from the east, and the German Socialists decided to defend themselves from czarist autocracy.

The manner in which war was declared was itself revealing of the peculiarities of German political life. The basic decision was reached by the chancellor, the emperor, and the general staff, with the last-mentioned having perhaps the decisive voice. The Reichstag was called on to ratify this decision when the government asked for war credits. The Socialists, after debating the issue in party caucus, decided to vote "yes," although some revolutionaries opposed this decision. Party discipline prevailed, and the Social Democrats voted in a bloc for war credits, much to the relief of the government. In addressing the Reichstag the emperor declared that he no longer saw parties before him, only Germans. A political truce was declared.

Whether a desire to escape domestic conflicts disposed the government toward war in 1914 is a question that cannot be answered conclusively for Germany any more than for Britain or France. Perhaps so; in the course of a speech in the Reichstag during the 1911 Moroccan crisis, August Bebel, the leader of the Social Democrats, deplored the disastrous effect that war would have, and a Conservative interrupted him with the claim, "After every war things get better." Germany's last war had brought unity; it was thought that the next war, particularly if Germany emerged victorious and dominated continental Europe, would finally consolidate the nation and put an end to domestic grumblings. Yet even German chauvinism and hope of victory could do no more than temporarily suspend internal disagreement. Under the strain of war the conflict between Reichstag and crown—translated into a struggle between the Reichstag and the military—and the divisions within German socialism reemerged in aggravated form.

Russia Between Revolution and War

Russia began an era of constitutional rule in 1906 with an election of delegates to the first of four Dumas that were to be chosen before 1914. For the first time in Russian history political parties were organized legally, and an electoral campaign was held. Several diverse political parties and factions emerged from the elections.

Political Groupings

The largest and most important of the political groups was the Constitutional-Democratic, or Kadet, party, representing the liberal, professional class. The Kadets hoped to convert the Duma into an effective instrument of government for Russia by insisting that ministers be responsible to it. They also favored an extensive land-reform program based on expropriations of larger estates. Their outlook was progressive by standards of western parliamentary practice, and indeed they thought of themselves as liberal democrats of a western stamp.

To the left of the Kadets three major factions represented the interests of workers and peasants. The Socialist-Revolutionaries maintained their belief in a rural socialism based on the commune as the foundation for a radical transformation of Russian society. Because this party decided to boycott the first Duma elections as a sign of contempt for the bourgeois institution, the size of their following was not reflected in the Duma. The second group to the left, the Social Democrats, was split into two factions—the Mensheviks and the Bolsheviks—which united for the elections, although divergent views on tactics continued to provoke controversy between them. The Mensheviks were disposed to support the "bourgeois-democratic" revolution as a preliminary to a subsequent proletarian uprising; thus they were willing to cooperate with democratic parties in the Duma in an effort to discredit and undermine the old regime. The Bolsheviks, led by Lenin, condemned any collaboration with bourgeois elements; such policy, Lenin argued, would blunt the revolutionary zeal of the working class. Lenin wished to preserve the faction's purity so that it could assume leadership of the new wave of revolutionary disturbances that the Bolsheviks considered imminent. The third group on the left was known as the "Labor group"; it was not explicitly Marxist but claimed to speak for the working class.

To the right of the Kadets a sizable group of moderate deputies, representing industrial and landowning interests and the upper echelons of the bureaucracy, had formed an Octoberist party. The name derived from the party's endorsement of the principles set forth in the Czar's October Manifesto. They embraced a conception of the Duma's function that was much more limited than that of the Kadets. Generally, the Octoberists supported the government, but they were outnumbered by the "hostile" parties ranging from the extreme left to the Kadets. Those delegates on the extreme right rallied behind the Union of the Russian People, an ultra-nationalistic group that proclaimed its dislike of the Duma and its proceedings. The Union demanded a restoration of the Czar's unlimited autocracy and became the most consistent champion of reactionary opinions in the Duma.

The First Duma: Conflict with the Czar

When the Duma met on April 27, 1906, its members presented a spectacle that reflected many of the contrasts and diversities that existed within Russian society. The assembly included peasants, workers, middle-class lawyers, intelligentsia, representatives from the national minorities, clericals, and aristocrats. As the Czar opened the first session in the Winter Palace, his imperial council, various court officials, and their wives looked on, presenting a uniformed and jeweled contrast to the motley crowd of elected delegates. From the outset the possibility of finding common ground for understanding amid this diversity seemed unlikely.

Different interpretations of the Duma's place in Russian politics promised sharp divisions between the Kadets and other parties of the left and the Czar's government. Between the October Manifesto of 1905 and the convening of the first Duma, the government had indicated its intention to circumscribe the powers of the elected assembly. The most important limitations were contained within a series of Fundamental Laws issued in the spring of 1906, when it became clear that the new Duma would be recalcitrant. By decree the Czar imposed a second assembly, the State Council, as an upper chamber. This body was far less representative than the Duma since half of its members were appointed by the Czar himself. Ministers were also to be appointed by the Czar and were not to be directly responsible to the Duma. The legislature had to approve all measures before they became law, but the initiative remained with the Czar's government. Another article in the Fundamental Laws enabled the ministers to enact temporary legislation by decree when the Duma was not in session. This legislation had to be approved subsequently by the Duma, but the emergency provision could be used against it, particularly when the Czar retained the right to summon and dismiss the legislature.

Outright conflict between the Czar's government and the Duma rapidly developed when the Duma presented its demands to the throne. These included political amnesty for those arrested during the revolution, a ministry that was responsible to the deputies, universal suffrage, and expropriation of larger estates to satisfy the peasants' land hunger. The government rejected all the proposals. This response provoked a violent scene in the Duma during which an outraged Kadet demanded that the executive authority submit to the Duma's will.

Irritated at the Duma's behavior, the Czar's government contemplated dissolving the assembly and calling for new elections. The break came over land reform. The Czar's minister of the interior announced that a program of agrarian legislation was under consideration, but before it could be presented the Duma called on the peasants to await its own proposal, which would be more comprehensive. The government declared that the Duma had exceeded its authority in making this appeal to the people. Two days later the first Duma was dissolved, having lasted seventy-three days. This was an unpromising beginning for Russia's experiment in constitutionalism.

In protest against the Duma's dismissal, many Kadets and a handful of deputies from the left-wing parties fled to Finland, where they were able to obtain immunity from the czarist police. From Vyborg in Finland they issued a manifesto calling on the Russian people to refuse to pay taxes or to be inducted into military service. The response to the "Vyborg manifesto" proved disappointing; although the countryside was disturbed by sporadic outbursts of violence in the summer of 1906, the people continued paying taxes and seemed immune to the liberals' call for determined opposition to the government. The failure of the Vyborg appeal showed that Russian liberals could not initiate revolutionary zeal on their own; they had to depend on spontaneous disturbances and a corresponding breakdown of governmental authority to press successfully for political concessions. The Kadet liberals found themselves on the defensive. Those who signed the Vyborg manifesto were banned as candidates for the coming election to the second Duma.

While preparations were being made for these elections, the government began an intensive repression of the disturbances in the countryside. Many areas were placed under martial law. In accordance with the Fundamental Laws, governor-generals of districts under martial law could order field court-martials for persons accused of political offenses against the Czar. Justice was summary. Military authorities conducted trials that lasted no more than forty-eight hours, and sentences were carried out within twenty-four hours of the verdict. There were no appeals. In the first eight months after the decree approximately one-thousand executions were carried out under its provision. Even more informal justice was administered by bands of right-wing groups that conducted a reign of terror in the country with official approval. This wave of persecution was also marked by government encouragement of anti-Semitism and officially instigated attacks on the Jews in the cities. The czarist government gained temporary control over revolutionary tendencies, at the cost of arousing widespread hostility to the regime. The minister of the interior, Peter Stolypin, confessed, "In no country is the public more anti-governmental than in Russia."

The Second Duma: Continued Opposition

The sentiments of the opposition found expression in the elections to the second Duma at the beginning of 1907. Despite the government's attempt to influence the outcome, the elections were as unfavorable to the government as those for the previous Duma had been. The Kadets lost half their representation, but other parties of the left and extreme left gained significantly. The left parties, including the Social Democrats, the Socialist-Revolutionaries, and the Labor group, formed the largest single bloc in the Duma. Over half the delegates were hostile to the government. Politicians on the right, who also increased their representation, engaged in deliberately provocative tactics, hoping that a stalemate between the parties on the left and the government would force another election under a more restricted franchise.

A stalemate was inevitable in the absence of any basis for compromise. The Duma attacked the government for emergency measures introduced between sessions and bitterly denounced the summary court-martials. The left-wing delegates promptly raised the land question; one peasant delegate stood up and announced that the poor man in Russia "cannot help demanding the land, even if it is against the law; his needs force him to demand it. A hungry man is capable of anything . . . ." When it became apparent that only continued wrangling with the Duma lay ahead, Stolypin, who had emerged as the most forceful of the Czar's ministers, decided on another dissolution and new elections under a restricted franchise.

The dissolution came when the government fabricated an accusation of treason against Social Democratic deputies; the evidence consisted of forged papers that the police "discovered" in the Socialists' party offices. The government then requested that parliamentary immunity be lifted so that the accused Socialists could be prosecuted. The Duma appointed a committee to investigate the charges, but before the committee could submit its report, an imperial decree dissolved the assembly and another decree altered the electoral law. The latter measure was illegal since it contradicted the Czar's own Fundamental Laws, which required that changes in the electoral law be approved by the Duma. In effect, this move amounted to a coup d'état on the part of the government.

The Third Duma: a Rubber Stamp

Elections for the third Duma in two years produced a progovernment majority. The revised electoral law virtually disenfranchised all urban workers and sharply reduced representation from non-Russian areas of the empire, which had supplied many opposition delegates in the first two Dumas. The third Duma became a rubber stamp for the Czar's government and lasted its full term of five years. With the Duma's eclipse as a power in Russian politics Stolypin found himself in the ascendancy. Order was restored to the countryside by continued harsh repression after 1907, while Stolypin launched a series of land reforms intended to eliminate sources of rural disaffection.

Stolypin's Land Reforms

Before the 1905 revolution the commune and the peasantry were regarded as pillars of traditional Russian society. Militant peasant uprisings had stunned the government and shaken its complacency, and the opposition views expressed by peasant delegates in the Duma further disabused the government of their illusions concerning the peasant's loyalty to the Czar. Stolypin concluded that the peasant commune was at once an economic liability and a breeding ground for revolutionary, anti-government sentiments. To break up the commune, Stolypin persuaded the Czar to publish a series of decrees that favored transfers of land from communal or family holdings to private, individual ownership. Credit facilities were expanded to help peasants purchase land, and some of the imperial lands were made available on generous terms. Consolidation of holdings was encouraged; at the same time those who wished to sell their rights in the commune and move to the cities were allowed to do so. Stolypin wanted to encourage the rise of a class of independent peasant proprietors with a stake in Russian society who would become loyal supporters of the Czar. This was, as Stolypin put it, "a wager on the strong." He also calculated that consolidation and private ownership would improve agricultural output.

His estimates proved correct. Rural disturbances declined sharply between 1907 and 1914, and overall production and output per acre increased steadily. The impact of Stolypin's reforms was impressive. By 1915 one-fourth of all communal households had received individual allotments of land and another fourth had made application for distribution of their communal rights. As an additional way of relieving land pressure, the government encouraged settlement on land opened up in Siberia; between 1906 and 1909 a wave of emigration toward the east took place.

With the land transfers remarkable progress had been made toward the formation of an independent peasant class. A rise in prices for agricultural goods and an increase in output brought a measure of prosperity to the countryside. Demands for better equipment created an internal market for farm instruments before the war. Yet Stolypin's reforms and the accompanying agrarian boom did not solve Russia's rural problems. Most of the consolidated farms remained inefficient compared with those in central or western Europe. Pressure on the land was only partially relieved by breaking up the communes and by new settlement in the east. Natural increases in population caused the proportion of the number of peasants to the land to remain constant or even to increase in some areas. Many poorer peasants became either agrarian or industrial laborers under unfavorable conditions. Even the more prosperous peasants often found themselves indebted to the state banks. At best Stolypin's measures ameliorated rural conditions without providing a definitive solution to a difficult question. But from the government's point of view the easing of rural discontent was a political gain. Less encouraging, however, was a rise of urban disturbance in the three years preceding the war.

Worker Unrest

For a brief period Russia's economic boom, which set in after 1907, brought tranquillity to the industrial districts as well as the countryside. The incidence of strikes reached a low in 1910, but the next year they increased. The government's suppression in 1912 of a strike among workers in the Lena goldfields, located in Siberia, touched off a wave of strikes elsewhere in Russia. The Lena strike had cost the lives of 200 workers, and some 500,000 workers went on strike during the month of April in protest against the massacre. The unrest continued throughout the year and lasted until the war. In the first six months of 1914 Russia experienced some 3400 strikes that affected more than a million and a half workers. Two-thirds of these strikes were protests against government policy; the others were motivated by economic grievances. The strike wave peaked in July 1914 with a general strike in the Baku oilfields and a general strike in St. Petersburg that led to fighting between workers and police. Barricades went up in the capital, and the uprising was suppressed by force only a few days before Russia declared war.

The government's attitude toward the working class was not always hostile. Some measures of social reform were inaugurated, including sickness and accident insurance; a number of provincial governments introduced improved educational and hospital services. But these measures were often inadequate, and working-class protests persisted. Because the strikes were illegal and thus undertaken at great risk, the increase in their number testified to the harsh conditions of industrial labor in Russia: wages barely provided subsistence. The strike movements were particularly intense in the large factories that had sprung up in the new industrial districts as well as in the suburbs of Moscow and St. Petersburg. The concentration of Russian industry in large factories enabled underground unions and political organizations to reach a great number of workers easily.

The political left could count only limited gains from the surge of industrial discontent. The Mensheviks concluded that revolutionary agitation and semi-conspiratorial activities brought little results. They turned toward winning a mass following by distributing propaganda and by instituting adult education classes for the factory workers. The process was regarded as a long-term one; gradually a broadly based movement would be created that would form the basis for a revolutionary upheaval. Lenin dismissed such tactics and continued to favor the formation of a disciplined elite that would provide the leadership for the proletarian revolution. Despite the encouraging evidence of industrial disturbances and the inroads made by Bolsheviks among St. Petersburg and Moscow factory workers, the Bolsheviks appeared to be in political and financial difficulties in 1914. Lenin himself despaired of seeing a revolution in his lifetime, although he continued his agitation and attacks on the government from Switzerland, where he had fled to avoid czarist police. A war, he predicted, would be favorable to revolution, but for the time being he discounted the possibility of war between Russia and either Austria-Hungary or Germany.

The Weakening of the Government

Meanwhile, the grip of the Czar's government began to weaken between 1911 and 1914. By 1911 Stolypin had accumulated a large number of enemies and was in conflict with all elements of the government. The left detested him for his repressive policies; the Socialist-Revolutionaries particularly disliked his rural program since it undermined the potentially revolutionary commune. Despite Stolypin's policy of repression and his appeal to nationalism by encouraging Russification in non-Russian areas, notably Poland, he was unable to overcome opposition to him in reactionary circles. Reactionaries at court considered his reforms daring and dangerous innovations, and they were jealous of his ability.

In addition, Stolypin won the disfavor of the imperial family by being highly critical of the so-called holy man, Gregory Rasputin, who had great influence with the empress because of his ability to relieve her only son from the suffering associated with his hemophilia. Rasputin's generally scandalous behavior and frequent debauches shocked St. Petersburg. Stolypin's suggestion that the Czar ban Rasputin from court gained him the hostility of the empress and was ignored by Nicholas II. In the summer of 1911 Stolypin's health declined, and he went into semi-retirement. Many predicted that he would resign from office, but his life was cut short when he was assassinated by a political revolutionary while making a rare public appearance that summer.

With Stolypin's death the Czar lost his most talented minister of the prewar decade. Stolypin's successors were mediocre men, and Rasputin continued to hold sway at court and to cast discredit on the government. The fourth Duma, elected in 1912 and still based on restricted suffrage, showed its restiveness at the government's weakness. Moderate and left parties began to discuss the possibility of forming a united opposition. The mild difficulties encountered with this Duma led extreme Conservatives to advise transforming the institution into a purely consultative council. In the background, the wave of strikes indicated that neither Stolypin's reforms nor the muddling through of his successors had tempered Russia's domestic conflicts.

Against this background of renewed tension the government learned of the events in Austria-Hungary that seemed to be pushing Europe toward war. As elsewhere in Europe domestic problems intruded on the calculations of ministers responsible for a decision to enter the war. The events of 1905 had demonstrated to Russian officials that there was a dangerous connection between war and revolution. During the various Balkan crises in his reign the Czar was reminded that Russia's wars in the nineteenth century had produced revolutionary disturbances at home. In the spring of 1914 similar admonitions came from a variety of sources. Within the Duma the Kadet leader warned the government that it could not pursue aggression abroad and repression at home; outside the government the former minister, Witte, repeated the warning he had made before 1904: the resources of the state could not stand another war. Even Conservative deputies, despite their strong nationalism, counseled seeking accommodation with Germany to prevent a war that would bring internal collapse and revolution.

But there were others who argued that Russia could not stand aside while Austria overran the Serbs. If the government failed to act, its weakness would be exposed and revolution would follow in train. A shameful defeat for Russia's Balkan policy carried more risks than the burdens of war. In the crisis of July 1914 the foreign minister, Sergei Sazonov, argued that in addition to the need for maintaining Russia's prestige abroad, general mobilization "was unavoidable also for internal political reasons." In making this statement he seemed to echo Plehve's earlier belief expressed in 1904 that Russia needed a "small, victorious war" to silence revolutionary opposition. The war that Russia entered in 1914 was, like the war with Japan in 1904–05, neither small nor victorious.

The Nationalities Crisis in Austria-Hungary

Domestic Conflicts in Austria

In the years after 1907 it became obvious that universal suffrage provided no solution to Austria's domestic conflicts. The Austrian legislature, the Reichsrat, was hopelessly divided along national and ideological lines. The electoral reform gave the Slavs a majority over the German delegates by 259 to 233, but the Slavs were unable to combine and dominate the assembly, largely owing to the favorable treatment that the imperial government accorded to Polish land-owners, thereby securing their loyalty. Differences between Social Democrats and Christian Socialists about the role of the church, among other things, further complicated the picture. Continued quarreling among national groups, particularly between Czechs and Germans, paralyzed the Reichsrat until the government in exasperation suspended its sessions in 1911 and sent the delegates home.

The disorders of parliament in Vienna were matched throughout the country. Demonstrations in Prague at the height of the Bosnian crisis of 1908–09, when the empire teetered toward war, were marked by shouts of "Long live Serbia!" and "Down with Austria!" Similar cries went up in the Italian districts of the South Tyrol where imperial officials discovered various dynamiting plots directed against the government by Italian irredentists, including an attempt to blow up the emperor's train during his visit to Trieste in 1909. Elsewhere in the Austrian provinces conflicts between disputing national groups brought government repression that left behind a measure of order and much bitterness.

The government hoped that new elections in 1911 would clear the legislative impasse. The results were discouraging, for the governmental parties, including the Christian Socialists and the Polish delegation, suffered losses. The Social Democrats replaced the Christian Socialists as the dominant political force in Viennese political life. The extremist pan-Germans also showed impressive gains. Since the socialists were revolutionary and the German extremists were opposed to any compromise with the Slavs, the parliament presented unlikely material for governing the country.

The government, headed by Count Sturgkh, managed to push through military reforms that increased the number of recruits each year and provided a potential mobilization of a million and a half men. Military organization was streamlined, mobilization timetables were accelerated, and armament expenditure was increased. These military reforms were justified as an essential precaution in view of rising international tensions, but they strained the financial resources of Austria. The military laws represented the ministry's only major pieces of legislation. Sturgkh had no more luck than his predecessors in calming nationalist disputes within the country.

Evidence of heightening disaffection from the empire could be seen in the growth of the neo-Slav movement under the leadership of Karel Kramer. The aim of this movement was to reconcile Slav differences in a common struggle for Slav supremacy within the Hapsburg domains. The neo-Slavs looked to their brother Slavs in Russia for moral support. Athletic organizations, or Sokols, which were organized among the Slav population, became forums for pro-Slav propaganda. International meetings of the Sokols, such as the one that gathered in Prague in 1912, produced declarations of Slav solidarity. In Galicia, pro-Russian sentiments increased among the Ruthenian peasantry, and pan-Slav propaganda flooded across the border.

Despite these efforts the various national minorities could not unite beyond making declarations of dissatisfaction with the status quo and opposition to Hapsburg policies. Real social and economic differences, to say nothing of perennial historical quarrels, divided the Slavs within the empire. Between Polish landlords and Ruthenian peasants there was little but mutual hatred; the Czechs were among the most advanced peoples of the empire in their economic progress and political talent and had little in common with the backward Ruthenes. Many Slavs in Austria, notably the Slovenes, showed little concern for the struggles of other Slavs and pursued their own affairs. Finally, among the most vocal critics of the existing system were the Italians, who had no interest at all in the Slavs' complaints but looked across the border to the Italian state for their salvation. Thus grievances mounted but no viable solution to them seemed possible.

This discord did not mean that Austria was destined to disintegrate. Except for the Italians, the outright secessionists within the nationalities were in a minority. Most nationalists realized that small, separate states could easily fall prey to the ambitions of the great powers.

What Slav politicians sought was simply greater autonomy within the empire. One proposal called for a reorganization of the empire into a triple monarchy with an autonomous Yugoslav state alongside the Austrian and Hungarian states. Although the precise boundary of this proposed state was unclear, its proponents believed that trialism would relieve internal tensions. Moreover, Serbia might be attracted to the empire and be induced into joining and profiting from the largest free-trade zone in Europe. But there were objections to the trialist solution. It would not, for example, solve the timeless dispute between Czechs and Germans in Bohemia. The greatest obstacle to the formation of an autonomous Yugoslav state was the hostility of the Hungarian Magyars, who feared a diminishment of their own importance. The Magyars opposed any policy that would give further weight to the Slavs within the empire.

Another alternative was to transform the Hapsburg domains into a kind of Danubian commonwealth—a federal state that would permit local autonomy for various nationalities in matters such as education but retain the economic unity of the empire as a whole and present a common military and foreign policy to the outside world. Associations were to be established that would look after minority rights throughout the empire, and the empire itself was to be divided along national lines as much as possible for administrative purposes. There were many persuasive advocates of this solution, including the Social Democrats. Another federal scheme called for the formation of fifteen autonomous units that would have their own legislatures for local affairs and elect delegates to an imperial parliament. Each unit would use its own language internally, but German would be retained for official business at the imperial level and in the army. This scheme found supporters in Vienna, and the heir apparent, Francis-Ferdinand, regarded it as an acceptable solution for reorganizing the imperial state under continued Hapsburg leadership.

But the Magyars remained intransigent in their opposition to any alteration of the imperial structure. If the monarchy were to be saved at all, the Magyars reasoned, it would be through greater, not less, Magyar influence throughout the realm. All hopes of reform foundered against the political egoism of the Magyar elite. At the same time, neither the Poles in Galicia nor the Germans in Bohemia were prepared for concessions to Ruthenian or Czech aspirations. The intense conflict between the Germans and the Czechs drove the government to the expedient of ruling by decree. In 1913 Sturgkh dissolved the provincial legislature in Bohemia after it had been reduced to impotence by German obstructionist tactics. In its place he appointed an imperial committee, thereby summarily ending any pretense at ruling through a representative assembly. When the Czechs retaliated by staging demonstrations in the Reichsrat in the spring of 1914, Sturgkh dismissed that assembly and resorted to arbitrary rule by decree for all of Austria.

Perhaps reform might have been forced on stubborn opponents by Francis-Ferdinand when he succeeded the aging Francis-Joseph —although some of his close associates doubted his resolution to push through constitutional changes of such a sweeping nature. In any event, his assassination in Sarajevo in 1914 ended whatever prospects for change his candidacy for the throne might have held.

Domestic Conflicts in Hungary

Although some modification of the franchise had taken place in Hungary, this reform had been arranged so that Magyar supremacy within the legislature remained intact. In relations with other national groups the Magyars showed an unwavering determination to impose their own cultural values and standards. Magyarization continued to be enforced, although such policies strained the foreign relations of the empire.* Magyar oppression of Rumanian inhabitants living in Transylvania brought repeated protests from Rumania and from Austria-Hungary's ally, Germany. The Germans feared, not without reason, that Magyar policies in Transylvania were driving Rumania away from its alliance with the central powers—Germany, Austria, and Italy. Such appeals were made in vain, however, and ill-feeling over Transylvania remained high on both sides of the border. Rumanian politicians were beginning to detest Hungary more than they feared Russia, and in some quarters in Rumania speeches were made in favor of a war of liberation to free Rumanians within the Hungarian state from the Magyar yoke.

Perhaps the area in which Magyarization caused the most severe strains was Croatia, which theoretically enjoyed some autonomy under Magyar rule. The Magyars' steady infringement on Croatian rights and privileges caused the Croatians to put aside their differences with the sizable (approximately 30 percent) Serbian population living within Croatia, despite contrasts in religion and customs between the two Slav populations. In 1905 Croatian and Serbian delegates met and agreed to join forces in common cause against Hungarian

---

* For an understanding of Hungary's geographical position in relation to the nationalities surrounding it, see the Balkans map in Chapter 9, p. 334.

pretensions. Shortly after this the Magyar government in Budapest required that the Magyar language be used on the railway service in Croatia; this move galvanized opposition to Magyar dominance. Elections to the Croatian provincial legislature produced an assembly that was unanimously hostile to the Magyar governor appointed by the Hungarian state government. The president of the assembly made an inflammatory speech praising the Italian *risorgimento* and was enthusiastically applauded.

The conflict between the government and the united Serbs and Croats came to a climax in 1909 when the governor brought some fifty Croats and Serbs to trial for allegedly engaging in treasonous activities. Although the accusation rested on forged documents, thirty-one of the accused were condemned to hard labor; the verdict was later dismissed on appeal. This sham trial further discredited Magyar authority, and it led may Croatians and Serbs to contemplate separation from Austria-Hungary in order to join an independent Yugoslav state under Serbian leadership.

Within Serbia itself changes had taken place that encouraged the Serbs and Croats within Hungary in their ideas of independence and liberation from Magyar domination. In 1903 the corrupt and dissolute King Alexander was brutally murdered; the conspirators involved in his assassination had been offended at his marriage to a commoner of questionable background and alienated by his high-handed dismissals of parliamentary delegates and judiciary officials. The assassination ended the Obrenovich dynasty in Serbia and brought the head of a rival family, Peter Karageorgevich, to the throne. Constitutional rule was reestablished in Serbia, but the army, which had engineered the coup d'état, exercised a powerful influence on Serbian policy. The army was highly nationalistic in its political views and pro-Russian rather than pro-Austrian in its foreign policy.

Soon Serbian nationalist societies were agitating for the creation of a South Slav state. Close ties were formed between Serbian organizations and disgruntled Serbs and Croats in Austria-Hungary. Though most Slav political leaders in the dual monarchy still thought primarily of obtaining autonomy within the empire, younger students turned toward the idea of full independence and association with Serbia. Slav students from the Hapsburg empire who spent time at the university in Belgrade were encouraged in such opinions. Serbian army officers claimed that Serbia would one day liberate the Balkans in the way that Piedmont had sparked Italian independence. The parallel was not a pleasing one to either Vienna or Budapest.

Growing separatist sentiment among Slavs in the empire gave

ammunition to the war party in Vienna, headed by Conrad von Hötzendorf. Since the time of the Bosnian crisis of 1908–09 Conrad had argued that the solution to Austria's nationalities dilemma lay in a preventive war that would silence those Serbs who encouraged separatist sentiments wthin the Hapsburg monarchy. After 1912 this militant war party gained increasing influence in Vienna, persuading the emperor that Serbia represented a permanent menace to the empire's security. Moreover, the war hawks wished to act quickly before the Russians rebuilt their army. Austria thus looked to a military triumph as a way to restore its prestige in the Balkans and put a halt to separatist tendencies within the empire.

The major opponent of this aggressive policy was Stephen Tisza, leader of the Hungarian parliament and, after 1913, premier, whose Magyarization policies had caused considerable disaffection within Hungary. Tisza remained faithful to the Magyar axiom that there were enough Slavs in the empire as it was; the inclusion of more Slavs would simply increase pressures for the establishment of a third, Slav state under the Hapsburgs, and this idea was anathema to all Magyar politicians. But the assassination of the heir apparent, Francis-Ferdinand, by a member of a Serbian secret society in 1914 gave Conrad an unparalleled opportunity to urge punishment of the Serbs. The Austro-Hungarian foreign minister, Count Berchtold, was prepared to go to war as was the Austrian prime minister, Sturgkh. After lengthy arguments, Tisza reluctantly yielded and Austria-Hungary prepared for war. At this point the empire's domestic political dilemmas melded into the international crisis that brought on the First World War.

SUGGESTED READING

Many of the books listed in the Suggested Reading for Chapters 3 and 4 are useful in studying European political life in the prewar decade. Politics in Britain are discussed in Elie Halévy's *The Rule of Democracy, 1905–1914* (New York: Barnes & Noble, 1961, 2nd ed. rev.), the concluding volume to his *History of the English People in the Nineteenth Century*. Another survey of the Liberal years is Colin Cross's *The Liberals in Power, 1905–1914* (London: Barrie & Rockliff, 1962). A book that has strongly influenced our interpretation of prewar England is George Dangerfield's *The Strange Death of Liberal England, 1910–1914* (New York: Putnam, 1961), which stresses the inability of the Liberals to deal effectively with the unrest engendered by labor, the suffragettes, and the Irish question. Labor's position is treated in E. H. Phelps-Brown's *The Growth of British Industrial Relations, 1906–1914* (New York: St. Martin's Press, 1959), and in H. A. Clegg, Alan Fox, and A. F. Thompson's *A History of British Trade Unions Since 1889*, Vol. I (Oxford: The Clarendon Press, 1964). Roy Jenkins discusses political conflict and rivalry among the Conservatives in *Asquith* (New York: Chilmark Press, 1965); the same author examines the constitutional quarrel in *Mr. Balfour's Poodle* (London: Heinemann, 1954). The acute phase of the naval race is the basis for Arthur J. Marder's study, *From the Dreadnought to Scapa Flow: The Royal Navy in the Fisher Era, 1904–1914*, Vol. I (London: Oxford University Press, 1961).

Insight into French politics of the right may be obtained from Eugen Weber's *The Nationalist Revival in France* (Berkeley: University of California Press, 1959) and from his *Action Française: Royalism and Reaction in Twentieth-Century France* (Stanford, Calif.: Stanford University Press, 1962), which carries his narrative into the postwar period. Gordon A. Craig's volume of essays, *From Bismarck to Adenauer: Aspects of German Statecraft* (New York: Harper & Row, 1965, rev. ed.), provides critical assessments of Germany's political leadership after Bismarck's fall. The pessimistic mood characteristic of German social thought is the theme for Fritz Stern's *The Politics of Cultural Despair: A Study in the Rise of the Germanic Ideology* (Berkeley: University of California Press, 1961). A description of the rebellious spirit of German youth on the eve of war may be found in *Young Germany: A History of the German Youth Movement* (New York: Basic Books, 1962) by Walter Laqueur.

A favorable view of Giolitti's politics may be found in William A. Salomone's *Italy in the Giolittian Era: Italian Democracy in the Making* (Philadelphia: The University of Pennsylvania Press, 1960). Also favorable to Giolitti and critical of the nationalist *literati* is John A. Thayer's *Italy and the Great War: Politics and Culture, 1870–1915* (Madison: University of Wisconsin Press, 1964). The minorities conflict in Austria is discussed by Elizabeth Wiskemann in *Czechs and Germans* (New York: St. Martin's Press, 1967, 2nd ed.). The political tensions in the empire as a whole that ultimately destroyed the experiment of a supra-national state are analyzed in Oscar Jaszi's *The Dissolution of the Habsburg Monarchy* (Chicago: The University of Chicago Press, 1929). William A. Jenks's *The Austrian Electoral Reform of 1907* (New York: Columbia University Press, 1950) is a study of the failure of the "leap in the dark."

The Russian left has been extensively treated; among valuable works on the subject are Samuel H. Baron's *Plekhanov: the Father of Russian Marxism* (Stanford, Calif.: Stanford University Press, 1963) and Bertram Wolfe's *Three Who Made a Revolution* (New York: Dial Press, 1964, 4th ed.). *The Russian Intelligentsia* (New York: Columbia University Press, 1961), edited by Richard Pipes, treats various aspects of this "superfluous" class that gnawed at the structure of czardom. Thomas

Riha provides a portrait of a Russian liberal in *A Russian European: Paul Miliukov in Russian Politics* (Notre Dame, Ind.: University of Notre Dame Press, 1968). Alfred Levin's *The Second Duma* (New York: Shoe String Press, 1966, 2nd ed.) discusses the difficulties of the constitutional system in Russia.

9

THE INTERNATIONAL
DISSIDENCE, 1907–14

While the European states were contending with
rising domestic tensions, dissidence on the international level was also mounting. In the prewar
decade a series of diplomatic crises, each resolved
just short of war, left an accumulation of mistrust
and rancor. Ultimately one such crisis provoked a
general European war of cataclysmic proportions.

The enormity of the war has since cast shad-
ows over the events that preceded it. Yet in the
prewar decade several developments seemed to
favor a continuation of the process of moving from
one crisis to the next, stopping short of war each
time. Even a lessening of the international tension
seemed possible. There was evidence of a rising
internationalism. Several peace groups pressed for
international agreements and cooperation, and
called for a reduction in armaments. The European socialist movement appeared committed to
extreme action that would halt the machinery of
European armies. In addition, the growing economic interdependence of European states lessened

the likelihood of a war that would disrupt a profitable exchange of goods.

But against these developments must be set other, more powerful ones. The various war scares provided nationalists and even many moderates with arguments for increasing military expenditures. The armaments race imposed burdens on each nation's material resources, and the frequent diplomatic alarms placed a psychological strain on European statesmen. The strong temptation to go to war and end difficult problems "once and for all" finally prevailed.

The growing tension that made resolution of international differences increasingly difficult after 1907 could be seen in a succession of crises. The first of these centered on the Balkans.

Balkan Quarrels and the Second Moroccan Crisis, 1908–13

After the Algeciras Conference in 1906 a calm settled momentarily on European diplomacy. The fact that Algeciras left the future status of Morocco in doubt perhaps should have been cause for alarm, but it did not seem ominous for the peace of Europe at the time. Furthermore, Russia's conciliatory mood after its defeat by Japan permitted the British government to compose some of its outstanding differences with Russia in the Levant, and Anglo-Russian rivalry in the Far East appeared to have dissipated.

Yet it was the frustration of Russian ambitions in Asia that led, in part, to renewed international tensions in the Balkans and produced a new storm in European diplomacy. Since 1897 Russia and Austria-Hungary had laid aside their traditional rivalry in the Balkans, and for over a decade the Balkan peninsula did not disrupt European politics. This understanding broke down after 1908, when the two empires renewed their quarrels over that area.

The Bosnian Crisis, 1908

The new Russian foreign minister, Alexander Izvolsky, saw an opportunity for achieving some success for Russian foreign policy by reviving the question of opening the straits at Constantinople to Russian warships. In practical terms, the policy had little to recommend it, for the Russian navy had been decimated in the Japanese war, but Izvolsky was anxious for a diplomatic triumph after the defeat in the Far East. The time seemed right because France and Britain, former opponents of Russian ambitions at the straits, were now on good terms with Russia. Izvolsky realized that Austria-Hungary, traditionally hostile to any evidence of an extension of Russian power into the Balkans, would object to Russian pressure at Constantinople, but he hoped that their mutually beneficial cooperation might be extended, particularly since the successful revolution of the Young Turks in July 1908 was creating common problems for Russia and Austria-Hungary. A rehabilitation of Turkish strength in the Balkans under Young Turk leadership would frustrate both Russian and Austro-Hungarian hopes for expanding their own influence in that area. Izvolsky thus considered making a bargain with the Austro-Hungarian minister, Alois Aehrenthal, who had his own reasons for wanting to score a diplomatic success for the Hapsburg empire.

Aehrenthal wished to put an end to Serbia's increasing overtures to the Serbian population under Hapsburg rule. The provinces of Bosnia-Herzegovina, which had been placed under Austrian administration by the Congress of Berlin in 1878, consisted predominantly of Serbs who had never been happy with this arrangement. They were particularly susceptible to the pan-Serb propaganda that began flowing across the border from Belgrade. Aehrenthal thought that a direct annexation of the provinces would eliminate any hope on the part of of the Serbs that Bosnia might someday escape Austrian administration and become part of a greater Serbia. Annexation also seemed desirable to forestall any notions the Young Turks might entertain about regaining this portion of the former Ottoman holdings in the Balkans.

In September 1908 the two foreign ministers met at Buchlau in Austria-Hungary and reached agreement on a proposal made by Izvolsky. In exchange for supporting Austria's annexation of Bosnia-Herzegovina, Izvolsky asked that Aehrenthal support Russian demands to open the straits. Both empires would gain at the expense of the Ottoman empire before the Young Turks could renovate this decaying edifice.

Because the opening of the straits and the annexation would alter existing international agreements, Izvolsky assumed that a conference would be called to discuss the proposed changes, and he set out on a tour of the European capitals to sound out other powers on these issues. He had just arrived in Paris when he learned that Aehrenthal had unilaterally annexed the provinces without warning anyone, least of all Izvolsky, of his intentions. Vainly the enraged Russian foreign minister tried to salvage something from the situation. He asked for compensation at the straits, but Great Britain found this strange demand unacceptable. Then he insisted that the annexation be taken up by an international conference, a suggestion that had more merit but was not acted on. He emerged as champion of Serbian interests in the provinces, after having bargained those rights away a few weeks before. Although Izvolsky felt that he had been betrayed, he could not reveal the nature of his deal with Aehrenthal without exposing his own duplicity.

The annexation provoked a heated response in Serbia. Angry crowds in Belgrade demonstrated against the Austrians, and the army prepared for war. In Vienna, the war party, led by Conrad von Hötzendorf, called for an attack on Serbia in order to muzzle the Serb nationalists in Belgrade. Europe appeared headed for war over the Balkans; the Austrians consulted their German allies while Serbia turned to Russia for aid. The Austrians were amply rewarded, and the Serbs were not. In January 1909 the chief of staff for the German army, General Moltke, assured Conrad that Germany would render full support to Austria if attacked by Russia. German support in fact went beyond Austrian expectations. In March, as Aehrenthal was showing a more conciliatory attitude toward Russia, the German chancellor, Bülow, demanded that the Russian government give a categorical "yes or no" reply on whether it acknowledged the annexation. Because of the weak state of their army, the Russians had no alternative than to answer the ultimatum affirmatively. The annexation was recognized and the crisis passed.

The Bosnian crisis marked a clear triumph for Austria-Hungary and Germany, but sober second thoughts might have given diplomats in Vienna and Berlin less cause for satisfaction. The Magyars were dismayed and irritated that more Slavs had been added to the empire, where they would continue agitating for an autonomous Slav state, if not outright independence. More important, Austrian and German diplomats had behaved recklessly for the future by discrediting Russia and France before their allies. Because Russia was left with no way of backing out of the crisis short of openly accepting humiliation, its credit among the Serbs fell and talk of protecting brother Slavs suddenly rang hollow. At the same time France's credibility was suffering among the Russians. Germany's humiliation of Russia was in fact intended to demonstrate the unreliability of Russia's western allies, Britain and France. In the crisis both states, particularly France, had cautioned Russia that their basic interests were not involved and, therefore, Russia could not assume military assistance in the event of war. The upshot of Germany's actions was that in the next crisis, in order to save face, Russia would be less reluctant to come to the aid of the Serbs and French statesmen would be under greater pressure to lend support to their ally, Russia.

Finally, Bülow's hard line and Moltke's unwavering assurances tied the German ship of state more firmly to the "leaky Austrian frigate" than at any time since the mid-nineteenth century. Germany's willingness to endorse Austrian ambition in the Balkans significantly altered the Dual Alliance, which Bismarck had designed as a purely defensive arrangement. The initiative passed from Berlin to Vienna.

Although the unpleasant aftereffects of the Bosnian affair are apparent in retrospect, at the time Germany appeared to be in a strong position on the Continent. In the aftermath of the Bosnian affair it seemed as if Britain, France, and Russia were courting German favor. At the height of the crisis, in fact, France and Germany had reached an accord in which Germany recognized French political interests in Morocco in return for French assurances that both countries would share in the economic development of Moroccan resources. French desires to improve relations with Germany were partly responsible for the restraint that marked the French response to Russia. An influential group within the French Radical party, led by finance minister Joseph Caillaux, favored reaching an understanding with Germany. In Britain, the left-wing members of the Liberal party were alarmed at the soaring estimates for naval expenditure, and they pressed the government to reach an agreement with Germany to limit the arms race. The negotiations were thwarted by the cross-purposes that characterized Anglo-German relations, but for a brief period there was a strong desire to find some accommodation with the German empire. Even Russia experienced a détente in relations with Germany after Izvolsky stepped down as foreign minister in 1910. But German diplomacy suffered during the second Moroccan crisis, which broke out in 1911. The event hardened British and French attitudes toward Germany and indirectly helped raise the threat of war again in the Balkans.

The Second Moroccan Crisis, 1911

Political conditions in Morocco continued to deteriorate after the Algeciras Conference. The Sultan proved incapable of controlling rebellious tribes in the interior of the country and along the Algerian border. Algerian authorities repeatedly appealed to Paris for the right of intervention in Morocco to curb marauding bands that operated across the border. In the spring of 1911 rioting in Fez, the Moroccan capital, brought a French military expedition into the city to protect the European residents. The French move violated the Algeciras accords, but the French calculated that the other European powers would acquiesce in what they described as an unavoidable intervention.

The German foreign office, sensing that a French protectorate was at hand, demanded some compensation from France. To enforce its claims, Germany sent a gunboat to the Moroccan port of Agadir, ostensibly to protect German business interests (there were two German businessmen, both of questionable repute, in the city). The new French premier, Caillaux, was placed in an awkward position, for he had favored a Franco-German reconciliation. The German foreign secretary, Kiderlen-Wächter, offered to give full approval to a French protectorate in Morocco in exchange for the French Congo, but Caillaux refused to submit to this blackmail. Instead he consulted the army on how well it was prepared to hold off a German invasion.

At this point Great Britain entered the dispute. Fearing that Germany might demand and obtain a naval port on Morocco's Atlantic coast as part of a bargain with France, Lloyd George made a strong speech at London's Mansion House in which he warned that Britain could not be treated as a "nation of no account" in matters that were of vital interest. Although Lloyd George directed his warning at both Germany and France, the Mansion House speech indicated to Berlin that Britain was prepared to back France in the quarrel with Germany. Kiderlen-Wächter had deliberately sought to display Germany's muscle in international affairs, but he recoiled at the prospect of war. He settled for a portion of the Congo, and the French obtained German approval for their Moroccan protectorate. Once more, a crisis had been resolved short of war.

The bitterness stirred by the Moroccan crisis offset the success of finally settling the question. German colonialists and nationalists believed that Germany had been forced to take less than was due for a final renunciation of Morocco. Public opinion deeply resented Lloyd George's tough lecture, and several members of the Reichstag attacked the government for giving way. In Paris the Germans' blunt behavior favored French nationalists who argued that any talk of reconciliation with Germany was nonsense, and that the country should prepare itself for a fight that was to come sooner or later. A sign of the times was the resignation of Caillaux, accused by French nationalists of dealing with the Germans behind the back of his own foreign minister, and his replacement by a convinced nationalist, Raymond Poincaré. French statesmen rather pointedly began repairing their relations with St. Petersburg as a counterweight to the German menace.

Finally, the second Moroccan crisis, like the first one, prompted military discussions between French and British officers. Not long after the crisis the British admiralty transferred part of the Mediterranean fleet to home waters and the bulk of the French fleet was stationed in Toulon. An informal understanding divided naval responsibilities between the two nations, although the cooperation was not sealed by a binding agreement.

The Balkan Wars, 1912–13

As France moved toward a Moroccan protectorate, the Italians prepared to invade Tripoli by declaring war on Turkey, the nominal suzerain of that African territory. The Italian war against Turkey in 1911 had immediate repercussions in the Balkans. Before embarking on the Tripoli venture, the Italian government had obtained Russian approval for their colonial campaign in an agreement signed in October 1909. In return for this approval the Italians agreed to support Russia's bid to have the straits opened to their warships. In so doing, Italy revealed that in Balkan affairs its interest and behavior ran counter to that of its nominal ally, Austria-Hungary.

Even more significant was the effect of the war on Ottoman power in the Balkan peninsula. The Italian military victory over the Turks encouraged the smaller Balkan states to exploit Ottoman military weakness for their own gain. With the Turks occupied elsewhere, Serbia, Bulgaria, and Greece formed a Balkan League in May 1912 and four months later attacked the Ottomans in the Balkan peninsula. The Balkan League triumphed on all fronts, and the peace treaty left Turkey with only a beachhead on the European shore around Constantinople. For all intents and purposes, the Ottoman presence in Europe was at an end; the coup de grâce had been delivered by a collection of former dependencies.

The eclipse of the Ottomans in European politics was an event of deep significance. The smaller states of the Balkans, no longer afraid of the Turkish army, had less reason than ever to look to the Hapsburgs for protection. The first Balkan war was a victory for local nationalism over a dynastic state, and other dynastic empires looked on with concern. Neither Russia nor Austria-Hungary was certain that the demise of the Ottoman empire in Europe was desirable, for it meant that a reorganization of the Balkans could not be postponed. Austria dreaded any success of nationalism in the Balkans and particularly disliked the aggrandizement of Serbia. Austria tried to limit the consequences of Serbia's success by calling for the formation of an Albanian state, based on a predominantly Moslem population, that

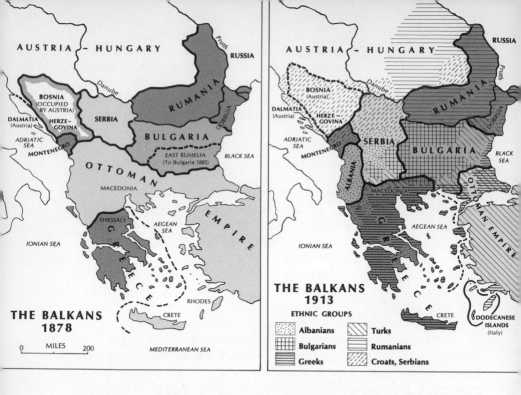

THE BALKANS
1878

0 ___MILES___ 200

THE BALKANS
1913

ETHNIC GROUPS

Albanians   Turks
Bulgarians   Rumanians
Greeks   Croats, Serbians

would block Serbian ambitions for a port on the Adriatic coast. The Russians also had interests to protect from the victorious Balkan states. At one point during the first Balkan war the Bulgarians threatened Constantinople itself; the Russian foreign minister, Sergei Sazonov, was not at all sure that another power at the straits would be preferable to a weakened Turkey. The European powers decided to take a hand in the provincial antagonisms of the Balkans by calling a conference of ambassadors in London to settle certain disputes arising out of the Balkan war. At this meeting an independent Albania was created to satisfy the Austrians, but otherwise the Balkan states were allowed to keep the spoils of their victory.

The settlement was little more than a truce, however. Even at the time of the London conference, the Balkan League was beginning to quarrel over the division of the spoils in the ethnically mixed region of Macedonia. After deciding that Serbia and Greece had gained too much from the war, the Bulgarians attacked those two states in June 1913. But the Bulgarians badly overestimated their capacity. Their former allies, joined by Turkey and Rumania, defeated them that summer in a decisive manner. The Treaty of Bucharest signed in August awarded Bulgarian territory to each of its opponents—Serbia,

Greece, Rumania, and Turkey. The settlement was as equitable as could be arranged in that part of the world, but it left some countries deeply discontented. The Bulgarians obviously resented the treaty, but even more serious was the reaction in Vienna. The Austrians had backed Bulgaria in the conflict and regarded the Treaty of Bucharest as a defeat for their Balkan policy. Austria's opponent, Serbia, had by this point doubled its size and was on the way to becoming a large Slav state. Conrad, back as chief of staff of the Austro-Hungarian army, was proclaiming that Austria's prestige and survival as a major power hinged on curbing Serbian pretensions, even if this meant war. Conrad and the war party in Vienna resolved not to miss another chance to punish the Serbs. The Balkan Wars had produced a highly volatile atmosphere in southeastern Europe by the end of 1913.

The Alarms of War

Military Preparations

The armaments race that accompanied the diplomatic crises did not suddenly seize the European governments: military expenditure had increased regularly since the end of the Franco-Prussian War in 1871 because of the greater costs of more advanced military technology and because of the requirements of colonial conquest. But the amount allotted for military purposes was sharply augmented in each European state after the turn of the century.

Germany's naval program imposed heavy demands on its budget, especially with the development of Dreadnought-type battleships after 1906. The German general staff also took steps to improve the technical efficiency of its army, already regarded as Europe's finest. The German budgets for 1911 and 1912 contained provisions for greater military expenditure for new weapons, particularly artillery, which subsequently proved their value. At the beginning of 1913, an army bill presented to the Reichstag called for an augmentation of the peacetime army from 623,000 to 820,000 men by October 1914. The general staff justified this increase by citing Austria's weakened position as a result of the Balkan Wars and Italian preoccupation with the pacification of Libya, which meant that the German army assumed a heavier responsibility for maintaining the military balance of the Triple Alliance.

Passage of the German military law in 1913 touched off a chain reaction. The French Chamber of Deputies, frightened by German behavior at the port of Agadir, voted an increase in length of military service from two to three years; the additional contingent would bring the French army, not including colonial troops, to some 750,000 men. Thus, despite having a population less than two-thirds that of Germany, France would have an army that matched the strength of its eastern neighbor. The Russian army, slowly recovering from the defeat of 1905, participated in the wave of military reforms. By 1917 Russia's army was to be raised to over 1,800,000 and efforts to improve the cumbersome structure of this massive force were introduced. French loans were advanced to extend the strategic railway network that would permit a rapid assembly of troops along the Austro-Hungarian and German borders. At the same time Austria-Hungary embarked on military reforms that raised the annual contingent from 103,000 to 160,000 men, assuring a mobilized Hapsburg army of some million and a half men in the event of war.

Two states resisted the trend toward military expansion despite pressures in this direction. The Italian general staff contemplated increasing the annual contingent 25 percent and raising the standing army from 275,000 to 375,000 men, but the government realized that a program to bring the Italian army up to the standard of other powers lay beyond the financial capacity of the state, whose resources had been strained by the Tripoli campaign. In Britain, efforts to introduce a program of national conscription failed, so that in 1914 Great Britain remained the only major power with an exclusively volunteer system. Nevertheless, military reforms assured Britain of a well-trained elite force that could send six divisions to the Continent at the outset of a European war. Although neither Italy nor Great Britain expanded their peacetime armies, military costs rose as dramatically in these two states as in other countries. Most of the increase for Britain went into naval expenditure, while the Italians had to pay off the costs of colonial conquest. Between 1870 and 1914, the costs per capita of armaments more than doubled in each European nation, with the exception of Germany where the cost per capita increased six-fold.

Debates over military expenditures inevitably drew the military into the political arena. Yet it was behind the scenes of parliamentary controversy that the military exercised its most important influence. Conversations between French and British officers strengthened the entente between those two nations during the prewar years and created informal obligations as significant as the actual treaties that had been signed. The deployment of French and British naval forces that was agreed on in 1912 gave Britain primary responsibility for defending the North Sea and France's channel ports from possible attack.

Britain was not technically compelled to aid France in the event of war with Germany, but if France were attacked, its channel ports would be vulnerable unless Britain fulfilled what was in fact a strong obligation to provide naval assistance. Military conversations between Paris and St. Petersburg strengthened the existing Franco-Russian political alliance after 1912, and French military pressure was a major consideration in the advance of French loans to build strategic railways in Russia.

Formal planning among the central powers was minimal. The Italians agreed at the beginning of 1914 to supply three army corps and two cavalry divisions in support of the German army in the event of war, and the Italian navy was to block the transfer of French troops from North Africa. But Italian military promises depended on the government's assessment of its obligations under the terms of the Triple Alliance. Between Germany and Austria there was some coordinated planning of a general nature. The Austrians were to assume a major role in holding back the Russian army in the event of a German offensive against France, but little provision was made for close tactical cooperation. Nevertheless, contacts between German and Austrian officers fostered a sense of common purpose, and at crucial points General Moltke gave the Austrians assurance of German support in case war broke out against Serbia. This entry of the military into the political realm went unchecked by the political leaders in Berlin. In the spring of 1914, Moltke observed to Conrad that the military balance was momentarily favorable for Germany and Austria, but he feared that any delays would reduce their relative advantage. Advice of this sort could only encourage the more belligerent spirits—notably Conrad himself—in Vienna, and it marked a significant change in the character of the Dual Alliance.

The strengthening of military forces throughout Europe reflected growing international tension, but these military preparations were designed primarily to discourage aggression and not to encourage war. Yet military strength has meaning only if governments are prepared to send their military forces into battle, or at least are able to convince their opponents that they will do so; therefore, the basic obligation of the professional military was to plan for war. In 1914 plans hinged on railroad timetables. European armies still traveled on foot and horseback, but they were assembled by train. The basic principles of generalship rested on Napoleonic precepts that called for a rapid assembly of superior forces at the point of battle. The Prussian armies had carried out these concepts to perfection in the wars of 1864, 1866, and 1870–71, by making effective use of strategic railways and by carefully preparing mobilization orders. Prussian success in these wars so dominated European military thinking between 1871 and 1914 that all armies had calculated the time needed to assemble and go into battle to the day and hour. A day or half-day could prove decisive one way or another, the military strategists predicted. As a result of this thinking, an order for mobilization amounted to a declaration of war. Once armies were set in motion, they could not be recalled without creating confusion and inviting attack.

The formation of the Schlieffen plan, which became the basis for German military action in the event of war on the Continent, left Germany with few alternatives in any war crisis. The plan anticipated a two-front offensive directed first against France and then against Russia; it assured that a war arising from a Balkan dispute between Austria and Russia would become a general European war as soon as Germany went to Austria's aid. By planning to send their armies into France across Belgium, the German generals violated long-standing political obligations to respect Belgian neutrality and made British intervention that much more likely.

By the time mobilization was decided on, military necessity would become the primary determinant of a nation's policy. Military preparations in Europe both heightened the tensions and reduced the scope for diplomatic maneuver.

Peace Movements

As the armaments race accelerated, several movements appeared in Europe urging that weapons be abolished and that international law and arbitration be substituted for armed conflict. Since the time of the Renaissance, legal theorists had searched for some basis for international law that would regulate the affairs of states; in the nineteenth century a growing number of international agreements on such matters as postal regulations, telegraph communications, and control of waterways had been signed. These were perhaps minor accomplishments, but they encouraged pacifists and others to believe that such agreements might be extended to political disputes. At the turn of the century a number of pacifist associations and private international organizations began publishing tracts in favor of a limitation and eventual abolition of armaments. These ideas found some favor among practical politicians who had become concerned at the costs of military technology.

A step toward peaceful resolution of international conflict was taken in 1899 with the convocation of a "peace conference" at the

Hague at the instigation of the Czar; he had called for a meeting that would try to find some basis for limiting the arms race and providing machinery for the arbitration of international disputes. The Czar's appeal stemmed in part from sincere humanitarian motives and in part from a desire to reduce the burdens of Russia's military outlay. The Hague Conference elicited platitudes and considerable skepticism among the powers. After several days of fruitless discussion, the delegates accepted a proposal for the creation of an international court of arbitration at the Hague; the weakness of this institution was that there was no means of compelling quarreling parties to make use of its offices.

A second "peace conference" in 1907 at the Hague proved even less productive; those measures that were accepted were generally designed to make war more humane—by providing for protection of neutrals and prisoners of war—rather than to abolish it. Meanwhile, several nations, including Britain, France, the Scandinavian states, and Italy, committed themselves to the concept of arbitration of specific disputes among themselves, but the limited scope of these accords meant that they were little more than tentative steps toward the acceptance of international law. Organizations such as the Interparliamentary Union and the Universal Peace Congress held annual sessions to formulate proposals that would foster international cooperation. Although animated by men of high principles and intelligence, these organizations lacked authority to translate their resolutions into enforceable rules. No nation was willing to abandon more than a very small part of its sovereignty. In the absence of any supranational authority there was no way of enforcing sanctions against nations that violated the proposed measures, a dilemma that was to plague international organizations later in the twentieth century.

Encouragement for the beliefs of the internationalists was found in the writings of men who argued that the complexity of the European economy made modern war inconceivable or too costly to contemplate. In 1900 Jean de Bloch, a Warsaw banker, published a six volume study, *La Guerre,* in which he predicted that the next war would become stalemated in siege operations that would produce widespread starvation and a collapse of the economic order in Europe. Bloch's views on the economic consequences of modern warfare had some influence, notably on Czar Nicholas II, who accorded him a personal interview. An even more popular expression of a similar thesis appeared in Norman Angell's *The Great Illusion* (1910), in which the author marshaled impressive evidence to prove that war did not pay. The economic disruption caused by war would affect victor and vanquished alike, so that there would be little distinction between the two. The popular reception given to Angell's book indicated the extent to which public opinion apparently wished to be persuaded of the unprofitability and obsolescence of war.

The middle-class liberals and wealthy philanthropists who supported private peace organizations believed that peace served the political and economic interests of all states. They believed that sooner or later this common interest would be recognized and then practical measures toward the elimination of war policies would be taken. These assumptions reflected liberal confidence in the eventual triumph of reason, a certainty that all nations shared the same basic concerns, and an optimistic faith in progress. There is no reason to doubt the sincerity of this feeling. But these hopes had to be placed beside the reservoir of popular chauvinism that existed within each country, a sentiment that even pacifists sensed might be a more profound force than the desire for peace.

International Socialism: the Peace Debate

Even as the reformist-revolutionary controversy persisted within socialist parties, the question of peace and of opposition to militarism came to occupy an equally important place in the debates of the European Socialist Congresses during the prewar years. For European socialists the search for peace stemmed from a conviction that war was a bogey created by militarists and arms manufacturers for their own selfish interests and was used to distract the working class from its goals. The workers' common interests were best served by peace, and the Second International repeatedly admonished its members not to be deceived into fighting each other. The real conflict cut across national boundaries and pitted working class against capitalists. Delegates to the international congresses devoted considerable energy to debating the tactics that socialists could employ to prevent war; however these debates only exposed the internal divisions in the International.

Debates of the Stuttgart Congress, 1907

Resolutions condemning war and imperialism had been passed at every International Socialist Congress since the 1890's, but the debates at the Stuttgart Congress of 1907 were particularly illustrative of the dilemmas that the socialists faced in choosing tactics that would effectively oppose war preparations and prevent armies from marching if war should break out. The German hosts of the congress hoped that debate over concerted opposition to war could be avoided since they did not want to provoke the German authorities with speeches that could be interpreted as incitements to treason. When a French delegate, Gustave Hervé, introduced a resolution that would require all socialist parties to greet a war declaration with a general strike, the issue could not be avoided.

A number of other proposals came up for debate. The mildest position was taken by August Bebel, leader of the German socialists, with support from the French Marxist Jules Guesde. They claimed that the path to peace was to be found in the triumph of socialism and the abolition of standing armies. Socialists should devote themselves to achieving the victory of the working class; there was no need for the Second International to decide on anti-war tactics other than a general statement that all socialists should take whatever measures seemed appropriate to prevent its outbreak. Bebel wished to avoid a more specific obligation, and Guesde trusted in the course of history to eliminate capitalism and thereby remove the cause of all wars.

The vagueness of this position disappointed Jean Jaurès. Although a moderate reformist in domestic policies, Jaurès tended toward a more radical position on the question of socialist opposition to war. The humanitarian Jaurès recoiled at the horror of war, and he was willing to embrace Hervé's idea of a general strike in the higher interests of peace. A third position, expressed at Stuttgart by Lenin and by Rosa Luxemburg, deplored war but called for workers to exploit the economic crisis war would bring to overturn the capitalist order. This revolutionary appeal went beyond the demand for a general strike, which was aimed at blocking military activities without necessarily producing a social upheaval.

The peace resolution that the Stuttgart Congress adopted was an unwieldy motion incorporating the major views expressed. The downfall of capitalism eventually would remove the dangers of war; in the meantime socialists were urged to oppose military expenditure and insist on the abolition of standing armies as a matter of principle. The International's Brussels office, the executive secretariat, was called on to coordinate socialist opposition to war in any crisis. Each party pledged itself to use "all means" to prevent the outbreak of war. Most delegates assumed that all means included a general strike, but this step was not specified. The last sentence of the resolution embodied the radical position that favored using a war crisis "to hasten the abolition of class rule," but most deputies took the statement as largely a rhetorical one. The resolution received unanimous approval, and the Stuttgart Congress produced a widespread hope that socialism had become an instrument for securing peace in Europe.

A major weakness of the Stuttgart resolution was the vague and often contradictory nature of its provisions. The lack of any machinery to enforce these provisions was another weakness, one that could also be found in other attempts to regulate peace. The Brussels office was without coercive powers, although the range of its activities had expanded since its creation in 1900. Despite practical limitations on common action, socialists believed that they would unite if threatened by a European war, and they pointed to occasions, such as the Fashoda crisis, when cooperation across national lines had induced moderation. In 1911 German and French socialists actually did restrain their governments during the second Moroccan crisis. Whether socialist influence was decisive during this crisis could not be determined, but their conduct enabled socialists to take satisfaction in the movement's potential strength. The failures of socialists to halt belligerence were less encouraging; a majority of the Italian socialists, for example, opposed the war against Turkey in 1911 to no avail.

Obstacles to Socialist Cooperation

The consistent gains of socialist parties encouraged socialists in their hope that common opposition might prevent war, but in no country did they command a majority. The success of an anti-war campaign or an opposition to mobilization rested on cooperation with other parties or on the willingness of the working class to conduct a general strike. Adherence to revolutionary doctrine blocked the prospect of an alliance of parties on the left in opposition to war preparations, although in France in the elections of 1914 there was a tacit cooperation between Socialists and Radicals based on hostility toward the three-year draft law passed the previous year. This combination dominated the French Chamber, but its potential for effective action was offset by the fact that the French Socialists continued to withhold support for bourgeois ministries, even those that might support a return to the two-year draft. In Germany the electoral success of the Social Democrats, who had consistently voted against military credits, did not block military legislation—quite the contrary. In order to get a tax reform, the German Socialists accepted the 1913 military budget, which, they reasoned, would pass in any event. In addition, the structural weaknesses of the Reichstag within the German empire further reduced the effectiveness of German socialism as a counterweight to German militarism.

As for a general strike, there was little assurance that German or French workers would respect it. The general strike, even as a threat, was socialism's most potent weapon, but socialist leaders hesitated to advocate its use. A general strike would be taken by socialists and conservatives alike as a call to revolution and a confrontation with established authority. In western and central Europe socialists sensed, without admitting it, that they risked losing the political achievements of a generation if they ventured in this dangerous direction. This reluctance hardened into patriotic loyalty when invasion threatened the country in which they had won a place. A general strike, moreover, would fatally weaken a country in time of crisis and perhaps prepare the way for a triumph of reactionary powers within the country. There was no guarantee that the socialists of Russia, for example, would be able to stop the Czar from sending his army to curb them. No party was willing to risk defeat and endanger its own existence.

Nationalist sentiment proved to be a formidable and critical obstacle to effective socialist cooperation. Despite declarations of class solidarity, national antagonisms created friction within the socialist movement itself, particularly in those countries where the nationalities question had become acute. Rumblings of dissatisfaction came from the Polish minority within the German Social Democratic party; the Poles complained that the German-speaking majority showed little sensitivity to their problems. The issue was even more serious in the Austro-Hungarian empire, where the Czech socialists broke with the Viennese leadership and established a separate organization; their separation was recognized by the Second International's congress at Copenhagen in 1910.

The mutual suspicion of the British Labor party and the German socialists paralleled the naval and commercial rivalry between the two countries. The British questioned the sincerity of the German socialists' commitment to disarmament, while the Germans wondered aloud if the British Labor party were really socialist at all. Jean Jaurès sincerely believed that cooperation between French and German socialists was the surest path to peace. His enemies on the right in France accused him of disloyalty because of his admiration for German socialism. Yet Jaurès remained a patriot who was proud of his country's democratic institutions; he argued that socialists might be forced to take up arms in defense of their country—an argument that was taken up by most European socialists in 1914. Thus the comradeship that marked the meetings of the Second International was counteracted by deeper passions of national loyalty.

The strength of nationalist feeling did not mean that the socialist search for peace was artificial during the prewar years. Many workers looked on the party as a guarantee of peace, and the meetings of the Second International rang with deeply felt expressions of fraternity. Few socialists believed that ordinary citizens of the European states could be brought to shoot at one another. The immediate response to the crisis in the summer of 1914 was to seek, desperately, some way to avoid catastrophe. The socialist press condemned the behavior of governments that were risking the peace of Europe. Mass meetings were held in Germany and France to protest the war danger evoked by the Serbian crisis. But when the socialist executive bureau met on July 29 with major representatives from all socialist parties, little was achieved. Léon Jouhaux, the head of the C.G.T., indicated that he was willing to call a general strike, but he was uncertain whether the Germans would follow suit. The response of the Austrian socialist Victor Adler indicated the dilemma that the socialists faced. He deplored the crisis, which already meant war between Austria and Serbia, but he indicated that nothing could be done to stop it. The mood of the Viennese workers was belligerent, and the Austrian Socialist party would have to go along with them. Jaurès returned from the meeting discouraged though not yet disheartened. He spent the last day in July urging his government to restrain the Russians, but that evening as he dined in a restaurant he was assassinated by a distraught super-patriot. His death has served as a symbol for the Second International's struggle for peace, although it may be doubted that even Jaurès, had he lived, could have withstood the fever that was sweeping over Europe.

The Force of Nationalism

Within all socialist parties there were those who could find reason for going along with their own governments. Orthodox Marxists had argued for years that there was an inevitability to historical development; socialists built their parties and nurtured parliamentary strength as preparation for the upheaval that would occur when conditions were right. Socialist doctrine and practice thus favored a kind of inertia. When the war crisis broke, the socialists in each country drew back from the prospect of a general strike that would lead to revolution and perhaps prepare for their country's military defeat. After some soul-searching, the socialist parties decided to vote the war credits demanded by their governments. By endorsing these credits European socialism confessed to the deep nationalism within its ranks.

Nationalism was at once a creative and a potentially destructive force in European history. It helped unite the European nations into centralized governments of impressive strength; but it also divided the Europeans from one another. In 1914 nationalism turned the Europeans toward destructive purposes, despite the proclaimed intention of European socialism to prevent such a calamity from occurring.

The Coming of War, Summer 1914

The Assassination of Francis-Ferdinand

Rumors of war had been current for a decade before the crisis broke out in the summer of 1914 that brought on the war. There was no reason to believe at the time of the crisis that the danger of war was any greater than it had been in the recent past. The event that set into motion the diplomacy of war was the assassination of Francis-Ferdinand, the heir apparent to the Austro-Hungarian throne, during a state visit to Sarajevo on June 28. The visit was a provocation in the eyes of Serbian nationalists, for Sarajevo was the capital of the recently annexed province of Bosnia, and the visit coincided with the anniversary of the battle of Kossovo, which had resulted in a Serbian defeat at the hands of the Turks in 1389 and ended Serbian independence. The assassin, Gavrilo Princip, was an Austrian subject of Serbian extraction who had received weapons in Serbia; the plot had been planned in Belgrade. Princip and his fellow conspirators had slipped across the border with the connivance of Serbian border guards a few days before Francis-Ferdinand's arrival. The head of Serbia's military intelligence section, Colonel Dimitrievich, knew of the plot and had aided the conspirators. Even the Serbian prime minister, although uninformed of the actual attempt, suspected that some rash act might be carried out and had vaguely warned Vienna against allowing Francis-Ferdinand's visit.

The extent of Serbian involvement in the assassination was not fully known in Vienna at the time, but there was reason to condemn Serbia because the Serbian press and various nationalist associations had openly preached violence against the Hapsburg opponents of Serbian national claims. The event shocked public opinion throughout Europe; sympathy for Austria and a corresponding condemnation of Serbia were widespread. Even czarist Russia, Serbia's protector among the major powers, deplored the assassination of a member of a European ruling house. The Austrians realized that they had an excellent opportunity to settle accounts with Serbia and end anti-Hapsburg agitation in Belgrade. Moreover, the outcome of the Balkan Wars had damaged Austrian prestige in southeastern Europe. If the Austrian government failed to act, Austria-Hungary's standing as a great power would be discounted. Considerations of this sort led Berchtold, the foreign minister, to plot a small war against Serbia; the government contemplated dismembering Serbia, distributing southern Serbia to Greece and Bulgaria and administering the northern portion without directly annexing it.

Had the Austro-Hungarian army marched promptly, the other powers might have confined themselves to protests, and a conference might have been called to regulate the quarrel. By then Austria would have been in occupation of Belgrade and in a strong bargaining position. But the government delayed. The army required weeks for preparation, even against Serbia. Meanwhile, the Austrian government consulted Berlin in search of diplomatic support that would be as useful as that offered during the Bosnian crisis. An Austro-Hungarian mission reached Berlin July 5 and met with William II and Chancellor Bethmann-Hollweg. William assured the delegation that Germany's full support could be counted on, and he urged them to take advantage of this favorable moment. Both the emperor and the chancellor believed that Austrian hesitation would seriously damage the Hapsburg empire's tottering prestige in the Balkans and lead to a weakening of Germany's one firm ally. In giving this encouragement the German government assumed that punitive military action against Serbia was being considered, but they also assumed that the Austrians would act quickly and that the war would be contained as a local conflict between Austria-Hungary and Serbia.

The Austrian delegation returned to Vienna with what has been described as a "blank check," but the government encountered further delays in cashing it. A week was consumed in wearing down the opposition of Stephen Tisza, the Hungarian premier. Tisza raised objections to military action that would only add more Slavs and more problems to the empire. Tisza also detested war and hoped to find a way to achieve a diplomatic and not a military triumph over Serbia. He finally relented to a proposal for giving Serbia an ultimatum after he won a lightly given promise from Berchtold that "not one inch" of Serb territory would be added to the empire. Additional time was taken in an investigation of Serbian complicity in the assassination—an investigation that did not establish Serbian guilt.

By this time the opportunity for punitive action against Serbia had become less favorable. The attitude of Austria's potential opponents stiffened. The circumstances of the Bosnian affair, when Germany and Austria had forced the western allies to accept annexation, seemed unlikely to be repeated. Russia had recovered from the effects of the Japanese war and was prepared to take a more aggressive stance than before. The Russian government warned the Austrians that Russia would not tolerate Serbia's humiliation and would oppose any military measures taken against it. Behind the Russian warning was the confidence of the Russian foreign minister, Sazonov, that in this crisis he could count on British and French support. Since 1912 the French government had been strengthening its ties with Russia, and the French president, Raymond Poincaré, and the French premier, René Viviani, during a state visit to St. Petersburg, pointedly reminded the Austrians that Russia had a firm ally in France.

The hardening of Russian and French attitudes had little effect in Vienna, where Berchtold proceeded with composing a strong ultimatum to be given to Serbia. But he delayed delivery of the note until Poincaré and Viviani had completed their visit in Russia and embarked on their return voyage. Berchtold hoped to profit from the absence of easy communications between the French government leaders at sea and their Russian allies.

The Austrian Ultimatum

Late in the evening of July 23, nearly one month after the assassination, the Austrian ambassador in Belgrade delivered the ultimatum to the Serbian government. The terms were deliberately made severe so that Serbia would reject them and Austria would then have a pretext for declaring war. Serbia was called on to suppress all Serbian groups that promoted subversive activities in Austria-Hungary; anti-Hapsburg publications in Serbia were to be banned; the control and surveillance of the passage of arms and persons across the mutual border was to be strengthened; those responsible for the plot were to be prosecuted, and Austrian officials were to be allowed to participate in the investigation. An answer to the ultimatum had to be given within forty-eight hours. The Serbs replied within minutes of the deadline on July 25. All of Austria's demands were satisfied, save the requirement that Austrian authorities take part in the investigation, which the Serbs judged, with good reason, as a violation of their sovereignty. Although the full ultimatum had not been accepted, the reply appeared to both Germany and Austria to be remarkably conciliatory. William II, when he read the response, declared that all pretense for war was gone—a judgment that proved hasty.

The Austrian ultimatum awakened Europe to the severity of the Serbian crisis. The assassination had been regarded as a serious matter, but not excessively grave. Ministers and politicians had gone on vacation in July—William II went off for a cruise after giving Austria the "blank check"—and most states seemed preoccupied with internal matters. But the ultimatum indicated that Austria was prepared for war in the Balkans. News of it produced a flurry of activity in European capitals. Germany tried to restrict the potential conflict by sending a circular to the European powers emphasizing that the affair should be resolved between Austria and Serbia. The intervention of other powers, the circular warned, would bring "grave consequences." Yet other powers showed an interest. When the Russian government learned of Austria's ultimatum, military advisers urged that an alert be issued to the army as a preliminary step toward mobilization. On July 25, the Czar agreed that thirteen army corps might be mobilized along the Austrian border if and when that gesture appeared useful. At the same time, the Russians advised Serbia to accept the Austrian demands for the time being and to await action by the major powers.

In London on July 26 Sir Edward Grey, the British foreign secretary, proposed that the matter be referred to arbitration by the four powers not directly involved—Germany, France, Italy, and Great Britain. All but Germany welcomed this suggestion; the Germans refused to haul their Austrian ally before a "European tribunal." Both Austria and Germany hastened to anticipate diplomatic intervention by the other powers. Four hours after receiving Serbia's reply to the ultimatum, the Austrians ordered mobilization, and Bethmann pressed Berchtold to act before the powers intervened. A more prudent course, suggested by William II, recommended that Austria use the Serbian reply as the basis for a negotiated settlement, but by the time this sensible proposal reached Vienna late in the evening of July 28, after having been delayed by Bethmann, Austria had already declared war on Serbia.

The declaration of war deepened the crisis to the point where peace seemed irretrievable, but efforts to avert a wider catastrophe were continued. William II proposed that the Austrian army should peacefully occupy Belgrade. With the Serbian capital as a hostage, the Austrians would have "punished" Serbia, and time would be gained in which the powers could reach a final solution to the crisis in conference. This approach was welcomed by Sir Edward Grey since it corresponded to his earlier appeals for consultation, but by the time Bethmann urged moderation on Berchtold, Austria-Hungary was at war and unreceptive to this new-found caution. At the same time, William II and the Czar exchanged telegrams in which they expressed alarm at the crisis and beseeched each other to halt the fatal rush toward war. Time had become compressed and crucial decisions were made—or abandoned—as communications between governments crossed one another. Panicky desperation characterized the chancelleries of Europe's capitals after July 28. In central and eastern Europe the initiative began slipping away from the emperors and their diplomats and into the hands of the generals.

Mobilization for War

The Austrian declaration of war roused the Russian government to begin the cumbersome process of assembling its huge army. When news of the declaration and of the subsequent bombardment of Belgrade reached Moscow, Sazonov, in accordance with decisions reached three days earlier, decided to mobilize the army along the Austrian border. But late the same day Sazonov discovered that the Russian army had no plans for partial mobilization. If there was to be any mobilization, the entire army would have to be assembled along the German as well as the Austrian border; this plan could not be altered, the Russian general staff insisted, without causing fatal confusion and inviting attack. On July 29, Sazonov informed the Czar that the entire army would have to be called up. Sensing the responsibility that he would bear for taking this drastic step, the Czar hesitated, but by July 30 Sazonov had worn down his reservations, arguing that Russia had to be prepared for a war that was coming in any event. That day the order for full Russian mobilization was given.

The German general staff was alarmed at the Russian maneuvers, for Russia appeared to have gained a head start in calling up its army. This impression was heightened by a misleading telegram that Nicholas II sent to William II, in which he indicated that partial mobilization had been decided on five days earlier, although this had been only a preliminary alert and not an order for mobilization. General Moltke argued that even partial mobilization meant a war between Austria and Russia in which Germany would be involved. Any delay jeopardized Germany's chances for victory. More important, Germany's war plan was as inflexible as Russia's mobilization plan. The Schlieffen plan called for the defeat of France before turning on the lumbering Russian forces in the east. Thus no plan had been devised for a partial mobilization along the eastern frontier, as William II discovered when he suggested to Moltke that the army mobilize only against Russia. The last word was with the military: war with Russia meant war with France.

News of Russia's full mobilization gave further urgency to the military arguments. By 1914 the view that mobilization meant war had become an axiom of European politics. On July 31, Bethmann sent an ultimatum to St. Petersburg demanding that mobilization orders be canceled within twelve hours; at the same time, he sent an ultimatum to Paris demanding that the French government promise neutrality in the event of war between Russia and Germany, and that they cede to Germany two major fortresses—Toul and Verdun—as guarantees of good faith. These two ultimatums were more imperious and unanswerable than Austria's demands on Serbia a week earlier. Anticipating unfavorable replies to both, the German general staff took preliminary steps toward mobilization.

Even at this late hour Bethmann was, as he put it, "grasping every straw." On July 30 he had sent a telegram to Vienna once more urging negotiation; but when this telegram was shown to Berchtold, Conrad produced another from Moltke in which the German chief of staff called on Austria to order general mobilization against Russia as well as Serbia. "What a joke!" Berchtold exploded, "Who rules in Berlin, Moltke or Bethmann?" The Austrians took advantage of Berlin's confusion to follow the advice of Moltke, which most suited their own intentions anyway.

By the end of the day of July 31, the decisive steps toward war had been taken in eastern Europe. Russia and Austria had started to mobilize, and the German army was preparing to strike westward. On his return from Russia, on July 29, the French premier, Viviani, had discovered an excited crowd in Paris clamoring for war. Yet the French government at first tried to warn the Russians against taking action that would be provocative. The French ambassador in St. Petersburg, Maurice Paléologue, was more sympathetic to Russian intransigence than his superiors in Paris, however, and he advised the Russian foreign office against giving way. He assured them that if Russia were attacked by Germany, the French would meet the obligations of their alliance.

In Paris, Viviani's only reply to the German ultimatum was the ominous comment that France would pursue its own interests. On August 1, Germany made a formal declaration of war against Russia and ordered full mobilization; the same day the French government called for a general mobilization and proclaimed a state of siege in

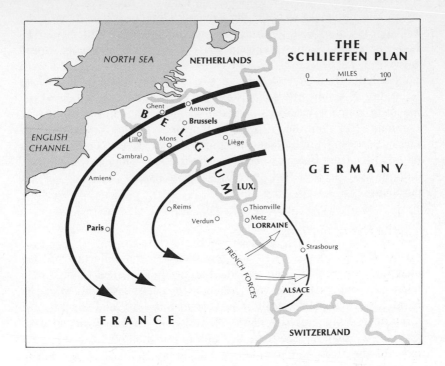

THE
SCHLIEFFEN PLAN

0   MILES   100

NORTH SEA   NETHERLANDS

NETHERLANDS

ENGLISH
CHANNEL

Ghent
Antwerp
Brussels
Lille   Mons
Liège
Cambrai
Amiens

BELGIUM

LUX.

GERMANY

Reims   Thionville
Verdun   Metz
LORRAINE

Paris

FRENCH FORCES

Strasbourg

ALSACE

FRANCE

SWITZERLAND

the country. Anxious not to appear the aggressor and thereby risk losing British support, France had initially drawn its troops back ten kilometers from the frontier. But with the German ultimatum, the time for such prudence had passed.

On August 2 Germany invaded Luxemburg. That evening the German ambassador delivered a note to the Belgian foreign ministry demanding passage for German troops through Belgian territory. An answer had to be given within twelve hours; if unfavorable, the German government would regard Belgium as an enemy. The next day, August 3, the Belgians rejected the demand and requested aid from the powers—other than Germany—that had guaranteed the country's neutrality in 1839. But the German army was already invading Belgium along routes sketched by Schlieffen and his staff in 1905. On the pretext that French planes had bombarded Nuremberg, the German government declared war on France the same day. A few hours before, the French government, fulfilling its alliance obligation to Russia, had declared war against Germany.

Only Great Britain remained outside the general European conflagration, but not for long. Sir Edward Grey had hoped until the last moment that Britain could arrange a negotiated settlement. His behavior caused some doubts in Paris as to whether Britain would provide naval assistance and an expeditionary force if France were attacked by Germany. Bethmann also may have hoped for British neutrality. Even members of the British cabinet were uncertain of the extent to which Britain was obligated to aid France in the event of a German attack. But the violation of Belgian neutrality tipped the balance decisively. London sent an ultimatum to Berlin: Germany was to withdraw from Belgium within five hours. This demand was refused, and on August 4, 1914, the British government declared war on Germany.

The End of Illusions

As Europe plunged into war few imagined the suffering that lay ahead. Here and there were poignant scenes that seemed to anticipate what was coming. The German ambassador broke into tears when he handed Germany's declaration of war to Sazonov, and Sir Edward Grey uttered his famous remark: "The lamps are going out all over Europe: we shall not see them lit again in our lifetime." But the great mass of the European population, caught up at once in the heady emotion of the moment and the adventurous compulsion of military duty, went into battle in a holiday spirit. Crowds poured into the streets of European capitals singing patriotic songs and cheering for victory. Both sides thought the war would be won rapidly—by the end of the year anyway.

For a month the war developed according to schedule—at least according to German planning. The German army marched through Belgium and into France, pressing down toward Paris. Then plans went awry, and the universally shared illusion that the war would be brief proved false. German military plans outreached the capacities of the army. Outside Paris the German troops, disorganized after their long march through Belgium and northern France, paused to regroup. The French army had, meanwhile, recovered from its initial defeats and, aided by the British expeditionary force, counterattacked and halted the German westward thrust. The war in the west stalemated as the armies entrenched themselves in a battle line that ran from the English Channel to Switzerland. The military planners had not foreseen this deadlock, nor had they digested the implications of technological improvements in firepower that gave the advantage to soldiers defending positions against attack. During the first days of the war the French army, according to its own plan, launched suicidal infantry attacks against entrenched German positions in Lorraine with disastrous losses. Military strategists on both sides suffered a painful disillusionment with their prewar assumptions, and the ordinary soldier paid heavily for this miscalculation.

The illusion that war was glorious proved equally false; 1914 was the last year that Europe cheered declarations of war. The war did not produce rapid, brilliant victories, nor did it provoke immediate revolution or lead to an economic collapse, as some radical socialists anticipated. Pacifists and socialist revolutionaries alike had underestimated the capacity of governments to organize their states for war. Few had foreseen that Europe's formidable industrial and technological capacity would be converted to destructive purposes or that future victory would be mortgaged on immediate sacrifices in men and material strength.

Debates on the Causes of the War

The war that broke out in 1914 had such a devastating effect on Europe that historians have devoted a great amount of energy to sorting out its causes. The effort has produced a wealth of evidence and detail along with a variety of interpretations. The archives continue to be sifted for new information on which further revisions of interpretation are made. The debate over the causes of the First World War has been lively and sometimes acrimonious, and it is still very much alive. At the risk of oversimplification—and without pretense about resolving a continuing debate—some of the interpretations of the origins of the war will be indicated here.

The main actions that led to war have been known for some time. Arguments among historians turn on two issues: the relative importance of underlying and immediate causes of the war, and the question of responsibility for its occurrence.

Underlying Causes

In seeking long-range explanations much has been written about the economic and imperial rivalries that poisoned relations among the European states. Military preparations, including armaments increases, the naval race, and the formation of inflexible military strategies, have also been cited as major influences that propelled Europe toward an armed conflict. The growth of military power made the alliance system more menacing. Although created for defensive purposes, these alliances increased the danger of war by dividing Europe against itself.

Relations among European states were embittered by the experience of frequent diplomatic confrontations after 1905, and this tension made the peace of Europe unstable. Because of the alliance system, all powers could be drawn into any European quarrel, and there was no international system capable of mediating national disputes. Unlike the European "concert," which aimed at preventing war from breaking out, the alliances were made in anticipation of some future war. Critics of the prewar alliances therefore claim that their existence made war more likely, and they were not a "system of peace" but simply evidence of international anarchy.

Recent studies have emphasized the deep, unsettling effects that Germany's rise to power had on the balance of European politics. Propelled by the momentum of an expanding industry and population, Germany threatened to dominate the European continent. The French alliance with Russia was designed to contain Germany and preserve the status quo. Only by turning to an eastern ally could France hope to match German military strength. For their part Russian statesmen grew alarmed that Germany might gain decisive influence at Constantinople and use its influence to close the straits to Russian commercial shipping out of the Black Sea grain ports. Great Britain, already sensitive to a growing commercial rivalry, entered into European commitments to restore the balance that Germany's growth threatened to upset. While these powers were allying to contain Germany, the Germans were, according to the German historian Fritz Fischer, engaged in a "grasp for world power." From the point of view of German imperialists, this policy was simply an attempt to gain Germany's rightful place of pre-eminence in the world, and the allied powers were deliberately seeking to frustrate this goal by drawing an iron ring around Germany and Austria. Between Germany's "world policy" and the fears of the European powers ranged against it, a serious conflict developed that pointed to a showdown.

Other underlying causes of tension have caught the attention of historians. France longed to recover Alsace-Lorraine, and it was only a realistic appraisal of French chances in a war of revenge against Germany that tempered such thoughts. A desire to escape the dilemmas posed by domestic political disputes may have disposed certain European statesmen toward welcoming the distractions of a patriotic war. All these latent forces surfaced during the decade prior to 1914, and they contributed to the strained atmosphere in international relations during these years.

But this atmosphere did not seem to point irretrievably to war. Instances of economic cooperation and agreements, of interpenetration and flexibility in the alliance blocs, of accords signed between presumed rivals, and the like, offset a totally pessimistic assessment of European international politics before 1914. Moreover, the alliance system and Bismarck's system before it had given the European powers a long era of peace. Finally, it is difficult to maintain that such causes determined that war would occur precisely in the summer of 1914. The breakdown of peace resulted directly from one long-standing difficulty—Austria's frustration with Balkan nationalism—and the immediate events of the summer of 1914.

Immediate Causes

The war began, as the American historian Laurence Lafore has reminded us, with a Balkan conflict between Austria and Serbia. Berchtold, Conrad, and the imperial government of Austria-Hungary decided to go to war and reduce Serbian pretensions once and for all. There was even a serious issue—the assassination of a member of a ruling house—to lend righteousness to the Austrian cause. These men deliberately sought war and could not be restrained. They received support and encouragement from Germany at a critical moment. The German government apparently believed that firm support and a strong policy would discourage the other powers from taking a hand in this Balkan quarrel.

The configuration resembled the Bosnian crisis with the crucial differences that Russia also was prepared to risk war with a mobilization order and France was less vigorous than in times past in restraining Moscow. The alliance system did not cause the war but it enabled a small war to escalate into a general conflict. There was nothing inevitable about the process; much depended on individual decisions of men acting under stress. Once Austria declared war, however, escalation moved rapidly. No state followed the letter of its alliance agreements, but the prewar crises had accustomed statesmen to looking for support within the context of alliance patterns.

The Responsibility for War

Closely linked to the question of causes of the First World War is the question of responsibility. In 1919 the peacemakers at Versailles inserted a clause in the treaty signed with Germany that assigned "war guilt" to the German nation. In the next few years historians, particularly in the United States and in Germany, tried to correct this misreading of history. In some instances the effort to relieve German guilt led to a condemnation of France and Russia. According to this view, in its most exaggerated form, Russian and French statesmen conspired to provoke war during Poincaré's visit to St. Petersburg July 20–23, 1914, and French Ambassador Maurice Paleologue goaded the Russians toward an intransigent position. This argument no longer commands a very wide following; whatever faults the French committed lay in not demanding more emphatically that Russia rescind the order for mobilization, a demand that would have been difficult to push to extremes if the alliance between the two countries were to be taken seriously in Paris and St. Petersburg. Paleologue did not accurately reflect his government's caution, but this cannot be made into a conspiracy.

Some historians place blame on Great Britain for Sir Edward Grey's behavior during the crisis. The case against Grey faults him for failing to make clear to the Germans that Britain could be drawn into a continental war, and for keeping his own cabinet in the dark on Britain's obligations to France. A left-wing faction within the Liberal government disliked the entente with France and wanted to keep Britain out of continental complications; this division in the cabinet, added to a preoccupation with domestic issues, gave an impression of uncertainty in London about whether Britain would assist France in the event of war. Yet Grey indicated to his cabinet at the height of the crisis that Britain would not remain neutral, although he hoped until the last minute that a compromise solution might be found. Efforts to build a case against the entente of the allied powers seem less persuasive than they did during the 1920's or 1930's. More recent studies emphasize the mistakes that were made in central and eastern Europe.

Since the war arose from the conflict between Serbia and Austria, these two states must share the major responsibility for the outbreak of a European war. An important official in the Serbian government conspired in the assassination of the archduke, and the prime minister of Serbia had some inkling that a plot was afoot. His vague warnings to Vienna now seem to have been inadequate and even irresponsible. But what of Austria's behavior? The archduke's visit was a provocation, although scarcely a justification, for a political assassination. After the assassination Conrad and Berchtold were determined to have war with Serbia. Perhaps they saw war as the only possible salvation of the empire. If Austria did not act, the empire would be discredited as a major power, and Austrian impotence would encourage further turbulence among the nationalities within the Hapsburg domains.

The responsibility for the escalation of the conflict may be assigned to Germany and Russia. The German government gave its Austrian ally every assurance of support; its subsequent attempts to hold back the Austrians may be described as too little and too late. The Germans did not deliberately seek war, but when the war crisis came, they were prepared to assume the burdens of a general European conflict. They believed that their alliance with Austria and their geographical position between the hostile states of France and Russia required that they enter the conflict. They may also have seen a chance to win world power or European hegemony or to break the "ring" forged around them. The German reading of their own obligations was rigid, and it made escalation of any war in which Austria was involved much more probable. Equally serious was the rather unthinking way in which Russian officials decided on mobilization. Certainly the Russian government understood that this was a drastic step; yet Sazonov yielded rather quickly to—indeed he welcomed—the argument of military necessity. Thus if the burden of responsibility must be placed, it lies more heavily with the eastern monarchies than with the western powers, although mistakes abounded throughout Europe during those summer days.

Finally, the military arguments that prevailed in eastern Europe, and at crucial points in the crisis, played a decisive role in bringing about war. For this reason the military leadership has been severely criticized for its aggressiveness. Yet it has been argued that the military gained importance because the political leaders of eastern Europe were prepared to and wanted to follow their advice. Sazonov in Russia and Berchtold in Austria were as irresponsible in their willingness to turn to violence as their military advisers. In Germany, General Moltke increasingly had the decisive voice; Bethmann offered ineffectual restraints and, in any event, concurred in offering the Austrians a "blank check" and in encouraging them to take decisive action. The military had a duty to prepare for war; criticism of the generals is valid insofar as they failed to plan in a way that would leave options open to their governments. But the basic failures of 1914 were political ones.

The summer's crisis revealed weaknesses within the European state system, which succumbed to the weight of national divisions, and it exposed the frailties of those men in power who made grave miscalculations at a critical moment in history. The First World War, moreover, had an enormous impact on the course of European history. Three empires tumbled during the war. Social and economic dislocations arising from the war prepared the way for the Bolshevik triumph in Russia and for the rise of fascism and totalitarian political movements in central and eastern Europe. The costs of war diminished the power of the European states in the world. The war exacerbated nationalist hatreds within the continent and produced disillusionment and pessimism among many intellectuals. An understanding of why Europe switched onto the track leading to war is of continuing importance for knowledge of the past as well as for a better comprehension of human behavior. But the war cannot be seen as the sole root for Europe's twentieth century history. The search for the causes of the First World War has distracted students of the period from other significant aspects of the prewar years. A one-dimensional picture of European diplomats and soldiers marching steadily toward catastrophe is misleading—the period 1890–1914 should be seen as a time in which some of the characteristic features of contemporary Europe appeared, and not as simply a background for the war. The writings of Freud, for example, had very little to do with the outbreak of war, but they have had a great deal to do with the way in which men have looked at themselves and one another in the twentieth century.

*   *   *

What does a rapid glance back at Europe in 1914 show? In many respects the European people were more prosperous then and had more reason for contentment than at any time in the past. The European economy had been booming for over a decade. Production increased steadily while prices and business confidence were on the upswing. Trade among the European states was thriving, and British banking houses provided convenient means for balancing accounts among European states and between Europe and the non-European world. There were many more contacts among European peoples. Restrictions on travel were virtually nonexistent; passports were used only in Russia; and government regulation of individual lives was minimal by the standards of the latter part of this century.

The potential of the technological and scientific revolutions was being realized. A great variety of new goods appeared on the market, ranging from the automobile to electric lamps for the home. The airplane caught the popular imagination as the French pilot Louis Bleriot flew across the English Channel. Bleriot's flight symbolized the drawing together of Europe, linked by an efficient, rapid communications system. The European nations seemed to dominate the world; at least European power was exercised on a global scale, and European culture radiated toward foreign lands.

For the European working class, conditions of labor steadily improved, and government-sponsored social services relieved some hardships associated with industrial, urban life. A sense of participation in society could be obtained through membership in unions or in the growing socialist movements, and an expansion of the franchise offered a channel for popular political expression. Literacy had become nearly universal, and sports and the cinema provided opportunities for diversion.

But this was not entirely a golden age, despite its later reputation; there was a less auspicious side to Europe in 1914. Serious imbalances existed in the prosperity that emanated from the industrial order. The rise in prices after 1900 offset—and in some areas more than offset—wage increases for many workers so that purchasing power remained static or even declined. By and large the middle classes profited most from the prewar economic surge. Workers registered gains, but distinctions between classes remained that created resentment within the proletariat, evoking alarm among the lower middle classes and the more well-to-do. Acute political conflict, in part emerging from class differences, caused each government to struggle to find means for preserving stability amid pressures for change; in 1914 the prognosis was for continued political and social tension within the European states. Indeed, the prospect of serious domestic upheaval may have inclined Europe's leaders toward a "clearing of the air" in a short, triumphant campaign.

European political power overseas seems less overwhelming in retrospect than it did at the time. The strains of maintaining world supremacy had already emerged before 1914, as resistance to European rule appeared in parts of the European empires and as some non-European states gained the means to challenge Europe's industrial and economic ascendancy. The intense nationalism of the European states also posed difficulties in an age in which industrial and economic developments placed emphasis on interdependence of nations. All these problems were to become much more intense later in the century, but their outlines took shape before 1914.

If the prewar European world may be summed up in a very general way, it may be seen as a period in which the pace of change quickened at an astonishing rate. Innovations in science and technology provided concrete examples of a kinetic energy that could be found throughout European society. Indeed, innovation, experimentation, and diversity seemed to be the hallmarks of the age. In science, the arts, even in politics, men were reaching out in new directions. But without some skill at adaptation, European society and politics often suffered severe strains from the frenetic pace of change. For all the remarkable achievements of the age, there were those who questioned the desirability of innovation for its own sake. They began to suspect, if contemporary trends were any indication, that the future might not be to their liking. Europe in 1914 was at once dynamic, resourceful, and not a little anxious about its future.

SUGGESTED READINGS

Elie Halévy's essay "The World Crisis of 1914–18: An Interpretation," republished in his *An Era of Tyrannies,* tr. by R. K. Webb (New York: New York University Press, 1966), presents the view that Europe in 1914 was headed for either war or revolution, and "the forces making for war" prevailed. In a similar vein, Arno J. Mayer has looked at the domestic tensions across Europe on the eve of the war in his essay, "Domestic Causes of the First World War," in L. Krieger and F. Stern (eds.), *The Responsibility of Power: Essays in Honor of Hajo Holborn* (New York: Doubleday, 1967).

A recent re-examination of the evidence has led Laurence Lafore to concentrate on the problems arising from southeastern Europe and the emerging nationalities in *The Long Fuse: Interpretations of the Origins of World War I* (Philadelphia: Lippincott, 1965). Two older diplomatic histories still offer guides to the complexities of Balkan diplomacy: Bernadotte E. Schmitt's *The Annexation of Bosnia, 1908–9* (Cambridge: Cambridge University Press, 1937) and E. C. Helmreich's *The Diplomacy of the Balkan Wars* (Cambridge, Mass.: Harvard University Press, 1938). The "young Turk" revolt and its attendant complications are discussed by E. E. Ramsur, Jr., in *The Young Turks* (Princeton: Princeton University Press, 1957). The Moroccan crisis of 1911 is the subject of Ima Barlow's *The Agadir Crisis* (Chapel Hill: University of North Carolina Press, 1940). Milorad M. Drachkovitch in *Les socialismes français et allemand et le problème de la guerre, 1870–1914* (Geneva: E. Droz, 1953) has some critical comments on the socialists' "peace debate."

Assignment of responsibility for the war excited a generation of scholars in the 1920's and 1930's and has recently been revived as a subject of lively debate. Among the older interpretations, Sidney B. Fay's *The Origins of the World War,* 2 vols. (New York: Macmillan, 1930), tries to correct the "war guilt" view that saddled Germany with responsibility for the outbreak in 1914. For many years Fay was considered the standard guide. Published at the same time, Bernadotte E. Schmitt's *The Coming of the War, 1914,* 2 vols. (New York: Scribner's, 1930; Fertig, 1958), is less sympathetic to the central powers. Another standard account, Luigi Albertini's *The Origins of the War of 1914,* 3 vols. (London: Oxford University Press, 1952–57), is filled with information and is considered by many historians to be the most objective of the three accounts, although Albertini was an Italian interventionist and much of his book justifies Italy's entry into the war. The revival of interest in the origins of the war is due in large part to the publication of Fritz Fischer's controversial *Germany's Aims in the First World War* (New York: W. W. Norton, 1967), which emphasize that Germany was more than willing to take the risk of war as it sought to "grasp at world power" (the title of his book in the German original). Some of the main issues of the debate may be found in "1914," *The Journal of Contemporary History,* Vol. 1, no. 3, 1966, reprinted by Harper & Row in a paperback edition, *1914: The Coming of the First World War, 1967.*

The incident that precipitated war is discussed in Joachim Remak's *Sarajevo; the Story of a Political Murder* (London: Weidenfeld & Nicolson, 1959), and in the detailed analysis, sympathetic to the Serb position, of Vladimer Dedijer, *The Road to Sarajevo* (New York: Simon & Schuster, 1966). The rigidities of German military planning are apparent in Gerhard Ritter's *The Schlieffen Plan* (London: O. Wolff, 1958).

INDEX

Page numbers in *italics* refer to illustrations.

362

India, 94, 95; Anglo-Russian border rivalry in, 177, 182, 192; British in, 198, 200, *214, 215*; nationalism in, 229–31
Indian National Congress, 229, 230
Indo-China, 184, 211–13, 231–33
Industrial order: changes in, 9–10; conditions inducing development of, 5–6; and imperialism, 199; rise of, 3–8, 43; variations in development of, 6–8
Industrial revolution, 3–8; and growth of cities, 36–39; in Russia, 156; second, 8–14
Industrialization, 4, 6–8; in 1890, *7;* spread of, 19–20; and urban expansion, 36–39
Industry, consolidation of, 16–17
International socialism. *See* Socialism
Internationalism, 327, 338–40
Irish home rule, 87, 88, 89, 90, 287, 291–92
Iron industry, 6, 10–11, 19
Irredentists, 318
Ismail, Khedive of Egypt, 204
Italian army and navy, 336, 337
Italy: anarchism in, 49, 52, 53; art in, 254; Chamber of Deputies in, 112, 113, 116, 294; domestic conflicts in, 283, 292–98; economic problems in, 114, 115; education in, 294; emigration from, 36; in Ethiopia, 115–16; General Confederation of Workers (C.G.L.) in, 56, 62, 296; industrialization in, 6, 7, 19; and Libya, 335; literature in, 266; in Mediterranean agreements, 174; parliamentary triumph in, 117–19; political parties in, 295–96, 297; politics in, 80, 85, 111–20; social reforms in, 118, 293–94; socialists in, 70–71, 114, 116, 118, 295–96, 342; suffrage in, 80, 294, 295; syndicalism in, 56; tariff in, 16, 33; in the Triple Alliance, *see* Triple Alliance; Tripoli invasion by, 187, 296, 297–98, 333; and Tunisia, 202, 203; unification of, 111–12, 171; war of, with Turkey, 296, 298, 333–34, 342
Izvolsky, Alexander, 192, 328, 329, 330, 331

Jameson, Leander Starr (Dr. Jameson), 92
Japan, 4, 16; art in 241; and Britain, 161, 181–82, 194; defeat of China by, 228; in Manchuria, 161, 162, 213, 217; Meiji government in, 227–28; modernization of, 226–28; Tokugawa regime in, 226–27; and war with Russia, *see* Russo-Japanese War; as a world power, 228–29; world trade of, 94
Jaurès, Jean, 71, 72, 76, 107, 110, 301, 303, 341, 343, 344
Jews: in France, 302; in Russia, 155, 157, 160, 312

Joffre, Joseph, 302
Joyce, James, 264, 265
Junkers, 31–32, 128, 132, 136, 304, 305, 308

Kadet party (Russia), 158, 309–10, 311, 312, 313, 317
Kafka, Franz, 264, 265–66
Kandinsky, Vasily, 251; *Winter* by, *250*
Karageorgevich, Peter, 322
Kautsky, Karl, 67, 68–69, 71, 72
Khartoum, battle at, 185
Kiderlen-Wächter, Alfred von, 332
Kipling, Rudyard, 291
Kirchner, Ernst Ludwig, 254
Kitchener, Horatio Herbert, 92, 185, 209
Korea, 161, 213
Kornfeld, Paul, 262
Kossuth, Francis, 148–49
Kossuth, Louis, 148
Koumintang, 233, 234
Kramer, Karl, 319
Kropotkin, Peter, 53–54
Kruger, Paul, 92, 210, 211
Krupp, house of, 10
Kulturkampf, 127

Labor force, 5, 9; migration of, 36, 221; in Russia, 156
Labor group (Russia), 310
Labor movement: in Britain, 58–59; in France, 299–301
Labor party (Britain), 59–60, 70, 343; militancy in, 289–90, 292
Labor Representation Committee (Britain), 59–60
Labor unions. *See* Trade unionism
Laissez-faire, 44, 46, 86
Land ownership: and agrarian crisis, 30–33; feudal pattern of, 33; and peasantry, 34–35; Polish, in Austria, 318; in Prussia, 136; Russian reforms in, 314–15
Landed aristocracy, 31–33
Landes, David, 14, 15
Lansdowne, Henry Charles, 181, 182, 186
Laos, 184, 212
Latin America, 18, 50, 219–22, 224, 225
Lawrence, D. H., 266
League of Unions (Russia), 163
LeBon, Gustave, 273
Legien, Karl, 61, 69
Lenin, Nikolai, 47, 69, 157, 198, 199, 310, 316, 341
Leo XIII, Pope, 103
Leopold II, of Belgium, 205
Levant, 218–19, 240, 328
Liberal party (Britain), 59, 80, 85–87, 183; and armaments race, 331; eclipse of, 87–88; and Indian nationalism, 231; and Liberal Unionists, 89; return to power of, 90–91, 95–96, 284
Liberal party (Hungary), 148

Rasputin, Gregory, 316–17
Ravachol, François, 51
Red River Valley (Tonkin), 212
Reform Act of 1867 (Britain), 86
Reformism, 295, 296
Reichsrat, 318, 321
Reichstag, 124, 126, 127, 128, 129, 130,
  133, 135, 136, 137, 179, 188, 304, 332,
  335, 342; and political reform, 306–08;
  progressive tendencies in, 304–05
Relativity theory, 278
Renoir, Auguste, 243, 244
Representative institutions, 83–84, 123,
  274. *See also* Parliamentary system
Revisionism, 68–72
Revolutionism, 47; in Russia, 157, 158
Rhodes, Cecil, 92, 207, 210–11
Rhodesia, 210
Ricardo, David, 44–45
Rimsky-Korsakov, Nikolai, 259
Risorgimento, 111, 112
Roberts, Frederick, 92, 93, 291, 306
Roentgen, Wilhelm, 277
Romagna, Italy, 296, 297
Rome Congress, 71
Roosevelt, Theodore, 223–25
Rosenberg, Harold, 279
Roseberry, Archibald Philip, 90
Rouault, Georges, 251
Rousseau, Jean-Jacques, 48
Rudini, Antonio de, 117
Ruhr basin, 11, 32, 37
Rumanians, 140, 147, 321, 335
Russia, 123, 124–25; agriculture in, 153,
  315; anarchism in, 49, 52, 53–54; art
  in, 254; Balkan interests of, 172, 174,
  317; in Bosnian crisis, 318, 323, 328–
  31, 346, 347; and Britain, *see* Anglo-
  Russian rivalry and entente; bureauc-
  racy in, 150–53; challenges to state in,
  153–55; class distinction in, 26; communes in, 310, 314, 315; cooperatives
  in, 33; in Crimean War, 151, 171, 191;
  Czar's government in, 311, 313, 316–
  18; Duma in, *see* Duma; economy in,
  155–56, 315; emancipation of serfs in,
  151–53; in Far East, 161, 180, 181,
  192, 328; first reform efforts in, 151–
  53; and France, 176–78, 186, 347;
  French investments in, 18, 20, 159, 192;
  German ultimatum to, 350; grain exports from, 21, 30, 114, 156; industrialization in, 6–7, 19–20, 153, 156, 159;
  land ownership in, 32–33, 152–53; land
  reforms in, 314–15; in Manchuria, 180,
  182, *see also* Russo-Japanese War;
  mobilization of, 349, 350; peasantry in,
  35, 158; political parties in, 309–10;
  political power in, 83, 84; politics in,
  80, 123, 124–25, 150–65; population
  growth in, 152, 153; and Reinsurance
  Treaty, 174, 175–76; Revolution of

1905 in, 146, 162–65, 284; revolutionary societies in, 154, 157, 158; suffrage
  in, 80; syndicalism in, 56; in Three
  Emperors' League, 173; unions in, 63,
  156–57; at war with Japan, *see* Russo-
  Japanese War; at war with Turkey,
  171, 173
Russian army, 336, 349, 350
Russian navy, 162, 178
Russian Revolution of 1905, 146, 162–65,
  284; and October Manifesto, 163, 164,
  310, 311
Russian Social Democratic party, 158,
  310, 313
Russification, 155, 316
Russo-Japanese War, 76, 160–62, 182,
  188, 191, 192, 194, 217, 225, 228, 347
Russo-Turkish War, 171, 173
Ruthenes, 140, 319
Rutherford, Ernest, 278
Rye and steel alliance, 32, 136, 138

Sahara, 208, 240
Saigon, 232
St. Petersburg, 37, 63, 162, 163; strikes in,
  157, 315, 316
Saint-Simon, Henri, 46, 48
Salandra, Antonio, 298
Salisbury, Robert, 88, 89, 90, 91, 93, 175,
  181, 185, 207
Sarajevo, 345
Sarrant, Albert, 232–33
Sazonov, Sergei, 317–18, 334, 347, 349,
  352, 357
Scandinavia, 16, 30, 33, 34, 61
Scheurer-Kestner, Auguste, 105
Schlieffen, Alfred von, 177; war plan of,
  338, 349–50, *351*, 352
Schoenberg, Arnold, 259, 260
Schumpeter, Joseph, 201
Sciences: physical, 276–79; social, 239,
  270–76, 279
Sculptors, 240
Second International, 73–76, 343
Senegal, 198, 207
Serbia, 172, 322; assassination of Francis-
  Ferdinand in, 345–47; and Austria, 320,
  329, 330, 335, 344, 347–49; in Balkan
  League, 334; in Battle of Kossovo, 345;
  nationalists in, 345; at war with Bul-
  garia, 174; war responsibility of, 356
Serbs, 140, 147, 317, 321, 322, 323
Serfs, emancipation of, 151–53
Sergei, Russian Grand Duke, 162
Seurat, Georges, 245
Shuster, Morgan, 219
Siam, 184, 187, 212
Siemens-Martin steel process, 10
Sino-Japanese War, 213, 228
Slavs, 124, 142, 143, 148, 155, 318, 319,
  320, 322, 330
Slovaks, 147

Triple Alliance, 115, 173–74, 176, 177, 190, 335, 337
Tripoli, 187, 296, 297–98, 333
Tunisia, 202–03; French occupation of, 101, 173–74, 202–03; Italian settlers in, 202, 203
Turati, Filippo, 70, 296
Turkey, 151; and Balkan Wars, 334–35; and Battle of Kossovo, 345; at war with Italy, 296, 298, 333–34, 342; at war with Russia, 171, 173. *See also* Constantinople; Ottoman empire

Uitlanders, 91, 92, 210
Ulster and Ulstermen, 291–92
Umberto I, of Italy, 53, 117
Union of the Russian People, 310
Union of South Africa, 210, 211
Unions. *See* Trade unionism
United States, 4, 5, 10, 94; anarchism in, 50, 52, 53; and Boxer Rebellion, 161; economic growth of, 222–23; emergence of, as world power, 223, 225; expansionism, 223–25; foreign investments in, 18, 200, 222; grain exports from, 16, 21, 30, 114; immigration to, 36; navy of, 187; and open door policy, 94, 214, 218, 225; and Russo-Japanese War negotiations, 225; socialism in, 74; in Spanish-American War, 159, 194, 223
Universal Peace Congress, 339
Upper class, 23–25
Uranium, 277, 278
Urban planning, 37–38
Urbanization, 35–39; in 1910, *21*

Vaillant, August, 50, 51
Van Gogh, Vincent, 245, 247–49, 250, 252; *The Starry Night* by, *247*
Vatican, 108–09, 112, 295
Verne, Jules, 241
Victor Emmanuel III, of Italy, 117
Victoria, of England, 86, 89, 181, 306
Vienna, 37, 62, 139, 140, 141, 143, 318, 320, 322, 323, 330

Vietnam, 184, 211, 212, 232
Vishnegradsky, I. A., 155, 156
Viviani, René, 299, 302, 347, 350
Vladivostok, 161, 162, 213
Vorticism, 254
Vyborg manifesto, 312

Wages, 28, 45
Wagner, Richard, 258
Waldeck-Rousseau, René, 107, 108
War: abolition of, 74, 75–76; and peace, 169–70. *See also* First World War
Weber, Max, 274–75
West Africa, 101, 137
Whigs (Britain), 85, 284
William I, of Germany, 53, 125, 129
William II, of Germany, 94, 125, 130, 131, 132, 133, 135, 136, 137, 138, 176, 180, 181, 188–89, 191, 225, 249, 304, 306, 307, 348, 349, 350
Wilson, Henry, 291
Winter Palace, 162, 311
Witte, Sergei, 6, 156, 159, 160, 163, 164, 317
Witwatersrand, 91
Women's suffrage (Britain), 290, 292
Workers' International, 71
Working class, 27–30, 43; in Britain, 285; in France, 299–301; in Russia, 156–58, 315–16
Working hours, 29
World trade, 16, 199
World War I. *See* First World War
Wright, Frank Lloyd, 257, 258

X-rays, 277

Young Turks, 234, 329
Yuan Shih-K'ai, 234
Yugoslav state, 320, 322

Zabern affair, 307–08
Zanardelli, Giuseppe, 117, 118
Zemstva, 153–54, 158, 159, 160, 163
Zola, Emile, 106, 263

A 0
B 1
C 2
D 3
E 4
F 5
G 6
H 7
I 8
J 9